OUTLINES
OF
HISTORICAL JURISPRUDENCE

BY

SIR PAUL VINOGRADOFF, F.B.A.
CORPUS PROFESSOR OF JURISPRUDENCE IN THE
UNIVERSITY OF OXFORD

Volume One

Introduction *Tribal Law*

THE LAWBOOK EXCHANGE, LTD.
UNION, NEW JERSEY
1999

ISBN 1-886363-64-1

Third reprinting 2001

Printed in the United States of America
On Acid-Free Paper

The Lawbook Exchange, Ltd.
965 Jefferson Avenue
Union, New Jersey 07083-8605

Please see catalogue at rear of this volume
or our website www.lawbookexchange.com
for a selection of our other fine facsimile reprints
of classic works of legal history.

Library of Congress Cataloging-in-Publication Data

Vinogradoff, Paul, Sir, 1854-1925.
Outlines of historical jurisprudence / by Sir Paul Vinogradoff.
p. cm.
Originally published: London : Oxford University Press, 1920.
Includes bibliographical references and index.
Contents: v. 1. Introduction. Tribal law.
ISBN 1-886363-64-1 (cloth : alk. paper)
1. Historical jurisprudence. 2. Law, Primitive. 3. Law, Greek
4. Law—Philosophy. I. Title.
K325.V56 1998
340'.09—dc21

98-42298
CIP

OUTLINES

OF

HISTORICAL JURISPRUDENCE

BY

SIR PAUL VINOGRADOFF, F.B.A.

CORPUS PROFESSOR OF JURISPRUDENCE IN THE
UNIVERSITY OF OXFORD

Volume One

Introduction *Tribal Law*

OXFORD UNIVERSITY PRESS

LONDON EDINBURGH GLASGOW NEW YORK
TORONTO MELBOURNE CAPE TOWN BOMBAY

HUMPHREY MILFORD

1920

PRINTED IN THE UNITED STATES OF AMERICA

TO

ALBERT VENN DICEY

THIS VOLUME IS

DEDICATED

IN

ADMIRATION AND GRATITUDE

PREFACE

The introduction to this work has grown to such a length that the Preface may well be cut short: I should merely like to explain why I have undertaken a most complicated task. In the course of my legal and historical studies one great problem has presented itself over and over again—the problem of the relation between conditions and efforts, between aims and fate. It is in the sphere of law that this problem assumes its most definite aspect. Law, both customary and enacted, is intended to be a direction of conduct, but its actual application is a compromise between intentions and circumstances. As Aristotle has put it, we have to take account in human affairs both of what is desirable and of what is possible. From this point of view, attempts to arrange society on reasonable lines culminate in conceptions of jurisprudence, while, on the other hand, all theories of jurisprudence have necessarily to start from some basis of given fact. Some knowledge of historical jurisprudence is needed by historians, because it helps to arrange the data of political and social life in accordance with consistent schemes of law. For lawyers historical jurisprudence is the best introduction to the social interpretation of the innumerable technical rules and doctrines of their profession. Unfortunately collaboration between jurists and historians, though highly desirable, is not often achieved in practice. Historians have not yet come to realize that private law may be more important for social development than constitutional arrangements. And as for lawyers, they often have to be content with the stereotyped statements of more or less antiquated textbooks. There is nothing for it but to step into the breach in the hope of reopening the discussion. A task of this kind is naturally beset with great difficulties. I have only attempted to trace its outlines, for a general survey of the ground seemed primarily wanted. Many particulars may have to be rectified, many points will have to be worked out in greater detail. But something will have been achieved, if readers obtain a kind of bird's-eye view of the subject.

It is to be hoped that a second volume, on the Jurisprudence of the Greek City, may follow without much delay. Further instalments, though contemplated, are not yet in a fit state to be mentioned in this preface.

It is my pleasant duty to express my sincere thanks to many kind friends who have encouraged and supported me by their expert advice. I am especially indebted to Professor J. A. Smith of Oxford, Professor H. D. Hazeltine of Cambridge, Miss M. A. Czaplicka of Lady Margaret Hall, Oxford, Mr. C. K. Allen of University College, Oxford, Miss Neilson of Mount Holyoke College, Mass. (U. S. A.), and Miss M. F. Moor, formerly of Somerville College, Oxford.

TABLE OF CONTENTS

INTRODUCTION

Part I. Law and the Sciences

Part II. Methods and Schools of Jurisprudence

TRIBAL LAW

Part I. The Elements of the Family

Part II. Aryan Culture

Part III. The Clan and the Tribe

INTRODUCTION

PART I

LAW AND THE SCIENCES

CHAPTER I

LAW AND LOGIC

WHY should there be a special study of jurisprudence? Every one knows why there should be a study of law. It is obvious, for instance, that in order to draw up a will, or to enforce claims arising out of an agreement, one has to know the law. Some lawyers will say that they must attend to the actual rules of law and to the requirements of their clients and have no time to read books on general topics. But the craftsman's point of view can hardly be carried very far. Even in pleading as to the rescission of a contract you may have to rely on considerations of morality and of public utility.[1] It will, I suppose, be conceded that a wide range of culture and knowledge is desirable in the case of the legislator and of the judge; but then barristers and solicitors prepare the way for judicial decisions and deal with the same elements of right as the judges, although their arguments are presented from more one-sided points of view. Some practising lawyers will nevertheless—as Leslie Stephen has put it—consider all theory of law with "serene indifference"; if so, they will have to be left to their own devices. Jurisprudence addresses itself to those who study law as a part of a system of knowledge.

The lawyer's craft.

The subject has an interest of its own apart from any consideration as to immediate utility. Law is one of the great departments of human thought and of social activity. As such, it claims the attention not only of the jurist but of the student of social science, of the philosopher and, in a wider sense, of every educated man. We may systematize our knowledge of the world from two different points of view: either by reducing complex phenomena to their causes and ascertaining, as far as possible, the laws of their recurrence, or by using our knowledge as a guiding light for our

Theoretical and applied sciences.

[1] An interesting survey of the influence of ethical considerations on early Common Law and Equity is given in AMES' lecture on *Law and Morals, Lectures on Legal History* (Cambridge, Mass., 1913), pp. 435 ff.

actions. In the first direction, when we study things as they are, there arise theoretical sciences, such as mathematics, physics, economics. In the other direction, when we study the means of making things as we want them to be, we have to turn to applied sciences, such as engineering, medicine, law. Comparing laws with medicine, we may say that both aim at providing a rational background for a vast body of practical precepts; both are indispensable for the intelligent exercise of an art; both derive their teaching from the application of various sciences to the concrete problems of health and disease, of civil intercourse and crime. The physician combines for a specific purpose doctrines of physics and chemistry, of biology and psychology; the lawyer draws on the study of logic, of psychology and of social science in order to co-ordinate and explain legal rules and to assert rights. Our enumeration of the sciences on which the lawyer has to rely may seem scanty at first sight. Why is ethics not mentioned among them, why not history and philosophy? As to ethical doctrines, they are, of course, closely related to jurisprudence, but they present themselves to jurists chiefly in their practical aspect as influencing conduct.[1] In this sense the data of ethics form a most important chapter of psychology, as the operations of the mind bearing on conduct.

Of the connection between history and jurisprudence we shall have to speak on many occasions. It may be sufficient to state now that history cannot be contrasted with the theoretical study of law because it provides one of the essential elements of legal method. As for philosophy, its influence is all-pervading and is bound to make itself felt in the treatment of any subject: it forms, as it were, the atmosphere for all scientific studies. At the same time it cannot and ought not to direct the investigation of any particular point, for the very reason that it aims at a synthesis of all. Every jurist is left to face the problems of law in his own way, and by such help as he can derive from those branches of special knowledge which have a

[1] Cf. on the relation between morals and law, LORD HALDANE, *Higher Nationality*, an address delivered before the American Bar Association in Montreal in 1913, pp. 22 ff.

direct bearing on legal questions. And these are logic, psychology and social science.[1]

Fallacies and logical concepts.

Logic supplies the formal framework for all varieties of reasoning, and its relation to legal thought is obvious. The rules of reasoning are certainly not different in law from the rules recognized in the ordinary interchange of thoughts. In this sense the usual rules as to concepts and conclusions remain in full force as regards legal deductions. Indeed, juries attending to the arguments of parties have to be careful not to be misled by fallacies. Archbishop Whateley, for instance, has very appropriately illustrated the sophistical trick called *ignoratio elenchi* (irrelevant conclusion) from its frequent use by barristers.[2] This sophism consists in substituting for the proposition to be proved some other proposition irrelevant to the problem of proof. Another fallacy much favoured by sharp pleaders is the substitution of the absolute affirmation for a conditional one (*a dicto secundum quid ad dictum simpliciter*). In an amusing little book, published in 1588, a versifier of Spenser's circle, Abraham Fraunce, who happened also to be a barrister of Gray's Inn, treats of a "lawyer's logicke" on a pattern supplied by Pierre la Ramée's textbook of formal logic. He illustrates his teaching by alternate references to agricultural practices, or other occurrences of daily life, and to cases from the Year Books, the Abridgements, Dyer and Plowden. The passage concerning the *secundum quid* fallacy is worth quoting:[3] the legal illustration is taken from a trial in which the question arose whether the issue of a man was entitled to inherit property granted in special tail to a man and his wife and their issue. "A double elench (sophism) lurketh in this place, one of composition, another of division, for composition thus. Humfrey Crowther is a

[1] WUNDT, *Logik*, II, 2, p. 24.

[2] MILL, *Logic*, II, pp. 468, 469: "If any one has pointed out the extenuating circumstances in some particular case of offence, so as to show that it differs widely from the generality of the same class, the sophist, if he finds himself unable to disprove these circumstances, may do away with the force of them, by simply referring the action to that very class, which no one can deny that it belongs to, etc."

[3] *The Lawyer's Logicke*, p. 64.

good fiddler, therefore he is good. And this fallacy is from the whole, because those two things so joined together seem to make a whole, whereupon afterwards the part may be concluded, as though in this example Humfrey Crowther were a whole integral thing, made and consisting of these two parts, goodness and fiddlery. Some others call this *a dicto secundum quid ad dictum simpliciter,* when we apply that absolutely and generally which was spoken in part and in respect, as here Humfrey is called good, not generally, for his good conditions, but particularly in respect of his gitterne. In 9 *Henry VII* 19a, 'he who is heir to father and mother, is heir to the father, and yet to say that the issue of a husband from his second wife in the case of special tail is heir to father and mother generally and absolutely would not follow, because the father could have had a son by his first wife. *Vavisor, J.:* state the major premise, and the fallacy will be apparent: he, who is heir to father and mother joined is heir to father and mother each separately—and this is false.' "[1]

Logical categories.

Of course, it is not only sophistical traps that may be studied in lawyer's pleadings, but also perfectly justified operations of reasoning. Fraunce, for instance, devotes some of his first chapters to discussing the relation between cause and effect, and classifies causes according to the best approved logical patterns of his time.[2] Under the heading "efficient cause" he refers to a curious case reported in Plowden's *Commentaries*, in which the widow of a man who had committed suicide contested the forfeiture of his estate on the ground that a dead man could not be charged with felony. The reply was that death was only an effect, while the cause of death consisted in the felonious act committed during lifetime. "The cause efficient either maketh or destroyeth. Maister Plowden, folio 262a. They said that

[1] Issint in 9 *Henry VII*, 19a: "Cestuy qe est heire al pere et mere, est heyre al pere, mes l'issue del baron et sa seconde feme donees in speciall tayle est heyre al pere et mere, ergo il est heyre generalement al pere et mere et simpliciter, non sequitur, car le pere poet aver fils par le primer feme. *Vavisor* expone mayorem et apparebit fallacia. Cestuy qe est heyre al pere et mere conjunctim est heyre al pere diuisim, or ceo est false."

[2] *Lawyer's Logicke,* p. 12.

the forfeiture would be connected with the time of the original offence which caused death, and this is the putting him into water, and this was done in his lifetime, and this was a felony. . . . Thus Sir James Hales being alive caused the death of Sir James Hales, and the act of the live man effected the death of the dead man."[1]

Although every rule of logic may be illustrated from legal practice, on the other hand there is a considerable admixture of technical requirements which differentiates this mode of thought from other species of the same kind.

Rules of pleading.

As the conclusions of legal reasoning are directly translatable into practical results, and as they influence the status, rights, reputation and possibly the existence of persons, law is not satisfied with the general guarantees of good logic against fallacies and errors of judgment, but imposes rules devised to fit the average requirements of fairness and common sense, even at the risk of brushing away exceptional claims and imposing minor hardships. This modification of the logical framework is very noticeable in procedure. The history of Common Law procedure[2] presents special opportunities for watching the peculiar combination between rules of logic and the requirements of practical life as conceived and formulated by lawyers. The reason is that the legal profession did not strive in this country to construct a purely technical apparatus for conducting trials, but built up its administration of justice as a compromise between the professional element of the Bench on one side, and the popular element of the jury on the other. The first was supposed to deal exclusively with the *law* in the cases, while the latter was called up originally for a verdict as to the *facts* of the

[1] Issint que Sir James Hales esteant en vie causa Sir James Hales estre mort, et l'act del vive home fist le mort del mort home. Cf. PLOWDEN, *Comm.*, ed. of 1761, *Hales v. Petit*, Mich. 4/5 Eliz. in C. B.

[2] An excellent introduction to the special treatment of logical problems in Common Law is provided by THAYER, *A Preliminary Treatise on Evidence in Common Law.* On the technical rules of reasoning in Equity, see LANGDELL, *Summary of Equity Pleading.* Cambridge, Mass., 1877.

trial. Without concerning ourselves with the rather intricate development of this fundamental opposition between law and fact, let us notice that the introduction of popular opinion, as a factor in deciding the trial, made it necessary for the judges to take special care that the moves of the opponents in the legal struggle should be reduced to their simplest and most regular expression. It was important in a contest before the Court that the parties should not be allowed to beat about the bush and to confuse the jury by irrelevant assertions and arguments. Historically the growth of Common Law procedure was chiefly directed towards keeping pleadings within reasonable bounds and conducting them along definite logical avenues. The Year Books show how the judges of the fourteenth and fifteenth centuries gradually developed the technical framework of pleading, a framework which in spite of a certain artificiality and rigidity proved an excellent school for conducting disputes in an orderly way. It stood the test of practice so well that it remained in force until the middle of the nineteenth century, and towards the end its principles found an admirable exponent in Sergeant Stephen. His textbook on pleading deserves attention even now, though a great part of the technical framework has been removed in deference to the unconventional habits of discussion in our democratic age.[1] The principal feature of this system was the joining of issue, the reduction of matters in dispute to a definite contradiction between assertion and denial, between *yes* and *no*. If A claimed the payment of a debt from B, the latter could *traverse* the plaintiff's declaration by denying that he owed the money. Or else B might demur and challenge a decision on the ground that the claim was based on a wagering transaction and void at law. A third possibility would arise in case the defendant *confessed* the fact alleged by the plaintiff, but *avoided* the claim arising out of it by pleading a valid *exception:* e.g., A brings an action against B for distraining a horse of his; B confesses the distress, but pleads that the

[1] On modern pleading as shaped by the Acts of 1834, 1852, 1873, etc., see ODGERS on *Pleading* (8th ed. 1918), pp. 155, 171, 175.

horse had broken into his close and was grazing there to his, the defendant's, damage.

It is obvious that the grouping of allegations within certain classes by *traverse, demurrer,* or *confession and avoidance* made it possible for the Courts to proceed with great regularity and logical accuracy. The detailed rules as to the application of demurrer, traverse and avoidance were in keeping with the main object of reducing the dispute to the simplest forms of logical contradiction. With this object in view the issue was allowed to be taken, according to strict rule, only on one single point, although in many cases there may have been several debatable points in the trial. Yet, in order not to confuse the mind of the jury by a multiplicity of issues, one of these points had to be selected by counsel for the defence for a special issue.[1]

The same principle of regularity in the struggle underlies such rules of pleading as that by demurring to a point of law a party admits the truth of an opponent's allegations as to fact,[2] or that in traversing an accusation the denial must be a denial of fact, and not a defence on the ground that an act was not wrongful,[3] or again, that two affirmations do not make a good issue.[4] This last rule looks rather cryptic at first sight. It is really a branch of another and wider rule prohibiting *argumentative* traverses, that is, traverses based on *inference* instead of direct denial. For instance, if it were alleged by the plaintiff in a trial that a party died seised in tail and the defendant traversed the declaration by alleging that he died seised in fee, this would not be good issue, because the denial would not be a direct one but based on the inference that he who held in fee did not hold in tail.

The Acts of 1852 and 1854 and the Judicature Acts of 1874 and 1876 have freed counsel from the shackles of a rigid system of pleading. This has made litigation

1 *Coke upon Littleton,* 126a, note 4. As to the relation between general and special issues, see WILLISTON'S preface to his edition of *Stephen on Pleading,* pp. 4 ff.

2 *Stephen on Pleading* (2nd ed.), pp. 176 f.

3 *Ibid.,* p. 180.

4 *Ibid.,* pp. 423 f.

much more pliable and more dependent on intuition and imagination—with all their good and bad characteristics. On the whole, these changes make for an increase in substantial justice. But it must be admitted that they have lessened the hold of pure logic on the administration of the law, in as much as they have removed many of the firm pegs from which compelling deductions could be started.

Evidence. A similar process may be observed in a domain closely connected with pleading, namely, in the law of evidence. As a result of the preliminary encounters in pleading the parties have sooner or later to fight for a decision on some issue of fact or law. In the first case everything would depend on the proofs which could be mustered in favour of the contending claims. Now, in order to realize the peculiar character of legal proofs one must keep in view two guiding considerations:

(1) The two litigants in a trial at Common Law do not hold a position of equality. The maxim—*beati possidentes*—has a wider scope than the protection of possession: it means also that the defendant in a trial can take advantage of the previous state of equilibrium and challenge the *actor* or plaintiff to overcome the inertia of existing order by irrefutable evidence.[1]

(2) In estimating the relative value of evidence, Courts cannot be guided by the methods and standards of criticism which obtain in daily experience or in historical investigation. They have, to be sure, certain privileges by way of examination and cross-examination which ordinary persons and historians are debarred from using. On the other hand, the practical consequences of their decisions

[1] THAYER, *Cases on Evidence*, 2nd ed., 1900, p. 69: "In general, he who seeks to move a court in his favour must satisfy the court of the truth and adequacy of his claim, both in point of fact and law. But he, in every case, who is the true *reus* or defendant, holds, of course, a very different place in the procedure. He simply awaits the action of his adversary, and it is enough if he repel him. . . . It may be doubtful, indeed extremely doubtful, whether he is not legally in the wrong and his adversary legally in the right; indeed he may probably be in the wrong, and yet he may gain and his adversary lose, simply because the inertia of the court has not been overcome, because the *actor* has not carried his case beyond an equilibrium of proof, or beyond all reasonable doubt. Hence the importance of assigning the *burden of proof*."

are so important, that they must draw the line between the possible, the probable and the certain much more strictly than persons responsible merely to their own conscience, or guided by their own interest. As a matter of fact, the treatment of evidence by historians is quite different from its treatment by lawyers: writers like Gibbon and Macaulay were not hampered in their judgment by meticulous rules as to ascertained evidence.

On the other hand, the judge has to take care not only of the appropriateness of his decision as to the case in hand, but of its relation to former and future cases, of the soundness of the principle proclaimed and enforced in meeting the average requirements of fairness and public utility. Hence peculiar standards of admission and exclusion of evidence, devised to provide firm pegs for deductions in the responsible task of sifting evidence. This leads, among other things, to the rules as to *admission* and as to *relevancy*.

Burden of proof.

It is out of the question for us to plunge into a special discussion of all these interesting doctrines, but it is well worth while to point to some characteristic examples. As regards the *burden of proof,* the leading notion is quite simple and indisputable.[1] He who is allowed in the course of procedure to make an affirmation as to facts is called upon to prove it by sufficient evidence. This means that in the ordinary course of events, the burden of proof rests on the plaintiff (demandant or claimant).

However, in cases where a plea of confession and avoidance is put forward, it is the defendant who, granting the facts alleged by the plaintiff, seeks to put them in a different light, and therefore assumes the part of the *actor* and with it the burden of proof. Another apparent shifting of the burden of proof arises when the plaintiff can refer in support of his attack on the defendant's position to some general assumption of the law bearing on a whole class of facts, for example the assumption that a child born in wedlock is the legitimate issue of the husband or that a person making a will or a contract is presumed to be sane

[1] The expression may be taken in two different ways. See THAYER on *Evidence*.

unless the contrary can be proved. These are *presumptions* of the law intended to obviate wanton attacks on the reputation and welfare of families and individuals. Now, although the existence of such a *presumption* provides the plaintiff with a *prima facie* case and makes it incumbent on the defendant to produce evidence to the contrary, it cannot be said that the principle of the incidence of proof as regards claimants has been subverted. The use of the *presumption* is in itself an attempt to fall back on general admission instead of particular evidence, and, in case of substantial opposition on the defendant's side, the plaintiff will have to produce particular evidence if he does not wish to lose his case.

As an example of the importance of the proper treatment of the matter I should like to cite the case of *Hingeston v. Kelly*. "This was an action for work and labour. At the trial before Lord Denman, C.J., at Dorchester . . . it appeared that the plaintiff was an attorney, and . . . acted for the defendant as an election agent in a contest for the borough of Lyme Regis. . . . It also appeared from the evidence . . . that the plaintiff had voted for the defendant at the election, although a paid agent is not permitted by law to vote. The defendant produced evidence to show that it was agreed that the plaintiff's services were to be given gratuitously.

His lordship in summing up told the jury that the plaintiff, having proved the services rendered, was *prima facie* entitled to be paid, and that they should find for the plaintiff unless the defendant had distinctly proved to their satisfaction that the services were to be gratuitous, in which case they ought to find for the defendant. The jury found for the plaintiff.

A rule for a new trial was obtained.

In the Court of Exchequer, Parke, B., stated his opinion:

'The great difficulty in my mind is whether, looking to Lord Denman's summing up, the jury understood that the burthen of proof still lay on the plaintiff. The burthen of proof was never altered. The plaintiff being a professional man, and performing professional services, was *prima facie* entitled to remuneration. His voting, indeed, was an act which amounted to a statement by himself that he was not to be paid. Still, if the case had rested there, the jury, notwithstanding the voting, might have believed that the contract was that the plaintiff was to be paid. Then came the evidence for the defendant to show that the plaintiff should not be paid. After this was given, the question for the jury still remained, whether on the whole evidence the plaintiff had made out his title to remuneration. I think, if I had been a juryman, that in the facts of this case I should have found my verdict against the party, whether the plaintiff or the defendant, on whom I was told by the judge that the burthen of proof lay.

Alderson, B. If the case was left in doubt, the plaintiff ought not to succeed.

Rolfe, B. . . . He (Lord Denman) appears to have said that the plaintiff has proved something which entitled him to a verdict, unless the defendant proves a discharge. I think the jury must have understood from this, that it lay on the defendant to make out his case. There must be a new trial.'[1]

Exclusion of Evidence.

As regards rules restricting the admission of evidence, their object is not merely to prevent the main threads of argument from being confused by the introduction of matters which have no direct bearing on the case: in this respect, although it is the duty of the judge to keep the course of the trial firmly in hand and to stop irrelevant digression, it would be impossible to formulate precise general rules. There are, however, certain classes of statements which are excluded on the strength of such general rules, because, though in particular instances they might be helpful in discovering the truth, on the average it is deemed to be dangerous and mischievous to admit the corresponding evidence. A well-known restriction of this kind consists in the exclusion of hearsay evidence, and the reason of it is not far to seek: if the Courts allowed such evidence to be produced, it

[1] 18 *L.J.* (Exch.), p. 360: THAYER, *Cases on Evidence*, p. 76 (Exch. 1849).

would be impossible to require a strict examination of the circumstances under which the original testimony had been obtained.

I should like to draw special attention to the exclusion of evidence as to former offences or accusations against persons on their trial. A characteristic case occurred in 1851.[1]

The defendant was indicted for felony, at the Leeds Borough Sessions, before the Recorder of Leeds. The first count charged the defendant with breaking into a warehouse and stealing on the 3rd of March, 1851, fifty yards of woollen cloth; the second count charged a simple larceny on the same day; the third count charged the defendant on the same day and year of having received the same property knowing it to have been stolen. The counsel for the prosecution proposed to prove that on the 13th of December, 1850, the defendant had been in possession of four other pieces of stolen cloth. The Recorder admitted the evidence and told the jury, on the summing up, not to apply the evidence to either of the first two counts; but he told them that it was evidence of guilty knowledge under the third count. The jury found the defendant not guilty on the first two counts; guilty on the third count. The defendant was sentenced to seven years transportation, but respited until the question as to whether the disputed evidence was receivable and whether the direction to the jury was correct had been decided. The Court held that the evidence ought not to have been received. In the course of the trial Lord Campbell, C.J., said: "The moral weight of such evidence in any individual case, would no doubt be very great; but the law is a system of general rules, and it does not admit such evidence because of the inconvenience which would result from it."

In delivering his decision Lord Campbell, C.J., said: "In my opinion there was no more ground for admitting the evidence under the third count than there was under the first and second. Under the two latter, it would have been

[1] *Reg. v. Oddy* (1851) 2 Den. C. C. 264.

evidence of the prisoner being a bad man, and likely to commit the offence there charged. But the English law does not permit the issue of a criminal trial to depend on this species of evidence. So under the third count, the evidence would only show the prisoner to be a bad man; it would not be direct evidence of the particular fact in issue. . . ."

Alderson, B. "I am also of the opinion that this evidence was inadmissible. To admit of such evidence in the present case would be to allow a prosecutor in order to make out that a prisoner had received property with a guilty knowledge, which had been stolen in March, to show that the prisoner had in the December previous stolen some other property from another place and belonging to other persons. In other words, we are asked to say that in order to show that the prisoner had committed one felony, the prosecutor may prove that he committed a totally different felony some time before. Such evidence cannot be admissible."

To sum up, the rules of Common Law procedure, although based on logic, disclose in their technical framing the preoccupation of the lawyers to fit their action to the requirements of average situations and prevailing social views, even though many solutions based on probability may have to be rejected in the process.

Interpretation.

The part played by dialectics in the elaboration and application of substantive law is not less conspicuous than its share in procedure. In fact, all the principal operations of juridical thought necessarily contain elements of logical analysis. When the problem has to be solved by reference to a legislative enactment—a statute, the clause of a code, a regulation or by-law—the correct solution generally depends on interpretation, that is, either on the definition of terms or on the co-ordination of various parts of the law in such a way that they are logically coherent. In the case of definition, a peculiar difficulty arises from the fact that legal rules are conservative in their essence, while the terms used by them are bound to be affected by gradual changes in the meaning of words. Mill deals with these linguistic changes in a valuable chapter of his *Logic.*[1]

Interpretation based on context, and on ordination of various clauses and rules under leading points of view may be illustrated from *Attorney-General v. West Riding of Yorkshire, Ex parte Grenside.*[2] The case turned on the meaning to be attached to the obligation of local educational authorities under the Education Act of 1902 to "maintain and to keep up the school within its area in a state of efficiency." The West Riding County Council considered the words from the point of view of the twofold grouping of schools as national elementary schools on the one hand and as voluntary schools with a special board of managers under trust deeds on the other, and contended that it was bound to provide for the efficiency of both kinds of schools merely in those respects which were common to both, namely, for general secular instruction, while leaving all care and charges connected with denominational teaching to the denominational boards of managers. The House of Lords decided otherwise: by combining, among other things, clause 76 with clause 97, of the Act of 1902, they came to the conclusion that the maintenance of a school in a state of efficiency included provision for the teaching of religion. It cannot be asserted that the authoritative interpretation of the House of Lords in this case was purely the result of superior reasoning: the West Riding County Council was not guilty of a palpable logical blunder, and the Lords were certainly actuated by their general view as to the policy of the Act of 1902. But they were bound to bring this conception into harmony with the text itself, and this they achieved by co-ordinating the clauses round the conception of general efficiency.

In the application of Common Law rules the process of interpretation is more involved and requires greater skill on the part of the lawyer, because in many cases it is not only the application and interpretation of the rule that is

[1] MILL, *Logic,* II, p. 144; cf. VINOGRADOFF, *Common Sense in Law,* p. 125.

[2] (1907) *A.C.* 29 ff.

in question, but its very formulation. It would be out of the question to go into this matter in detail, as it forms the substance of a great part of the Common Law development. I should like, however, to point out as an illustration of the process the famous Rule in Shelley's Case, by which it was laid down that when the ancestor, by any gift or conveyance, takes the estate of freehold, and in the same gift or conveyance an estate is limited to his heirs in fee or in tail, the term *heirs* constitutes words of limitation of the estate of the ancestor, making it fee simple or fee tail, and not words of purchase giving a separate right to the heirs.[1]

Even apart from interpretation every case before the courts may be considered from the point of view of the dialectical processes which underlie the arguments and the decisions. The most common method used is that of *subsumption*—the bringing of the facts of the case under the influence of some recognized rules. Take a recent case—*Macmillan and another v. London Joint Stock Bank Ltd.* (1917) 2 K.B. 439, and (1918) A.C. 777. Subsumption.

A clerk of a London publisher had taken advantage of the fact that he had been entrusted with a signed cheque in which the space for the words had been left blank, though the figures £2 had been written at the bottom: he inserted the words one hundred and twenty and the corresponding figures. The bank paid the money, but refused to assume responsibility for the payment of £118 in excess of the amount intended to be paid by the firm. "The governing principle had been stated by the plaintiff to be that a man could not take advantage of his own wrong . . . a man could not complain of the consequences of his own default against a person who had been misled by that default without any default of his own." It cannot be said that the decision in the case was easy to find. There were very strong grounds for the argument of the appellant, who tried to bring the facts under the operation of the rule that no

1 Coke, I, p. 233. Lieber, *Legal and Political Hermeneutics* (Boston, 1839), contains many interesting observations on the methods of Interpretation in English Law. Thibaut's little book, *Theorie der logischen Auslegung des römischen Rechts* (Altona, 1799), is still the most thoughtful and clear treatment of the subject as regards Roman Law.

one could take advantage of his own wrong,—in this case the careless manner in which the employer had drawn up the cheque. The Court of Appeals, however, took another view of the rule to be applied: it drew a distinction between the proximate or effective cause of the loss and the more remote circumstances attending the issue of the cheque. In the opinion of the Court these circumstances did not suffice to shift the responsibility from the forger to the firm in whose employment he had been acting. "A customer owed a duty to his banker not to mislead, but such duty was not broken by negligently drawing a cheque in such a manner as afforded another person an opportunity of misleading. Negligence in order to estop must be negligence in the transaction itself, and the proximate cause of the loss." The chain of reasoning as stated by Swinfen Eady, L.J., is presented in plain literary language, but it might be converted by a pedantic schoolman into a *sorites*—a sequence of syllogisms in accordance with Aristotle's precepts. Such a sequence would ultimately rest on two fundamental syllogisms, a negative and a positive one. The first may perhaps be expressed in the following words: (1) No one can take advantage of his own wrong. (2) The incomplete manner in which the cheque was drawn up by the principal is not a wrong in the above sense. (3) This being so the principal is not responsible for the fraud of the clerk. The second syllogism may be stated as follows: (1) The risk in the acceptance of a fraudulent cheque falls on the bank which accepts it. (2) The cheque presented to the bank was a document which had been tampered with by the clerk. (3) Therefore the whole matter lies between the bank and the clerk.

The Court of Appeal pronounced in favour of the publishing firm. The House of Lords, however, looked at the matter in another way. The Lord Chancellor (Lord Finlay) in delivering his decision, brought the case under the operation of the rule as to negligence. He said among other things:

"As the customer and the banker were under a contractual relation in this matter, it appeared obvious that in drawing a cheque the customer was bound to take usual and reasonable precautions to prevent forgery. Crime was, indeed, a serious matter, but every one knew that crime was not uncommon. If the cheque was drawn in such a way as to facilitate or almost to invite an increase in the amount by forgery if the cheque should get into the hands of a dishonest person, forgery was not a remote, but a very natural consequence of negligence of this kind. *Young v. Grote* was decided nearly one hundred years ago. It had often been approved of by many of the greatest judges, and, with the exception of a recent case in the Privy Council, there had never been a decision inconsistent with it but for that now under appeal.

The sole ground on which *Young v. Grote* was decided by the majority of the Court of Common Pleas was that Young was a customer of the bank owing to the bank the duty of drawing his cheque with reasonable care, that he had delegated the performance of that duty to his wife, that she had been guilty of gross negligence in having the cheque filled up in such manner as to facilitate an increase of the amount, and that the fraudulent alteration of the cheque by the clerk to whom, after it was filled up, it had been entrusted by her for the purpose of getting payment, would not have taken place but for the careless manner in which the cheque was drawn. The duty which the customer owed to the bank was to draw the cheques with reasonable care to prevent forgery, and if, owing to neglect of this duty, forgery took place, the customer was liable to the bank for the loss. As the negligence of the customer caused the loss, he must bear it."[1]

Generalization.

While in cases similar to that we have been discussing the course of reasoning runs in the direction of subsumption to a certain rule, the logical process may also develop in the other direction; the problem would consist in such a case in combining scattered rules or decisions under more comprehensive principles. Legal reasoning on those lines

[1] In *Young v. Grote*, (1827) 4. Bing. 253, the wife of the plaintiff had ordered a clerk to insert the text of the cheque left in blank by her husband to the amount of £50. He wrote the text as directed,

leads to extensions of juridical concepts, or to their co-ordination. An example may be adduced from the history of the action of *assumpsit.* The Year Books of the fifteenth century show the Lancastrian lawyers at work on the doctrine of liability arising out of implied agreements. They were busy discussing the cases of a doctor harming a patient by mistaken treatment, of a smith spoiling a horse by shoeing it wrongly, etc., and they came to the conclusion that malfeasance in carrying out the undertaking amounted to a tort and entailed liability to compensation. But how about a carpenter who had promised to build a house and had failed to do so? The millmaker who having promised to construct a mill by an appointed day had not finished his work according to promise? The original view was that such cases of *nonfeasance* "sounded in covenant" and required a written contract to protect the parties. A case of 1425 shows the judges of the Common Bench divided in opinion on this point. (Y.B., 3 Henry VI, 36). Some ten years later, however, a more comprehensive view of the principle of *assumpsit* prevailed, as is shown in a decision by Paston and Jeune (Y.B., 14 Henry VI, 18, 58); liability for carrying out an undertaking was extended to cases of nonfeasance as well as malfeasance.[1]

Dogmatic construction.

The logical co-ordination of juridical ideas reaches a still higher level when the object is not to interpret, to apply or to formulate a rule, but to set up a doctrine, that is, a complex of mutually dependent rules. Such doctrines are apt to grow out of the settlement of particular problems, when practice or reflection induces lawyers to survey a whole section of their subject: the influence of such dogmatic constructions on the actual administration of justice can hardly be exaggerated, and the intellectual subtlety displayed in building up these logical schemes is often very remarkable. I should like to point out as an example the treatment of contractual obligation in modern systems of law. It will be convenient to start from the English

but subsequently made use of spaces left blank to alter the sum from £50 to £350.

[1] W. Barbour, *History of Contract in Early Equity*, pp. 45 ff., in Vinogradoff's *Oxford Studies in Social and Legal History*, Vol. IV (1914).

doctrine, as the more familiar one. The keystone of this doctrine consists in the requirement of a valuable consideration in cases of agreements not made by deed under seal.

"A valuable consideration in the sense of the law may consist in some right, interest, profit, or benefit accruing to one party, or some forbearance, detriment, loss, or responsibility given, suffered or undertaken by the other."[1] One of the principal consequences of this doctrine is that the "liberal intention" of one of the parties is not accepted as a sufficient ground for a valid promise. There must be an inducement to the promise in the shape of some valuable advantage, unless the transaction is carried out as a deed. The strict formulation of the doctrine was not achieved without misgivings. Lord Mansfield was in favour of admitting the validity of promises conditioned by moral obligations. But Common Law eventually settled down in requiring consideration in the present or in the future. "A promisor cannot be sued on his promise if he made it merely to satisfy a motive or wish, nor can he be sued on it by one who did not furnish the consideration on which the promise is based."[2] To be sure the greatest latitude is given to personal opinion in matters of consideration. As Hobbes has expressed it (*Leviathan*, pt. 1, c. 75): "The value of all things contracted for is measured by the appetite of the contractors, and therefore the just value is that which they may be contented to give."[3] Nevertheless the fundamental idea is the requirement in the case of "parol" agreements of some equivalent by way either of direct acquisition or of a limitation imposed on the other party. A distinction between consideration and motives is drawn in the English theory in the sense that no motives are recognized except those derived from material profit and loss.[4]

[1] *Currie v. Misa*, L. R. 10 Exch. 162. This definition is not quite complete in so far as it does not take note of the fundamental rule that consideration moves from the promisee. A more exact, but abstract definition is given by AMES, *Lectures on Legal History* (Cambridge, Mass., 1913), p. 323: "Any act or forbearance or promise by one person given in exchange for the promise of another."

[2] ANSON on Contract, p. 104 (14th ed., 1917).

[3] Cited by POLLOCK, *Principles of Contract*, p. 171.

[4] ANSON, *ibid.*, p. 102: "Past consideration is not consideration,

The test is simple and effective, but it cannot be said that it gets rid of difficulties: the weak side of the doctrine becomes apparent in the inadequate way in which it meets the cases when promises are given and obligations undertaken from motives of disinterested friendliness and affection. As "gratuitous liberality" does not find express recognition, its natural and unavoidable manifestations have to be disguised under fictitious pretences of consideration [1] or by treating agreements in the nature of a deposit or *mandatum* as exceptional and contriving some protection for them under rules derived from kindred doctrines.[2]

Continental systems have treated the same problem of agreement from the opposite point of view in so far as they have allowed a wider scope for motives. Historically and theoretically this treatment was suggested by certain features of Roman law. When the latter ceased to consider contracts in their purely formal aspect as relations established by the correct performance of certain solemn acts,[3] the means for ascertaining the will and intention of the parties naturally assumed a primary importance for the recognition and enforcement of agreements. Obligations which could not be referred to a *justa causa* were exposed to attack and revocation. In bilateral contracts, such as sale, the cause of the obligation of each party was easily discernible in the corresponding obligation of the other party: if you let a house, the rent promised to you in return is the cause of your obligation to the lessee. In agreements such as donation, gratuitous deposit or *mandatum,* the cause was recognized in the liberal intention of the promisor to benefit the promisee.[4]

and what the promisor gets in such a case is the satisfaction of motives of pride and gratitude."

[1] In *Thomas v. Thomas,* (1842) 2 Q. B. 851, the moral motive which prompted the husband in providing his widow with a home was not recognized, but the payment of a nominal rent was considered to be sufficient to uphold the validity of the agreement.

[2] Cf. Sir W. ANSON's remarks on gratuitous bailment, *Contracts,* pp. 103 ff.

[3] One of these forms was "verbal" but not in the sense of the English *informal* "parol" agreement. The stipulation was considered a binding solemnity. Cf. GIRARD, *Manuel de droit romain,* 3rd ed., p. 452.

[4] See BRINZ, *Pandekten,* II, § 248, note 28; DERNBURG, *Pandekten,*

The doctrine was worked out definitely in French Law.[1] Art. 1131 of the Code Civil lays down that: An obligation devoid of cause, or provided with a false cause, or an illicit cause, has no effect whatever. (*Une obligation sans cause, ou sur une fausse cause, ou sur une cause illicite ne peut avoir aucun effet.*)

The development of the idea and its co-ordination with other rules of the Code gave rise to an interesting dogmatic construction. One of the consequences drawn from the requirement of a *causa* was the distinction between cause and motive. An attempt had to be made to draw a line of demarcation between the two.[2]

But the distinction, though plain enough in theory, proved to be difficult to apply in practice. If the Courts had rigidly followed the view that *cause* is the professed reason of a contract, they would have been obliged to lend the assistance of public power to transactions prompted by immoral motives if these motives, though sufficiently obvious, did not constitute a technical element of the contract. Cases in point arose, for instance, when Courts were asked to uphold donations made to concubines for the purpose of keeping up immoral intercourse. The Courts refused to do so on the ground of Art. 1131, but that meant that they found it necessary in the above-mentioned cases to overlook the distinction between cause and motive.[3]

Other difficulties arose from the necessity of harmonizing Art. 1131 with Art. 900. The latter rule lays down that if an illegal condition has been set to a promise, the promise remains valid while the condition is annulled. In applying Art. 900 the French Courts inquire whether the condition

§ 95, p. 220, 7th ed., II, § 315, applies to the modernized theory of Roman Law which tends towards the admission of "abstract" obligations apart from any *causa*. WINDSCHEID, *Pandekten*, II, § 319.

[1] It owes its origin there to the great seventeenth-century jurist Domat (*Lois Civiles*, Livre 1, t. 1, s. 1, nn. 5, 6).

[2] The *cause* is the aim or the intention inherent in the contract and therefore known, or supposed to be known, by both parties. The *motive* is the impulse that prompted the transaction. In unilateral contracts the cause consists either in a former service, or purely and simply in the liberal intention (BUFNOIR, *Cours de droit civil*, II, 528. Cf. COLIN et CAPITANT, *Cours de droit civil* (1915), II, 313.

[3] BEUDANT, *Cours de droit civil*, II, p. 115.

in question is so substantial as to form the *cause* of the contract or whether it can be treated as a *mode,* admitting of alteration. The decision in each case depends on a consideration of the circumstances of the case and must therefore be regarded as a point of fact.[1]

In this way the French doctrine tends more and more to pass from a conception of the cause as the professed reason of agreement to a view which makes cause equivalent to intention.

One might almost feel inclined to consider the complete abandonment of the requirement of a *cause* in the German Civil Code as the final result of the development of continental jurisprudence which, starting from the formal contracts of Roman Law and clinging for some time to the abstract notion of a juridical cause as distinguished from motive, has eventually reached a stage in which the Law deals directly with intentions and consent, and has abandoned the requirement of a technical cause.[2] On the whole it may be said that the English doctrine, insisting on a tangible justification of agreements, has been obliged to seek such a justification in valuable consideration, while the continental doctrines opposed to such a material test have been gradually led to reject altogether the technical requirement of cause. Thus under the influence of a logical deduction distinctions have been made and consequences have been drawn in all directions, but the predominance of the logical method has led to a one-sided treatment of principles and to conflicts with practical requirements which arise from the complications of actual life.

Exaggeration.

English law, so conspicuous for its common sense and attention to practical needs, is probably less liable than any other to have its rules perverted by an excess of abstract dialectics.[3]

[1] BUFNOIR, *Cours de droit civil,* I, p. 543; COLIN et CAPITANT, *Cours de droit civil,* II, p. 318.

[2] Cf. survey of the fluctuations of German Law on this subject in R. HÜBNER, *Grundzüge des deutschen Privatrechts* (1908), pp. 493 ff.; SALEILLES, *De l'obligation en droit civil allemand;* PLANIOL, *Cours de droit civil,* II.

[3] I may mention that the notion of *public policy* is bound to introduce a powerful element of practical reflection restraining abstract

Yet, even here, matters may sometimes assume an aspect which reduces rules to absurdity. Sir F. Pollock gives an amusing instance in connection with the discharge of obligations.[1] "It is the rule of English law that a debt of £100 may be perfectly well discharged by the creditor's acceptance of a beaver hat or a peppercorn, or of a negotiable instrument for a less sum at the same time and place at which the £100 are payable, or of 10/- at an earlier day or at another place, but that nothing less than a release under seal will make his acceptance of £99 in money at the same time and place a good discharge. The rule in *Pinnel's Case*,[2] though paradoxical, is not anomalous. It is the strictly logical result of carrying out a general principle beyond the bounds in which it is reasonably applicable."

The danger of such an abuse of dogmatic construction is much greater under the sway of continental systems. French jurists have lately[3] entered emphatic protests against its deadening influence.

As regards Germany, I will restrict myself to a reference to Ihering, who, himself a brilliant dialectician, has ridiculed the extravagant use of dogmatic construction by pedantic colleagues. A few extracts from his *Scherz und Ernst in der Jurisprudenz* will suffice:

"I had died. A form of light met my soul on its leaving the body.

"You are now free from the ties of the senses that chained your spirit to the body. You need only think of the place you want to go to in order to be there.

"I will try. Where shall I put myself by means of my thought?

deductions. On the meaning of public policy, see *Davies v. Davies* (1886) 36 Ch. D. 364.

[1] *Principles of Contract*, p. 179.

[2] 5 Coke's Rep. 117.

[3] GÉNY, *Méthode d'interprétation*, p. 133: "By substituting for the real elements of juridical life—for the moral, psychological, economic, politic and social motives—technical, abstract, cold notions deprived of fruitful reality, our interpretation of law has created a system of pure formulæ and categories which, in conjunction with the exaggerated influence attributed to a modern code, has rendered the scientific practice of our courts not only sterile, but often harmful."

"As you are a student of Roman Law you will proceed to the heaven of juridical concepts.—Is it dark there?—Quite dark. Here is the apparatus for constructions. It is nice that it should be acting just now. Let us see what is the object of the spirit who is working it.—Mighty spirit, allow us to ask what are you doing just now?—I am constructing contract.—Contract? But that is quite a simple thing; what is there to construct?—A good deal—just because it's simple.—But then what will happen in the case of concepts like rights as to rights, the *hereditas jacens,* the gage in one's own property?—All trifles! I have finished these things off long ago. The only things that interest me beside Contract, are Obligation and Direct Representation.—May I ask what results you have reached as regards them?—As to Obligation—it is a right to an act to be performed by the debtor.—I cannot conceive this at all. As long as an act has not been performed, it does not exist: therefore there can be no right concerning it.—Exist! One sees that you do not belong to our set. What we think—exists, etc."

Logical system of Law.

One form of logical exaggeration has played a particularly important part in the history of juridical thought—it is the assumption that there is a completeness in a legal system which enables the jurist to discover legal principles and to formulate rules even when there is no positive basis for them in statutes or precedents. According to this view there are no gaps in a rational system of law—say the Roman, the French or the English; law, even if not expressed, is latent *in gremio judicum* and will be formulated by the Courts called upon to produce it. This doctrine has been taught by German jurists, for example by Brinz, and it has been used by English lawyers to support the fiction that there is no such thing as "judge-made law" and that Common Law is the logical exposition of pre-existing principles. A modern writer on jurisprudence has attacked this fallacy with great vigour. "The whole science of Jurisprudence does not claim to be anything but a system of rules for the guidance of the judge, for surely no one has ever been foolish enough to imagine that the law embodies a complete system of rules whereby the course of human action in all possible circumstances can be settled beforehand. Jellinek has already noticed that the dogma of the logical completeness of our legal system does not apply to public law, but only to those branches of the law in which the final decision rests with the judge. The case does not differ when the decision does rest with the judge . . . He is obliged to discover some solution, but this solution is certainly not the product of a logical legal system complete in itself. The only practical object of such a system is to supply the judge with an ample provision of rules to aid him in pronouncing judgment in all possible cases."[1]

The fictitious character of the doctrine of the latent completeness of law, let us add, becomes especially apparent when one reflects that its consistent application would lead to the admission that our existing Common Law system was, apart from statutory innovations, in existence in the time of Bracton and of Martin of Pateshull. Those who shrink from such a paradox have to make room somewhere for creative innovation, and can hardly look to any other source of inspiration for the law-making judges than their sense of practical requirements.[2]

However, exaggeration in the use of an effective method ought not to obscure the value of the method when applied with proper caution. When all has been said about the barrenness of pedantic logic, it must be remembered that what we have to deal with in actual reasoning is not formal exercises in school logic, but the *dialectical* treatment of materials, instinct with vital problems and issues. Utility, public interest, morality, justice, are constantly claiming their share in the thoughts of the lawyer, while logic provides him with a solid framework for his reasoning.

1 EHRLICH, *Grundlegung der Soziologie des Rechts*, p. 15.
2 Cf. J. C. GRAY, *Nature and Source of the Law* (1909), § 489, p. 217.

CHAPTER II

LAW AND PSYCHOLOGY

THERE is an aspect of law which brings its close dependence on psychology into a particularly strong light; namely, the fact that law deals with the human will.

The operation of will in testaments and agreements.

Both in civil and in criminal proceedings lawyers are constantly confronted by this mysterious conception of the will, and although they have tried to simplify the subject for convenient manipulation, they are often reminded of the awkward psychological background stretching behind their conventional formulæ.

This is obviously true of the law as to *testaments.* From the most remote antiquity the principal condition imposed on testators by the legislators and courts is the requirement that the testator should be of sound mind at the time when he makes his will. Not only downright insanity or senile debility, but morbid submission to influence is considered in all countries to be a reason for invalidating a will. In Athens, leave to make a valid testament was refused to the insane, to people who had fallen into dotage, to men under the influence of women (*μανιῶν, ἢ γέρων, ἢ γυναικὶ πειθόμενος*). No wonder the law reports are full of cases turning on the question, What is to be understood by the notion of a "sound mind" in relation to civil incapacity?—and one cannot but feel that the whole subject is in a state of uncertainty and transition. I will merely refer to one case in which the will of an insane person supposed to have been made during a lucid interval was granted probate, although the same person had been previously refused leave to execute a deed. (*Re Walker, Watson and others v. Treasury Solicitor.*)[1] "The deceased suffered from delusions, and when under those delusions she would become passionate, violent, and even

[1] (1912) 28 T.L.R. 466.

dangerous. Her obsessions were entirely recognized by herself as morbid and did not prevent her from taking an intelligent interest in general topics. She kept up a correspondence with her relatives and friends, with the Visitors in Lunacy and the Master in Lunacy, and in other respects was a shrewd and clever woman, and her memory was excellent.'' In 1904 she executed a deed creating a trust for the benefit of some relatives, but the Master in Lunacy refused to recognize the validity of the deed and the Court of Appeal confirmed his decision on the ground that the interests of a lunatic so found by inquisition were to be protected by the Committee in Lunacy under the Crown and that the creation of a trust would lead to dual control and a conflict of authorities. Nevertheless, when Mrs. Walker made a will in a lucid interval, this will was granted probate.

It is even more difficult to come to a conclusion as to the dependence or independence of mind of a person, who is not a recognized lunatic.

One of the leading cases on this matter is *Norton v. Relly.*[1] It originated in a bill against Relly, a dissenting preacher, and others, as trustees in a deed of gift executed by Mrs. Norton, granting an annuity of £50 a year to the defendant, praying that it might be delivered up to be cancelled.

The Lord Chancellor in giving judgment for the plaintiff said: "I could easily have told what by the proofs of his cause, and his own letters he appears to be—a subtle sectarian, who preys upon his deluded hearers, and robs them under the mask of religion; one itinerant who propagates his fanaticism even in the cold northern countries, where one should scarcely suppose that it could enter. Shall it be said in his excuse, that as to this lady she was as great an enthusiast as himself when he first became acquainted with her and consequently not deluded by him? It appears indeed that she wrote some verses 'on the mystery of the

[1] (1764) 2 Eden 286. Cf. *Lyon v. Home*, 6 Eq., pp. 655 ff. (1868): "A widow of seventy-five was induced by a 'medium' to adopt him and to make various gifts and a will in his favour. The relation between them implied domination over her mind." The rule is different in the case of simple contracts.

union of the Father, the Son and the Holy Spirit.' It is true that it appears by this that she was far gone, but not gone far enough for his purpose. She advanced step by step till she became quite intoxicated, if I may use the expression, with his madness and enthusiasm. Inasmuch as the deed was obtained in circumstances of the greatest fraud, imposition and misrepresentation—the defendant, Relly, shall execute a release."

The responsibility for crime.

Even more momentous issues are involved in the necessity of estimating the action of intellect and will as regards the responsibility of a person for crime. The development of criminal law is highly characteristic of a gradual change of views on the subject of individual responsibility. One need not look very far back in history to discover an appalling barbarism in the treatment of criminal offenders. Eighteenth-century England, whose legal system was described and extolled by Blackstone, built up its criminal law on an indiscriminate application of the death penalty, and on purely external tests of responsibility. The spread of humanitarian doctrines embodied in Beccaria's famous book,[1] in Howard's activity and the utilitarian agitation of Bentham, brought about great changes in all directions. But the psychological grounds of criminality remained unexplored and the legal tests of responsibility were still of the most rudimentary kind even in the middle of the nineteenth century. In 1843 a pronouncement of the judges was made in *M'Naughten's Case*[2] with regard to criminal responsibility. It was laid down, among other things, that to establish a defence on the ground of insanity, it must be clearly proved that at the time of committing the act the accused was labouring under such a defect of reason from a disease of the mind as not to know the nature and quality of the act he was doing, or if he did know it, that he did not know it was wrong.[3]

Up to quite recent times the legal doctrines applied by the Courts in attributing responsibility even in the case of mental disease did not go further than the admission that

[1] *Dei Delitti e delle Pene* (1764).
[2] *Reg. v. M'Naughten*, 10 Cl. & F. 200.
[3] J. F. Stephen, *History of Criminal Law*, II, p. 153.

a person incapable of distinguishing between right and wrong could not be punished for a crime. "Moral insanity" in the shape of uncontrollable ideas was not recognized as a ground for sending an accused person to an asylum.

Take the case of *Reg. v. Haynes.*[1]

"The prisoner, a soldier, was charged with the murder of Mary MacGowan, at the camp of Aldershot. The deceased was a woman with whom the prisoner had been on the most friendly terms up to the moment of the commission of the offence. No motive was assigned for the perpetration of the act. . . .

"Bramwell, B., in summing up to the jury, said: 'As to the defence of insanity, it has been urged for the prisoner that you should acquit him on the ground that, it being impossible to assign any motive for the perpetration of the offence, he must have been acting under what is called a powerful and irresistible influence, or homicidal tendency. But I must remark as to that, that the circumstance of an act being *apparently* motiveless is not a ground from which you can safely infer the existence of such an influence. Motives exist unknown and innumerable which might prompt the act. A morbid and restless (but resistible) thirst for blood would itself be a motive urging to such a deed for its own relief. But if an influence be so powerful as to be termed irresistible, so much more reason is there why we should not withdraw any of the safeguards tending to counteract it.' "

Later on English law has shifted its point of view.[2] Let us take a simple case which started in the assizes in Leeds. (*R. v. Jefferson.*)[3]

In the Court of Criminal Appeal, an appeal was brought against a conviction for the murder of a woman. It was proved that the accused cut the woman's head in the presence of witnesses and made no attempt to escape, and also that he took certain articles of clothing not worth a penny and brought them away with him. In delivering

1 (1859) 1 F. and F. 666; KENNY, *Cases on Criminal Law*, pp. 52 f. Cf. VINOGRADOFF, *Common Sense in Law*, pp. 131 f.

2 See e.g. Lord Esher in *Hanbury v. Hanbury* (1892), 8 T.L.R. 559.

3 (1908) 24 T.L.R. 877.

judgment Mr. Justice Lawrence said that there was no doubt that the verdict given was unsatisfactory, and in his judgment it ought not to stand. There was strong evidence called before the jury which showed that the man was not in such a state of mind as to make him responsible for his act. The sentence must be quashed, and the order would be that the prisoner should be detained as a criminal lunatic during His Majesty's pleasure.

The general principle which governs the subject at present was summarized by Mr. Justice Bray in *R. v. Fryer.* (24 Cox C.C. 403.) The circumstances of the case were very similar to those in *Reg. v. Haynes.* A soldier had, without any apparent motive, strangled a girl who had been engaged to him. Bray, J., said in his charge to the jury: "For the purpose of to-day I am going to direct you in the way indicated by a very learned judge, Fitzjames Stephen,—if it is shown that he (the accused) is in such a state of mental disease or natural mental infirmity as to deprive him of the capacity to control his actions, I think you ought to find him what the law calls him—'insane.'"

The crucial question of responsibility has to be decided by a jury guided by the general directions of the presiding judge. In this way a small body of laymen representing public opinion in the country have to formulate verdicts as to innocence, guilt and responsibility. They have to make up their minds not only as to the evidence of witnesses and the value of circumstantial indications, but also as to the relative importance of statements by experts, such as doctors in cases of mental disease or morbid influence. From a technical point of view such a method is open to objections, and, though the creation of the Court of Criminal Appeal makes it possible to correct flagrant errors, the verdicts of juries do not always show a high standard of perspicacity.

According to English ideas, however, no better means can be found for submitting cases to the opinion of the community. In spite of all its failings, the jury represents public opinion and gives expression to the common sense of disinterested citizens. In this matter as in many others, law aims not at perfection or refinement, but at a definite solution on considerations which appeal to average members of the community. For this very reason it is immensely important that popular notions should be brought up to a level with the broad results of scientific study. By imperceptible degrees scientific discoveries are making their way into popular consciousness, and it is the duty of those who are in closer touch with progressive thought—lawyers as well as scientists—to promote by all available means the spread of knowledge on these subjects.

Scientific and juridical treatment.

People are often shy of approaching the psychological study of legal phenomena, especially of crime, because they are afraid of undermining the practical premises of social security by investigating closely the psychological motives of criminals. This apprehension seems based on a pure misunderstanding: the principle of social self-preservation requires adaptation to altered scientific views rather than adherence to antiquated theories and the grappling of juries in every single case with the perplexing problem of responsibility. Tarde has some pertinent remarks on the subject.[1]

Measures of isolation and prevention adopted at the right time may safeguard society from dangerous outbursts on the part of degenerate subjects. In any case, it is obvious that the point of departure of any thorough analysis of the *mens rea* must be sought in psychology.

On the other hand it would be idle to contend that modern psychologists can treat such problems without taking heed of the lawyers' requirements and limitations. For one thing, the latter aim not at discussion, but at a decision. It would never do in practice to dismiss cases as insufficiently ripe for a verdict. Social justice holds the accused in a vice and must direct him either to the right

[1] "A medico-legal expert, Mendel, has published a work intended to prove that his colleagues, in answer to the question 'Was the accused in the possession of his faculties?' should refrain from giving any answer. . . . It becomes more and more easy for a lawyer, with the writings of alienists at his disposal, to demonstrate the irresistible nature of criminal impulse which carried his client off his feet."—*Penal Philosophy*, p. 15.

or to the left, must declare him either guilty or not guilty, although in a number of cases there may be great doubts on the point. A *non liquet* verdict in the shape of a disagreement of the jury, only delays final decision and throws the responsibility for it on another set of doomsmen. Now this is not a chance peculiarity nor one which can be easily improved upon. Even in a system like the Scotch, where a "not proven" verdict is possible, it is considered as an exceptional occurrence, and the aim of the proceedings is to reach a definite *yes* or *no* solution of the dispute.

This state of things corresponds to the fundamental difference between theoretical investigation and practical action: the first strives to reflect all shades and niceties of the material, while co-ordinating them as far as possible in accordance with underlying principles; the latter steers according to its best lights towards an end, however incomplete and contradictory the information at hand may be. A pilot navigating a ship, a physician attending a patient, a lawyer conducting a case cannot break off their operations at pleasure: this means in the case of the lawyer that he frequently has to be content with average estimates and approximate truths, sometimes even with artificial presumptions which help to bridge over insoluble difficulties and awkward gaps. Bearing these facts in mind, we shall be in a position to understand the peculiar mixture of theoretical and practical considerations presented by law. In the department of criminal justice from which we started, this mixed character is especially noticeable.

Definitions of crime.

Modern judges and juries cannot be content with a slavish rehearsal of statutory rules. It seems out of the question at present to adopt Bentham's definition of crime as an act which it is deemed necessary to forbid,[1] and yet the superficial character of this statement is still traceable in the definition proposed by Austin and improved upon by an eminent professor of English law in our days: "Crimes are wrongs whose sanction is punitive, and is remissible by the Crown, if remissible at all."[2] One might wonder

[1] *Works,* I, p. 81. (*Principles of Morals and Legislation,* ch. xiv.).
[2] KENNY, *Outlines of Criminal Law,* p. 15.

why the possibility of remission is both inserted in the definition and declared not to be essential to it. But the principal objection to such a definition seems to be, that it is purely "extrinsic," and that to that extent it begs the question it is supposed to answer. We start from the fact that certain acts are punished by the State, but we want to know *why* the State assumes such a power in respect of its citizens. It is not enough to point to certain peculiarities and contradictions of positive law, as it has been shaped in the course of history, in order to render an intrinsic definition unnecessary or impossible. As a matter of fact, the principal "intrinsic" definitions (among them those of Blackstone and of Stephen) are not so widely different or so incomplete as it might seem at first glance. Crime is generally understood to be *a revolt of the individual against society*, and the questions as to the methods of reacting against such revolts and of the measure of sensitiveness in the social body towards them are subsidiary questions which do not go to the root of the matter.[1]

Modern teaching as to ideas.

It is out of the question to review all the theories brought forward by modern psychologists: we have to leave their discussion to specialists. But it is desirable to point out whom we intend to follow, as there are many roads towards the goal and a jurist has to make up his mind which to take. The teaching as to the association of ideas, developed by Locke, Hume, J. S. Mill and Bain may serve as a starting-point. It showed the necessity of analysing perceptions in a way entirely different from the logical one, and to explain their combinations by contact in the course of experience rather than by subdivision and subsumption under abstract categories. The associationists dealt, however, in a one-sided way with ideas as phenomena of cognition, and when they took up the problems of emotion and volition, they approached them from an intellectualistic point of view, as products of formulated thought.[2]

[1] On the literature of criminal law see, e.g., BEROLZHEIMER, *Strafrechts Philosophie*, 1907.

[2] WUNDT, on "Psychology," in WINDELBAND'S *Philosophie im Beginn des XX Jahrhunderts*, p. 6: "In Wolff's *Deutsche Psychologie* and in the writing of his successors we find the meanings of the words 'to think' and 'thought' extended in a remarkable way to

Reflex and Energy.

The next stage was reached by a materialistic synthesis on a physiological basis, as represented by Fechner, F. Maudsley, Ribot, etc. The aim was to establish a direct dependence of the mental process on the physical one. All facts of consciousness were considered as *epiphenomenal reflexes* of physiological processes stimulated by the impact of outside objects on the receptive organs of the nervous system. From this point of view ideas could be compared to the movements of the meter registering the pressure of steam on the engine—not productive in any way, but merely manifesting the organic process.[1] James, Lange and others have carried the psycho-physiological hypothesis even further into the domain of feeling and of volition. In their view, the feelings of joy, sorrow, anger, fear, are consequences of changes produced directly by impressions from the outside world. These impressions call forth reflexes in the shape of accelerated action of the heart, a stiffening of the muscles, tears and the like; the sentiments which were supposed to call forth these physiological changes are in truth only consequential emotions produced by physiological reflexes.[2] In the same way, the exertion of the will was supposed to be only a phenomenon of consciousness, producing a mistaken notion of activity where in truth there is a passive state of the organism reflecting impulses which come to it from the outside. This reversal of the usual meaning of terms and of common-sense experiences is not called for by the necessities of analysis and leads to absurd conclusions. As James Ward has put it: "Let Professor James be confronted first by a chained bear and next by a bear at large: to the one object he presents

all kinds of psychic values; similarly the word 'idea' is used in the works of English and French psychologists of this and the preceding period in an all-embracing sense; these are eloquent and tangible proofs of the tendency to resolve all actual qualities and differences in one and the same medium of logical reflection."

1 E.g. Ribot, *German Psychology*, p. 215.

2 E.g. Lange, *Les Émotions*, trad. par G. Dumas, 1902, p. 10: "Emotion then is the outcome on the one hand of more or less localized sensations, on the other of vascular and muscular states; let us not therefore speak any more of these mysterious entities which are called fear, anger, joy, or, if we speak of them, let us clearly recognize that they express the ill-defined consciousness of a certain number of movements. It is a matter of pure mechanism."

a bun, and to the other a clean pair of heels. Professor James would remind us that in his nomenclature 'it is the total situation on which the reaction of the subject is made.' But there is just a world of difference between 'object'= stimulus transformed by preorganized mechanism into an efferent discharge, and 'object'=total situation to which the subject reacts."[1]

Altogether it may be said that the physiological school in its eagerness to establish an immediate connection between mental states and their physiological substrata has gone beyond the mark. It is not necessary and not admissible to eliminate the mental process in order to assign the physical process its due share. In psychology we can no more do without the subjective side of our thoughts and emotions than we can do without their objective premises. Consciousness once created becomes a powerful agent in itself and one of the means for carrying on evolution. This has been emphasized in every way by Alfred Fouillée.[2] Rightly construed, his theory of ideas as forces gets rid of the supposed passivity of the mind and lays stress on the most elementary form of its conscious reaction against the outer world.

Mental unity.

In the present stage of psychology, its most influential exponents may be said to have adopted the view that the mental process presents a unity (*psychosis*) distinct from the physiological process, though intimately connected with it. In its relations to the outside world the mind is both receptive and active, receptive in so far as it receives impressions, and is excited by them to emotion; active in so far as it transforms its impressions and emotions by reasoning and volition. The vital knot between reception and activity is formed by *attention*, that is, by the selection of certain facts for mental treatment.[3]

Such a view excludes the old subdivision of the mental

[1] *Enc. Brit. Art. Psychology* (1st ed.), XXII, p. 586.

[2] A. Fouillée, *L'évolutionnisme des idées-forces*, p. 196: "This development of energy is not a creation of energy, nor a free direction of energy; physically it is the passing of one kind of energy into another, of the force of tension into the force of translation; psychologically it is the passing of a conflict of ideas and of desires into determination." Cf. Wundt, *Logik*, I, p 24.

[3] J. A. Ward, *Psychological Principles* (1918), p. 57.

current into *faculties.* It regards consciousness as the subjective aspect of the mental process itself and prepares the way for it by selective attention. James (*Principles of Psychology,* I. 400) rightly notices the insufficient treatment of attention by rival psychological schools: "Empiricists ignore selective attention, because they wish to account for all products of experience by laws of association which cluster things together independently of the activity of the subject, and idealists, in the interests of the ideal order, regard experience as dictated by the objective selection of pure thought."[1]

The fundamental change of point of view has led to a revision of all the principal doctrines as to the functions of the mind. As regards the intellect, it cannot be considered any longer as the predominant partner in the mental process. The assumption of metaphysical rationalism and of empirical intellectualism about *ideas* as primary elements of human consciousness have been shown to be erroneous both as to the insoluble character of these supposed elements and as to their combinations.

We have now to guard against the opposite exaggeration. We understand that mental processes cannot be treated as mere physiological reflexes: such a view would result in absurdity—in denying the special character of psychic phenomena; or else would claim for these phenomena the position of effects without causes.[2] But although such a materialistic conception may be said on the whole to have been abandoned by leading psychologists, a tendency to dwell chiefly on the animal processes in the human mind is still very prevalent. It has its natural explanation in the extensive study of animal societies and of savage tribes, but it ought to be balanced by considering the progressive

[1] Wundt's theory of apperception brings into strong relief the element of selective activity, but contains doubtful points from the philosophical point of view. See article on "Apperception" in HASTINGS' *Encyclopaedia of Ethics and Religion.*

[2] FOUILLÉE, *op. cit.,* p. 164: "When consciousness exists, outside the conditions of unconscious phenomena, a new condition is added to the previous ones, the condition of consciousness, whatever this may be; otherwise this would be a case of an effect without physical causes."

aspect of human history and the immense difference between human and animal development taken as a whole. The decisive cleavage in this respect is marked by *language:* it provides the human race with an instrument for mental intercourse and reflection to which there is no equivalent in the animal world. While animals possess means of expressing their emotions by varied cries, man alone has elaborated speech as a method of intellectual formulation. The importance of language in logic has been sufficiently appreciated and explained by writers on the subject. But its importance in psychology is certainly as great. It makes it possible for the individual to communicate not only with his immediate neighbours, and not only in respect of elementary wants and feelings: it raises individual consciousness to social consciousness in all tribes and all nations of the world. And as the chief operations in forming language are logical operations, language tends necessarily to increase the share of the intellectual function in human life far beyond the spiritual range common to man and the animals.[1] Once this step in the growth of speech has been achieved, the influence of reasoning and reflection proceeds in human development with ever-increasing and cumulative force. Through the power of formulating ideas man obtains a greater control over the unformulated impulses of his nature, and this certainly contributes to the setting up and to the enforcement of moral standards; reflection as well as imagination find vent in religious beliefs and religious worship. Altogether, the evolution of human civilization is unthinkable without the guiding thread of intellectual intercourse and speculation.[2]

Spiritual development.

1 TARDE, *Psychologie économique*, 1902, p. 113: "It is impossible to account for the superior designs of art, luxury, truth, justice, or to define the notions of credit or of value without invoking the constant interchange between human sensibilities, intelligences, and wills in their perpetually changing impressions.—They cross each other's lines ceaselessly."

2 WUNDT, *Lectures on Human and Animal Psychology* (translated by Titchener, 1894), p. 350: "It seems that the entire intellectual life of animals can be accounted for on the simple laws of association. Nowhere do we find the characteristic marks of a true reflection of any active functioning of the imagination or the understanding—you may remember the story in Pliny's *Natural History*

Emotions and Instincts.

This principle should be firmly borne in mind when we come to consider the modern aspect of the theory of *emotion.* It was recognized long ago that a purely intellectualistic interpretation of human life would reduce it to a colourless scheme of premises and conclusions. Tone and rhythm are imparted to it by the currents of appetite and satisfaction which run through every moment of human as well as animal existence. And the discoveries in the field of heredity and development have shown that these emotional currents are not restricted to the life of single individuals. In combination with cognitive processes they form inheritable tendencies, habits and instincts which themselves serve as stepping stones for further evolution.[1] By observing the animal world, this feature is made especially clear in its final results and sometimes in its gradual stages. We all know what remarkable effects the accumulation of experience, together with hereditary transmission, has produced in the habits of bees and ants, and it is a legitimate surmise that similar processes have played a great part in preparing the various customs of human tribes.[2]

of the elephant who was punished during a performance for his bad dancing, and who secretly set to work to practise in the night so as to do better next time? Are we likely to accept the story and the explanation?"

P 357: "The criterion of intelligent associative action and of intelligent action proper can only be this—that the effect of association does not go beyond the connection of particular ideas, whether directly excited by sense impressions, or only reproduced by them, while intellectual activity, in the narrow sense of the word, presupposes a demonstrable formation of concepts, judgments and inferences, or an activity of constructive imagination." Cf. the authoritative summing up of BOAS, *The Mind of Primitive Man* (Annual Report of the Smithsonian Institution, 1901, pp. 451-60). See also HOBHOUSE, *Mind in Evolution,* 321 ff.

1 MACDOUGALL, *Introduction to Social Psychology,* 8th ed. (1914), p. 29: "[Instinct] an inherited or innate psycho-physical disposition which determines its possessor to perceive and to pay attention to objects of a certain class, to experience an emotional excitement of a particular quality on perceiving such an object, and to act in regard to it in a particular manner, or at least to experience an impulse to such action." Another definition of instinct in HOBHOUSE, *Mind in Evolution,* 70 ff.

2 MACDOUGALL, *ibid.,* p. 7: "The truth is that men are moved by a variety of impulses whose nature has been determined through long ages of the evolutionary process without reference to the life of man in civilized societies. The problem is, how can one account

The real difficulty arises when we try to apportion the share of emotional and of cognitive functions in accounting for the complex results. It has to be recognized, to begin with, that it is impossible to make a clear distinction between instincts as such and inherited habits or capacities: one variety shades off imperceptibly into the other, and their fluid differences depend entirely on the greater or the lesser degree of unconscious determination. Cats and dogs have a proverbial repulsion one to the other, and yet it has often happened that kittens and puppies have been brought up to live together in perfect amity. Gipsies are well known vagabonds and horse-thieves, but many scions of the gipsy race have managed to live the life of ordinary law-abiding citizens.

Besides, the variety of combinations of nature and environment are so great that we can only strive to mark off the principal tendencies of development, but not their innumerable ramifications. For this very reason it is misleading to attempt a permanent tabulation of primitive instincts on an emotional basis: such a tabulation is bound to be arbitrary and confused at the same time. Is there, e.g., sufficient reason, for surmising a primitive instinct of *self-abasement*, though a dog generally slinks with his tail between his legs when he meets a redoubtable specimen of his kind? Surely the instinct of self-preservation with its natural consequence of fear is sufficient to explain such occurrences. Or is it absolutely necessary to tabulate the opposite feeling of self-assertion (pride, vanity, etc.) as a special primordial instinct? The sentiment of self is wide enough to embrace this and other expressions of an egotistic state of mind. *Curiosity* again can hardly be understood without introducing the element of cognition.[1] The only motive for establishing these complicated distinctions seems to be the wish to reduce the forms of civilization to developments of habits common to men and animals. But, whatever may be our speculations as to the connecting links between apes and primitive man, there is after all the vast

for the fact that men so moved ever come to act as they ought, or morally and reasonably."

[1] MacDougall, *Social Psychology*, pp. 49 ff. holds a different view of these matters.

world of experience as to subsequent stages of human history to be accounted for.[1]

Altogether, it seems scarcely scientific to build up an edifice of more or less differentiated "instincts" in order to prove the influence of heredity and custom on social life. If, however, we set out to trace hereditary habits to their ultimate sources we shall hardly get beyond modifications of selfishness and altruistic attraction on the one hand, and the substitution of unpremeditated reflexes for reasoned action on the other: such a substitution can, of course, take place in the experience of an individual—say, in learning to walk—as well as in that of a hereditary group, e.g., in the formation of peculiarities of dialectic speech.[2]

The Will.

The idea of the *will* as a special faculty separated from cognition and feeling has been abandoned by modern psychological analysis. It is recognized only as the appetitive side of the mental process and, as such, it appears in the germ in every manifestation of feeling whether we call it conation, desire or appetite. In so far as any fact of attention is conditioned by a certain stress of mental activity, the will takes part in all the various stages of the process of cognition—in perception, reflection, reasoning, exertion of memory and imagination. The illusion of a faculty distinct from the intellect and from feeling is created by the fact that the manifestation of the will being a final act, a solution of the previous psychical tension, it is reflected in consciousness as a movement in opposition to motives, as a creative act in opposition to its preparation.[3] This reflection of the will in self-consciousness is at the root of the famous controversy between the upholders of a free will and the determinists. In spite of self-consciousness, no

1 MacDougall, *op. cit.* Cf. the curious explanation of self-consciousness, pp. 247 f.

1 *Ibid.* Cf. the curious explanation of self-consciousness, pp. 247 f.

2 Wundt, *Völkerpsychologie*, I, 1, p. 11: "The domain of voluntary actions derived from considered motives lies outside the range of social psychology. The latter is confined to the domain of instinctive action."

3 Giddings, *Inductive Sociology*, p. 269: "Psychical determination is the *free exercise of will not the exercise of free will*—in so far as volition is the expression of one's own mental constitution—from hereditary tendency and present sensations to reason and conscience. It is an internal and psychical as distinguished from external and physical necessity."

action and no will can be thought to be causeless. In fact, the will appears as the last link in an endless chain of causes ranging from the immediate impulses which led to the exertion of will-power—to the remote conditions shaping character and circumstances. In this way it may be taken for granted that every act of a man is pre-established by previous states and events. If, however, the point of view is shifted and we reflect on our will as the efficient cause of change, and on our actions as springing from our resolve, we are conscious of this resolve as of a *choice* between possibilities, and sometimes we may watch the conflict of motives which prompt us in various directions. The conception of free will is therefore a fact of consciousness in which, though unable to ascertain the exact combination of factors, we oppose the various influences preceding action to the resolve which initiates it. The appeal to reason in the choice of possibilities is perfectly justified, and the formula of *free will* comes to mean in substance that men do not follow impulses blindly, but are normally able to act in accordance with their reason and morality.

The discussion as to free will has brought us to a general problem which has been the subject of inquiry ever since men began to reflect philosophically—namely, to the problem of the origin of the moral ideas. The problem is undoubtedly of such fundamental importance that it cannot be considered exclusively as a special topic of psychological investigation: all the schools of human thought approach it in connection with their general conceptions of the world and of the destiny of man, that is, under the direct influence of their systems of synthetic philosophy. For our purpose, it may be sufficient to treat the subject as a necessary premise of the jurisprudential doctrine of right and duty. It may be taken for granted that the extreme view which goes to deny the existence of any but selfish motives in human nature must lead, if consistently developed, to a revolt against all social conventions. Moralists.

The diatribes of Nietzsche are eloquent expressions of the contempt of the "superman" for the human herd: he deems himself a god and an animal at the same time. These views do not only account in a striking manner for present development, but they are at the same time a reduction to absurdity of the struggle for power in the moral world. It may be appropriate to consider some pronouncements of the prophet of natural license. "To train an animal that may make promises—is this not the aim which nature has set itself as regards man? We find as the ripest fruit of the tree the sovereign personality—emancipated from customary morality, the autonomous supermoral personality—briefly, the man endowed with his own independent, far-reaching will, who may make promises. Being such a free man, this lord of his free will, the sovereign, how should he not know to what extent he is superior to every one that may not make promises and affirmations in his own right? The free man, the holder of a far-reaching indestructible will, has his own standard of value; looking out from his own self to the others, he treats them with respect or contempt. He honours his equal, the strong, the trustworthy—but he will kick the whining curs who promise without leave, and he will flog the liar who breaks his word at the very moment when he utters it." (*Works, VII,* 343, 344: *Die Genealogie der Moral,* 2, aph. 1, 2.)

"Naturalistic morality, that is healthy morality, is ruled by the instincts of life. Unnatural morality, that is morality as it has been almost always taught, respected and preached until now, is directed against the instincts of life, it is a condemnation of these instincts, either a concealed or an open and impudent condemnation." (*Works, VII,* 88: *Götzendämmerung, Die Moral als Widernatur,* aph. 4.)

"Selfishness is worth what the person manifesting it is worth from a physiological point of view; it can be worth a great deal and it can be worthless and contemptible. Each individual has to be considered as the representative of growing or of waning life. Altruistic morality, a morality that cripples selfishness, is a bad sign under all circumstances. This applies to the individual. It applies even more to nations." (*Works, VIII,* 140, 142: *Götzendämmerung, Streifzüge eines Unzeitgemäszen,* aph. 33, 35.)

Utilitarians.

It is something of an anticlimax to survey the pale statements of popular utilitarians after having caught a glimpse of the fierce glare of Nietzsche's invectives. The utilitarian doctrine starts with a characteristic attempt to build up ethical precepts on a speculation as to blessings in the life to come. Listen to Paley (*Moral Philosophy,* ed. 1838, III, bk. ii, chap. iii): "Why am I obliged to keep my word? The answer will be: Because I am urged to do so by a violent motive, namely, the expectation of being after this life rewarded, if I do, and punished for it if I do not, resulting from the command of another, namely, of God. Therefore private happiness is our motive, and the will of God is our rule."

"The method of coming at the will of God concerning any action by the light of nature, is to inquire into the tendency of that action to promote or diminish the general happiness" (III, bk. ii, ch. v).

"Whatever is expedient, is right. It is the utility of any moral alone which constitutes the obligation of it" (bk. ii, ch. vi).

Hardly more satisfactory are the modifications of "hedonistic" doctrine advocated by Bentham and his school. It has often been shown that the notion of the greatest happiness of the greatest number is vague in all its elements. The calculus of happiness could not be effected on anything like scientific principles even if we had made up our minds as to the unit of measurement: how are accumulations of welfare in some cases to be balanced against diminutions of welfare in other cases? And, what is worse, what is happiness to consist of, and to what unit are ideas of happiness to be reduced in order to apply a computation? The only possible unit that suggests itself to Bentham is the enjoyment of material goods, and this is obviously too narrow a basis in the case of the moral world.[1] The standard of success suggested by the "pragmatists" is not of a more abiding nature. What is success in social life? We all know how little value is to be attached to

[1] Cf. WUNDT, *Ethik,* p. 362.

external prizes. And if spiritual benefits and achievements have to be taken into consideration, then the question arises again, what is the unit and measure of success?

In view of the evident failure of doctrines derived from individual egoism, and of the fact that selfishness is absolutely inadequate to explain the existence of society, the utilitarian doctrine has been modified in two directions: on the one hand sympathy has been claimed as a basis for *altruistic* behaviour, on the other, social pressure in the shape of various forms of education has been recognized as the principal factor in the formation of moral ideas.

The original conception of sympathy, as developed by Hume, may be reduced to a kind of derived and enfeebled egoism; and it cannot be said that the reproach of trying to counterbalance strong psychological motives by weak ones can be removed from subsequent developments of Hume's theory.[1]

A certain modification was introduced by Adam Smith, who laid stress on *objective* participation in the feelings and suffering of our fellow-men, as distinct from any *subjective* putting of oneself into one's neighbour's place.[2]

The assumption of independent emotions of affection and tenderness certainly contributes to a fuller understanding of human thought and behaviour, although it destroys the unity and simplicity of a psychological theory of morals.

[1] HUME, *A Treatise on Human Nature*, Pt. II, Lect. II (ed. by Green and Grose, 1874, II, 271): "It is only from the selfishness of man and the scanty provision nature has made for his wants, that justice derives its origin. Though in our actions we may frequently lose sight of that interest which we have in maintaining order, and may follow a lesser and more present interest, we never fail to observe the prejudice we receive either mediately or immediately from the injustice of others. . . . We partake of their uneasiness by *sympathy*. The general rule reaches beyond those instances from which it arose, while at the same time we naturally *sympathise* with others in the sentiments they entertain of us."

[2] On the contrast between Hume's and Hutcheson's conceptions see WUNDT, *Ethik*, p. 286: "According to Hume this sympathy which we feel for actions that do not concern us personally, springs nevertheless from egoism, because we should not feel sympathetically towards virtue if we did not put ourselves in the place of those who draw an advantage from their virtuous actions. Hume's sympathy is therefore a very different thing from those feelings of benevolence and general love of humanity which Hutcheson has made the basis of his ethical doctrines."

In order to get rid of the uncomfortable contrast between egoism and altruism and to reduce the two sets of motives to one principle, psychologists have been led to *social utilitarianism.* According to this doctrine altruistic habits and feelings are produced in man, as well as in animals, by the growth of instincts tending to the conservation and the success of the species. Mimicry might be cited as a biological example of such adaptation promoting the success of a group in the struggle for existence, namely, the mimicry illustrated by the survival of animals which assume the shape and colour of their surroundings. Even more significant are the effects of combination: birds which congregate and hold together have a better chance of crossing the sea in their migrations than those which do not; ants and bees have been taught by experience and instinct to work together and to sacrifice themselves for the common interest of the ant heap or of the beehive.[1] Social utilitarianism.

The history of man from this point of view presents all kinds of varieties of individual adaptation to social needs and requirements. Such adaptations may have been partly intentional, and partly unconscious results of the survival of individuals endowed with qualities contributing to success in the struggle for life: the fierce and courageous, the wily and prudent, would have advantages which are transmitted to subsequent generations by means of heredity. Such instances are most obvious, and, of course, all traits making for closer alliance, for mutual support, are sure to contribute to success in the competition between social groups. Still, no one is likely to maintain that motherly care or the affection between lovers is primarily attributable to survivals of competitive advantages.[2]

[1] ESPINAS, *Des Sociétés animales*, p. 57: "Mankind accomplishes its first stage of evolution—in the individual and in the species—invents and perfects its first arts without manifesting reason in its analytic and explicit form. Why should not the animal do the same during the entire course of its evolution?"

[2] On the elementary altruistic impulses in human nature see WUNDT, *Ethik*, p 229: "We have found [the psychological] elements [of morality] to be certain moral instincts which may develop on different lines and therefore manifest themselves with great variety in practice, but remain intrinsically identical They have produced the two great spheres which we have found to be the chief

Social Education.

The educational aspect of social utilitarianism is certainly of great importance. The point has been urged very strongly by Ihering in regard to morals as well as to law. He calls attention to the various rules imposed by social groups on their members by way of convention and custom, all tending to organize and discipline individuals for the sake of carrying out various forms of common undertakings. The habits of a set of men in regard to clothing, forms of address, etiquette, fashion, form themselves into rules of conduct which single persons find it difficult to transgress.[1] Codes of honour and of professional behaviour are even more exacting. Religious bodies enforce conformity with their confessional tenets and with their moral requirements. The State formulates its claims by means of compulsory laws. Rules of moral obligation and conceptions of moral right are of the same origin. All the varieties of moral restraint are originally either the outcome of instincts useful to the species, or the results of reflection and experience on the part of social groups as to their aims and requirements. Such reflection and experience carried a step further by education and custom form a body of rules of conduct entirely distinct from the aspirations of individual egoism and providing the necessary checks on the latter.[2]

There is a good deal of truth in these observations, but they do not constitute the whole truth. As in the case of sympathetic altruism, we are confronted in the case of social requirements with a principle which, in itself, could be regarded only as supplementary or secondary in comparison with the innate force of selfishness. People may be drilled into docility to some extent by the associa-

and never-failing expressions of moral life, namely *religious ideas* and *social intercourse.*

"Corresponding to these two great, universally recognized, groups are two *psychological elementary motives*, the general recognition of which rests on the constancy with which they are active in human consciousness, namely the feelings of *veneration* and of *affection.*"

[1] IHERING, *Zweck im Recht*, II, pp. 258 ff.; VINOGRADOFF, *Common Sense in Law*, pp. 19 ff.

[2] IHERING, *Zweck im Recht*, I, p. 43 (popular ed.); LISZT, *Strafrechtliche Aufsätze*, I. pp. 144 ff.; DURKHEIM, *Les règles de la méthode sociologique*, IX, p. 11.

tion of ideas, by influence and custom, as animals are drilled to obey their tamer, but the universal prevalence of moral restraints must have its roots in individual nature in order to stand the strain put on it by interests and desires. It is only when a starting-point for a controlling force has been discovered in the nature of every individual that the complicated machinery of moral ideas can be set in motion by the pressure of social requirements.

Conscience.

The solution of the problem was supplied long ago by the common opinion of mankind: it lies in the fact that man, as a reflecting being, is constrained to judge his own acts as well as those of others. *Conscience* is not a new notion, but it is not an antiquated notion either. Whatever we may desire and do, our eyes are open to our own doings and we estimate them more or less explicitly at their value in accordance with principles, distinct from the particular motives which may have prompted our action. This necessity of reflection, the appeal to impersonal verification, holds good not only in the case of reasoning but also in that of conduct. Of course, men sin against conscience, as they err against logic: the modern Attila proclaimed his righteousness, mercy and piety at the very time when he plunged the world into a hell of lawlessness and cruelty. But sin and error are not to be wiped out by impudence. *Securus judicat orbis terrarum!* Conscience is inherent in the human mind, it is as much a necessary form of appreciation of actions as space and time are necessary categories of our experience of phenomena. To Kant belongs the great merit of having expressed in philosophical terms the foundation of moral ideas. The process of judgment entailed by it necessarily takes the shape of a comparison between the given act and the ideal act, between what *is* or *has been* and what *ought to be* or *ought to have been*, between the concrete achievement and the general rule.[1] Where there is judg-

[1] SIMMEL, *Kant*, p. 54: "If we recognize as a fact a categorical ought, a compelling law in ourselves above our will, and obedience to it as the foundation of all morality—how can we reconcile this with the thought that freedom is the greatest of all values? The deepest sense of Kant's Ethics lies in the assertion that this

ment as to past or present, there are imperative obligations as to the present or the future. Such obligations are categorical, because free reason decides not on the arbitrary choice of the persons concerned, but on the strength of universal requirements. The fact that imperatives of this kind are often disregarded does not in any way alter their nature as rules of conduct. The general direction for the individual in connection with moral problems is to act in such a way that his rule of conduct may be accepted as a law of universal application.[1]

It may be added that the gradual shading off from judgments of conscience on a high level of human development to rudimentary forms of moral reflection in children and animals, is in no way an argument against the existence of the category of duty in conscious beings. With children and animals the working of the mind in this groove is usually prompted by acquired habits or by inherited instincts, but this only means that the contents of their moral judgments are supplied by these methods. The *possibility* of providing such contents is conditioned by the faculty of estimating conduct. This faculty cannot but differ widely in the case of different species and of various individuals within each species—a familiar instance is supplied by the difference in this respect between dogs and cats. All our surmises as to the working of animals' minds are necessarily hypothetical in the extreme, as we have no means of communicating with animals in the same way as we do with our fellow-men. Our observations of the self-sacrificing devotion of bees to the hive community or of the household virtues of birds are merely external and devoid of the background of psychological introspection. Under these circumstances it is hardly allowable to make the supposed limitations of the animal

contradiction does not really exist . . . Man can exert his free will only according to an absolutely general law and conversely only a will acting according to the categorical 'ought,' can be called free It is Kant's leading strain [*Leitmotiv*] that this general law imposes itself on every one from within, and is produced in the very wellspring of personality"

[1] Cf. Caird on *Kant*, II, pp. 142 ff.

mind an argument against the development of conscience in man.

Form and Content in Morals.

A most important feature of the "subjective idealism" formulated by Kant, and taken up again by modern thinkers who do not wish to surrender to sensualism and rationalism, is the distinction between the *formal* and the *material* elements in morality. The imperative of *duty* is a category of the human mind, but the actual precepts as to duty are not innate in any sense. They are suggested by historical circumstances in the widest sense of the term, including personal surroundings, inherited habits, social customs, educational ideals, laws.[1] They vary from age to age, from country to country, from school to school, although the conditions of human intercourse and the similarity of fundamental problems ensure a good deal of traditional continuity and some universality of principles.[2] I should like to emphasize at this point that although historical evolution and social influence come fully to their right in such combinations, it would be erroneous to suppose that the framing of moral ideals is to be always regarded as a direct response to social requirements. We undoubtedly have to recognize the power of national consciousness and of universal sense of right to make men face privations of all kinds and give their lives for a good cause, but we should not forget that most powerful moral impulses in the history of mankind have come from personalities who stood not for the common agreements of their contemporaries, but for a burning ideal of truth and righteousness. Moses and Buddha did not receive their inspiration from the Philistines or from the Sophists of their day, and their ideas did not achieve victory by the help of the ballot.

1 NATORP, *Sozialpädagogik*, p 39

2 BRUNO BAUCH (Windelband's *Philosophie im XX Jahrhundert*): "Evolutionist morality arrives at a similar conclusion although it does not lay stress on the necessary connection between the category of duty and the concrete duties." See, for example, DURKHEIM, *Le Suicide*, p. 226: "All this super-physical life is awakened and developed not by cosmic but by social means It is the action of society that has excited in us these sentiments of sympathy and solidarity which incline us towards one another; this it is which, fashioning us after its image, has penetrated us with these beliefs, religious, political and moral, which govern our conduct." Cf. p. x.

This does not mean that the prophets and martyrs are detached from the history of their time: on the contrary, they reveal its most intimate needs and aspirations. But they have to break through the crust of prejudices and recognized interests, and to give shape in a distinct form to the confused cravings of nations.[1] Prophetical activity may be said not only to discard old rules, but to introduce new values, in as much as it obtains currency and influence for new ideas. And it is not only in such exceptional cases that the freedom, the sovereignty of personal spirit over surrounding conditions manifests itself, but also in countless instances when smaller men obey the dictates of their conscience in opposition to commands imposed by social authority: the three youths who refused to worship the statue of the King, the Christian confessors who gave their lives for the sake of their faith, the assertors of free thought and political liberty who did not shrink from the Inquisition, have expressed by their actions the claim to oppose outside pressure in the name of conviction and conscience, and their opposition is to be considered as much a social fact as the pressure brought to bear on them, quite apart from its success or failure in given circumstances.

It would be superfluous to point out the close connection of the psychological and ethical doctrines just mentioned with the theory of law. No teaching on the theory of law can afford to ignore questions as to the interdependence of the functions of the mind, the analysis of instinct and passion, the study of the will, the cross currents between morality and law, etc. We shall have to revert to these questions again and again when we come to examine the development of systems of jurisprudence.

[1] CARLYLE, *On Heroes and Hero Worship* (The People's Library, pp. 49, 50), "The Hero as Prophet": ". . . Such a man is what we call an original man; he comes to us at first-hand. A messenger he, sent from the Infinite Unknown with tidings to us. We may call him Poet, Prophet, God:—in one way or other, we all feel that the words he utters are as no other man's words. . . . It glares in upon him. Really his utterances, are they not a kind of 'revelation';—what we must call such for want of some other name? It is from the heart of the world he comes."

Stages in the development of criminal law.

Let us come back to the evolution of criminal jurisprudence and look at it in the light of modern psychological research. Although crime and punishment have faced one another right through history, the manner in which the two notions have been adjusted as regards each other has varied in a significant way. In the beginning of civilization punishment was a violent reaction against harmful acts, a form of self-defence. This gave rise to the blood feud and to revenge for personal injuries. The action of the avenger may be spontaneous, or induced by common opinion, but the correspondence between injury and the recoil is obvious in both eventualities. In a second stage political communities of various kinds assumed judicial authority and carried out retribution in the name of the government. In a third stage, after the great progress achieved by human individuality with its lofty ideals of freedom and justice, the problem has been shifted from the sphere of struggle with the offender into the sphere of justification of the judge. Instead of being a form of instinctive self-defence criminal punishment became a measure of social education.[1]

As Liszt has very properly expressed it, punishment gradually comes to be understood as a means towards an end, the end being to counteract criminality.[2]

The new developments in scientific psychology were bound to affect the theory of crime and punishment, and they are beginning to react on penal legislation. Commissions instituted to review the field of prison management and penal servitude have come to the conclusion that when punishment renders the persons subjected to it worse than they were before, it defeats its own purpose.[3] It is widely recognized both in England and on the Continent that the present system of a machine-like correspondence between abstract entities designated as crimes, and penalties graduated on external standards, leads to a formal casuistry

[1] On the general evolution of ideas as to criminal law, see MAKAREVICZ, *Einführung in die Philosophie des Strafrechts,* 1906.

[2] LISZT, *Strafrechtliche Aufsätze,* p. 83.

[3] FERRI, *Criminal Sociology* (English translation), p. xii.

against which healthy moral feeling and social experience rise in revolt.[1]

Anthropological researches in criminal law.

One of the Italian writers who have done so much of late to throw light on these momentous problems has described in striking words the general effect of the fermentation which is spreading in the midst of society at large in connection with questions of criminal responsibility. "It was natural to suppose that by means of the condemnation of the guilty to several years of imprisonment, society was sufficiently protected against him and his like. But when, over and above these causes, one discovers still deeper ones, of which the former are only the result, when, for example, one is concerned with the perversity of the thief's predecessors, his education, his shameless mendicancy, the petty larcenies which were his apprenticeship during his childhood, his shameful loves, and his sorry associates . . . then society feels less secure because it feels itself the more threatened. On the whole, free will being denied, society understands that it has not a single force, accumulated and isolated in a single individual, to contend with, but that it stands face to face with a complexity of forces converging in an individual; its anger against him becomes less, and its peril is thereby increased."[2]

Yet when one takes stock of the whole range of modern

[1] TARDE, *Penal Philosophy*, p. 30: "Penal law . . . was degenerating into a sort of fictitious casuistry, where the classifying of entities makes us lose sight of realities, and where we are engaged with offences, with the manner of being of offences, and their relation to penalties, and never with the offenders and their relation to good people Here we have neither psychology nor sociology, nothing but ontology." Cf. GAROFALO, *Criminology*, p. 55: "The jurist studies crime only in its external form; he makes no analysis from the standpoint of experimental psychology. . . . What concerns him is . . . the classification of facts according to the rights which they infringe—the quest for the punishment which proportionally, and 'in abstract,' is a just punishment, not for the punishment which experience has proved efficacious for the diminution of crime in general." The change of treatment in Great Britain is reflected among other things, in the recent legislation as to penalties, which leaves a wide scope to the discretion of the Court. See, e g, Criminal Justice Administration Act, 1914 (4 and 5 Geo. V, c 58), Cl. 10, 12, 16, etc.

[2] CARNEVALE, *Critica penale* (Lipari, 1889), ref. to by TARDE, *Penal Philosophy*, p 15.

criminological inquiries, one finds that there is no reason for disquietude on the part of lawyers or of the public. The movement is certainly part of a great crisis which has come over the civilized world, and in so far its course will be affected by the progress of thought in all the higher regions of human speculation. But, apart from that philosophical atmosphere which is common to all branches of study, the specific evolution of criminal jurisprudence does not present insoluble difficulties and fatal contradictions.

A kind of panic was produced by the discoveries of alienists and neuro-pathologists such as Despine, Morel, Maudsley, Krafft-Ebbing on the one hand, by Lombroso's hypothesis as to atavistic relapses into savagery on the other; lastly by Liégeois' observations on hypnotic suggestions as a source of crime.[1] But these uncomfortable manifestations of the mysterious background of unconscious and subconscious influences lurking behind healthy and well-ordered life have been reduced to their true proportions,[2] and, while necessitating a revision of rough-and-ready methods of attributing criminal responsibility, they are entirely unlikely to subvert the fundamental notion of responsibility.

Kant's teaching.

Some conclusions are clearly apparent as the results of unprejudiced investigation. To begin with, it has been recognized that there was a substantial core of truth in older theories which have been superseded or modified in recent years. The idea of personal expiation, for instance, which lies at the root of religious conceptions of criminal retribution, has its full justification in cases when some strong moral influence brought to bear on the culprit or some powerful revulsion of feeling in his inner self has produced a craving for regeneration and atonement.[3]

The same idea lies at the bottom of Kant's much-decried

1 FERRI, *Criminal Sociology*, p. 26; GAROFALO, *Criminology*, p xxx.

2 A most important contribution in this respect has been made by COLOJANNI.

3 TARDE, *op. cit.*, p. 42.

doctrine of retaliation. Just because moral life centred for Kant in the individual consciousness of duty, the only conception of punishment consistent with individual freedom was the idea of atonement as the natural consequence of crime.[1] The fatal objection to this unlimited idealism, as well as to the more vulgar forms of expiation practised by the Church, lies in the fact that while transgression and remorse are individual, punishment and purification come from the State or from the Church in the shape of external compulsion and external purification. Expiation and atonement have too often served as pretexts for suppression and traffic in indulgences. And yet modern penal reformers might do worse than take to heart this moral tendency of old theories and try their skill at the creation of real reformatories in which incipient and occasional criminals might have a chance of retrieving their false start in social life by atonement.

Social reaction. Another train of thought suggested by former aspects of criminal law points to the decisive importance of *social reaction* against acts which injure the commonwealth either directly or in the person of its members. The feuds of former epochs as well as the wars of the present are states of conflict with enemies, and in a sense each criminal is an enemy threatening the safety of the commonwealth.[2] This broad ground of social defence is so incontestable that even the most extreme of those who plead for extenuating circumstances admit the necessity of adequate measures of self-preservation on the part of society, e.g., Ferri.[3] It is more interesting, however, to watch how the operation of this principle of social reaction is understood and traced by modern determinists who recognize that the world of criminal law has not been discovered as a new continent by the disciples of Lombroso and Ferri, but existed a long time before, although its maps may have been defective in important

[1] CAIRD, *Kant*, II, pp. 343, 377. The moral meaning of expiation has been brought home to all those who care to read by TOLSTOY'S *Resurrection* and by DOSTOIEVSKY'S *Crime and Punishment*.

[2] TARDE, *op. cit.*, p. 57: "The '*defensive reaction*' of a society is always the same thing at bottom, whether it be against an aggressor from within or one from without."

[3] *Sociologia criminale*.

respects. Garofalo, for instance, points to the moral sense of the community, as a complex of inherited feelings of sympathy and repulsion which the criminal finds arrayed against him in consequence of his act;[1] while Tarde rightly remarks that the feelings in question are themselves a consolidation of innumerable social experiences which settle down into habits and instincts. This growth of social ideas and habits, again, cannot be considered merely in contrast with the passions which have prompted the criminal to infringe the existing social rules; they are, in another sense, part and parcel of the consciousness of the criminal himself.[2] This suggests Tarde's own doctrine of responsibility as the outcome of a person's *identity* and the *similarity* of his mental attitude with that of the members of some social group. This doctrine, though somewhat scholastic in its wording, expresses the great truth that responsibility for crime rests on the attribution of a set of recognized rules to all reasonable members of a community. The exceptions derived from anomalies of the mind or from anomalous social situations serve to confirm the significance of the main principle. According to a leading German criminologist, Liszt, crime is the result of two factors—social influences and individual predisposition. It really comes to this, that as the reasonable individual ought to follow the direction of moral duty, society is reasonably bound to maintain and to enforce a certain number of positive rules which safeguard its existence. On the other hand, there is no necessity to keep up antiquated forms of compulsion and punishment when

[1] GAROFALO, *op. cit.*, p. 102: "The existence of non-pathologic anomalies, and, among these, the absence of the moral sense, must be taken as established. . . . The expression 'moral insanity' is utterly indefensible. . . . When no derangement of the physiologic functions can be detected, the case is not one of disease, however great may be the incompatibility of the individual with the social environment." P. 104: "Criminal anomaly is therefore a deviation from the type of civilized man; in this it differs from disease, which is an anomaly in relation to the human species as a whole."

[2] TARDE, *op. cit.*, p. 107: "The malefactor who, after all, has breathed the social air since his birth . . . is bound logically, after having blamed such and such a criminal, to blame himself, in the commission of a crime of a similar nature."

their inadequacy and corrupting influence have been revealed by scientific inquiry.

Problems of the policy of punishment.

In this way the immense change brought about by the experimental study of criminals raises primarily problems of legislation as to penalties. Undoubtedly, the spread of crime in definite directions—say as regards property or in infringement of sexual morality—ought to claim the attention of students of social science as well as of legislators, but very few thinking men would endorse Ferri's projects of unlimited changes in law and civic intercourse.[1] Garofalo is certainly right in his criticism of these Utopian declamations, when he points out that it would be hardly practical to renounce the use of money in order to make forgery impossible, or to abolish marriage in order to put an end to bigamy. Reforms and even revolutions have to deal with the entire body of society and must take into account the whole complexity of social relations. Penal legislation deals with moral anomalies and must be directed towards the best means of restricting, if not suppressing them.

It is significant that some of the most thorough students of penal anthropology, like Garofalo and Calojanni, advocate measures of most stringent repression on the strength of the investigations of the experimental school. Garofalo is not only in favour of a frequent recourse to the death penalty for incorrigible criminals, but he recommends swift and harsh bodily punishment for impulsive and brutal criminals and elimination by deportation of recidivists and other corrupt subjects.[2] His theory may be regarded as a violent reaction against a sentimental leniency to which he ascribes the increase of crime in European society.[3]

Yet reformers are not more likely to commit themselves to a revival of systematic cruelty than to be carried away by a sympathy towards criminals, which would make honest citizens the victims of violent and lawless ruffians. While both extremes have to be shunned, the general trend of the new methods is becoming more and more clear every

1 *Sociologia criminale*, pp. 215, 328.
2 *Criminology*, pp. 191 ff.
3 *Ibid.*, pp. 200 f.

day. As crime is recognized as a social anomaly, punishment is bound to take the shape of treatment rather than of retribution. *Treatment* is a term which reminds one both of medical cure and of the precautions against infection. Apart from the weeding out of cases that have to be dealt with in asylums and hospitals, responsible convicts must naturally be subjected to measures of isolation and discipline. The death penalty may still be necessary in extreme cases, but society must exercise special care in order that the awful power of putting an end to the life of its members may not be misused in application. In the vast majority of cases the most effective measures indicated by modern penology are (1) material reparation of the injury (indemnification), (2) disciplinary colonization, and (3) variation of penalties dependent on good behaviour. Of all methods of penalizing culprits the one most usual in our days, imprisonment, appears to be the most unsatisfactory.[1] There is nothing to recommend it but the ease of its application to large numbers of delinquents. It has been described by all competent observers as an active incitement to further wrong-doing, and it is to be hoped that the difficulties attending other methods will not prevent civilized countries from introducing and carrying out improved systems of penalties. In any case, the fruitful development of the methods advocated by reformers is dependent on the recognition of one great principle—the idea of the *individualization of the penalty.*[2] This means that the punishment has to fit the moral case of the criminal as the drug has to fit the pathologic case of the sick man. No abstract equations will do: the judge stands to the criminal in the position of the doctor who selects his remedy after diagnosing the disease and the resources of the patient's organization.

Such a task is immensely difficult to fulfil; but is it not the blessing as well as the curse of the modern student that he is conscious of being confronted on all sides by tremen-

[1] F. LISZT, on Criminal Law, in P. HINNEBERG'S *Kultur der Gegenwart.*

[2] See SALEILLES, *De l'individualisation de la peine,* 2 éd , 1909. Cf. Prevention of Crime Act, 1908 (3 Edw. VII, c. 59, s. 1).

dous problems, instead of facing in happy ignorance obvious dangers and mistakes? It requires courage and self-denial to approach the problems of crime, but the problems of destitution, of education, of sexual relations are no less perplexing. In any case, we may envy the blind who do not notice them, but it is not proper for those who see to shut their eyes on purpose.

Psychological treatment of motives.

In general, the wider range obtained by modern psychology in considering mental movements and, more especially, the importance attached to emotions in explaining conduct, has naturally led to a different treatment of motives of action. Professor Petrazicki[1] of Petrograd argues that it would be wrong to suppose that all conduct is directed towards definite aims. In a great number of cases it is not the *aim*, but the *cause* of emotion which directs the appetite and the will. Altogether the "solution" of emotions assumes a leading part in the psychology of behaviour. Petrazicki draws a distinction between two currents of impulses essential to the explanation of morality and law. Purely selfish motives are certainly insufficient to explain morality; even the addition of sympathy does not suffice to explain the growth of ethical and legal systems. By the side of the two classes springing from egoism and sympathy he places the instinctive response to calls which are obeyed automatically as a result of habit and influence. In the case of legal rules the habit of obedience is usually accompanied by the recognition of obligations and the attribution of rights. The customs of submission on the part of subjects are matched by habits of command on the part of rulers. Whatever we may think of the share assigned to these various feelings and of their co-ordination, it cannot be denied that habit, custom and instinct of rule and submission do play a prominent part in the smooth working of institutions. We have recently witnessed cases when these bonds have snapped, and we are well able to judge how difficult it is to reconstitute authority and morality by means of appeals to reason or to physical compulsion.

[1] In his *Lectures on the Theory of Law and Morality* (Russian).

CHAPTER III

LAW AND SOCIAL SCIENCE

Individual psychology as a source of social life.

THE original domain of psychology is confined to the study of the individual mind in its conscious, subconscious and unconscious life. The methods of this study are introspective and may be supplemented by observation of self and of other individuals in their normal and abnormal state, and in various stages of development, as well as by experiments concerning mental phenomena, and comparison with animal life. It is obvious, however, that such a study, if centred entirely on individuals taken singly, would be incomplete and artificial. The essence of human personality has been correctly defined in the saying, that man is a social being. Hence scientific psychology is bound to extend towards a consideration of the effects of relations between men, while social science is bound to start with the elements of social intercourse ingrained in human nature.

A particularly energetic assertion of the claims of individual psychology in explaining the social process has been put forward by G. Tarde. In his view, social life has to be explained chiefly by *"intermentality,"* by the intercourse between minds, and the most important of such processes is *imitation.*

The most obvious examples occur in the case of the communication of ideas by means of speech: it ensures the suggestion of ideas by one person to another, even if there are great differences in the respective surroundings of the two persons. It is needless to dwell on the results produced by conversation, by oratory, by lessons, by letters and books. Nor are we likely to minimize the effect of delivery, of temperamental warmth,[1] of examples of moral *infection* or

[1] TARDE, *Les lois de l'imitation* (2 éd., 1895), p. x: "To say that the distinctive character of every social relationship is the faculty of

prestige. In the case of hypnotic phenomena and of morbid suggestion, this process of *infection* reaches an extreme stage, but ordinary social intercourse is permeated with transfers of the same kind in various homely and attenuated forms. Indeed, no analysis of social life based on the consciousness of isolated individuals can be sound or productive of positive results. Social intercourse depends essentially on "intermental" cross currents of attraction and opposition, of suggestion and submission. Leaders exert their authority more through these mental[1] fluids than through direct command or by force. Followers do not only submit, but react in many ways, and the results of mutual adaptation produce a peculiar fusion of elements which cannot be treated as a heap of fragments, but as a manifestation of new life: just remember the synthesis of Saxon and French elements in English speech or the permeation of German law by the reception of Roman doctrines. Altogether this aspect of influence and imitation is quite as vital for legal development as the aspect of tradition or the aspect of modification by circumstances.

Tarde's brilliant synthesis culminates in the sentence, "society is imitation, and imitation is a kind of somnambulism." It is not difficult to discover the weak points of this theory, and they have been criticised with some asperity, for example, by Tarde's rival in France—Émile Durkheim. "Sometimes all that is not original invention has been called imitation. On this reckoning, it is clear that nearly all human acts are facts of imitation, for inventions properly so-called are very rare. But precisely be-

imitation, is to say that in my eyes there is no social relation, no social fact, no social cause other than imitation."

1 TARDE, *op. cit.*, p. xi: "These social relations, thus various, gather themselves into two groups: on the one hand, people tend to transmit from man to man, by persuasion or by authority, a belief, and on the other hand a desire. It is precisely because human actions when imitated have this dogmatic or imperious character that imitation is a social bond, for it is dogma or power that binds men. Only part of this truth has been perceived, and it has not been clearly perceived, when it has been held that the characteristic of social bonds was constraint or force. This means ignoring the spontaneous elements in the credulity and docility of the masses of the people."

cause the word imitation comes to designate almost everything, it designates nothing definite." [1]

But certainly imitation, although not possessing the properties of a magic formula which will solve all social problems, undoubtedly plays a great part in the formation of social ties.

Social psychology.

In view of such undeniable influences, where can we place the dividing line between social science and psychology?

Societies of all kinds are composed of individuals, and have no independent existence as conscious beings in the same sense as individual persons are known to possess conscious existence. True, historians, philosophers and jurists have often spoken of the "soul of a nation," of the "self-consciousness of a people," and far-reaching conclusions have been drawn from such expressions. But, in common sense, it would be preposterous to attribute personal life to social bodies in the same way as to individuals. Society is constituted by a complex of relations and not by physical unity. Its consciousness is the collective result of social intercourse and the summing up of innumerable individual beliefs, desires and emotions.[2]

It would therefore be wrong to deny the importance of concentrating the investigation of the nature and conditions of such intercourse into a special department of scientific study. Such attempts have sometimes been made by psychologists, who have pleaded for an extension of their branch of study to social phenomena under the denomination of *national* or *social psychology*.[3] . .

[1] DURKHEIM, *Le suicide*, p. 114, note.

[2] PAUL, *Prinzipien der Sprachgeschichte*, p. 12: "It stands to reason that we cannot operate with the mind of the community and with elements of this mind of the community. The 'psychology of nations' can only consist in relations between individual minds produced by their reciprocal action."

[3] *Ibid.*, p. 7: "Cultural science is identical with social science. Society makes culture possible and makes man an historical being. A completely isolated human soul would certainly also have a history of its development, including relations to its body and its environment, but even the most gifted would only attain very primitive culture which would cease with death. Only through transmission of what an individual has gained to other individuals, and through co-operation of several individuals towards the same aims, can these narrow limits be extended. Not only economics, but every kind of culture, is based on the principle of division and co-operation

Exaggerations of the psychological treatment of social facts.

There are thus weighty reasons for an extension of the borderline between both departments, namely, as regards the influence of social factors modifying the instincts, habits and desires of individual man: such modifications have begun right from the time when the species *homo sapiens* detached itself from its original animal stock, and they are going on unceasingly in the process of recorded history. But this appropriation by the psychologists of a special set of questions on the borderland of both studies is after all only a matter of convenience and should certainly not lead to the absorption of sociology by psychology. And yet it is at such a rectification of frontiers that the more ambitious among the psychologists are aiming: they claim the right to subject social phenomena and relations to their own results and standards, and, for the purpose of such an annexation, they are ready to discard the most conspicuous features of psychological observation—introspection, and to extend the definition of psychology to the study of human behaviour in all its aspects. The consequences of such a shifting of ground cannot be said to justify the claims of the initiators of social psychology in this wide sense. Social creations, like language or religion, are approached with more valour than discretion, and instead of a critical examination of data and of careful inferences, we are treated either to sweeping assertions about instincts or to a restatement of facts gleaned from occasional linguistic, mythological or folklore studies.[1]

of labour. The particular study of cultural principles and the right it claims to co-ordination with other sciences, consists therefore in the investigation of the intercourse between individuals; it presents to us the relation of the one to the many, in 'give and take,' in influence and being influenced; it shows the younger generations entering into the inheritance of the older."

Cf. WUNDT, *Völkerpsychologie*, I, 1, pp. 16 ff.

[1] W. MACDOUGALL, *Introduction to Social Psychology* (8th ed., 1914), p. 3: "The department of psychology that is of primary importance for the Social Sciences is that which deals with the springs of human action, the impulses and motives that sustain mental and bodily activity and regulate conduct." P. 18: "Social psychology has to show how, given the nature, propensities, and capacities of the individual human mind, all the complex mental life of societies is shaped by them and in return reacts upon the course of their development and operation in the individual."

The heterogeneous aspect of the social process.

The fundamental misunderstanding at the root of this aggressive policy seems to consist in the fact that a sufficient distinction is not made between the elements of individual thought from which all spiritual relations spring, and the social synthesis which eventually results from the process of intercourse. Social formations set up standards of their own and require for their scientific study peculiar methods in keeping with the subject itself. Before one can speculate on the *psychological* factors of language, one has to study the conformation of existing languages and the laws of their development, and a linguist who would boldly derive the laws of phonetics from imitation, or the philological peculiarities of conjugation from inherited habits or feelings, would remind one of those writers on natural philosophy who deduced light and sound from the metaphysical properties of matter. One of the most famous exponents of national psychology, Wundt, did to a great extent realize the necessity of starting on a new track as regards social relations.[1] He insisted, at any rate, on the heterogeneity of social as contrasted with individual psychology. The "heterogeneity"[2] pointed out by him may

[1] *Völkerpsychologie*, I, p. 1: "*Völkerpsychologie* is based on the fact that society creates independent psychic values which are rooted in the mental characteristics of individuals, but are themselves of a specific kind and provide the individual life with its most important content."

[2] É. DURKHEIM, *Le suicide*, p. 359: "Either morality is derived from nothing which is given in the world of experience, or it is derived from society. . . . This is in no way astonishing for the student who has recognized the heterogeneous character of individual and social states. . . . Doubtless in proportion as we make only one in a group and in proportion as we live its life, we are open to their influence; but conversely, in so far as we have a personality distinct from its personality, we rebel against the group and try to escape. And every one leads this double existence at the same time; each of us is animated at the same instant by a double movement. We are bound by the social sense and we tend to follow the bent of our nature. The rest of society therefore presses upon us to check our centrifugal tendencies, and we on our part concur in pressing upon some other individual to neutralize his."

Cf. the same, *Les règles de la méthode sociologique* (1895), p. 124: "Since the essential characteristics of sociological phenomena consist in the power which they have of exercising pressure from without upon individual consciousness, they are not derived from it, and thus sociology is not the corollary of psychology."

P. 127: "Society is not simply the sum of individuals, but the

be noticed in all sorts of natural processes. The sensation of "white" is not original, but is produced by the fusion of the various fundamental colours of the spectrum, and yet the sum of the blue, yellow, red and other component colours is not felt once the fusion has taken place, and "white" appears with its own distinctive features.[1] Again, water is quite distinct in its properties from the oxygen and hydrogen which go to the making of it. In the same way, social intercourse, though arising between individuals, develops on lines of its own and does not simply follow the promptings of individual psychology.

Sociology.

To sum up, social science moves in a department which, though intimately connected with psychology, nevertheless requires independent methods of observation and generalization.[2] If we turn to this particular field of social science, we have to ask ourselves, first of all, whether it can be treated as a connected whole and what kinds of investigation may be and have been co-ordinated under this generic term. It is hardly necessary to state that the conception of a social "science" analogous to natural science like physics, chemistry, biology, has been evolved within very recent times, chiefly by Comte and Spencer: on the whole, it may be said to have substantiated its right

system formed by their association presents a specific reality which has its own character."

[1] Cf. SIGWART, *Logik,* transl. by Dendy, III, p. 124.

[2] DURKHEIM, *Le suicide,* p. ix: "The sociological method which we follow rests entirely upon this fundamental principle, that social facts ought to be studied as things, that is to say, as realities outside the individual. There is no precept which has been more contested by our opponents, but there is none more fundamental. For, in short, in order that sociology may be possible, it is necessary before all that it should have an object and one which belongs to it alone. It must treat of a reality and one of which other sciences are not cognizant. But if there is nothing real outside particular consciences, it disappears through lack of matter proper to itself. The only objects to which observation can henceforward be applied are the mental states of the individual, since nothing else exists. Now these belong to the province of psychology. From this point of view, indeed, all that is substantial in marriage, for example, in the family or in religion, is the individual needs to which these institutions are held to respond: it is paternal affection, sexual appetite, what has been called the religious instinct, etc. As for the institutions themselves and their various and complex historical forms, they become negligible and of little interest."

to independent existence. The more special studies of social relations are older in order, however; it is enough to point to political economy, which can be traced a long way back to the physiocrats and Adam Smith; comparative religion and folklore was initiated by Vico; comparative politics and comparative law may even be said to start with Aristotle and to have been rejuvenated by Macchiavelli and Montesquieu. This precedence of the special branches has great significance in itself: it shows that it is in the field of such particular studies that original and fruitful investigations have been conducted before generalizations could be framed which allowed access to a higher plane of development, namely, to an attempt to construct a *sociology*, or general science of society. It may be added, perhaps, that even now the advance in the special branches is far more conspicuous and productive of greater results. This has been emphasized by one of the leading sociologists of our time, Émile Durkheim.[1]

In special studies on social subjects we have to do with new ideas applied to concrete facts which must be not only full of scientific significance, but in direct touch with realities. In the books devoted to general sociology we

1 É. Durkheim, *Le suicide*, p. v: "Unfortunately there is a good reason why sociology does not afford us this spectacle [of progress]; it is because in most cases it is not faced with definite problems It has not got beyond the period of construction by philosophic synthesis"

P. vi: "Books of pure sociology can scarcely be used by any one who makes it a rule to limit himself to definite questions, for the greater part of them are not included in any particular framework of research, and, moreover, they are too poor in documents of any authority."

Cf *Règles de la méthode sociologique*, p. 96: "It seems as if social reality could only be the subject of an abstract vague philosophy or of purely descriptive monographs."

Even more pessimistic is the pronouncement of Jellinek, *Allgemeine Staatslehre*, I, p. 90: "Sociology in the widest sense of the term embraces all manifestations of human society. This is the reason why sociological researches are without limitations of any kind; it takes away the possibility of a healthy, methodical progress directed towards attainable aims. The material of facts which modern Sociology proposes to take as a basis for its doctrines, is a screen which can only conceal for the ignorant the fact that aprioristic constructions founded on incomplete observation are lurking behind."

are often met by lifeless abstractions hardly disguised by artificial phraseology and scholastic disquisitions. Take, e.g., the definition of the subject in Simmel's work (*Soziologie*, pp. 7 f.): "It seems to me that the one and the whole possibility of creating a special study of Sociology is to detach ideas underlying contents from the forms which mutual influences in social life assume, and look at them as a whole from a scientific point of view. Social groups which are in substance as dissimilar as possible nevertheless manifest in their form identical influences of individuals on each other. Domination and submission, competition, imitation, division of labour, formation of parties, representation, consolidation—internal and external—etc., manifest themselves in political as well as in religious communities, in a band of conspirators as well as in trade-unions, in a school as well as in family-life."

For our purpose, however, namely for establishing the connection between social science and jurisprudence, it is not necessary to follow prolix variations on the theme of the contrast between matter and form, or to construct a theory of cultural science round the supreme conception of *unity*.[1]

The elaborate terminological exercises of De Roberty, the painstaking programmes of R. Worms and De Greef sometimes recall to one's mind Mephistopheles' instructions to the freshman: "When concepts fail, words may turn out of good avail." (*"Denn eben wo Begriffe fehlen, da stellt ein Wort zur rechten Zeit sich ein."*) The more or less paradoxical fancies of Lester Ward provide, perhaps, more interesting reading, but the thought which suggests itself forcibly in the perusal of this writer's volumes is that his excursions into all the sciences are the very reverse of careful scientific inquiry: why should such random disquisitions pretend to be contributions to a new science?

In truth, apart from the well-known achievements of the great pioneers of the study—A. Comte as to the classi-

[1] E.g. STAMMLER, *Wirtschaft und Recht*, p. 13; NATORP, *Soziale Pädagogik*, p. 37.

fication of sciences and Herbert Spencer as to the application of the principles of physical evolution to social life,[1]—the best contributions to general sociology have been obtained by applying purposely one-sided theories to the investigation of society.

I have already had occasion to speak of Tarde's doctrine of imitation; no less one-sided in its way is the treatment of the subject by Durkheim, who opposes social pressure and compulsion to Tarde's shibboleths of individual invention and imitation. Giddings rightly pleads for a combination of both elements. But Giddings' own theory of the "consciousness of Kind" is hardly free from the same taint. Surely social life in material and spiritual intercourse does not consist exclusively of the conflicts and cross-influences of socially conscious groups—neither economic intercourse, nor religion nor science, nor literature could be explained on these lines. However, such arguments have had their value as throwing a strong light on one or another feature of the subject; and by combining the various explanations, we may not only find that they supplement one another, but even sometimes that they result in mutual corroboration. For example, Durkheim's study on the Division of Labour[2] may serve as an introduction to Giddings' teaching as to consciousness of kind, while, on the other hand, Durkheim's monograph on elementary forms of religious life[3] presents, in a way, the systematic culmination to studies of group

[1] For a good summing up of their main results, see BARTH, *Die philosophie der Geschichte als Soziologie*, I, and GIDDINGS, *Principles of Sociology*. Two principles formulated by Comte and Spencer are especially worth attention: see BARTH, *op. cit.*, p. 34: "Evolution in the intellectual sphere moves side by side with that in the social sphere. Although the intellectual is by nature weaker than our 'affective capacities' (IV, pp. 387, 388; V, p. 28): although it so greatly needs the incentive supplied by the appetites, the passions, and the feelings; and although it exists in order to modify rather than to dominate (*pour modérer, non pour commander*, V, p. 170; cf. V, pp. 219, 229): yet it is the leader, and the other activities of the mind are subject to it. '*Réorganiser d'abord les opinions, pour passer aux moeurs, et finalement, aux institutions*' (VI, p. 521). (The object is, first to organize opinions, then customs, and finally, institutions.)"

[2] *La division du travail* (1902). SPENCER develops a theory of natural right of freedom—*Social Statics*, 94 f., *Man versus the State* (ed. 1886), p. 84 ff.

[3] *The Elementary Forms of the Religious Life*, trans. by J. W. Swain.

psychology. Indeed Giddings has attempted to justify the extremely one-sided character of such studies in general sociology by the requirements of scientific monism, the necessity of co-ordinating all parts of the scientific inquiry round one guiding principle. Undoubtedly such monotony of treatment helps to make an inquiry clear and coherent: it is a pity, however, that in subjects like sociology there is such a variety of elements and such a wealth of possible combinations that the reduction to unity of principle is almost certain to subject the facts to a kind of Procrustean mutilation. Durkheim's work is especially characteristic in this respect: it is remarkable for incisive and suggestive thought, steeped in extensive learning and presented to readers with great skill of exposition. But one feels all along the pressure of a heavy dogmatism, and on every page plain truths are manipulated in an artificial manner for the sake of theoretical coherence. However much we may concede to analytical investigation, the subject of "Sociology" at large is synthetical in its very essence, and some means must be found to do justice to this characteristic peculiarity.

Statistics. A necessary supplement and correction of abstract sociology is presented by statistical investigation. The best means of estimating the impression produced by a scientific treatment of numbers in the study of social life is to turn to the work and outlook of the first pioneers of statistical observations, for instance Quételet. He remarks in his *Physique sociale* (1869) on the heights of French conscripts recognized as proper for military service: "By means of the known groups, it has been possible to calculate *a priori* those not included. I have thus been led to the opinion that a notable fraud has been perpetrated in rejecting men for defect of height, a fraud which I have been able to illustrate by a table."

The remarkable regularity observed from year to year in the number of such apparently disconnected cases as the posting of letters without address [1] or the number of

[1] BUCKLE, *History of Civilization in England* ("The World's Classics"), I, pp. 24, 27.

suicides, suggested to Quételet and to his disciples the view that individuals in society become grouped round certain central or average types (Quételet's *homme moyen*) whose inclinations and character produce the results registered in the statistical tables. This explanation had to be modified in the course of subsequent researches. Knapp, for instance, arrived at the following conclusion: "The observation that the number of acts of the same kind within the limits of a given district is subject to such slight variations from year to year, finds its explanation in the fact that men are very much alike both as regards the motives by which they are actuated and also as to the circumstances of their environment from which motives are mainly derived."[1]

The fundamental fact remains that all forms of social activity create results which, when amenable to enumeration, present an incontestable regularity and persistency. As Sir R. Giffen has expressed it (*Statistics,* p. 3): "It seems to be quite unnecessary to debate whether the whole field of statistics thus dealt with or a portion of it can be treated as a distinct science. There are people who think that the study of man in societies by means of mass observation is entitled to rank as a distinct and separate science, which they call Demography. Others vehemently dispute the claim thus put forward, maintaining that the method of statistics is useful to many sciences, and especially to sociology, but that there is no separate science entitled to the name. I confess that controversies like this, purely verbal, as it seems to me, are to my mind devoid of interest. It is not disputed that there are great masses of sociological facts which must be treated and handled by statistical methods, and that there is a group of scientific facts in consequence which can only be appreciated by those who follow such methods. Hardly anything can turn upon the question whether we give the name of a distinct science to such groups of facts, or not."

In a general way it is certain that the statistical method has become indispensable to social studies and that it may

[1] *Jahrbücher für Nationalökonomie und Statistik,* XVI (1871), 245 ff.

be used both for descriptive purposes in order to characterize a situation or a course of development, and for analytical purposes in order to ascertain the working of certain factors, when the fluctuations in their working can be subjected to definite observation.

History.

Another department of knowledge intimately connected with sociology is the study of *History*. It presents, as it were, the highroad to general sociology, in as much as it is directed primarily to establishing the facts of social development.[1] In the terminology of Spencer's school it is the necessary introduction to *social dynamics*. History, however, had existed for ages before *sociology* in the modern sense was thought of. Historical aims and methods have been mapped out independently of any direct connection with social laws or any substitutes for them. Let us notice to what conclusions the historians themselves have come in respect of these aims and methods.

Natural science has been contrasted by modern thinkers[2] with cultural science based on history. The aim of natural science is to discover laws, that is, abstract principles to which the actual facts may be subordinated without residuum. The aim of cultural science is to ascertain what is important in the concrete and the individual.[3] The standard in this case is not the standard of recurrence, but the standard of *value*. The course of history is said to be the struggle for cultural values in economics, politics, literature, art and religion. The Renaissance or the sway of Napoleon are great events in themselves, quite apart from their place in the scheme of social evolution. The stress falls on individualization as against generalization. How is such a

[1] BARTH, *Philosophie der Geschichte als Soziologie*, I.

[2] WINDELBAND, *Naturwissenschaft und Geisterwissenschaft Begriffsbildung;* H. RICKERT, *Die Grenzen der Naturwissenschaftlichen Erkenntniss;* the same, *Naturwissenschaft und Kulturwissenschaft.*

[3] In the view of RICKERT, an historical event cannot be isolated from its circumstances, none of which will ever recur. Cf. GEO. TREVELYAN, *Clio* (1913), pp. 7, 12, 15: "The deeds themselves are more interesting than their causes and effects and are fortunately ascertainable with much greater precision. It is possible that when Professor Seely said: 'Break the drowsy spell of narrative. Ask yourself questions, set yourself problems,' he may have been serving his generation. But it is time now for a swing of the pendulum."

view to meet the following simple question: granted that history has to deal with individual states and events, can it try and does it try to assign *causes* to these states and events? And how can one assign causes to effects without instituting express or concealed comparisons with similar though not identical combinations,—without analysis and generalization? The force of these queries cannot be disregarded, and the chief exponent of the above-mentioned view, Professor Rickert, cannot help reintroducing the element of generality in this connection after expelling it from the domain of concrete history. It cannot be said, however, that he has found a right place for it, and writers who stand very close to him in other respects, for example Edward Meyer and Herman Paul, make allowance for the generalizing tendency as well as for the individualizing one.

An apt and incontrovertible illustration of the necessity of reckoning with scientific generalization as well as with artistic individualization in historical processes is presented by the history of language.

Considered as a store of words and phrases serving the purpose of expressing various meanings, language is undoubtedly a product of innumerable acts of invention. In its phonetic aspect, as a combination of sounds and in its grammatical framework of forms and syntactic rules, it is amenable to generalization and to scientific treatment. And is the case so entirely different in folklore, in myth, in religious beliefs, in morals, in economic arrangements, in political institutions? A common-sense summing up of the position may be taken from Giddings' syllabus of *Inductive Sociology*.[1]

Synthetic and analytical functions of history.

Yet the attacks of the literary and cultural school are not without a substratum of truth. They bring out strongly one fundamental peculiarity of historical thought. It is primarily *synthetic* in character: so far as it deals

[1] *Op. cit.*, p. 8: "The historian has seldom attempted to dissociate the constant elements in history from the unique, the individual, the personal. On the contrary, he very properly has tried to grasp history in its concrete entirety and, in recording the life of any people or age, to make clear the vital connection between those things that are universal and those that are peculiar or distinguishing."

with social realities it has to treat of complex states and complex processes, and its main object is to estimate and reflect the peculiar concentration of various elements in the shape of individuals, nations, events. In any case it must pave the way for such estimates by a careful examination of evidence. And as for the final reconstruction, it will depend both on reflective comparison and deduction, and on artistic intuition.

This synthetic outlook of history gives it a peculiar value in combination with other studies. It enlarges the field of personality from individual life to that of social bodies—political, national, religious, literary, scientific. History opens a unique vista of *synthetic* treatment. In a sense, it may be regarded as the complement of general sociology, because it strives to represent the intimate connection between the different sides of social life; it appears in this way as a continuous illustration of the interdependence of different factors which constitute Society as distinct from the State or any other human group.

There is another side of historical knowledge that seems no less important. Leslie Stephen has remarked[1] that the aversion of the Utilitarians for history has vitiated their whole system, because it has deprived the school of empirical philosophy of the main material of social experience, namely, the data of past development.

There is profound truth in this remark. It would be a sad matter if we were debarred from using historical experience in forming judgments on the problems of social science and politics which surround us. I do not suppose any one is likely nowadays to question the immense political value of such a work as Tocqueville's *Ancien régime.* Indeed when, under passing influences, historical data have been disregarded for a time, as, e.g., in economics, the omission has had a damaging effect on the whole trend of the inquiry. In this sense it may be said that history, besides being a department of synthetic knowledge by itself, takes a place as a method in the development of all branches of social science in their analytical work.

[1] *The English Utilitarians,* I, pp. 297-301.

From our point of view, the departments of social studies may be classified into five principal groups: (1) anthropology, (2) the study of cultural intercourse, (3) economics, (4) politics and (5) jurisprudence. The first group would comprise: (*a*) geography in its anthropological aspect, the study initiated by K. Ritter and by Ratzel (anthropogeography), (*b*) ethnography, as a review of racial and tribal divisions, and (*c*) physical and social anthropology and prehistoric archæology. The latter finds its principal place in this first group because its scientific treatment is dependent on its intimate connection with natural sciences, —especially with comparative anatomy and geology—but it is obvious that it presents at the same time connecting links with the treatment of origins in the four other groups. Classification of social studies.

The section of cultural intercourse embraces comparative philology, religion and philosophy, literature, art and folklore in general. The place of the other sections in such a classification is sufficiently indicated by their names. Now, undoubtedly both primitive institutions and cultural studies, e.g., the study of religion, have a bearing on the development of law: let us only think for a moment of Brahmanic and Mohammedan jurisprudence. Yet we may leave the discussion of cross-currents in these to the treatment of particular problems. It is different with economics and political science. These branches of social science are so closely allied to law that it is necessary to ascertain from the start in what way they react on jurisprudence and how the lines of demarcation between their respective domains have to be drawn.

The position of political economy requires special attention in many ways. The study has reached a high scientific level and, in spite of many controversies and doubtful points, presents the best proof of the possibility of bringing social phenomena within the scope of exact analysis and of generalizing reflection. Such results have been achieved primarily through the isolation of one set of facts and their analytical arrangement under the sway of one simple motive—the striving towards the acquisition of material goods. Political economy.

This fictitious simplification enabled the classical school to build up, with the help of deduction, a coherent and comprehensive doctrine; the dialectical analysis of economic concepts such as value, price, capital, wages, rent, has been used as the chief method of economic investigation. No doubt, it has yielded rather incomplete results: in actual life the motives of economic action are far more complicated —education, customary standards of welfare, social ideals, and feelings, religious impulses, etc., have exerted and are exerting their influence on production, distribution and exchange. Even within the special range of economic enterprise, it would be quite wrong to reason on the assumption of purely mechanical processes of competition and co-operation between individuals supposed to be equal one to another in quality, in will power, in character, in aims. And yet such a reduction of economic society to a collection of uniform atoms, led by the same forces to similar aims, has formed the basis of political economy as understood and taught by the classical school. It has found its most remarkable exponent in Ricardo, a thorough intellectualist and utilitarian, who set the stamp of his mechanical doctrines on the English and continental economics of the first half of the nineteenth century.

The famous disquisitions on rent, wages and prices are certainly tainted by mechanical atomism.[1] Yet, it must be said emphatically of these thinkers that once you grant their premises you are bound to follow them to their conclusions, and it cannot be doubted that the work of Adam Smith, Ricardo, Malthus, J. S. Mill has advanced the cause of social science more than any other line of study. As, after all, the desire of acquisition and profit does act as one of the principal elements in economic life, the analysis of its working is bound to explain a great deal in the phenomena of production, distribution and exchange.[2] The

[1] SCHUMPETER, *Literary Survey* in the *Grundriss der Sozialökonomik* (1914). *Epochen der Dogmen- und Methoden-geschichte,* I, p. 65. Cf. E. CANNAN, *Theories of Production and Distribution.*

[2] A. MARSHALL, *Principles of Economics* (6th ed., 1910), p. 27: "They deal with a man, who is largely influenced by egoistic motives in his business life. Being concerned chiefly with those aspects of

peculiar combination of deductive reasoning and empirical observation has made it possible to evolve a system adequate to explain real facts from the point of view of a most important period—that dominated by individualistic liberalism.

Improved methods.

Vital defects were perceived by those who revolted against the intellectualism and the selfishness of this economic movement. Not only reactionaries and romantics, but all those who believed mainly in intuition, imagination, organic and unconscious or half-unconscious development, criticized the narrow-mindedness and barrenness of the classical school of political economy. Carlyle in England, A. Comte and Le Play in France set themselves to prove that the life of society even in its economic expressions depends on many feelings and tendencies which have nothing to do with personal greed and, in fact, that it is impossible to build up a society by the action of selfish motives. In political economy itself the standpoint of organic growth was represented by Roscher and that of the "heterogeneity" of elements by Knies,[1] while Schmoller's school became a centre of historical research opposed to the dialectical and speculative methods of classical economists. In spite of many compromises and much overlapping, the students in this department grouped themselves in a characteristic way round the two poles of abstract doctrine and concrete observation as to development.[2] It is important to note that modern progress in this field has not removed this polarization, but rather accentuated it. Jevons and the so-called Austrian and American schools have shifted the group of discussion and introduced new principles: instead of concentrating on the problems of value in exchange, they have placed in the foreground the problems of value in use and of supply and demand.[3] Yet

life in which the action of motive is so regular that it can be predicted, and the estimate of motor forces can be verified by results, they have established their work on a scientific basis."

[1] Cf. MAX WEBER, *Roscher und Knies* in *Schmoller's Jahrbücher für Gesetzgebung, Verwaltung und Volkswirtschaft*, vol. xxvii ff.

[2] SCHUMPETER, *op. cit.*, pp. 55, 62, 99.

[3] JEVONS, *Theory of Political Economy* (3rd ed., 1888), p. xxxii. A. MARSHALL, *op. cit.*, p. 93: "Law of *satiable wants or of diminish-*

the analytical method is still used in contrast with the historical as the natural weapon of economic theory. Nothing could be more explicit than the statement of one of the leaders of the new school, F. von Wieser.[1] "The consciousness of man in his economic capacity presents a stage of experience possessed by every one who does business in ordinary life, and the theorist finds it ready for use in his own self without having to resort to special means for collecting it. The theory of national economy goes as far as, and no further than, common experience. The theorist's task ends with the general experience. But where science has to collect evidence in the way of historical or statistical work, or by any similar accepted method, it must leave studies of this nature to those working in other departments of economic science, who are able by means of their method to throw further light upon the results of their researches. He will, however, not be able to get away from the relation with historical development. There are numerous historical economic processes which, after having filled decades and centuries, are still unsettled, and which become clearer in the light of common experience. Among these must be reckoned the development of the division of labour, or the accumulation of capital, or the raising of ground rents or even the superseding of natural husbandry by cash-nexus." There is undoubtedly a great deal of truth in this frank recognition of the merits of an analytical isolation of the elements of social life and of their study in the concentrated light of typical idealization. The combination between such dialectical treatment and the study of concrete facts supplied by history and statistics remains, however, a vague "desideratum" and it is evident that further progress must depend on the bridging over of this gulf.

ing utility: the total utility of a thing to any one increases with every increase in his stock of it, but not as fast as his stock increases. The part of the thing which he is only just induced to purchase may be called his *marginal purchase.* The utility of his marginal purchase may be called the marginal utility."

[1] *Theorie der Gesellschaftlichen Wirtschaft* in the *Grundriss der Sozialökonomik,* I), p. 133.

Economic materialism.

A daring and interesting attempt has been made to solve this fundamental difficulty. Karl Marx and his school have not been content with appropriating the results of Ricardo's teaching on value and wages in order to show that it involves a profound social antagonism. They claim to have established a direct connection between dialectical theory and historical development by help of the formula of "economic materialism."

According to this theory the phenomena of spiritual life in the history of mankind are nothing but reflected images of economic conditions. Only the latter are the true realities of social life. "It is a mistake"—asserts the materialistic conception of history—"to regard ideas as independent entities and as existing by their own weight." The social materialist compares ideas to the rainbow which is not a substantial phenomenon, but a reflection, attributable to the passage of light through a certain *milieu*. You may investigate the appearance and significance of social conceptions and observe the birth and decline of ideas and their influence on history: but you must clearly realize that these observations do not represent the true objects or the laws underlying historical movements.

While you believe yourself to have got hold of ideas, you are only speaking of images, not of the real objects of which those ideas are the reflection.[1]

This is how, for instance, Engels explains the rise of Calvinism.

"Calvin's creed was one fit for the boldest *bourgeoisie* of his time. His predestination doctrine was the religious expression of the fact that in the commercial world of competition success or failure does not depend upon a man's activity or cleverness, but upon circumstances uncontrollable by him. It is not of him that willeth or of him that runneth, but of the mercy of unknown superior powers; and this was especially true at a period of economic revolution, when all old commercial routes and centres were replaced by new ones, when India and America were opened

[1] R. Stammler, *Wirtschaft und Recht*, p. 33.

to the world, and when even the most sacred economic articles of faith—the value of gold and silver—began to totter and to break down."[1]

"Recognizing the futility of his attempts to conquer matter by his own labour, the human being is wont to regard nature's resistance in the light of a hostile force, as the emanation of a will superior to his own which by prayers and offerings he seeks to render propitious. . . . It is therefore in no wise strange that the religious sentiment is thus developed as the psychological product of isolated and co-actively associated labour."[2]

We are confronted with an attempt to unite economic analysis and the concrete process of history into one comprehensive scheme, which, once recognized, cannot remain a mere piece of learning, but ought to serve as a direction and an incitement to practical action. To those who are drawn by the attraction of a coming change the formula of historical materialism appears a tempting pronouncement. If, however, we do not surrender to the *vertige* of a popular cataclysm, but inquire fearlessly into the symptoms of truth, the "dynamic" formula of the Marxists discloses both positive and negative features. On the positive side must be set the fact that in its treatment of history it leads to some extent to the same kind of useful isolation which modern theory has assigned to the analytical method in economics. It considers the life of humanity from a single point of view—that of the production and distribution of the means of existence; and by doing so it undoubtedly throws a strong light on the importance and influence of the economic factor in the process of evolution. And as the "means of existence" is, after all, the most general and the simplest requirement of life, the dialectical work performed by the materialists in this respect has had a far-reaching influence even apart from their peculiar aims. The negative side is no less obvious to all unprejudiced observers. By wilfully curtailing our range of view, by

[1] *Socialism: Utopian and Scientific*, p xxi

[2] A. LORIA, *The Economic Foundations of Society* (1907), (transl. by L. M. Keasbey), pp. 22.

following one train of thought and treating all other interests—political, religious, artistic, scientific, philosophical—as mere adjuncts and reflexes, the Marxists expose themselves to the certainty of miscalculation and misinterpretation.

Materialism and law.

In one respect such miscalculation is especially dangerous, both from a scientific and from a practical point of view—I mean the destruction of the domain of law by the Marxists under the pretext that law is merely a reflex manifestation of the preponderance of one or the other economic class. We shall often have to come back to the close connection between economics and law in the life of societies, but it is advisable to enter a protest from the very beginning against the one-sided explanation tendered by Marx's school. One or two elementary observations may help to show how little it corresponds to historical reality. The *régime* of slavery in ancient society and in the New World was not simply the result of economic factors, but a combination of economic exploitation with moral and political views which had a development of their own and crystallized in a definite body of law. It gave way before movements of mind which again could not be attributed exclusively to material considerations, but also to a change of opinion as to human nature, the State, the duties towards fellow-men, etc. These various currents of thought combined to produce the legal changes which transformed opinions and sentiments into rules of conduct. Or take the movement towards protection and development of national industries so conspicuous in recent times: it is evident that its motives are not suggested simply by the interests of certain influential groups and persons, but produced to a large extent by the intensified consciousness of national unity as against outside interests, although the free play of these interests may be profitable to individual citizens as consumers. Altogether, legal rules, by which all social intercourse is framed and contained, cannot be treated as mere corollaries of economic stages. Machinery, organization, co-operation have their own requirements, and to simplify the action of the social process by reducing the political and legal factor to the rôle of mere consequences of class struggle would be about the same as eliminating one of the factors in accounting for a process of multiplication. *Five* is as material an element in the formation of *thirty-five* as is *seven*.

Idealism in social movement.

In a sense it is strange that the campaign against idealism should be carried on so strenuously by representatives of the socialist movement, which, after all, entirely depends on the spread of self-consciousness and on the propaganda of political ideas among the labouring classes.[1] As far as numbers are concerned, these classes have always been preponderant, and yet the huge majorities of slaves or serfs never had a chance against their masters until the advance of political thought taught them to formulate their claims and to organize; while, on the other hand, within the classes superior to them in education and experience, theories favourable to the recognition of the claims of labour have been initiated and developed from moral sources—in connection with ideals of justice and political reconstruction.

The error of materialistic fatalism does not merely falsify the historical and scientific theory of the Marxists. It threatens the policy of practical socialism with a reduction to absurdity. If the life of organic evolution tends to war and to the levelling of society on the standard of the lower classes, it is obvious that it will lead to degradation in all respects and that all complex tasks requiring skilful handling will suffer in the process. Problems of engineering, of medicine, of law, of economics cannot be solved by mere appeals to communism. You do

[1] Cf B. KIDD, *Social Evolution* (1894), p. 218: "If we are to have nothing but materialistic selfishness on the one side leagued against equally materialistic selfishness on the other, then the property-holding classes being still immeasurably the stronger, would be quite capable of taking care of themselves, and would indeed be very foolish, if they did not do so. Instead of enfranchising, educating or raising the lower classes of the people (as they are now doing, as the result of a development which Marx has not taken into account), they would know perfectly well, as they have always done in the past, how 'to keep the people in their places,' i.e., in ignorance and political disability.

not build a railway bridge by the light of Marxist doctrine. We have lived to witness the blessings of the rule of workmen who do not work and of soldiers who do not fight in a great country confronted with every kind of difficulty and danger. Let us hope, at any rate, that the catastrophe of the Soviets may serve as an object lesson to illustrate the truth that it is not by discouraging education, industry and credit in favour of moral license, violence and corruption that the Socialists can hope to regenerate the world. If they want a serious trial for their views, they ought, like every other great movement of opinion, to strive for a commanding position in the domain of thought, and to justify the preponderance of the working class by its educational achievements.

CHAPTER IV

LAW AND POLITICAL THEORY

The State and Law.

We have now to consider another aspect of social studies, namely, political science, in the sense of a survey of institutions and of doctrines concerning public life. It is obvious that we tread here on ground which is indissolubly connected with the operation of law. It is not the particular problems of constitutional law, legislation, judicial organization, state interference in private affairs, that we need discuss now, as all these matters will appear automatically in their proper places when the legal material comes to be examined in detail. The first question to be answered at this juncture concerns the relation between State and Law: are their functions combined, and in what respect have they to be treated separately and in contrast to each other?

I may start with an explicit affirmation as to their interdependence. It is impossible to think of law without some political organization to support it; nor is it possible to think of a State without law. The first alternative is absurd, because law requires for its existence and application an organization to put it into force. The action of such an organization may be limited to recognizing and supporting rules framed by other agencies, say by priests, or by jurisconsults, or by experts in commerce or in folklore; in other cases the political element will be contributed by agreement between independent states. We may, again, have to deal with more or less autonomous associations subordinated or co-ordinated to the State, e.g., with churches or with local bodies, exercising authority over their members for the purpose of carrying out specific functions. All these cases, however, resolve themselves into varieties of the ordinary and fundamental position in which social order is maintained by laws enforced in the last resort by political unions. Although from a wider aspect the function of law may be attributed to all forms of social organization, it cannot exist anywhere without leaning directly or indirectly on some kind of political union acting as a safeguard of social order. In this sense law requires the State as a condition of its existence.[1]

On the other hand, neither the State, nor any other political or quasi-political body, can exist apart from Law, in the sense of a set of rules directing the relations and conduct of their members. The individuals who appear in the last resort as the component elements of these political bodies are not welded together by physical forces, and have therefore to be united by psychical ties ranging from occasional agreement to more or less permanent rules of conduct; and in the case of any society organized as a political union these ties are bound to take the shape of laws, customary or enacted, complete or imperfect, but all tending to establish order and to apportion rights and duties. When, as in the case of international law, the basis of the machinery rests on agreement, the whole structure is undoubtedly imperfect and shaky, but theoretically it is intended to embody rules recognized by the States as members of the international world, and therefore, in spite of flagrant breaches of faith and trust, it has a standing claim to support and enforcement by the common action of the political bodies which have taken part in its formulation. In short, law and the State are to that extent interdependent that it would be idle to derive one from the other. From this point of view the State may be defined as a juridically organized nation or a nation organized for action under legal rules.[2]

Marxists are apt to speculate on a complete disappearance of State and Law. Engels, for instance, thinks that "as soon as there is no longer any social class to be held in subjection, as soon as class rule and the individual

1 GIERKE, *Johannes Althusius*.

2 GIERKE, *Grundbegriffe des Staats* in the *Zeitschrift für gesammte Staatswissenschaft*, XXX, p. 160.

struggle for existence based upon our present anarchy in production, with the collisions and excesses arising from these, are removed, *nothing more remains to be repressed,* and a special repressive force, the State, is no longer necessary."[1] Is this scientific or Utopian? More practical Socialists do not share these illusions. According to Sidney Webb, "The necessity of the constant growth and development of the social organism has become axiomatic."[2]

Might and Right.

The necessary alliance between State and Law becomes even more apparent when one examines each of these conceptions in itself. As regards the nature of the State, three principal views have been formulated by political thinkers: it may either be considered as the embodiment of power, or as an organic growth, or as a juridical arrangement. I may say at once that there are elements of truth in each of these interpretations, although the share to be assigned to each is bound to vary in accordance with the epoch and the country. Any political organization, in so far as it has to appeal to power for its maintenance, can be considered as the resultant of forces seeking to obtain sway in the community: when, for some reason, the interests represented by these forces cannot be adjusted or reconciled, conflict may assume an acute form and lead to open and

[1] ENGELS, *Socialism: Scientific and Utopian,* p. 76. Cf. ACHILLE LORIA, *The Economic Foundations of Society* (1907), p. 16: "In order to prove that the ethics of love will be spontaneously established within the final society, it is not necessary to suppose with Bellamy and other Socialists, that egoism will cease to be active under this final economic *régime,* and that each will take pleasure in working for others. This would only be admissible under the supposition that the final society would succeed in changing human nature—a thing at least very problematic. . . . We have simply to take account of the fact that, within an economy where equality prevails, especially if it be associative in character, respect for the well-being of another is in conformity with the egoism of the individual, because every injury and every benefit accorded to others reacts inevitably to the disadvantage or advantage of the agent himself."

[2] *Socialism in England* (1890), p. 5: "The point of view expressed in the text explains the following protest against criticism by individualistic Liberals: When the higher freedom of corporate life is in question, they become angrily reactionary, and denounce and obstruct the most obvious developments of common action, as 'infringements of individual liberty, municipal trading,' or, dreadest of all words—'bureaucracy.'"

violent struggles in which the sovereignty in the State constitutes the spoils of victory. I need hardly recall the cynical conclusions drawn from such observations by Sophists or their pupils (e.g., Plato's Thrasymachus or Callicles), or by modern worshippers of brute force like Gumplovicz.[1]

It is more important to notice that a modification of the doctrine makes it more acceptable as an explanation of actual facts. The most famous advocate of the absolute State, Hobbes, derived it not from an assertion of brute force, but from the recognition of a sovereign umpire by selfish individuals. The notion of a contract of subjection is out of date, but the idea of the suppression of strife by a sovereign umpire is reasonable and based on experience. Let us go one step further and notice that the state of equilibrium obtained by this suppression of strife is the normal state of human communities. Of course, the enforced peace by which such equilibrium is conditioned does not prevent competition and conflict in regularized forms between individuals and social groups within the State, and therefore the equilibrium obtained cannot be described as a stable one, but rather as a series of oscillations round a common centre. Nevertheless the notions of peace and order that pervade this normal arrangement are inseparable from ideas of compromise and adjustment. The rule of the strong when it ceases to be a conquest or a revolution, is bound to settle down normally into a rule of law.[2]

The State an organism.

Another way of considering the State is to lay stress on its continuity, its historical development, the vital connection between its aims and its functions, the slow and partly unconscious growth of its tissue and organs. These

[1] *Der Rassenkampf*, 1883.

[2] MERKEL, *Juristische Encyclopädie:* (par. 35) "The ascertaining and safeguarding of spheres of power does not take place for the sake of justice, but the aim in this regard is only achieved through justice. The reason is to be found in the mischief of the struggle . . . ; but a lasting check on this mischief can only be an order that assigns to every one what is due to him according to accepted views."

(par. 40) "The contents of the law are generally in the nature of a compromise that has to be modified and revised in connection with changes of social circumstances."

features have sometimes suggested elaborate comparisons with biological organisms.[1]

But even apart from such analogies, the habit of approaching political problems as manifestations of quasi-organic processes has had a profound influence on the thoughts and actions of statesmen and citizens. In Burke and Wordsworth, for instance, this estimate of the sensitiveness and organic transmission of social life produced a violent reaction against the reckless manner in which the revolutionists were dissecting and resettling living nations.[2] Law comes in for its share in schemes of such organic interpretation, in as much as its evolution could be shown to depend on profound peculiarities of national outlook and temper and is not amenable to sudden and arbitrary changes.

In this way, though the first of the above-mentioned theories lays stress in an exaggerated manner on the catastrophes in the formation of States, while the other dwells on the superindividual life of national units, both views tend towards the establishment of a legal frame for society: the formation of a system of rules and rights appears in any case as one of the characteristic manifestations of the process of government.

Is the State a Corporation?

Naturally, therefore, political doctrine has tried to express in juridical formulæ the nature of the State as a special kind of society. We need not concern ourselves with attempts to represent the State as the agent of a theocracy or as the object of princely sway. Two other solutions deserve greater attention. According to one the State is a variety of the juridical concept of corporate life.[3]

It is pointed out that the essence of a State organization

1 SCHÄFFLE, *Bau und Leben des socialen Körpers.*

2 BURKE, *Reflections on the Revolution in France,* p. 31 (Everyman's Library). "Have not politics founded upon hereditary descent the merit of being 'the happy effect of following nature, which is wisdom without reflection, and above it'?"

3 JELLINEK, *Allgemeine Staatslehre,* pp. 162 ff., 581.

lies in the fact that its existence surpasses the existence and interests of its individual members while forming at the same time a most important element in the life of each one of them.

As Aristotle said long ago, man is a "social animal." It is impossible for him to live an isolated life: he is bound to associate with his fellow-men. All associations created by individuals—the family, the local group, etc.,—tend ultimately toward a self-sufficient union called the Commonwealth or State. Government and law give expression to the corporate will and mediate between the corporation and its members. It is out of the question for us to dwell on the differences between various exponents of the doctrine under discussion, especially as to the contrast between those who regard the corporation as an artificial or fictitious device for systematizing a complex of legal rules, and those who impart to corporations in general and to the State in particular the attribute of "reality."[1]

It may be sufficient to note that the conception of the State as a subject of right may sometimes lead to mystic views which it would be difficult to reconcile with individual "self-determination" or freedom. It is not, however, such extreme forms of the theory that interest us at present, but the general idea that in analysing the notion of the State we ought to apply to it the juridical attributes of the corporation and of the subject of rights. Undoubtedly such a subsumption of the species "State" under the genus "Corporation" is helpful and suggestive in many ways.

Even in its moderate forms it meets, however, the resolute opposition of a group of thinkers who contend that the key to any reading of political theory has to be sought in the fundamental fact of human life—in individual personality.

[1] GIERKE, *Das Wesen der menschlichen Verbände* (1902), pp. 17, 21, 22. THALLER, GÉNY and others, *L'œuvre juridique de R. Saleilles*, p. 330: "The conception of reality appears to us as the only conception admitted by the juridical consciousness of the masses, and interpreted by learned men, jurists and doctors. Everywhere the capacity and personality of collective, organized groups is seen to impose itself as a fact which people are content to state, and not as a refined and subtle invention whose origin is artificial or statutory."

All corporations have to derive their existence either from combined action by their founders or from delegation by some already existing authority, and the State cannot pretend to another origin. If it exists by nature (φύσει), it is not a corporation, if it exists by agreement (νόμῳ) it has to be deduced from the will of individuals. This means that in a juridical sense the dogmatic construction ought to fall into the class of "relation" and not into that of "personality." As men combine for commercial, educational, or religious purposes, so they combine in order to defend themselves, to settle disputes, to suppress crime. Their combinations in the latter cases are naturally more lasting and complex than in the former, but they are of the same kind, and it is only by realizing the vital connection between the rights of the State and the interests of individuals that we can hope to build on a secure political foundation and to further social progress by means of a healthy state organization.[1]

The State as a juridical relation.

Limits of analogies from private law.

It would be difficult to make a decisive choice between these rival claims. The competing theories present at bottom figments of the mind intended to describe and to summarize actual facts, and not to govern them. More than this; in so far as these formulæ draw on concepts devised originally for other purposes, they are merely analogies, and cannot be taken to apply to all the conditions and consequences which are to be observed whether in the case of corporations or in that of legal relations, in the sense attached to these terms by private law. Such analogies are most useful, as they suggest inferences, but in using them one must be careful to remember that the abstractions of public law brought into line with them stand on their special basis. It is obvious that, e.g., *consent* cannot play in constitutional law the decisive part it plays in the private law treatment of legal relations. Again, it would be absurd to regard citizenship from the point of view of membership in a corporation, or to derive sovereignty from the function of management of corporate interests. As for the doc-

[1] DUGUIT, *Études de droit public*, I, pp. 196, 258. LÖNING, *Handwörterbuch der Staatswissenschaften*, 3rd ed., VII, p. 701.

trinal idea of a *general will*, it has been the stumbling-block of political theories which have attempted to work out the notion of the State as a subject of right too closely on the pattern of moral personality.[1] The same may be said of the notion of *natural rights* as the basis of political combination.[2]

When all this is well understood, there is no objection to using both juridical doctrines—that of the corporation and that of the legal relation—to illustrate the working of the State in its different aspects; and, in practice, these analogies have contributed greatly to elucidate the bearing of such institutions as the fiscus, proceedings against the Crown, the responsibility of officers, the line of demarcation between crime and delict, the problem of the rights of the individual, etc. In fact, any topic of public law may be made the subject of interesting examination either from the point of view of the doctrine of *corporation* or from that of *legal relation*. The detailed discussion of this point must, however, be left to students of public law. What I should like to emphasize in conclusion as regards the general relations between political science and law, are the following two points derived from

[1] Cf. DUGUIT, *Les transformations du droit public*.

[2] BENTHAM, *Traité de législation*, ch. xiii (*Works*, I, p. 136): "To maintain that there is a natural right and to impose it as a limit to positive laws, to say that law cannot go against natural right, to recognize, in consequence, a right which attacks law, which overturns and annuls it, is at once to render all government impossible and to defy reason." "Right is the creature of law" (I, p. 135—*Sophismes anarchiques*). Cf. MICHEL, *L'idée de l'État*, pp. 83 ff.; THALLER and others, *L'œuvre juridique de R. Saleilles*, p. 333. Yet the notion returns in Spencer's teaching. BARTH, *Philosophie der Geschichte als Sociologie*, p. 116: "This [Spencer's] law of nature is by no means primitive law, nor is it the law of the strongest as evolved by Nature alone and without the admixture of any essentially human considerations. It is an ideal system, built up by means of philosophical deduction, and claiming freedom and equality for every member of the community. Nevertheless, this conception of natural law appears to furnish Spencer with a motive for maintaining the sovereignty of nature in society. In defiance of the Utilitarians, he clings to natural law and to 'natural rights.'" [*Social Statics*, ch. v, par. 3; *The Man v. the State*, pp. 87 ff.] "Every human being has a right to develop, in perfect liberty, all those faculties which do not trespass on the similar liberty appertaining to every other human creature." [*Social Statics*, p. 94.]

the above discussion. (1) The attempt to define the nature of the State in juridical terms is not a quibble of the lawyers. It is an obvious consequence of the view that State and government in a civilized country, in spite of all their might, have to conform to a rule of law,[1] and that the more closely their functions are subjected to the application of ordinary legal rules and methods, the better will be the guarantees against oppression, corruption and arbitrary measures. (2) On the other hand, as the permeation of the State with juridical principles can only be regarded as an approximation to the standards of law, dependent in the last resort on conditions of fact and on the distribution of real forces, all attempts to follow the possibilities of wrong, resistance and conflict to their ultimate consequences are bound to transcend the framework of positive law and of regular State institutions. Eventually persons and nations aggrieved by acts of State have to appeal to extra-legal means, to emigration, to passive or active resistance, to revolution. Apart from such desperate cases they can appeal, and they do appeal constantly, to public opinion—by way of the press, of meetings, of public and secret agitation. In this form we have the stream of criticism and of opposition to government and even to the State ever flowing in front of us. These appeals are extra-legal, though not necessarily illegal. They are addressed to *society*. Just because the State is so intimately bound up with law, it is unable to satisfy the pressure of the varied currents of economic, religious, cultural aspirations by its exclusive action. Even in its own sphere—in the domain of political life—it is dependent both for the initiation and for the ultimate defence of its rules and institutions on the action of society. All great movements of reform and legislation start from public opinion, and obedience to law and government could not be enforced for a moment if people failed to support them or stood up against them. It has been often pointed out that public order in the broad sense of the word is maintained not by a few police-

[1] Cf. DICEY, *Introduction to the Law of the Constitution*, 6th ed., pp. 180 ff.

men, but by the more or less explicit approval of the public at large.

Of course there is the army. But what would become even of the mightiest army, if, in addition to external discipline, there was not the moral resolve of the soldiers to defend the country and to uphold its laws? The Russian Army of 1917 counted its soldiers by millions, but it could not have inscribed the epitaph of Thermopylæ on the tombs of its dead. Summing up this discussion as to the nature of the State, we may say that it is an organization enforcing social order by means of legal rules.

Aims of the State-Protection.

The dependence of State machinery on the requirements, feelings and opinions of society becomes even more apparent when we proceed to examine the *aims* of the State. The question as to the aim of the State is a necessary complement to the question concerning the nature of the State.

It may be said at once that the aims of the State are not always the same. It is only the *minimum* requirements that recur under all circumstances. All States and even all rudimentary governments aim at *protecting* their members from outsiders, and to some extent, from the disorderly conduct of fellow-citizens. The measure of that protection varies greatly; one may say that the action of the State for this elementary purpose develops on the line of a spiral. At the start it increases with the progress of society involving more complex relations, more active cooperation and better methods for arranging political machinery and putting it into motion; later on, it generally diminishes, as people get more used to arranging their affairs themselves, develop capacities of individual enterprise and begin to resent government interference. Then, it may increase again in order to lessen the evils of bitter competition and class struggle. The tendency towards restricting the State is essential to individualistic liberalism and has been expressed in the history of political thought by the *laissez faire* policy. It is characterized in doctrine by pronouncements like that of Thomas Paine, that government is a necessary evil.[1]

[1] SPENCER, *Man versus the State* (1884), p. 33: "If, without

Welfare.

Within the range of this view of restricted State influence we are made to feel that the solution of the problem depends on a certain conception of social intercourse: the State is assigned purely negative duties, because the numerous positive requirements of human life ought to be met by the energy of individuals and by their co-operation on non-political lines. In practice, however, there are no States which hold themselves strictly within the limits of negative protection. All historical commonwealths attend more or less to the positive requirements of their subjects—to their *welfare*. They are driven to it even by considerations of finance: taxpayers have to be shorn, but the process of shearing depends largely on the quality and quantity of wool, in other words on resources and economic conditions. For this reason the care of the people's welfare came to be treated as a distinct aim of government by the most callous of "enlightened" despots. Frederick II of Prussia was a great husbandman of his kingdom, efficient not only in pressing unwilling recruits into his regiments, but in the thrifty and systematic exploitation of his subjects: his finance was based on State protection of colonization and industry. No wonder the policy of welfare developed into a systematic branch of knowledge at the same age as the policy of security.[1]

The liberal movement diverted the course of this evolution for a short time, but State interference set in again with increased strength in consequence of the spread of socialistic views. It is no longer a matter of theory in our time. German State socialism sacrifices liberty to the ideal of State-controlled well-being, and as for the more advanced factions of social democracy, they discard the

option, he has to labour for the society and receive from the general stock such portion as the society awards him, he becomes a slave to the society. Socialistic arrangements necessitate an enslavement of this kind: and towards such an enslavement many recent measures, and still more the measures advocated are carrying us." An interesting formulation of the restrictive doctrine as regards the State was made by Wilhelm v. Humboldt in his treatise, *Ideen zu einem Versuch die Grenzen der Wirksamkeit des Staates zu bestimmen* (1792). Cf. Haym, *Wilhelm von Humboldt*, pp. 46 ff.

national State altogether, but agitate for a social organization which will place private life under the constant supervision and direction of an organized society possessing all the qualifications of a sovereign State.

It is characteristic of the progress of the social functions of the State on the Continent that continental political science has been gradually shifting its ground in order to fit in its teaching with the various attempts and measures to organize social welfare. Lorenz Stein, a disciple of Hegel and a rival of Marx, made the contrast between government and society the basis of his theory of public law. It became the dominant doctrine in German universities, and eventually the idea of a *cultural* guardianship (*Kulturpflege*) in matters of religion, of literature, of science, of education and of economics led to the growth of a distinct department of political science supported by special administrative institutions and a specialized branch of public law. It is not without interest to listen to the programme of this study as sketched by Professor Edmund Bernatzik of Vienna:[1] "We realize nowadays that the poor must be protected by the State in a much greater measure than has happened up to now. Among other things, this knowledge has made necessary far-reaching changes in police laws and measures which all countries have started according to their respective state of civilization and with which they will continue far into the twentieth century.

"The experiences which we have gathered from the social struggles of the nineteenth century, have taught us that the mere issuing of laws is of little use unless their observation is entrusted to the right persons and carefully watched. During the period of liberalism we were only too easily content with merely issuing protective police-laws. It was a cardinal fault in the judicial organization of police that, while there was ample protection against too much police activity, there was hardly any against inactivity and laxity, from which the poor suffer particularly. The second half of the last century is characterized by the

[1] *Kultur der Gegenwart*, VIII, pt III, p 396.

creation of departments whose special function it is to see to the carrying out of the social public laws, namely, the so-called 'inspectorates' (of factories, trades, mines, sanitation and housing). The extraordinary importance which has since then been attached to statistics is closely connected with this."

Modern tendencies in England. The Western democracies are fully aware by this time of the possibilities and character of State action and control in social matters. The new orientation of social studies in England is, for instance, illustrated by the activities and writings of Sidney and Beatrice Webb. Their works on trade unions, on the reform of the Poor Law, and on Local Government are meant to provide not only theoretical but practical instruction. They are remote from the Utopian dreams of Stateless mankind: it is the function of social welfare that stands in their foreground. In *Industrial Democracy* for instance, we read:[1] "Above all these, stands the community itself. To its elected representatives and trained Civil Service is entrusted the duty of perpetually considering the permanent interests of the State as a whole. When any group of consumers desires something which is regarded as inimical to the public wellbeing . . . and when the workers concerned, whether through ignorance, indifference or strategic weakness, consent to work under conditions which impair their physique, injure their intellect, or degrade their character, the community has, for its own sake, to enforce a National Minimum of education, sanitation, leisure and wages. We see, therefore, that industrial administration is, in the democratic state, a more complicated matter than is naïvely imagined by the old-fashioned capitalist, demanding the right to manage his own business in his own way. In each of its three divisions, the interests and will of one or other section is the dominant factor. But no section wields uncontrolled sway even in its own sphere. The State is a partner in every enterprise. In the interests of the community as a whole, no one of the interminable series of decisions can be allowed to run counter to the consensus

[1] SIDNEY and BEATRICE WEBB, *Industrial Democracy* (1902), p. 822.

of expert opinion representing the consumers on the one hand, the producers on the other, and the nation that is paramount over both."

It is not our business to discuss the merits of these programmes. Our object is merely to show that welfare as the aim of the State supposes the closest interdependence between political and social organization.

It is not necessary to take sides in the momentous controversies between Individualism and Socialism, between syndicalism and State doctrine, in order to feel that modern jurisprudence is bound to take stock of the movements of opinion and of the collisions of interests that surround it on all sides. The Courts constantly have to pronounce decisions in the social struggles of the time and to formulate rules in order to harmonize and to define conflicting interests. Nor can the theory of law remain an indifferent onlooker in the crisis. It becomes more and more evident that the time-honoured opposition between private law and constitutional law is not appropriate to the present state of legal thought. Even the insertion of administrative law on the American or the French pattern could hardly satisfy the requirements of contemporary jurisprudence. What is really indicated by the examples of the treatment of the subject on the Continent is the development of the conception of *Public law* on the lines of a comprehensive treatment of the rights and duties of various social organizations—municipal, ecclesiastical, professional, educational, literary—that have stepped in between the individual and the State and are daily growing in importance in their task of organizing scattered individuals into conscious and powerful groups. The specialization of such a department of law is rendered necessary by the fact that jurists have in these matters to operate not so much with the concepts of equity and of direct command, but with the concepts of public utility and social solidarity, and it is not conducive to a fair and broad-minded treatment of these subjects to entrust it exclusively to lawyers brought up on an entirely different range of ideas. The great traditions of English Law preclude sudden or extreme changes in this respect, and such root and branch changes are not wanted. What is wanted is the growth of a specialized legal theory, of differentiated legal teaching and of corresponding practice of Bar and Bench.

Moral aims of the State.

One more aspect of political life remains to be considered, namely, the *moral* aim of the State. History is full of examples of measures for promoting morality and virtue by laws and political institutions. This aim was emphatically put forward by the Greek philosophers; it was the root of many measures of Roman statecraft—the *cura morum,* the censorial jurisdiction, etc. It is inherent in any political construction under the influence of theocratical ideas: Catholicism, Puritanism, Islam, Brahmanism, Buddhism, have all influenced legislation with this view. In our secular polity it manifests itself mainly by educational experiments and by the conflicting propaganda of political theories. There is one side of this ethical aspect of the State which deserves special notice even in our days, namely, the tendency to regard the State as the main agent in raising the individual from the selfishness and narrowness of his private existence to the interests, feelings and habits of an enlarged personality.[1]

The idea of the enlargement of personality involved in social life is a profound and fruitful idea. Consciously and unconsciously a man is lifted by this process of expansion from the level of his immediate appetites to a comprehension of duties, of rights, of justice, to a practice of self-control and self-sacrifice. But there is no reason for assigning this momentous evolution exclusively or even principally to the domain of the State. The process in

[1] See, for example, the idealistic characterization of the State based on Hegel and Green's teaching in BOSANQUET'S *Philosophical Theory of the State* (1910), p. 150: "The State is not only the political fabric, . . . it includes the whole hierarchy of institutions by which life is determined, from the family to the trade, and from the trade to the Church and the University. Pp. 187 f.: "We supposed ourselves prepared to do and suffer anything which would promote the *best life of the whole*. . . . The means of action at our disposal as members of a State are not *in pari materia* with the end. It is true that the State as an intelligent system can appeal by reasoning and persuasion to the *logical will* as such."

question is the *social* process at large, with all its ramifications in family life, in social co-operation, in educational and literary intercourse, in religious organization, as well as in political grouping. Thus we are led again from political doctrine to social science as a whole.[1]

As a result of this survey of the connection between social science and law it may be stated that, apart from the many special occasions in which both have to meet, the solution of two great problems will entirely depend on an active co-operation between these two branches of knowledge: (1) the problem of the relation of State and Law to the individual and his sphere of interests, rights and duties: (2) the relation of State and Law to the various groups in which human solidarity finds expression—family, local centre, business unions, educational institutions, literary circles, churches, states, international relations.

These studies ought to form the backbone of a general science of society, of the sociology discovered by Comte and Spencer.

[1] IHERING, *Zweck im Recht*, I, p. 67; DUGUIT, *Transformations du droit public*, xvii.

PART II

METHODS AND SCHOOLS OF JURISPRUDENCE

CHAPTER V

THE RATIONALISTS

The main currents of thought.

It is time to enter on our special field of study and to ask: What shape have the aims and methods of Jurisprudence assumed under the influence of the various sciences with which it is connected? The best way of treating the matter will be to examine the most important conclusions arrived at by leading authorities on the theory of law, and to define the ground we consider right to occupy in the midst of conflicting views.

There can be no question of following in detail the windings of the innumerable controversies on the subject of jurisprudence:[1] this would be a task of great promise and interest which requires special treatment in a history of juridical literature. I must restrict myself to a more modest scheme, namely, to pointing out in what respects contemporary conceptions of jurisprudence have been prepared in a direct way by previous thinkers. For this purpose it is not necessary to go very far back in tracing the course of development, although the Greeks, the Romans, mediæval schoolmen and Renaissance scholars have contributed largely to laying the philosophical and technical foundation of our study. But the vital results of their

[1] There is no satisfactory account of the general development of jurisprudence. BERGBOHM, *Jurisprudenz und Rechtsphilosophie*, (Leipzig, 1892) teems with details, but is confused and bewildering. R. POUND'S survey in the *Harvard Law Review* may help to trace distinctions, but suffers from lack of perspective and of organic connection between the parts. An excellent treatment of the German literature on the subject is presented by STINTZING and LANDSBERG'S *Geschichte der deutschen Rechtswissenschaft* (3 volumes in 5 parts, 1880-1910). The development of political doctrines in France is well traced by H. MICHEL, *L'idée de l'État* (1896). The methods and schools of Comparative Jurisprudence as treating the origins of law, are characterized by P. VINOGRADOFF in the article on Comparative Jurisprudence in the 15th volume of the *Encyclopædia Britannica* (11th ed.). LESLIE STEPHEN on the *English Utilitarians* is important for the understanding of the Rationalists.

doctrines have been appropriated and digested by more recent inquirers. We shall have to deal with these results in the shape and in the measure in which they have been "received" by leaders of thought within the last three hundred years.

Looking back on the glorious efforts of European philosophy and science, one certainly has not to fear lack of material, but rather to guard against overcrowding and confusion. In the case of a theoretical inquiry, it is especially important to follow clearly defined tracks and not to lose the guiding threads on account of tempting digressions. There are conspicuous landmarks that will help us to find our way in the maze of doctrines: broadly speaking, the course of juridical theory has proceeded in three main channels formed by the movements of general European thought: it started with the predominance of *rationalism* in philosophy and science; a decisive *Romantic reaction* set in against the narrow standards of the rationalistic methods and, eventually, the idea of *evolution* spread over the whole field of natural and social sciences. Let us examine the characteristic features of these three stages of development and conclude by noticing the main threads of contemporary jurisprudence.

Rationalism and empiricism.

It is common knowledge that the remarkable progress of mathematical and natural sciences in the seventeenth and eighteenth centuries impressed upon the minds of European thinkers the conviction that facts of human politics, morals and law could be and ought to be subjected to the same methods of observation and deductive reasoning as the facts of astronomy, mechanics, physics, etc., and that analysis and systematization on scientific lines had to replace statements founded on authority and tradition.

In the "humane studies" the rational side of the inquiry was even more prominent than in natural science, because the material to be operated upon was not amenable to direct observation by the senses in the same way as the planetary system or the phenomena of hydrostatics.

In consequence, it was not so much observation as ratiocination (reasoning) that served as a lever in the inquiries of the period of enlightenment. "The French encyclopædists of the eighteenth century imagined they were not far from a final explanation of the world by physical and mechanical principles; Laplace even conceived a mind competent to foretell the progress of nature for all eternity, if but the matter, the positions and the initial velocities were given. The world conception of the encyclopædists appears to us as a kind of mechanical mythology in contrast with the animistic mythology of the old religions."[1]

Both sides of the scientific process are represented in the rationalistic philosophy and science of these times—the mathematical method building up its conclusions on the basis of initial postulates by evolving consequences and relations of symbolic concepts, and the physical method discovering the properties of facts ascertained by human experience and co-ordinating these facts as causes and effects under scientific laws.[2]

This double aspect of rationalistic thought has to be clearly realized and kept in view. It establishes a fundamental difference between abstract reasoning in the domain of the "natural philosophy" of the age of enlightenment and the activities of mediæval schoolmen, who were also masters of dialectical reasoning, but, as Bacon had shown with decisive effect, were quite unable to do justice to experience as the great storehouse of substantial knowledge.

On the other hand, the bold attempt to obtain an intellectual mastery of nature—physical as well as human—forms the general characteristic of the period even though it was embodied in two distinct currents—the rationalistic group proper, led by Descartes, drawing deductions from *a priori* principles: and the empirical group, starting with Bacon and looking to experience as the foundation of human ideas.

Let us notice more particularly that the representatives

[1] A. MACH, quoted by Whetham, *The Recent Development of Mechanical Science* (4th ed., 1909). The subject is discussed in detail by A. S. LAPPO-DANILEVSKY in the *Bulletin of the Russian Academy of Sciences* for 1918 (Russian).

[2] MERZ, *History of European Thought*, I, 100, 314 ff., 396 ff.

of the *empirical* school—Locke, Hume, Adam Smith, Bentham—were themselves rationalists in so far as they trusted to purely intellectual interpretation of the facts of mind and society.

The psychology of the associationists, the political economy of the classical school, the social science of the utilitarians were governed by rationalistic conceptions. This is strikingly apparent in the treatment of psychological problems. Locke's and Hume's ideas are the results of introspection into the activity of the intellect. Feeling is hardly sketched by this psychology, which attempted to explain the working of the human mind by analysing the chance combinations of *ideas* called forth by impressions from the outside world.

As introspective inquiry was concentrated on the intellectual side of the associative process, it did not lead to greater results in the field of psychology than those achieved by the purely abstract theory of "faculties" built up by the school of J. Chr. Wolff. The difference between the two branches of the study consisted in their metaphysical implications and in the manner of grouping ideas into accidental or permanent combinations, more than in a fundamental contrast in the conception of mental life.[1]

Educational theories.

The movement of moral ideas is especially characteristic in the domain of education, one of the favourite subjects of eighteenth century society. The article on education in the Encyclopædia of Diderot and D'Alembert is composed in a spirit of purely rationalistic Sensualism.[2] It starts from the axiom—*je sens, donc j'existe.* It sets its faith in logic, and recommends reasoning as the unfailing method of imparting truth to pupils. It prohibits fables and fairy

Practical application.

[1] LESLIE STEPHEN, *The English Utilitarians*, II, p. 290: "Philosophy is by some people supposed to start from truths, and thus to be in some way an evolution of logic. According to Mill it must start from facts, and therefore from something not given by logic. For Mill the ultimate facts must be feelings. The *Penser c'est sentir* or the doctrine that all 'ideas' are transformed sensations is his starting point." For a transition see JAMES MILL'S *Analysis of the Human Mind.*

[2] *L'Encyclopédie; dictionnaire des sciences, des arts et des métiers*

tales. The prophet of the second half of the century, J. J. Rousseau, on the contrary scorns pedantic reasoning and appeals to emotion. But his *Émile* nevertheless remains a product of intellectualistic thought, with this difference, that instead of the pupil, it is the instructor who proceeds by clearly devised plans and methods. The pupil is a kind of lay figure in which impressions, associations and sympathies are called forth by a skilful master.[1]

Abstract method in political economy.

In political economy the influence of rationalistic thought was deeper and productive of greater results. The simplification achieved by restricting the inquiry to the working of the one motive of seeking profit led to a brilliant display of dialectical skill and to many important generalizations. And yet even here the cogency of argument and the scientific character of the treatment were obtained at the price of a wilful narrowing of the range of observation and the abstract treatment of the subject.[2] Modern students of economics have often called attention to Ricardo's one-sided but powerful analysis as the most characteristic expression of the rationalistic frame of mind.[3] Although his work falls into the first half of the nineteenth century, he is in spirit a thorough-going representative

(1775), p. 402: "It is Philosophy's constant axiom that our thought adds nothing to what the objects are in themselves. . . . Each individual perception must have its particular cause or its own motive."

1 MORLEY, *Rousseau*, II, p. 213: "One day Emilius comes to his beloved garden, watering-pot in hand, and finds to his anguish and despair that the beans have been plucked up, that the ground has been turned over, and that the spot is hardly recognizable. The gardener comes up, and explains with much warmth that he had sown the seed of a precious Maltese melon in that particular spot long before Emilius had come with his trumpery beans, and that therefore it was his land; that nobody touches the garden of his neighbour, in order that his own may remain untouched; and that if Emilius wants a piece of garden, he must pay for it by surrendering to the owner half the produce. Thus, says Rousseau, the boy sees how the notion of property naturally goes back to the right of the first occupant as derived from labour."

2 LESLIE STEPHEN, *The Science of Ethics*, pp. 14, 15: "If we had but a single passion, if we were but a locomotive stomach like a polyp, the problem would be simple. . . . Who can say what is the relative importance of the various parties in the little internal parliament which determines our policy from one moment to another?"

3 BRENTANO, *Die klassische Nationalökonomie*, 4 ff.

of the deductive method originated by eighteenth century enlightenment.

In *social science* the method of rationalistic reflection was equally conspicuous, although much more difficult of application, and therefore it did not yield scientific results similar to those achieved by political economy.

It is sufficient to mention the doctrine of the "state of nature" which has inspired so many "Robinsonian" speculations of eighteenth century philosophers and statesmen. It hinged on the notion that the natural relations between a man and his fellows could be discovered by careful introspection, freed from the distortions produced by prejudice and sinister interests.[1] Natural law had, of course, to be reconstructed on lines traced by reason.

Rationalistic individualism.

It was necessary for this purpose to start from the single individual and to build up society as a combination of reasonable beings.

The fatal tendency of rationalistic thought towards the simplification of experience by the isolation of the single individual[2] explains the indifference and even hostility towards the principal source of social experience, namely, history. The latter is not only ignored, but treated with hatred and contempt, as a source of superstition and mischievous authority.[3]

[1] BENTHAM, *Principles of Judicial Procedure*, ch. ii (*Works*; ed. Bowring, 1843).

Book of Fallacies, Pt. II, ch. ii (*Works*, II, p. 420): "I am a lawyer [would one of them be heard to say],—a fee-fed judge—who, considering that the money I lay up, the power I exercise, and the respect and reputation I enjoy, depend on the undiminished continuance of the abuses of the law, the factitious delay, vexation, and expense with which the few who have money enough to pay for a chance of justice are loaded, and by which the many who have not, are cut off from that chance,—take this method of deterring men from attempting to alleviate these torments in which my comforts have their source."

[2] LESLIE STEPHEN, *The English Utilitarians*, III, p. 315: "A difficulty arises from the defective view which forces Mill to regard the whole process as taking place within the life of the *individual*. The unit is then a being without moral instincts at all, and they have to be inserted by the help of the association machinery."

[3] BENTHAM, *The Book of Fallacies*, Pt. I, ch. ii (*Works*, II, pp. 339, 400): "On no one branch of legislation was any book extant, from which, with regard to the circumstances of the then present times, any useful instruction could be derived: distributive law,

Funda-mental Selfishness.

Having got hold of the individual as the isolated subject of analysis, rationalistic thought proceeded to examine the guiding motives of his conduct and came to the conclusion that all these various motives could be derived from one main principle—the pursuit of happiness, that is, the striving for pleasure and the avoidance of pain.[1]

There were also other views, but they did not obtain anything like the influence achieved by the doctrine of selfishness. The experience of life transforms selfishness into morality as regards others. The leading moralists laid stress on different considerations in order to explain the transition from egoism to altruism: the derivation of

penal law, international law, political economy, so far from existing as sciences, had scarcely obtained a name: in all those departments, under the head of *quid faciendum*, a mere blank: the whole literature of the age consisted of a meagre chronicle or two, containing short memorandums of the usual occurrences of war and peace, battles, sieges, executions, revels, deaths, births, processions, ceremonies, and other external events, but with scarce a speech or an incident that could enter into the composition of any such work as a history of the human mind—with scarce an attempt at investigation into causes, characters, or the state of the people at large. Even when at last little by little, a scrap or two of political instruction came to be obtainable, the proportion of error and mischievous doctrine mixed up with it was so great, that whether a blank unfilled might not have been less prejudicial than a blank thus filled may reasonably be a matter of doubt."

Cf. *Principles of the Civil Code*, Pt. I, ch. xv (*Works*, I, p. 318): "I cannot refrain from noticing here the ill-effects of one branch of classical education. Youth are accustomed from their earliest days to see, in the history of the Roman people, public acts of injustice, atrocious in themselves, always coloured under specious names, always accompanied by a pompous eulogium respecting Roman virtues. . . . The history of the Grecian Republics is full of facts of the same kind, always presented in a plausible manner, and calculated to mislead superficial minds. How has reasoning been abused, respecting the division of the lands carried into effect by Lycurgus, to serve as a foundation to his warrior institution, in which, through the most striking inequality, all the rights were on one side and all the servitude on the other."

[1] HOBBES, *Elementorum philosophiae*, sectio tertia: "De Cive," cap. II, i: "Est igitur lex naturalis dictamen rectae rationis circa ea quae agenda vel omittenda sunt ad vitae membrorumque conservationem quantum fieri potest, diuturnam."

Cf. MORLEY, *Rousseau*, II, p. 219: "He repeats again and again that self love is the one quality in the youthful embryo of character from which you have to work. From this, he says, springs the desire of possessing pleasure and avoiding pain, the great fulcrum on which the lever of experience rests."

morality from utilitarian motives remains common ground for most empirical intellectualists. It is highly characteristic that none of the older utilitarians attached much importance to the educational influence of social surroundings in moulding morality and transforming individual interests into social habits and rules: this aspect of development was bound to attract attention when historical conditions came to be taken into consideration, and eventually it did lead to the formation of the group of the so-called social utilitarians.

But history had no value for the rationalists themselves, and as social development was for them merely the sum of individual experiences, the entire transformation from selfishness to morality had to be effected by means of the calculus of utilities.[1]

Rationalistic thought reached its highest point in Bentham's ideal of the greatest happiness of the greatest number, an ideal which in its quantitative formulation necessarily tended towards an accumulation of material goods for equalized individual units.

Rationalistic enlightenment forms, as it were, the background for the jurisprudence of the utilitarian stamp, which is still religiously kept up in the law schools of twentieth-century England.

Idea of Freedom.

Before analysing the main points of that jurisprudential doctrine, let us mention briefly a group of theories which, though constructed on rationalistic lines, form a contrast to the utilitarian school. It may be said on the whole that the rival views are in conflict because one takes its stand on the principle of individual liberty while the other starts from the idea of State coercion: the opposition has to be formulated on broad lines and does not exclude a good many compromises and transitions, but I do not think the general drift of the contending schools of thought can be mistaken. What may be called the liberal orientation is represented most effectively by Locke, Rousseau and

[1] Bentham's position in this respect is well known. But it should be noticed that utility forms the keystone not only of the classical school in political economy, but also of Jevons' teaching.

Kant. Their teaching culminates in the idea of contract, as the basis of political and legal organization. It is sufficiently known how the compromise settlement of the English revolutionary period found its theoretical exponent in Locke and was adapted to the requirements of Common Law by Blackstone.

It may be worth noticing that the historical foundations of that course of development were wider than the struggle between King and Parliament, between monarchical discretion and the rule of traditional law: the declarations of Right of the American Colonies embodied in the Constitutions of single States and of the Union, provide eloquent testimony to the profound meaning of the struggle for individual liberty and for a government founded and supported by agreement.[1]

Rousseau's position is more complex: he started from the notions of natural freedom and of an original contract, but he is aware of the difficulty of building up a commonwealth from individualistic materials; and in his attempt to distinguish between the will of that commonwealth (*volonté générale*) and the aggregate will of its members (*volonté de tous*) he was driven to a unification of the State in the shape of a "moral person,"[2] endowed with absolute control over its component parts. In the last resort there is not much to choose between Rousseau's ideal democracy and Hobbes' ideal monarchy.[3]

[1] JELLINEK, *Erklärung der Bürgerrechte* (1895).

[2] BOSANQUET, *The Philosophical Theory of the State*, pp. 98 ff.: "Each individual may consider the moral person which constitutes the State as an *abstraction* (*être de raison*), because it is not a man; he would enjoy the rights of the citizen without consenting to fulfil the duties of a subject—an injustice, the progress of which would cause the ruin of the body politic. In order then that the social pact may not be a vain formula, it tacitly includes the covenant, which alone can confer binding force on the others, that whoever shall refuse to obey the general will, shall be constrained to do so by the whole body, which means nothing else than that he will be forced to be free."

[3] Cf. HOBBES, *op. cit.*, cap. ii, par. 2: "Actiones omnium a suis cujusque opinionibus reguntur. Quare illatione necessaria et evidenti intelligitur pacis communis interesse plurimum, ut nonnullae opiniones vel doctrinae civibus proponantur, quibus putent, vel se jure non posse legibus civitatis obtemperare, vel licitum sibi esse ei resistere, vel majorem minore sibi neganti, quam praestanti,

The roots of the dogmatic construction are obviously to be found in a rationalistic individualism incapable of conceiving any other motives than those derived from personal interest and therefore incapable of making room in a social life for any power but that of a strong personality—either individual or collective.

Conscience and duty.

Kant introduced yet another factor. He was much impressed by the works of Rousseau.[1] But the principal factor in his estimate of the world was the recognition of the imperative claim of individual conscience.[2] His famous ethical formula combines the idea of personal *duty* and of universal *law*. In his view the ultimate sanction of social order and of its rules lies in its justification before individual reason. In so far as *freedom* appears as the fountain of law and of the State men ought to obey rules because they are free to set them up in accordance with their reason (*Verstand*). Kant was not very successful in working out this magnificent principle of "self-determination" in detail,[3] but his speculations were anything but mere professorial exercises. They reflect the innermost aspirations of continental idealists in the great crisis of the eighteenth century. The Declaration of the Rights of Man of 1789 was dictated by the same idea of freedom, and though frustrated on many occasions by harsh realities, it has remained the great landmark and beacon of high-minded liberalism in the world.[4]

obsequium. Si enim unus imperet aliquid facere sub paena mortis naturalis, alius vetet sub paena mortis aeternae uterque jure; sequetur non tantum cives, etsi innocentes, puniri jure posse, sed penitus dissolvi civitatem. Neque enim servire quisquam duobus dominis potest; neque is, cui obediendum esse credimus metu damnationis, minus dominus est, quam is cui obeditur metu metus temporalis, sed potius magis. Unde sequitur erga illum unum . . . cui commissum est summum in civitate imperium, hoc quoque habere juris, ut et judicet quae opiniones et doctrinae paci inimicae sunt, et vetet ne doceantur."

[1] CAIRD on *Kant*. LANDSBERG, *Geschichte der deutschen Rechtswissenschaft* (1910).

[2] The categorical imperative; SIMMEL, *Kant*, p. 85.

[3] LANDSBERG, *op. cit.*

[4] BEUDANT, *Cours de droit civil, Introduction* (1896), p. 8: "An entirely different point of view was consecrated by a famous Act of the French Revolution: The Declaration of the Rights of Man [Oct. 2, 1789]. 'Right is a property inherent in human nature;

A second and entirely different current of thought must also be traced from the troubled times of the wars of religion: it culminates in the idea of *authority* as opposed to the idea of *freedom*. The terrible object lessons of civil dissensions taught Bodin to look for decisive *sovereignty*, as the pivot of political and legal arrangements.[1] The idea was not new: it had, for example, inspired Dante in his appeal for a monarchy towering over the feuds of mediæval Europe.[2] With Bodin the principle struck root in an abiding manner. Hobbes made it the central notion of his political system. It is needless to rehearse the well-known statements of his famous plea for the uncontested and absolute authority of the sovereign in matters of law and opinion.[3] Compulsion.

It is perhaps worth while to point out that Hobbes was by no means isolated in his contention that law and the State are to be governed by a sovereign will based on overwhelming force. The great Jewish thinker, Spinoza, in his detachment from practical strife, came to a similar conclusion.[4]

As rearranged by Samuel Puffendorf, Hobbes' doctrine became the gospel of enlightened police government in Europe.[5]

. . . it forms a part of human nature, and it is only the outcome and application of it. [Art. 4.] Liberty consists in doing everything that does not harm another; thus the only limits to the exercise of natural rights on the part of each man are those which ensure the enjoyment of these same rights for other members of society. These limits can be determined only by law.' . . . The State does not dispense rights; it is only a mechanism constituted for their protection. This is the modern idea of right [Bossuet, *Cinquième avertissement aux protestants*, par. 32]: 'There is no right against right.' Human right is before the law and is above the laws." Cf. BEUDANT, *Le droit individuel et l'État*.

1 BAUDRILLART, *J. Bodin et son temps*.

2 *De Monarchia*.

3 *Op. cit*, par. 14: "Neque sibi dare aliquid quisquam potest, quia jam habere supponitur quod dare sibi potest, neque sibi obligari: nam cum idem esset *obligatus* et *obligans*, obligans autem possit obligatum liberare, frustra esset sibi obligari, quia liberare se ipsum potest, jam actu liber est. Ex quo constat, legibus civilibus non teneri ipsam civitatem."

4 *Tractatus Theologico-politicus*.

5 LANDSBERG, *op. cit.* LAPPO-DANILEVSKY, *L'idée de l'État*, in *Essays in Legal History*, ed. VINOGRADOFF (1913).

In a sense its greatest triumph was achieved by the Napoleonic rule, when it restored order in France, broke the bonds of the feudal privilege in central Europe and settled the law of individualistic society in the Code Civil.

Bentham.

As regards law, the doctrine of absolute sovereignty was by no means confined to purely monarchical States: it was adapted by Bentham to the requirements of industrial democracy in England. Hobbes had already laid down that the form of government was not material in itself: monarchical despotism was most appropriate for the sake of unity, but other combinations were also possible, provided the uncontested authority of government over the subjects was maintained. Bentham, on his side, held that democratic institutions were desirable, but emphasized nevertheless the absolute power of compulsion as the necessary attribute of any government worthy of the name.[1]

He had no sympathy whatever with the vagaries of the French Revolution and strongly condemned all measures likely to produce dissensions and a decline of governmental authority.[2] But he advocated a rationalistic recasting of the laws in every direction—in private law, in criminal law, in the judicial and administrative system. The one method recognized by him as adequate was that of a systematic and rational legislation culminating in a Code. The historical fabric of Common Law and the process of casuistic expansion stood condemned as products of sinister interests and as fatal obstacles to a rational administration of justice.[3]

[1] *Constitutional Code*, Bk. I, ch. xv (*Works*, IX, p. 96).

[2] *Anarchical Fallacies*, Art. xvi (*Works*, II, p. 520): "Every society in which the warranty of rights is not assured [*toute société dans laquelle la garantie des droits n'est pas assurée*], is, it must be confessed, most rueful nonsense; but if the translation were not exact, it would be unfaithful: and if not nonsensical, it would not be exact.

"Do you ask, has the nation I belong to such a thing as a constitution belonging to it? If you want to know, look whether a declaration of rights, word for word the same as this, forms part of its code of laws."

[3] *Papers on Codification*, No. viii, Letter iv (*Works*, IV, p. 483): "The next time you hear a lawyer trumpeting forth his *common law*, call upon him to produce a *common law*: defy him to produce so much as any one really existing object, of which he will have the

Bentham was not content with a general revision of law for purposes of simplification and reduction to reasonable forms: he supplied a material aim for the action of the improved machinery. This aim was indicated by the doctrine of utility, which played so conspicuous a part in empirical philosophy. Mere forms without contents had no meaning for him, and he contrived to show to what extent the enlightened legislator could further the greatest happiness of the greatest number. In criminal law he tabulated, limited and justified the sanctions destined to deter people from breaking the law. His teaching on the subject, as well as legislation for simplifying procedure, has undoubtedly exerted a beneficial influence in throwing discredit on many barbarous practices of the English legal system. In this respect he worked in alliance with the powerful philanthropic movement represented by Beccaria, Howard, Haze, Grelet.

But he approaches this problem from a characteristic point of view, as a legislator dispensing carefully devised doses of painful remedies in order to assure the sanitation of diseased minds and to prevent healthy ones from catching the infection. The centre of operation is placed entirely in various forms of pressure from the outside—threats of condemnation by public opinion, threats of religion, threats of physical suffering, threats of coercion by the government. The treatment of private law is less interesting, but the tabulation of motives (security, liberty, etc.) is conceived and carried out in a truly rationalistic spirit.

Bentham in his long career provided the living link between eighteenth-century and nineteenth-century thought. The activity of his successor in the field of jurisprudence—Austin—fell into the first half of the nineteenth century, but in the direction of his mind he belongs entirely to the period of rationalistic enlightenment. He did not contribute any new ideas to the creed laid down by Hobbes and Bentham, but elaborated their ideas on jurisprudence Austin.

effrontery to say, that that compound word of his is the name. Let him look for it till doomsday, no such object will he find."

in a more systematic and technical form. He thought himself that he ought to have been born a mediæval schoolman or a German professor.

Might, as Sovereignty, is for him the characteristic sign of the State. All questions as to justice and as to the aims of law are consigned to the domain of *positive morality.*[1] The rigid distinction between them and the field of law makes it possible for the lawyer to dismiss troublesome inquiries as to political and social needs and claims. The general halo of the happiness of the greatest number is still hovering round the "province of jurisprudence," although it is impossible to make out what logical connection exists between the command of the Sovereign and the utilitarian watchword. Austin's statements, in their extreme barrenness, were the appropriate vehicle for a theory of law in the sense of a formal machinery. As the bailiff serving a writ or the policeman effecting an arrest is formally justified by his warrant and would meet all protests and complaints by a reference to that warrant, so the judge from Austin's point of view is merely the agent of the Sovereign who has appointed him and who guarantees the execution of his decisions. It is not of his office to consider independently the justice of any claims except those expressly reserved by law or logically derived from existing legal rules. It is curious that this formalistic doctrine should have flourished in the surroundings of English Common Law in spite of the fact that the best traditions of that system are bound up with a constant striving to extend substantial justice to litigants, and to take into account as far as possible not only technical formalities but underlying ideas of right. In England the cumbersome practice of judge-made law has been constantly and rightly defended as the means of ensuring a progressive adaptation to altered conditions combined with a traditional continuity. And yet Austin, in the same way as Bentham, was naturally opposed to the unsystematic processes by which case law is evolved. His rationalism de-

[1] *Lectures on Jurisprudence* (3rd ed., 1869), I, pp. 89, 175 ff., 183, 338.

manded direct legislation and codification, and he did not conceal his contempt for the historical traditions of Common Law.[1]

In one of the modern textbooks based mainly on the Austinian doctrine, the author (Salmond) finds it best to introduce a correction by modifying the famous definition of law as a command of the Sovereign. For Salmond laws are the rules followed by the judges in the administration of justice.[2]

This modification cannot be called a happy one: it begs the question. It does not attempt to explain the relation between the judges and statutory enactments or the function of the legislative power as such, but merely describes the function of the judiciary without referring it to any definite source. It could be maintained only if the judges were *eo ipso* legislators or the legislators judges. Austin was not guilty of such confusion, but simply declared all

[1] See, e.g., his severe condemnation of Blackstone, written in a style worthy of Bentham himself. "He owed the popularity of his book to a paltry but effectual artifice, and to a poor, superficial merit. He truckled to the sinister interests and to the mischievous prejudices of power; and he flattered the overweening conceit of their national or peculiar institutions, which then was devoutly entertained by the body of the English people, though now it is happily vanishing before the advancement of reason." Vol. I, p. 71. Cf. vol. II, pp. 547 ff., 670 ff. The disparaging estimate of the function of judges is clearly indicated in the treatment of the subject by the leading thinker of the school: HOBBES, *Dialogue between a Philosopher and a Student of the Common Law of England* (*English Works*, ed. Molesworth, 1840):

P "It is not wisdom but authority that makes the law. Obscure also are the words *legal reason*. There is no reason in earthly creatures, but human reason. But I suppose he means, that the reason of a judge, or of all the judges together without the King, is that *summa ratio* and the very law *which I deny*, because none can make a law, but he who has the legislative power.

Lawyer. To the gravity and learning of the judges, they ought to have added in the making of laws the authority of the King, which has the sovereignty.

P. It is very true, and upon this ground, if I pretend within a month or two to make myself able to perform the office of a judge, you are not to think it arrogant, for you are to allow to me, as well as to other men, my pretence to reason, which is the common law (remember this, that I need not again to put you in mind, that reason is the common law).

Lawyer. We agree then in this that in England it is the King, who makes the laws, whoever pens them."

[2] *Jurisprudence*. What should we think of the definition of a medicine as a drug prescrbed by a doctor? But though such a

the acts of the judges to be applications or derivations of the Sovereign's commands. And so they are—from a formal point of view. In order to get rid of the difficulty, one has to introduce the material point of view by the side of the formal: courts of law apply the law laid down by legislators, who are either Sovereign or empowered by the Sovereign, but they also administer justice,[1] that is, they consider conflicting claims in their substance and make use of their powers of formulation and application to supply gaps, to prevent miscarriages of justice, to remove crying abuses, to make way for urgent claims.[2]

And what the judges are certainly doing in the restricted sphere left open for their action, is at the bottom of the legislator's action in framing rules, although the latter are prospective while decisions are retrospective. This being so, jurisprudence cannot disregard the material aim of law without distorting one of its fundamental characters—the tendency towards justice, and substituting for it a mere reference to the machinery created for the attainment of this aim. Even from the technical point of view such a treatment would be inadequate as positive law does take cognizance of public utility, morality (*Gute Sitten*), good faith, etc. I should like in this connection to refer to the discussion of the methods of judicial interpretation carried on recently by French jurists: starting from the firmly formulated law of the Code Napoléon, the leading representatives of French legal thought urge the necessity of considering social aims for the purpose of the technical application of law and denounce the purely logical treatment of juridical problems.[3]

It is clear, therefore, that the Austinian definition

sweeping substitution of "wisdom" for authority cannot be justified, it is suggested by the sound feeling that law exists for the administration of justice and may be evolved from it.

Cf. Gray, *The Nature and Sources of the Law* (New York, 1909).

[1] Merkel, *Jurist. Encyclopädie*, § 14.

[2] Dicey, *Law and Public Opinion in England*, pp. 374 ff

[3] Gény, *Méthode d'interprétation.* Thaller, Gény and others, *L'œuvre de R. Saleilles.*

Definition of law.

of law [1] is inadequate and incomplete. *Laws* may be commands of the Sovereign in a formal sense, but *law* is not the aggregate of such commands but the aggregate of all rules directed towards ensuring order in the commonwealth, whether these rules are made by legislators, laid down by judges in their administration of justice or worked out by customary practice. *Law* exists for the sake of order, while *right* is essentially the measure of *power*. Hence an adequate definition of law is bound to reckon with the concepts of order and power.[2]

This expansion of the formal definition is obviously connected with the necessity of giving an account of the material aim of law. Order in the commonwealth has to be ensured by delimitation between the wills and interests of its individual members, a delimitation designated in ordinary speech by the term *justice,* while the share of interest and power claimed by the Commonwealth or the Sovereign in the legal arrangement takes into account the element of *public policy.* It is unnecessary to pledge ourselves to any particular form of rival theory in order to recognize that in one way or another room must be found in analytical jurisprudence for these conceptions, that the Austinian definition of law fails to account for them and that it is illogical to reintroduce them by the back door of positive morality.

Sanctions.

The barrenness of the rationalistic method is equally apparent when we analyse the teaching as to compulsion. Laws are formulated in order to be enforced: so much is perfectly true. But is the sanction of law to be always sought in coercion by the Sovereign? [3] We have seen that such coercion is in any case not the ultimate guarantee of legal order: it requires to be supplemented by the express or tacit acceptance and assistance of society at large, be-

1 AUSTIN, *op. cit.*, pp. 88 ff., 98.

2 Cf. VINOGRADOFF, *Common Sense in Law*, pp. 49 ff.

3 Besides direct coercion, law recognizes the sanction of *nullity,* which prevents people from drawing legal consequences from illegal acts. This kind of sanction operates in theory against members of the government as well as against subjects. But its practical importance depends entirely on social support.

cause, as has been said long ago, one can conquer by bayonets but one cannot sit on them. The hangman, the policeman and the soldier would not be strong enough to ensure social order and obedience to law for any length of time if the people at large were not disposed to back them.

Besides, supposing private individuals could be coerced to obey the law, could the government be compelled to obey it? Are we to agree with those who maintain that the will of a government representing sovereign power cannot be bound by law? Austin's position leads to this view, which was expressly discussed and accepted by Hobbes. It certainly does not constitute a satisfactory solution, however, because it collides with the existence of Constitutional Law, a necessary part of the legal order in civilized countries. In order to avoid the conflict, the theorists of coercion by the Sovereign are driven to maintain that Constitutions are arrangements of government adopted by the Sovereign for considerations of expediency, but lacking the essential character of legal obligation as regards the Sovereign himself.[1]

This plea of "confession and avoidance" can hardly be considered to have settled the difficulty, because although it very properly draws a distinction between government and the Sovereign, it cannot be asserted as a general principle that a Sovereign, even though he is free to alter constitutional laws, can disregard or infringe them at pleasure. The theoretical solution is not far to seek, as it corresponds with common-sense observation of what takes place in practice. Constitutional law creates obligations in the same way as private law, but its *sanctions,* as to persons possessed of political power, are extra-legal: revolution, active and passive resistance, the pressure of public opinion.[2] The sanction is derived from the threat of these consequences.

The ultimate appeal to social forces in the background is more strongly accentuated than in private law. And this is still more true of international law, which is en-

[1] SPINOZA, *Tractatus Theologico-politicus* (Hamburg, 1670), ch. v, p. 60; ch. xvii, p. 178 ff.; AUSTIN, *Province of Jurisprudence.*

[2] BINDING, *Die Normen und ihre Übertretung* (1890).

tirely formulated by agreement. Formally it is an agreement between Sovereign States, and therefore the parties are, according to the Austinian view, not to be bound by *legal obligation* to the Agreement. As there is no compelling sanction derived from superior authority, the rules of so-called International Law would be rules of positive morality.[1]

Such a conclusion is, however, not forced on us, if we recognize that rules may be statements of law even when their enforcement depends on extra-legal sanctions. We need not regard the treaty guaranteeing the neutrality of Belgium as a "scrap of paper" conditioned by the sense of expediency on the part of Prussia and other Sovereign States. We may deplore the "imperfect" effect of an obligation devoid of the sanction of superior force, but this need not prevent us from insisting on the legal character of a principle recognized by a solemn agreement between parties.

The third fundamental principle of rationalistic jurisprudence is the notion of Sovereignty. Here again matters are simplified to such an extreme extent that the principle becomes unworkable. The Sovereign is defined as the person or persons wielding supreme power in the State.[2] Sovereignty.

Two objections have to be urged in this respect. In our days of complicated political organization, it is not easy to distribute the members of a commonwealth into the two classes of rulers and ruled and to ascertain who wields supreme power in the State and who is in the habit of obeying commands.[3] In the case of the United States, for instance, it is certainly not the President or Congress who can assume the prerogative of Sovereignty. This prerogative may be attributed to a constitutional convention while it is in being, but what of the normal state of affairs when such a convention is not in being? Have we to say

1 HOLLAND, *Jurisprudence*
2 AUSTIN, *op. cit.*, I, pp. 226 ff., 236 ff.
3 DICEY draws a distinction between political and legal sovereignty, but it is evident that legal sovereignty, in so far as it is not a fiction (as in the triad—King, Lords and Commons), is derived from the political balance of power.

that the Sovereign in the United States is the people? This has been said not only by theorists, but by the United States themselves: "We, the people of the United States, etc." If this formula has a meaning, the quality of Sovereignty should be attributed not to any person or group of persons supreme in the State, but to a social entity—the people organized by a historical process into a commonwealth.

The second objection concerns the idea of finality of decision involved in the principle of Sovereignty. Such finality implies not only uncontested, but undivided power. But again there are numerous Federated States in the world in which Sovereign power is distributed in one way or another between the compound elements. Each State of the North American Federation or in the Commonwealth of Australia possesses a guaranteed share of Sovereign power, and the Union superior to all these fractional authorities is not a physical Sovereign in any sense, but an entity of Public Law supported, as we saw in the case of the War of Secession, by a possible appeal to extra-legal coercion by the people, that is, by society at large. Indeed, cases are conceivable, and have been actually observed, when political power within the State was divided not on the lines of local concentration, but on those of functional differentiation. This has often taken place in the shape of an opposition between Church and State; both are powerful centres of political attraction, and it has not always been the case that the secular government has succeeded in obtaining the final supremacy. *Imperium* and *Sacerdotium* did not only struggle with each other in the mediæval world, but had to combine in various ways, even in Protestant countries. The cross-influences of the Parliament and of the Kirk in Scotland led to a most curious constitutional compromise between the two powers, which stood the trial of some sixteen years wear and tear.[1]

It cannot be said that such experiments are the best means of arranging political society, but they show at any rate that the notion of Sovereignty ought not to be taken as

[1] DICEY, in *Scottish Historical Review*, XIV, No. 55.

an absolute principle, but as a generalization subject to various contingencies.

Altogether, critical examination of the results obtained by rationalistic jurisprudence reveals the fact that its solid achievements consist in the analysis of certain formal conceptions of positive law. It helps to explain the working of the machinery by which the legislative power puts the rules decreed by it into operation by means of Courts of Law and of the police. It does not solve the problems of the origin of legal rules and of their relation to the life of society.

CHAPTER VI

THE NATIONALISTS

Events and theories.

A REMARKABLE feature in the formation of social and legal doctrines is the fact that the principal schools of thought arise and displace one another under the influence of actual changes in world politics, as though the material struggle for power or property was reflected in the consciousness of thinkers and contributed substantially to produce change in the orientation of thought. The interdependence between the two courses of development may also be considered in the light of a verification of ideals by their practical consequences. Although ideals and arguments follow their own dialectical sequence, whenever they are put into practice, their practical consequences claim a place in the process, and this place is likely to be important indeed. Thus in the eighteenth century the irritation caused by obsolete feudalism contributed powerfully to produce rationalism, more particularly rationalistic politics and a rationalistic jurisprudence. On the other hand, the reaction against the idea that State and Law can be deliberately changed according to considerations of pure reason was reflected in the world of thought by a renewed reverence for the irrational, the unconscious and the subconscious elements of human nature and social life—for feeling, instinct, imagination, tradition and mysticism.

The disillusionment brought about by the excesses of the French Revolution obscured for a time the historical significance of the upheaval and brought discredit on the cult of reason as preached by the Terrorists.[1]

[1] WORDSWORTH'S *Prelude*, XIII, 20 ff.:

> I have been taught to reverence a power
> That is the visible quality and shape
> And image of right reason; that matures
> Her processes by steadfast laws; gives birth

The invasion of progressive militarism as represented by Napoleon's Empire was stemmed by the unexpected vitality of backward nations like the Russians, the Spaniards, the Tyrolese, by the tenacity of the British oligarchical *régime*, by the irrational revival of religion in France and of patriotism in Germany. A tide of romantic reaction set in towards a restoration of organic ties broken by the sacrilegious violence of rationalistic reformers.[1]

To no impatient or fallacious hopes,
No heat of passion or excessive zeal,
No vain conceits; provokes to no quick turns
Of self-applauding intellect; but trains
To meekness, and exalts by humble faith;
Holds up before the mind intoxicate
With present objects, and the busy dance
Of things that pass away, a temperate show
Of objects that endure; and by this course
Disposes her, when over-fondly set
On throwing off incumbrances, to seek
In man, and in the frame of social life,
Whate'er there is desirable and good
Of kindred permanence, unchanged in form
And function, or, through strict vicissitude
Of life and death, revolving.

XIII, 58 ff.:

The promise of the present time retired
Into its true proportion; sanguine schemes,
Ambitious projects, pleased me less; I sought
For present good in life's familiar face,
And built thereon my hopes of good to come.

With settling judgments now of what would last
And what would disappear; prepared to find
Presumption, folly, madness, in the men
Who thrust themselves upon the passive world
As Rulers of the world; to see in these,
Even when public welfare is their aim,
Plans without thought or built on theories
Vague and unsound, etc.

[1] LANDSBERG, "Pamphlet of 1830," *Geschichte der deutschen Rechtswissenschaft* (3rd Abt.), p. 101: ". . . the nineteenth century, begun with events of far-reaching consequences, and bowed down under the load of foreign oppression; newly awakened patriotism, raised to the pitch of enthusiasm, a higher sense of religion, the longing for national independence and for a state of social life built upon loyalty and religion, and finally the conviction that a philoso-

The Romantic Revival.

The literature of all the nations of Europe bears witness to the ardour and the creative force of the Romantic revival.[1]

The movement did not exhaust itself in efforts of imagination and mystic sentiment. It led to momentous results in the world of philosophical speculation and scientific method. Schelling tried to reconcile the two polar tendencies of the world—nature and thought—in his synthesis of identity. Hegel constructed a system with a similar object, but with much greater success. It is not our task to estimate the exact shares contributed by Rationalism and by the Romantic revival to his stupendous synthesis. It is sufficient to notice the necessary connection of Hegel's teaching with the new meaning acquired by history. The idea of the evolution of the Spirit in the world, which forms the key to Hegel's system, requires an embodiment in a historical sequence which has to take account of historical realities in their organic development: it substitutes the "cunning" of a Providence which operates through men's passions and strivings for the naïve schemes of deliberate arrangement propounded by rationalist thinkers and reformers.[2]

In the domain of positive knowledge the path of the Romantic movement is marked by the rise of a science of language, of comparative folk-lore, of the history of religion. The unity of these branches of study is perhaps best exemplified by the stupendous work of Jacob Grimm for the national self-discovery of the German people.[3]

Cultural consciousness assumed in its various branches the shape of schemes of universal scientific value and

phizing charlatanism in law and politics was exercising a pernicious influence, fixed the eyes of all patriots upon the old times of German strength and independence, and produced eager research in history which extended to all branches of scholarship; at times it produced over-estimation of the Middle Ages, mysticism and political fanaticism, but in the main it laid the foundation of new life in art and science and inaugurated a definite stage in the progress of the human mind. We owe the school of historical jurisprudence also to this movement."

[1] HAYM, *Die romantische Schule;* BRANDES, *Hovedströmninger i Litteraturen af det XIX Aarhundrede,* II.

[2] CROCO, *Filosofia della Pratica,* pp. 319, 401.

[3] LANDSBERG, *op. cit.,* III, pp. 2, 114 ff.

acquired a firm basis in appropriate technical methods. Comparative philology became the leading science of the group, revealing as it does the marvellous interplay of *individual* invention and *collective* thought, of logical categories, physiological factors and psychological peculiarities, of tradition and progress.

All these investigations were equally inspired by the belief in the expansion of personal life in the shape of a wider national consciousness requiring a psychology of its own.[1]

Such is the background against which stands out the rise of historical jurisprudence. In Italy the genius of Vico had discovered some of the main features of the organic process in history almost a century before they could be discovered by any one else.[2] The Historical spirit.

In England the protest against a reckless reshuffling of State and of law was sounded in clarion notes by Burke.[3]

In France the reaction in favour of history found a remarkable expression in St. Simon and his school.[4]

[1] PAUL, *Prinzipien der Sprachwissenschaft.*

[2] CROCE, *The Philosophy of Vico* (Eng. transl. by Collingwood 1913), p. 119: "Poetry, which ought to represent sense, and nothing else, came to represent sense already intellectualized . . . Barbaric civilization became a kind of mythological, allegorical representation of the ideal phase of poetry, and primitive tribes were transformed into 'crowds of sublime poets,' just as in the ontogenesis corresponding to this phylogenesis children had been made into poets"

[3] MORLEY, *Burke*, p. 240: "To him [Burke] there actually was an element of mystery in the cohesion of men in societies, in political obedience, in the sanctity of contract; in all that fabric of law and charter and obligation, whether written or unwritten, which is the sheltering bulwark between civilization and barbarism. When reason and history had contributed all that they could do to the explanation, it seemed to him as if the vital force, the secret of organization, the binding framework, must still come from the impenetrable regions beyond reasoning and beyond history."

[4] MICHEL, *L'idée de l'État*, pp. 187 ff. ST. SIMON, *Œuvres choisis*, I, pp. 146, 149 On *Le Play*, MICHEL, *op. cit.* pp. 529 ff MORLEY, *Burke*, p. 229: "Comte again points impressively to the Revolution as the period which illustrates more decisively than another the peril of confounding the two great functions of speculation and political action: and he speaks with just reprobation of the preposterous idea in the philosophic politicians of the epoch, that society was at their disposal, independent of its past development, devoid of inherent impulses, and easily capable of being morally regenerated by the mere modification of legislative rules."

The Historical School of Law.

It was in Germany, however, that the Romantic movement in political thought crystallized in its most influential form. It is represented mainly by the "Historical School of Law" initiated by Savigny.[1] The story of the literary conflict that led to the distinct formulation of its tenets has been told innumerable times. A proposal by a distinguished professor of Civil Law, Thibaut of Göttingen, to proceed to a general codification of the statutes and customs of the various German States in a logically coherent system on the pattern of Roman jurisprudence and of the Civil Code of France, called forth an indignant reply from Savigny, in which he contended that Law is as much a part of national inheritance as language or religion, that it cannot be treated as dead material to be cast and recast by professional jurists and statesmen according to their view of what is reasonable. The ground for codification had to be prepared by a careful study of national traditions and requirements as regards law. This conflict between prominent representatives of rationalistic and of historical conceptions of jurisprudence gave rise to a rapid concentration of interests and capacities for the purpose of the historical study of law. The directing principles of the new school were well represented by a new periodical publication, the *Review of Legal History*,[2] started by Savigny, Eichhorn and their friends. The programme of the school was as set forth in the first number: it distinguished two principal groups of juridical views and methods: the historical and the non-historical. The latter may lay the greater stress either upon philosophy and the law of nature or upon so-called common sense. It takes the view that each period has an existence and a world of its own, and therefore produces its own laws independently and arbitrarily out of its own

[1] We need not discuss the claims of Hugo to rank as the pioneer of the Historical School of Law. He was a precursor of Savigny as to method, but he did not achieve or contemplate the organization of legal knowledge characteristic of the *School*. Cf. LANDSBERG, III, 2, pp. 47 ff.

[2] *Zeitschrift für Rechtsgeschichte*.

insight and strength. History can only serve as a moral and political collection of precedents.

"The historical school on the other hand starts from the conviction that there is no perfectly detached and isolated stage of human existence. The present existence of every individual and that of the State develops with immanent necessity from elements furnished by the past. There is no question of choice between good and bad, in the sense that the approval of a given thing could be called good, the rejection bad, but that the latter was nevertheless possible.

Rejection of what is given is, strictly speaking, an impossibility; we are inevitably dominated by it, and we can only err in our judgment, but not change the fact itself.

The non-historical school holds that law is produced on the spur of the moment and in an arbitrary manner by those invested with the powers of law-making, independently of the course of law in past times, and purely according to the best of the convictions arising at the moment."

National conceptions of right.

The new departure was bound to lead to the reconsideration of the main position of jurisprudence as understood by the rationalists. Law was considered primarily not in its formal aspect as the command of a sovereign, but in its material content as the opinion of the country on matters of right and justice (*Rechtsüberzeugung*).

Instead of being traced to the deliberate will of the legislator, its formation was assigned to the gradual working of customs, the proper function of legislation being limited to the declaration of an existing State of legal consciousness, and not as the creation of new rules by individual minds. As regards the State, law was assumed to be an antecedent condition, not a consequence of its activity. In this way direct legislation was thrust into the background, while customary law was studied with particular interest and regarded as the genuine manifestation of popular consciousness.

Curiously enough, the historical school of law was confronted from the very outset by an awkward problem of German legal history; if law was a spontaneous manifestation of the national mind, how could it have happened that the German people had renounced a great part of its vernacular rules and customs in favour of the Corpus Juris of the late Roman Empire, compiled on foreign soil to meet conditions of social life entirely different from those obtaining in Germany? The founder of the "Historical School," Savigny, attacked the problem himself in his monumental work on Roman Law in the Middle Ages. He did not reach the critical period of "reception" in the fifteenth century, but his treatment of the previous epochs shows that in his view there was no break of continuity in the development of Roman Law at any time between the fall of the Western Empire and the rejuvenation of the Corpus Juris in the fifteenth century; the connecting threads are to be found in the transformation of Roman legal sources and rules by a process of "vulgarization" similar to that which led to the formation of Romance languages—Italian, French, Spanish—on the one hand, and a slow revival of legal learning in the Law Schools on the other.[1]

This investigation of the preliminaries of *reception* was not sufficient to explain the wholesale intrusion of Roman doctrines and of professional civilians in a field which had been cultivated for ages by the popular tribunals of the *Schöffen* and made to yield a harvest of Germanistic conceptions and rules. The question was treated from all sides by later writers, who dwelt on the antagonism between public and professional opinion in this respect and, though recognizing the value of certain improvements in technical matters and the helplessness of dispersed local customs before the unified body of the "Common Law of Rome" as practised in Germany (*Das Gemeine römische Recht*), insisted on the necessity of healing the grievous wound inflicted on the German people by the introduction of a body of foreign law.[2] The controversy was by no means confined to learned dissertations on the subject, but the conflict between Romanistic and Germanistic views

[1] Cf. VINOGRADOFF, *Roman Law in Mediæval Europe.*
[2] Cf. HÜBNER, *Grundzüge des deutschen Privatrechts.*

materialized into a struggle between their representatives in connection with a task of immense practical value—the drawing up of the Civil Code of the German Empire (*Bürgerliches Gesetzbuch*) which came into force on January 1, 1900. The first commission to which the elaboration of the Code had been entrusted, worked under the prevailing influence of Romanistic jurists, with Windscheid at their head. The result of their labours proved to be an adaptation of "Pandekten" learning to the conditions of modern Germany. It provoked a storm of indignation on the part of the "Germanists."

Conflict between Romanists and Germanists.

Beseler had already called attention pointedly to a contrast between popular law and lawyer's law. Now Gierke took up the cudgels against Windscheid and his followers and formulated many concepts which in his view were in contradiction to the historically recorded views of the German people.[1]

These protests received wide support, and led to the formation of a second commission which considerably revised the work of the first and concluded its labours by the preparation of the Code in its present shape.

The importance of this episode in the history of modern law-making can hardly be exaggerated. It shows to what extent theory and practice are intertwined in these matters. It shows also that the foundations laid by the "historical school of law" in Romantic surroundings were by no means obliterated by later developments, but have survived in certain respects up to our own times. This is only natural, as actual schools of thought cannot be separated by a clean cut one from another, but necessarily overlap the borders of the doctrinal changes of principles.

v. Gierke.

In fact, the champion of Germanistic codification, Gierke, stands altogether as a representative of the tradition of the "Historical School of Law" in its more recent and improved aspect. His staunch patriotism is both the reason and the consequence of his adherence to the standard of

[1] P. VINOGRADOFF, Introduction to the American translation of R. HÜBNER'S *Grundzüge des deutschen Privatrechts*.

national consciousness as regards legal institutions and rules. In all his works he tries to bring into strong relief juridical ideas which he considers to be peculiar to the Teutonic race or, in a more narrow sense, to the German people.[1]

An especially important case is presented by his theory of "associative" development.[2]

From the point of view of Roman Law such an entity as a town corporation is not a real person but a legal fiction adopted for practical purposes, while from the Germanistic point of view it is as much a reality as property. The "association theory" (*Genossenschaftstheorie*) in the ultimate form given by Gierke, showed that the two Roman categories of *universitas* and *societas* do not make intelligible the types produced by the Germanic law of association. It set in their place, by the side of corporate association, Germanistic "communities of collective hand," and pointed decisively toward the conclusion that the collective person possessed an actual existence in all the forms in which it was manifested. It has sharpened our

[1] SALEILLES, *Introduction au droit civil allemand*, 28 ff.

[2] O. V. GIERKE, *Das Wesen der menschlichen Verbände*, p. 21: "We deduce the existence of actively influential social ties uniting us, first of all from outer experience. Observation of those social events among which we pass our lives, and still more the study of the history of mankind, show that nations and other communities themselves shape the world of circumstances which lend them power and produce material and spiritual culture. All this is effected by individuals, because the communities are composed of individuals But individuals, in so far as their doings concern the community, are determined in their actions by physical and spiritual influences which spring from the ties that bind them together."

p. 22: "What outer experience teaches us is confirmed by inner experience, because the reality of the social life of the community exists also in our consciousness. It is an inner experience for us to find the place for our Ego in a highly developed social life. We feel ourselves to be self-contained units, but we also feel that we are part of a whole which lives and acts within us. Take away our relation to nation and State, to religious bodies or churches, to profession and family and all kinds of unions and guilds, and we should not know ourselves in the miserable remnant that would remain. When we realize this, we understand that all these things do not mean mere chains and bonds for us, but that they represent a psychic chain of experiences affecting our innermost life and forming an integral part of our being. We become conscious of the fact that part of the impulses directing our actions emanates from the sense of community in us, and that we are living the life of social beings."

discernment of the fact that juridical persons, even though not apparent to our sight, share this lack of physical existence with all other juridical facts and concepts. As we nevertheless ascribe reality to property or to an obligation, so too the State, the commune, the society (*Verein*), the endowment (*Stiftung*), are something real, not merely fictitious. If this realistic theory be adopted it is bound to lead to consequences which are not compatible with the adoption of the Roman point of view, for the corporation will, e.g., become responsible in the same way as physical persons in actions of tort: though malice cannot be attributed to a fictitious entity, it may, of course, influence the conduct of unions of live beings. Again, in Roman Law the property of the association is quite distinct from that of the members, but in the realistic conception—which, e.g., is very clear in regard to gilds—there can be no clear division between fictitious and ordinary property, and the rights of the members extend to the property of the craft as such. The gild-chamber, the gild furniture, the capital accumulated by contributions, entrance fees, penalties and gifts, served not only the ends of the association, but also the economic, social and other purposes of the members. Every associate might, for example, use the gild house for his convivial pleasures, each could demand support or loans from the capital of the gild, and so on. These benefits were not, however, indispensable to the gild members in the same way as the use of the "commons" was to the members of the "Mark"; the gild property was devoted in a far greater degree to the whole body as such. From the beginning, the entire body of gild members stood opposed to the individual in a far more pronounced manner than was originally the case in *Mark* associations; and this is explained by the fact that there was not in the case of the crafts, as there was in the case of rural communities, a complete coincidence of the purpose of the group with the aims of its members. The craft was not designed to further merely the interests of individuals,—it was precisely in the older period that it had to serve the interests of the association, the city, and the purchasing public.

Thus a moral person is in no way a fictitious being devised by lawyers in order to facilitate certain business operations: it is a real union, or a unit, in the sense that its existence and functions form a necessary part of the life of the group of live persons who are joined as its members. A craft-gild, a city, a State, are real beings, who live in the life of their members, possess a distinct consciousness and a common will, although their existence stretches over generations and is not interrupted by the disappearance of particular individuals included in it or by the appearance of others. This being so, the moral person is not only a necessary complement to the individual lives concerned, but it ought to be subjected to all the consequences of the notion of real personality.

All these features are attributed to the "real" corporation on the strength of a Germanistic tendency, although it is claimed at the same time that the interpretation of the juridical person has a basis in the nature of man and of society.[1]

Ihering's criticism and new departure.

The work of the "Historical School of Law" has not been done in vain, and later developments did not simply wipe it off the slate. If the rationalistic schools had cleared up the logical connection between the formal principles of positive law, the Historical School and the Romantic movement have established once for all the view of the organic growth of institutions and rules and have substituted for the rationalistic conceptions of the period of enlightenment a wider view of individual and social psychology. But the mystic nationalism of the Romantic theory has not stood the test of critical examination and of scientific progress. Nations are live beings in a certain sense, but not in the same sense as individuals: they are not circumscribed to the same extent in their development by unyielding forms, they react more freely against circumstances and command a wider range of adaptation. Tradition is a powerful factor in their life, but so is progress. The actual course of European history did not remain under the law of reaction and

[1] R. SALEILLES, *La personalité juridique* (1910), *passim*, especially p. 607.

conservatism: after taking a rest for a generation or two, it started again on the track of reforms and change. In the special field of jurisprudence we have already noticed some of the deficiencies of a rigidly nationalistic doctrine. But the best way of realizing the limitations of the Historical School of Law is to listen to the words of one who himself began as an adherent of the school, but eventually struck out a line of his own—I mean Ihering. No one was better qualified to appreciate the value of a historical study of the factors influencing law, than the author of the *Spirit of Roman Law.* But he felt more and more that the progress of law is not merely the result of an unconscious growth conditioned by innate character and by environment, but also the result of conscious endeavours to solve the problems of social existence. More perhaps than any other form of human activity, law is directed towards aims; it receives its orientation not only from the past but from the future. It may miss the mark or attain its objects in particular matters, but it is prospective and a function of consciousness in its very essence.[1]

This leading idea has played a part in the subsequent development of jurisprudence, and we shall have to revert to it by and by: at present it will help us to understand why the teaching of the Historical School of Law had to give way before new methods.

[1] IHERING, *Geist des römischen Rechts,* III, p. 296: "Juridical principles . . . are not merely logical categories, but forms for the concentration of material rules, and rules change with conditions"

CHAPTER VII

THE EVOLUTIONISTS

Darwinism.

No event in the history of scientific thought has had a greater influence in shaping the habits of mind of researchers and philosophers than the rise of Darwinism. The biological view of evolution focussed in that expression has come to dominate not only natural science, but also the study of man and of society.

The decisive feature of the Darwinian synthesis was the application of biological evolution to animal species; a further step led to the application to social groups of his views of the struggle for existence, of the survival of the fittest, of the processes of selection, of adaptation by heredity, of the unity of organic life. It has given a rude shock to many time-honoured prejudices and has naturally called forth fierce opposition. By the side of the supporters of confessional dogmas appeared idealists who believed that the spread of a doctrine starting from a biological basis endangered the dignity of man and the value of his creative power.[1]

Some of the shafts directed against Darwinian views struck home, but they reached only the more rash among his followers, who had come to regard the biological formulæ as rules of thumb fit for automatic application to all problems of history, ethics or social science.

Such pruning of the branches did not, however, harm the roots in any way. The main principles of the movement have proved a most potent ferment in the development of social studies. Three ideas emerge as especially powerful in this respect: the idea of gradual adaptation to circumstances, the idea of a continuous connection between the lowest and the highest forms of animal and human life,

[1] MERZ, *History of European Thought*, II, 624; III, 394 ff.

and the idea of a transformation of individual faculties through the life of social groups. In their combined effect these three leading ideas constitute the mainstay of the doctrine of evolution which has set its stamp on the scientific thought of the last seventy years. Needless to add, neither the special biological tenets nor the general views which accompany them were entirely and exclusively the personal products of Darwin's genius: their greatness and fruitfulness depend, of course, on the fact that they focus the strivings and intuitions of a whole period of scientific thought.

Teleological evolution in Law.

A saying of Ihering's may be taken as the appropriate epigraph to the Evolutionist movement in Social Science: "Law is not less a product of history than handicraft, naval construction, technical skill: as Nature did not provide Adam's soul with a ready-made conception of a kettle, of a ship or of a steamer, even so she has not presented him with property, marriage, binding contracts, the State. And the same may be said of all moral rules. . . . The whole moral order is a product of history, or, to put it more definitely, of the striving towards ends, of the untiring activity and work of human reason tending to satisfy wants and to provide against difficulties."[1]

The teleology of the legal process is underlined in these words by the side of its causality, and the fact that law is striving consciously to achieve social aims makes its study particularly interesting from an evolutionary point of view. To be sure, political and jurisprudential changes often lead to unforeseen results—witness the frequent cases when the excess of discipline has produced outbreaks of anarchy—but, apart from such cases of "heterogeneity" the effect of laws consists to a large extent in adaptation to conditions. Both invention and tradition play characteristic parts in this process.

Anthropology and prehistoric archaeology.

In the long history of civilization the first steps are in many respects the most decisive. Indeed, the proper expression would be "early stages" rather than first steps:

[1] IHERING, *Zweck im Recht*, II, p. 112.

when first steps were made, there was as yet no one to record them and to reflect on them, and the scanty material remnants of prehistoric archæology hardly justify the sweeping theories which have sometimes been constructed in accounting for them.

Nor has the study of savage races led to the discovery of primitive tribes immediately related to the higher apes which are supposed to be our nearest cousins among animals.

Yet, though even the most rudimentary forms of culture known to us are very complex and replete with various accomplishments, we are justified in considering them at early stages and in tracing the incipient forms of social organization and law in their arrangements. These cultural origins supply us not only with simpler combinations and more clearly defined natural conditions, but they possess the inestimable advantage of presenting themselves in a very great number of instances and varieties which shade off one into the other and offer welcome opportunities for comparative investigation. This is so much the case, that comparative jurisprudence has almost become synonymous with a study of primitive societies, although, of course, such a connotation is by no means rendered necessary by the aim of the study.[1]

Maine.

The attention of students was directed towards this "anthropological" origin in many centres at the same time. The atmosphere of social studies was literally charged in the second half of the nineteenth century with anthropological inquiries. It is sufficient to mention Bachofen's investigations on mother-right, Morgan's on classificatory

[1] VINOGRADOFF in the *Enc. Brit.* on *Comparative Jurisprudence;* THALLER, GÉNY and others, *L'œuvre juridique de R. Saleilles*, p. 108: "In short, it [comparative jurisprudence] will provide the jurisconsult with an entirely new field of observation, which will permit him to prove the value and the solidity of national constructions, to modify them, and even to make innovations among them, provided that the latter are in harmony with the body of internal law and do not interfere with its economy. If the result of the teaching of comparative law is that the same idea explains the juridical regulation of an institution in many legislations, will not this conception be singularly fortified?"

relationship, McLennan's observation on exogamy, Bastian's ethnographic parallels. Nor were the excursions of anthropologists restricted to particular problems of social intercourse. General surveys of evolution and attempts at formulating empirical laws made their appearance by the side of innumerable monographs. Among these a most conspicuous place may be claimed for Maine's work—not only in Great Britain, but among all students of legal anthropology in Europe.

It is not necessary to dwell on the conditions which contributed to give a definite direction to Maine's thought and to his writings. As a professor of Civil Law in Oxford he acquired interest in the historical formation of the legal system of Rome and presented the main threads of Romanistic study as an example of "Ancient Law" development in an attractive and suggestive book.[1] But Maine's principal contributions to jurisprudence were those volumes on Village Communities, on Early Institutions, on Modern Custom and Ancient Law which were written after his return from India, when his thoughtful mind had been awakened to the social aspects of law in its organic processes of adaptation revealed by a comparison between such vastly different bodies of custom as those of the Indian and Germanic village communities, of Slavonic joint families, of the clans and clientships of the Celts. In point of method Maine presented the greatest possible contrast with the abstract rationalism of Austin's analysis: he expressed his disagreement with the latter in a remarkable section of his book on Early Institutions.[2] As regards the Romantic school, he never took occasion to state an opinion, though the influence of Savigny may be clearly perceived in the book on *Ancient Law;* his method became, however, differentiated from that of the "Historical School of Law" in his later writings. No stronger contrast could be imagined than his treatment of Communities and that of Gierke: while the latter insists on the Germanistic

[1] Cf. Vinogradoff, *The Teaching of Sir Henry Maine.*
[2] *Early History of Institutions* (1875), pp. 345 ff.

peculiarities of the Mark and of the craft-gild, Maine uses v. Maurer's materials in order to impress on his readers the idea of a constantly-recurring combination which is no more German in essence than it is Indian or Slavonic, a combination produced by an undeveloped sense of individual right and natural union among the members of a village settlement. His interpretation of the evidence may be right or wrong, but it is certainly not the part played by the nationalistic element which he wants to emphasize, but the similarity in the methods of husbandry and land-tenure employed by different nationalities in similar conditions. Maine had a great following among continental writers—M. Kovalevsky, for instance, showed his adherence to Maine's views by the very title of his best book.[1]

Spread of anthropological jurisprudence.

Other students took up the same task without standing in direct connection with the British writer. R. Dareste[2] may be mentioned on account of his excellent sketches of legal customs and institutions from all parts of the world. Post[3] gathered an enormous mass of material from the life of savage and barbarian tribes.

J. Kohler, besides writing copiously himself on comparative law on anthropological lines, has formed an important centre of study in his Review of Comparative Jurisprudence.[4]

One feature of these works illustrating the natural history of legal customs and rules by comparison and analogy has been the attempt to formulate generalizations as to normal sequences of development, or what may be called empirical laws of jurisprudence. We read, for instance, in Maine's *Ancient Law* that the course of this development proceeds from status to contract.[5] A favourite scheme of social evolution starts with sexual promiscuity in the earliest stage, and marks the advance from anarchy to the horde, then to the clan, then to the family household which

[1] *Coutume contemporaine et ancienne loi* (1896).
[2] *Études de l'histoire du droit* (1882), *Nouvelles études* (1902, 1906).
[3] *Afrikanische Jurisprudenz*, etc.
[4] *Zeitschrift für vergleichende Rechtswissenschaft.*
[5] *Ancient Law*, ch. v.

itself is constructed first on polygamic and later on monogamic lines. From an economic point of view the commonly accepted sequence of stages consists in the transition from a society of hunters and fishers, to a nomad pastoral organization, then to an industrial and commercial, ultimately to capitalistic intercourse.[1]

These references may be sufficient to show on what broad lines comparative study has been carried out and from what different points of view legal problems have been approached by it. Marriage, husbandry, crime and punishment, succession, possession and contract have all been treated by the anthropological school as devices to meet varying social conditions, and the relative character of the solutions obtained has been as much to the fore as the analogies in the treatment of similar problems by nations and tribes situated in very different surroundings.

Sociological orientation. Ihering.

The work of the anthropological school as regards law has been largely descriptive and carried on rather in width than in depth. It was supplemented by another line of inquiry, akin to the former one in its premises and aims, but altogether different in technical method. I mean the *sociological* treatment of legal facts that became usual in the second half of the nineteenth century. The apostle of the sociological creed, A. Comte, did not pay much attention to law; it was absorbed for him in the general course of historical development.[2]

Spencer was led by his studies in descriptive sociology to consider customary rules and institutions among the materials for empirical generalization,[3] and his determined attitude in the controversy between the State and the individual made it necessary to formulate views as to the direction of social evolution ("the coming slavery"). But these fragmentary surveys do not count seriously in the history of juridical thought. An important departure was made, on the other hand, by Ihering. In his earlier writings he had

1 K. BÜCHER, *Entwickelung der Volkswirtschaft* (1904), pp 45, 54.
2 *Cours de philosophie positive*, IV, pp. 275-282; MICHEL, *op. cit.*, pp. 447, 448.
3 *Principles of Sociology.*

touched on several vital problems of general jurisprudence. He had contrasted in his *Spirit of Roman Law* the technical methods of the professional lawyer with the customary, half-religious formalism and the common-sense equity of popular legal lore,[1] and he had come to the conclusion that both methods are justified in their time and place, one in the initial stages of juridical formation, the other in epochs of advanced civilization and of complex intercourse. These observations suggested a different appreciation of national and international factors in jurisprudence and positive law: while in early periods legal rules grow more or less organically, like language and myth, later stages are characterized by universal and, as it were, impersonal conceptions, which, like coins of standard value, circulate without difficulty right through the world. In the Review of dogmatic Private Law which Ihering conducted with Gerber, he gave great prominence to the special craft of the lawyer and to methods of dialectical analysis and dogmatic construction. But he insisted energetically on the social aims of juridical activity, attacked with bitter scorn the tendency towards the self-satisfied exercise of juridical logic divorced from practical needs,[2] and represented the process of legal formation as a "struggle for right" among contending individual and social claims.[3] While illustrating forcibly the value of a stubborn assertion of the concrete will, he broke with the abstract conception of the will in itself (*an und für sich*) apart from aim and motive, and substituted in his famous definition of right the protected interest for the limited will.[4]

[1] *Geist des römischen Rechts*, III, p. 302: "Let us break the charm, the illusion which holds us captive. All this cult of logic that would fain turn jurisprudence into legal mathematics is an error and arises from misunderstanding law. Life does not exist for the sake of concepts, but concepts for the sake of life. It is not logic that is entitled to exist, but what is claimed by life, by social intercourse, by the sense of justice—whether it be logically necessary or logically impossible. The Romans would have been worthy to dwell in Abdera if they had ever thought otherwise, if they had sacrificed the interests of life to the dialectic of the school"

[2] IHERING, *Scherz und Ernst in der Jurisprudenz*. See *ante*, p. 25.

[3] *Kampf ums Recht*, p. 7.

[4] Cf. KORKUNOV, *Theory of Law*, transl. by Hastings.

The Aim of Law.

But Ihering's most important contribution to the general theory of law is given in his *Zweck im Recht* (the "Aim in Law"), a work which, in spite of its absence of symmetry and occasional lengthiness, presents one of the principal landmarks in the history of jurisprudence. It traces the conditions under which the individual and society co-operate in evolving rules of conduct. The governing ideas are that all human conduct being directed towards aims, these aims are bound to be determined by utility, the striving towards good and the avoidance of evil. The secret of history consists in the fact that good and evil are estimated in their values not by individuals, but by society, and that social aims are engrafted on individual consciousness by the educational action of society in fashion, in conventional rules, in moral training and ethical ideals, lastly and most effectually—in law. The history of juridical conceptions and institutions is devoted to tracing the evolution of this social education conditioned by all the varying influences of race, geographical situation, climate, economic arrangements, political organization, relations with neighbours, cross currents of religious and scientific ideas, etc., but ever tending towards a welfare achieved by social means. In the light of this orientation one comes to understand the meaning of the protest against the "Historical School of Law," a school pledged to the cult of rigid national personalities dependent on the past and barren as to the future.[1]

Juridical analysis. Jellinek.

I have already called attention to the revival of interest in juridical analysis and in juridical construction which characterizes Ihering's work. He always felt and spoke as a jurist, and did not want to exchange the sharp definitions and compelling inferences of the lawyer for the hazy descriptions and the fluid transitions of historians. This firm attitude of trained lawyers is very noticeable in

[1] LANDSBERG, *Geschichte der Rechtswissenschaft,* III, p. 816: "A juridical institution stands and falls with the achievement of its aim. It arises for the sake of aims, in the consciousness of aims, and in the struggle between aims. This is the reason why law cannot be explained either by mechanical processes or by blind growth. Its justification lies in its *ends,* as a means for their realization."

other works on sociological jurisprudence. I will select two as examples of a powerful current in the literature of the end of the nineteenth century. Jellinek's writings are devoted to problems of constitutional and administrative law. The book which immediately concerns us now is his *General Doctrine of the State* (*Allgemeine Staatslehre*); its chief aim is to ascertain the relations between political arrangements dependent on social conditions, on the one hand, and the rules which constitute the positive law of the State on the other. Apart from a valuable discussion of various theories bearing on the subject, the work is chiefly interesting on account of the light it throws on the part played by legal rules in upholding political systems.[1] It must be added, however, that the element of systematic construction predominates over the exact study of the facts in such a way as sometimes to distort the true meaning and perspective of institutions. This defect is very noticeable in the treatment of English Law, where Jellinek's rather arbitrary generalizations compare unfavourably with the masterly exposition of Dicey, derived from an intimate and profound understanding of Common Law.[2]

Modified doctrine of natural right.

Another significant current of thought connected with the evolutionist movement in jurisprudence may be seen in the revival of a modified conception of the law of nature—not in the rationalistic sense, of course, but in that of a striving towards ideals. If, as Ihering put it, law has not only to register actual rules and to explain their origin, but also to aim at the solution of social problems, it is not

1 *Allgemeine Staatslehre* (1905), p. 47: "The doctrine of a transformation directed towards aims sheds light on the fundamental error of the view that social phenomena arise and develop by a process of organic growth We ascribe to the organic process the facts that transcend our knowledge."

p. 176: "The critical question arising in regard to all social institutions: Why do they exist—springs therefore from the essence of our reasoning faculty First and foremost it holds good with regard to the State. Why does the State with its supreme power exist? Why must the individual suffer subjection of his will to another; why and to what extent ought he to sacrifice himself to the community?"

2 DICEY, *The Law of the Constitution.* In the work of Jellinek's pupil, HATSCHEK (*Englisches Staatsrecht*) these defects are magnified tenfold.

wrong or presumptuous to reflect on the general principles which in the present state of civilization we ought to accept as the guiding lights for legislators and reformers, and as the critical tests for approving or disapproving existing rules of positive law. The idea of constructing a sociological jurisprudence has been embodied recently in a work by Professor Eugen Ehrlich of Graz. He defines its scope in the following words: "The primary and most important task of sociological law (law on a sociological basis) is therefore to separate the component parts of the law ruling, regulating and determining human society, from mere decisions in individual cases, and to prove their organizing nature. This was recognized first in Constitutional and Administrative law. Indeed, no one doubts nowadays that State law means the organization of the State and does not exist for the purpose of settling quarrels but to define the position and tasks of the State-organs and the rights and duties of State officials. But the State is first and foremost a social union."[1] The principles of law are bound to be social in their essence.

Such principles are bound to be broad and general, but they cannot be universal and eternal: they appeal to the nature of men, not in the abstract, but as defined by circumstances. Every age will have its own ideals in this respect, although such ideals are bound to have some connection with each other. The ancient world ended by condemning slavery on the strength of the law of nature, the mediæval polity was overthrown when serfdom was condemned as being against nature, and present-day society is condemning ruthless competition as being against the law of nature. The appearance of such watchwords cannot fail to be ominous. They enlist strong sympathy when "there's something rotten in the state of Denmark." In this sense attention may be called to such works as Stammler's *Right Law* (*Das richtige Recht*) which has been hailed with approbation by many thinkers in continental countries, for example, by Saleilles, who accepted it as "a law of nature with variable contents."[2]

[1] E. Ehrlich, *Grundlegung der soziologischen Rechtswissenschaft.*
[2] Stammler, *Das richtige Recht.*

A similar idea is expressed in a suggestive volume by Saleilles' fellow-countryman Charmont.[1]

As in the case of Jellinek, the value of Stammler's book lies in the leading idea of the author and in the method advocated by him, much more than in the use he has made of his own suggestions. Instead of operating within the limits of a shifting scheme of ideals, Stammler proceeded to lay down a set of standard formulæ devised on a rationalistic pattern for all time. His four standards have no value for the advancement of juridical thought, and as for his *Theory of Law*,[2] with the pretentious epigraph *"non est mortale quod opto,"* it is hardly too much to say that it is presented in such a pedantic manner that it is almost impossible to read the big volume dedicated to it, and quite impossible to make use of for any definite purpose. It had been better if the author had taken to heart the admirable precepts of his own *Right Law*.

On the whole, there can be no doubt that the idea of evolution has had a potent influence on jurisprudential studies. It has not only supplied jurists with a suggestive explanation of the sequences of changes through which all systems of positive law pass in their history, but it has indicated a proper method for estimating the course of this development: we all recognize now that law has grown by conscious efforts towards the solution of social problems conditioned by causes which spring from previous stages of development and from the influence of surroundings. At the same time, the task of unravelling the sequence of evolution in law and right lies in truth at the source of all juridical activity. Evolution in this domain means a constant struggle between two conflicting tendencies—the certainty and stability of legal systems and progress and adaptation to circumstances in order to achieve social justice.

1 *Renaissance du droit naturel.*
2 *Theorie der Rechtswissenschaft.*

CHAPTER VIII

MODERN TENDENCIES IN JURISPRUDENCE

Critical tendency.

RECENT developments in the domain of jurisprudence have not yet assumed a sufficiently distinctive character to entitle them to rank as a new epoch in the history of that science. Nevertheless there are certain features, common to the work of writers of the beginning of the twentieth century, which deserve attention and are likely to advance the study towards new vistas.

To begin with, we have to notice a strong critical tendency: instead of the enthusiasm called forth by the earlier instalments of comparative study, an attitude of scepticism and searching investigation has been assumed by leading writers. Jellinek, for example, has expressed great disappointment as to the results achieved by anthropologists in their comparative surveys.[1]

Even more characteristic are the critical objections of the most brilliant legal historian of modern England—F. W. Maitland. He was a decided sceptic as regards many generalizations proposed by Maine—not, however, because of any opposition to relativism. On the contrary, he fully admitted that legal as well as social and political phenomena are produced by the flow of historical circumstances, but it seemed to him that writers had been guided in their work more by their wish to prove preconceived theories than by a careful consideration of the evidence. His developed sense of historical criticism rebelled against Maine's assumptions and lack of careful investigation of sources.[2] As regards primitive kindred, for instance, Maitland lays stress on the difficulty arising from the fact that ancient Anglo-Saxon and Germanic law recognized relationship on the female as well as the male side. In his

1 *Allgemeine Staatslehre.*
2 *Collected Papers*, I, p. 285.

view, there can therefore be no question of grouping the corresponding societies into patriarchal clans, which stand or fall with the conception of agnatic relationship. Again, in his criticism of Maine's theory of the village community, he held that there is no evidence of original communalism. Altogether, the theory of "stages" seemed unnecessary and misleading to him; why should one assume that all nations are constituted on the same lines and reproduce the same characteristic features in their treatment of economic and social problems? For Maitland, on the contrary, nations manifest such great differences of character and intellect that some national groups would be bound to skip certain stages, which other more backward units might pass through.[1] Obviously such criticism might be directed with even greater justice against the speculations of German writers like Kohler, than against the theories of Maine.

It is, however, important to notice that Maitland's opposition challenged not the method itself, but rather the indiscriminate way in which the comparative anthropologists worked out their ideals. He did not maintain that because there were so many fallacious analogies, all recourse to analogies is unsuitable.[2]

F. W. Maitland and the comparative method

As, however, the comparative method cannot be completely discarded, Maitland himself did use it repeatedly, and, in fact, he has shown by his very attacks how the same problems may be approached by a similar road while avoiding the pitfalls into which the former votaries of the school had stumbled.[3] For instance, the development of the idea of a corporation in England was studied by him in relation to German theories, and it was for this purpose that he translated a section of Gierke's work. In his

1 *History of English Law,* II, p. 237. *Domesday Book and Beyond,* p. 345.

2 *Collected Papers,* II, p. 4: "Only by a comparison of our law with her sisters will some of the most remarkable traits be understood."

3 *Op. cit.,* II, pp. 251, 312. *History of English Law,* I, pp. 486 *et seq.;* II, pp. 29-80.

analysis of kinship he protests against patriarchal theories, but goes a long way towards accepting the view of matriarchal origins of the process, etc.

The necessity for revising the comparative method is one of the lines on which modern jurisprudence has to take up the thread of investigation. Inferences must be preceded by a careful study of individual cases, and in this study juridical analysis ought to receive more attention than has been the case hitherto. This side is very poorly represented in the books on anthropological jurisprudence, which, even when written by lawyers, generally suffer from a tendency to put together things which are in reality unconnected.

The accumulation of somewhat indiscriminately collected facts like those presented by Post, Kohler, Kovalevsky, etc., had its justification in the necessity of preliminary surveys on broad lines. What is wanted now is to take our stand on the careful analysis of one or the other rule, relation or institution, as illustrated in its formation, development and decay by the facts of comparative jurisprudence. Steinmetz's monograph on crime and punishment in primitive society may serve as an example of the proper application of such a method.[1]

By the side of the critical tendency, there are signs of the appearance of a new *constructive* point of view. It is suggested forcibly by the great social crisis on which the world is evidently entering even now. The individualistic order of society is giving way before the impact of an inexorable process of socialization, and the future will depend for a long time on the course and the extent of this process. I should like to recall some remarkable pages by a German economist, who in 1890 looked on Great Britain as the land of promise for a "social peace": The social crisis.

"How could the inheritance which represents our highest spiritual and moral possessions and whose guardians we are, be considered entirely secure? If the movement which threatened to annihilate it, assimilates it in

[1] *Ethnologische Studien über die Entwickelung der Strafe* (1894).

such a way as (itself) to carry it towards the future; if instead of battling against existing society, it helps to develop it. But we seem farther than ever from such a solution; it demands an almost impossible amount of insight on both sides: it means that the *masses* should understand that the progress of mankind can only be gradual and peaceful, for it means indeed not the education of a few but of all, including every individual. Is it not thoroughly unscientific to advance the opinion in a century devoted to historical research and the doctrine of evolution, that an ideal state of society could be attained at one stroke, by means of external changes, and that progress means anything else than the development of what already exists? But the understanding demanded from the *upper classes* is not less hard, namely, to own that new times with new demands have now dawned and it is no longer possible to 'put new wine into old bottles.' Instead of such insight we find overbearing behaviour on the one side and suspicion and hatred on the other; the people are divided into two nations, out of contact, and without understanding for each other; they feel and think discordantly and, as Lord Beaconsfield said of his country, 'they are as much strangers to each other as if they had been born in different hemispheres'."[1]

It cannot be expected that the immense changes that are taking place in the domain of positive law should be accompanied by an easy and smooth transformation of jurisprudence. The process has, however, produced some remarkable speculations in that field, and they are distinguished in a characteristic manner as much by negative tendencies as by constructive features. Duguit's work in France occupies a prominent position in this respect.[2] He sets out as an uncompromising opponent of the juridical personality of the State, which he treats as a mere fiction, devised to conceal the matter-of-fact preponderance of

[1] G. von Schultze-Gaevernitz, *Zum socialen Frieden* (1890), p. viii.

[2] *Études de droit public; Droit constitutionnel; Transformation du droit privé; Transformation du droit public; Droit social.*

particular persons or groups. Instead of this "exploded" view he desires to set up the conception of social solidarity with public services and duties corresponding to it. It is not difficult to perceive that this change of attitude has been inspired by a general hostility to the State constructed on the lines of the conceptions of personality and will. It is more than doubtful, however, whether the author has succeeded in providing his nation of social solidarity with sufficiently definite attributes to enable it to act as a foundation for a system of law. We may extend or minimize the part played by the organized commonwealth in the life and conduct of its individual members, but it is difficult to see how even a socialistic commonwealth can get rid of the contrast between the personal and the public, the social and the individual. As a society organized for rule, it is bound to assume the form of a superphysical person.

Duguit's second position calls forth even stronger objections. He denies the existence of right as distinguished from law, the existence of subjective and individual claims of justice as distinct from objective rules.[1] (The subjective right, *Droit subjectif*, of Continental jurists.) He believes that men's position and activity in society are sufficiently defined by the duties imposed on them by social solidarity and points to the frequent cases when society demands the curtailment and sacrifice of the most elementary "rights"—e.g., claims to property and even to life. I will merely refer my readers to the pertinent criticism of Saleilles,[2] who, while recognizing the cleverness of Duguit's deductions, rejected them as subversive of the very essence of law. As long as society is made up of live individuals, its structure and order are bound to proceed from combinations between them, and if rights are assigned and limited by law, the latter appears, on the other hand, as a product of compromises and agreements which assume the technical shape of *rights*. The necessary renunciations and sacrifices are at bottom measures of expediency and of self-defence, and their apparent

[1] *Études de droit public*, I, ch i and ii.
[2] *Œuvre de Raymond Saleilles*, p. 32.

opposition to individual aspirations is in truth the surrender of casual licence for the sake of a reasonable assurance.

Another interesting symptom of the fermentation in the domain of jurisprudence is presented by Professor Eugen Ehrlich's book, *Elements of the Sociology of Law.* The writer seeks to show that the law administered by the courts of justice is only a small part, and the most external part, of the juridical process. The real roots of law rest in the soil of everyday intercourse, of social custom, and the greater the technical severance of legal rules from this broad social basis, the worse for society at large. All the misunderstandings, the encroachments, the pedantries of modern legal systems may be traced to this source. We are reminded of the arguments urged by von Bülow in his attack on the logical method of interpretation in German law, but the contributions of Ehrlich are stated in a much more comprehensive form, and connect themselves, in the past, with Puchta's teaching, while they point in the future to a recasting of legal rules and institutions to fit the requirements of a socialistic development. Subjective "right" has to suffer again in the process, because social needs and conventions are assigned the preponderant rôle in the forming of legal rules. Another Austrian, Professor A. Menger of the University of Vienna, has taken upon himself the task of criticising in detail the rules of the German Civil Code from a socialistic point of view, and has sketched the outlines of a socialistic legislation.[1] But his work, though very interesting, belongs rather to the field of positive law than to that of jurisprudence. There can be no doubt in any case that the socialistic movement cannot content itself with vague and sentimental attacks upon the existing legal order and the jurisprudence of the individualistic State. It is on the way to putting forward jurisprudential theories of its own.

We may like it or not, we may hail the recasting of social values or deplore it, but we have to make up our minds that

[1] ANTON MENGER, *Neue Staatslehre*, Jena, 1904. It would be out of the question to estimate in any way the possibilities arising out of the idea of a League of Nations.

the transformation is taking place as an episode of historical evolution. Let us remember the attitude of a great representative of an aristocratic civilization, Alexis de Tocqueville, before the advent of democracy. Something similar may be witnessed now in a book like Dicey's *Law and Opinion:* it sets before us in a concise and vivid contrast the elemental struggle between the individualistic tendencies, as illustrated by Bentham, and the rising tide of socialistic conceptions resulting in a crisis of English juridical thought and legislation.

From our point of view these ideas are expressive not only of the social anxieties and strivings of our time, but also of a scientific movement. Law has to be studied in constant reference to the movement of public opinion at large, because it is not only technical, but broadly historical: philosophers, naturalists, economists, students of political science, jurists, have all been thinking and talking of evolution. Its manifestations have been studied among the totem groups of Australia, the clans of the Celts, the communities of the Indians and of the Slavs, the towns of mediæval Germany. It is time that we should turn to the evolutionary crisis in which we are ourselves implicated nowadays. The ground is shifting under our feet and it is no use pretending that the province of law alone remains steady and immobile in the midst of the general transformation.

Scope of General Jurisprudence.

But is it not possible to put together a certain number of fundamental principles of jurisprudence derived from the universal requirements of the human mind, and to constitute in this way a formal[1] theory of law, independent of modifications brought about by national, geographical, political peculiarities? Such is really the claim of so-called "general jurisprudence." It may be observed at once, that such a claim seems rather odd on the part of writers who have renounced the conception of a law of nature and pin their faith to positive law. Though Wolff and Kant could map out schemes of universal jurisprudence, Austin and Holland have no right to do so. Nor does it make the

[1] HOLLAND on "Formal Theory of Law," *Jurisprudence*, p. 6.

attempt less inconsistent on the part of these latter writers, that they limit their province of jurisprudence to the law of the civilized world. What is the civilized world? When did it begin to exist? Is Christian civilization to be included in it? Is the law of the Roman jurists to be considered? Have Plato and Aristotle the right to speak on the philosophy of law? Are Mohammedan and Brahmanic conceptions to be excluded from consideration? Is it irrelevant for jurists to observe the beginnings of ideas of judicial authority, of public sanction, of private right, of family arrangements, of property, of possession, of co-operation? It would be difficult, to be sure, to embrace the whole range of human development by ideas of universal jurisprudence, but if we have to cut off arbitrarily parts of this development for the sake of unity of treatment, this surely shows that a scientific treatment of the subject ought to aim not at absolute and universal, but at relative constructions.

And when we examine modern textbooks of general jurisprudence in detail, we do find that the universal element in them is, at bottom, restricted to a statement of queries and a registration of disagreements. The setting of these queries is not accidental. All systems of law have to deal with rules and rights. All have to classify their material under the headings of public and private law. All consider delict and compensation, crime and punishment. All treat of status and contract, of things and obligations, etc. But suppose that, after drawing up your table of contents, you proceed to define law and right or property or crime? You will not only find that many of your colleagues disagree with you—this is inevitable in any case—but it will be difficult to deny that the ideas of the Greeks about justice as the end of law, or the Roman conception of absolute property (*dominium*) or the view of Canonists as to crime and sin, do not coincide with the teaching of modern jurists and are not likely to coincide with the doctrines of their probable successors.[1]

There is bound to be more substantial agreement as

[1] MERKEL, *Juristische Encyclopädie* (1885), par. 35.

regards *methods* of legal thought in so far as these rest on an application of *logic,* because formal logic is built upon universally accepted rules as to operations of reasoning. But in this department also, all the technical elements supplied by positive law as regards rules of presumption, of proof, of relevancy, of pleading, etc., will be "municipal" or relative and not universal or absolute. To sum up, the "general jurisprudence" of the nineteenth century can hardly stand for anything else than an encyclopædic survey of the juridical principles of individualistic society. In this sense it deserves full attention, because it expresses the tendency of the legal mind to co-ordinate and to harmonize its concepts into a coherent and reasonable whole on a given basis—the basis of individualism.

Legal history and historical jurisprudence.

Dogmatic or, as people generally say in England, analytical jurisprudence cannot claim to be more absolute in its tenets than the other departments of social science. It is conditioned by circumstances and therefore *historical* in its essence. But, of course, the term "circumstances" may mean different things. It may point to the ever-flowing course of actual history. In this case the most important features of the development have to be selected from the sequence of innumerable events by the legal historian. But the aim may also be to trace the life of juridical ideas in their action and reaction on conditions, and for that purpose the student of *historical jurisprudence* has to group his material in accordance with the divisions and relations of ideas rather than with dates. In other words, the order followed by legal history is chronological; that followed by historical jurisprudence is ideological. The significance of human evolution consists in the fact that such ideal lines can be traced in its progress: the saying, *vis consilii expers mole ruit sua,* does not apply to it.

The problem set to scientific method is how to utilize that characteristic feature of human evolution. Certain indications in this respect may be gathered from recent attempts in the study of political economy, which, as I have already had occasion to remark, stands for obvious reasons in the forefront of social research. After passing through the stages of abstract deduction and of vague historical synthesis, it has entered at present into a stage of intensive co-operation between the two.

Interesting suggestions have been made which have a wider bearing than the solution of purely economic problems. For instance, in a series of articles on the historical school in economics, as founded by Roscher and Knies, Max Weber pleads for a study of *types* of economic development.[1]

As an illustration of the manner in which the methodical principle of what may be called an ideological study of types may be applied, we may refer to K. Bücher's contributions towards a theory of economic stages.[2]

The use of the *ideological* method undoubtedly presents great difficulties and dangers: it is especially open to attack on the part of professional historians accustomed to the critical study of sources and to the ranging of facts within exact limits of time and place. Bücher's generalizations have, as a matter of fact, called forth very sharp objections from a leading historian, Edward Meyer.[3]

But this seems to be a case when *du choc des opinions jaillit la vérité.* If the besetting dangers are realized, it is not impossible to steer clear of them, and in any case, even if some of the diagrammatic simplifications may have to be materially supplemented, their sharply cut formulæ will have served a useful purpose by concentrating thought and starting it on fresh tracks. Quite apart from methodological speculation, we can point to a certain number of works that have played such a part in the literature of social science. Fustel de Coulanges' *Cité Antique* may be cited as a case in point. The deduction of all the details of civic life from ancestor worship is a palpable exaggeration of one aspect of ancient culture: it leads to a distorted perspective of the interplay of social functions. And yet there is hardly a book among the innumerable

[1] *Roscher und Knies* (SCHMOLLER'S *Jahrbücher für Gesetzgebung, Verwaltung und Volkswirtschaft im deutschen Reich,* xxviii [1903]).

[2] *Entwickelung der Volkswirtschaft,* pp. 102, 103.

[3] *Kleine Schriften zur Geschichtstheorie und zur wirtschaftlichen und politischen Geschichte des Altertums* (1910).

works on classical antiquities that brings home in such a powerful manner the typical grouping of the classical household and its bearing on social arrangements.

On a more extensive scale the same estimate may be applied to Mommsen's grand construction of Roman constitutional law around the idea of the *imperium:* it is also too forcible a simplification of a very complicated set of facts, but who can deny that the energetic elaboration of the dominant idea has illumined a maze of details with a directive light?

Stages and types of juridical evolution.

How are we to apply these methodological considerations to a systematic treatment of historical jurisprudence? It seems to me that the clue is to be found in the very attempts to build up a *general* jurisprudence for civilized mankind. Such attempts have turned out to be in truth constructions of a *typical* jurisprudence on *individualistic* lines. Taken in this sense they are justified and worthy of careful attention. They represent a concentration of the leading juridical principles in various departments of law round a central conception derived from the nature of the social tie—that of co-ordination of individual wills. Recent discussions make it abundantly clear that if individualistic civilization were to give way before one based on a *socialistic* conception of the social tie, all the positions of jurisprudence would have to be reconsidered. Nor is it doubtful that our individualistic jurisprudence has established its predominance after a prolonged struggle with *feudal* and *theocratic* conceptions derived from the social ties of human fidelity and of Divine guidance. Looking still further back, we may discern a great period of civilization in which the type of jurisprudence was settled by the social tie of *city* life. Previously to the antique πόλις, we have the records of *tribal* arrangements: they did not result in philosophical abstractions, but their unity and dialectical conferences can be sufficiently established in all directions.[1] And let us note that even a more primitive typical concentration of *totemistic* society has been discovered by

[1] *Essays in Legal History*, ed. by P. Vinogradoff, p. 10.

anthropological science, and has to a certain extent been subjected to a systematic treatment as a social type,[1] though, naturally, there is not much technical law at that stage. It might be tempting to tabulate the typical constructions of historical jurisprudence in the following manner:

1. Origins in Totemistic Society.
2. Tribal Law.
3. Civic Law.
4. Mediæval Law in its combination as Canon and Feudal Law.
5. Individualistic jurisprudence.
6. Beginnings of socialistic jurisprudence.

Such a scheme does not attempt to cover the whole ground. It leaves aside important variations, such as the juridical systems of Brahmanism, of Islam, of the Talmud. It is restricted in the main to the evolution of juridical ideas within the circle of European civilization. Yet in tracing earlier stages it is bound to take into account materials collected by anthropological inquiries from a wider range, in fact from all inhabited parts of the world. Only by this means can the complicated problems of early society be approached with any hope of solution. As the treatment is bound to be *ideological* and not *chronological,* the very important facts of Roman Law will have to be considered under various points of view—they help us to understand not only the civic state of the republican period, but also the archaic rules of Tribal law on the one hand, and the individualistic jurisprudence of the Empire on the other. This subject has received so much attention from the point of view both of legal history and of dogmatic study, that it is not difficult to arrange it on the lines of historical jurisprudence. A more difficult problem is presented by Mediæval Law. It might be theoretically correct to oppose as extreme contrasts feudal jurisprudence, based ultimately on the economy of the manor, and the world-wide expansion claimed for Divine guidance of

[1] For example, by DURKHEIM, *Elementary forms of religious life.*

Canon Law. The sources of the two systems are undoubtedly distinct and to a great extent antagonistic. But it is not a mere accident that the two laws—the feudal and the Canon—are found growing on the same soil. Their dualism is the necessary consequence of their extreme one-sidedness. Feudal law has too narrow and Canon too wide a basis: one starts from the estate and the other from mankind. Even technically the one cannot exist without being supplemented by the other. Feudal law has not attempted to develop a theory of justice, of equity, of crime. On the other hand, the Church has not worked out a system of land law or of status. In certain fields—like family law, succession, contract, corporation,—the two influences meet in conflict and in compromise. It would be impossible to do justice to this important period of juridical thought and activity by separating these divergent elements of the real world or by trying to effect a complete construction of the juridical system on the strength of either one or the other taken by itself. There is nothing left but to treat of them in conjunction.

Difficulties of ideological treatment.

So much as an explanation of my scheme. In conclusion I should like to submit two considerations which have to be borne in mind by any one who wishes to follow an attempt to sketch a historical jurisprudence on the above-mentioned lines. When we treat of facts and doctrines in *ideological* order we do not mean for a moment to deny or to disregard the conditions—geographical, ethnological, political, cultural—which have determined the actual course of events. Ideas do not entirely get their own way in real life; they are embodied in facts, and these latter appear influenced largely by material necessities and forces. It is not without importance for the development of legal principles whether the atmosphere surrounding them is that of a pastoral, an agricultural, or an industrial community; it is certainly of importance for public and private law whether a nation is living an independent life or has had to submit to conquest, etc. In a word, the chronological process of history cannot fail to affect the ideological deductions from a social type. We are bound, therefore, to make due allowance for the various cross-currents produced by actual conditions.

The second consideration is equally obvious, but perhaps even more difficult to put into practice. In constructing a typical theory of jurisprudence we are bound to present rules and institutions in a state of logical coherence and harmony, to establish a certain equilibrium between conflicting tendencies, to apportion rival claims as normal or exceptional, in a word, to consider jurisprudence from a *static* point of view. But then there is the *dynamic* one; ideas are mobile entities, passing through various stages—indistinct beginnings, gradual differentiation, struggles and compromises, growth and decay. It is not easy to do justice equally to both aspects of the process, and each individual worker will necessarily pay more attention to one or to the other. But we need not feel concerned about the ultimate outcome of such more or less inevitable limitations: the necessary corrections and synthesis are sure to be achieved by workers coming from different sides and converging towards a common aim.

The essential point is to recognize the value of *historical types* as the foundation of a theory of law.

TRIBAL LAW

PART I

THE ELEMENTS OF THE FAMILY

CHAPTER I

SELECTION OF MATES

HISTORICAL jurisprudence, as well as sociology, has to start from the axiom that man is a social animal (ζῷον πολιτικόν), i.e. that social intercourse is a necessary attribute of human nature. We need not repeat what has been admirably stated on the subject by Aristotle. Let us only take notice of the fact that tribal arrangements are the first application of this dogma. Ethnology and history describe numberless tribes: yet, in spite of all the variety of institutions and customs that pass before us, one fundamental feature asserts itself in all cases,—the fact that the earliest tribal moulds of society are based on conceptions of relationship and are derived from some form of family organization. As society expands, imagination, fiction, and artificial construction supplement and modify the natural ties of tribal life, but the notion at the root of all these excrescences is the notion of organic relationship. Marital Law.

Our survey therefore has to start from a study of the *marital union* as the initial institution which brings human beings together and provides for the growth of society. Whatever else men may become as tribesmen, citizens, landowners, traders, craftsmen, they are bound to be the offspring of some kind of union between a father and a mother, and the circumstances and conditions of such unions necessarily react on all the other sides of social organization—on kinship, succession, property, social status, etc.

In considering the evidence as to the forms and rules of primitive unions, let us bear in mind that even now, in our civilized society, marriage is a very complex institution, not to be explained by one or the other ruling idea, but representing a synthesis of several: consequently, it cannot give rise to one perfectly logical set of rules. It is not only an institution regulating sexual intercourse, and kept up by conjugal affection, but also an arrangement for the bringing up of children and a partnership for economic ends and social co-operation. Sometimes one side and sometimes another predominates. Married people who have long ceased to care for each other keep up the family tie for the sake of their children; considerations as to well-being and social standing, rather than sentimental motives, are often decisive as regards the formation of the union. No wonder that, even within the memory of modern generations, great changes have occurred in the framing of the law on the subject under the pressure of one or the other social force. In technical law, we can point out some very recent changes in the institution of marriage. Witness, for example, the great alterations effected in English Law as to the property rights of married women in the course of the nineteenth century, or the transition from the sacramental indissolubility of marriage in the law of the Church to the treatment of marriage as a civil institution under the control of the Courts.

If, in addition to this, one steps aside for a moment from the main track of European civilization and considers, for example, the polygamy allowed in the Mohammedan world, two considerations seem to suggest themselves at the very outset of our inquiry:

1. It is evident that marital union is a highly malleable institution;

2. It is very improbable that one rigid course was followed by mankind in the historical development of marriage law.

Theories of the evolution of marriage.

I insist on the second consideration even more than on the first, because it has been often and recently disregarded by some of the principal writers on the subject. Not to mention minor variations, there are now two diametrically opposed views as to the evolution of marriage. According to one set of thinkers, such as Bachofen, McLennan, Morgan, Kohler, and Frazer, the monogamous marriage of modern European civilization is the outcome of a slow progress starting from a state of sexual promiscuity or from irregular unions, which, according to some of these writers, gave way to group unions, the men of a group being recognized as the husbands of a corresponding group. Then comes a stage when families emerged from the group, families centred round the mothers, who gathered their children about them, but maintained only loose unions with the fathers of these children. Then the patriarchal system, with the predominance of the male as chief of the household, made its appearance and paved the way for the monogamic marriage to which we are accustomed nowadays.[1]

In sharp contrast with this sketch of development stands another scheme, outlined lately by Westermarck, Atkinson, and A. Lang. It starts from the position that primitive man, as well as the higher apes, was "patriarchal" through sexual jealousy and the instinct of appropriation. We have thus to start not from a state of sexual promiscuity, but from individual pairing: the male might acquire several wives when he had a chance, but he jealously guarded his mates against possible competitors. The "Cyclopæan family," as Mr. Lang terms it, was built up on the despotic sway of the sire over his wives and children, which involved the emigration of the younger males, who thereby became exogamous, that is, had to seek for mates outside their home. It is only by slow stages that these "patriarchal" methods gave way before more complex arrangements.[2]

[1] See, e.g., KOHLER, *Zur Urgeschichte der Ehe*, 1897; GIRAUD TEULON, *Origines du mariage et de la famille*, 1884; M. KOVALEVSKY, *Tableau du développement de la famille et de la propriété*, 1887.

[2] WESTERMARCK, *History of Human Marriage*, 2nd ed., 1894; A. LANG, *Social Origins*, and ATKINSON, *Primal Law*, 1903. The Cyclopæan theory is well summarized by Mr N W. THOMAS, *Kinship Organization and Group Marriage in Australia* (1906), p. 64: "At the point in the evolution of the human race at which Mr. Atkinson takes up his tale, man, or rather zoanthropos, was, according to his conjecture, organized, if that term can be applied to the grouping of the lower animals, in bodies consisting of one adult male, an attendant horde of adult females, including, probably, at any rate after a certain lapse of time, his own progeny, together with the immature offspring of both sexes. As the young males came to maturity, they would be expelled from the herd, as is actually the case with cattle and other mammals, by their sire, now become their foe."

Variety of arrangements.

Remembering to what extent solutions of the marriage problems vary nowadays, shall we admit as likely that either one or the other line of development sketched above was the sole highroad of evolution for all human tribes, whether scattered in the icy plains of the Arctic circle or clustering round the streams and wells of the desert, whether roaming over the prairie pastures or perched in the recesses of some mountain range? Considering the immense variety of conditions in ancient times, it is improbable that any exclusive theory will be true in all cases. We grant that there is some evidence that the institution of marriage may start from isolated pairs. A case which looks very significant in this respect is that of the Veddas of Ceylon; they wander through the forests in monogamous pairs, with their children and dogs, the father exercising a strong control over a small patriarchal household.[1] This is certainly an instance of primitive isolation, and there are many other cases in which the tendency is the same—as, for instance, in great forest-lands, where the population naturally spreads out in isolated homesteads. But is the soil favourable for such arrangements where the population is drawn together by the influence of natural environments —for instance, by the scarcity of water, or by mass hunting and mass fishing?[2] Under such conditions human beings naturally tend to congregate round water-courses, and gregarious instincts are bound to assert themselves. In these cases it would be difficult if not impossible to arrange families on the Cyclopæan pattern. Witness, for example, the communistic practices among the Indians of North America, or the Malayans, who are sometimes gathered together in communal houses one hundred and fifty feet or more in length.[3] We must be prepared to find materials for different forms of the marriage institution, as well as for the feelings and customs which naturally accompany

[1] C. G. and B. Z. Seligman, *The Veddas* (1911).

[2] See, e.g., C. Wissler, *American Indians*.

[3] Fallaize in Hastings's *Encyclopædia of Religion and Ethics*, 1917; C. Hose and W. McDougall, *The Pagan Tribes of Borneo* (1912), pp. 50-2; Hill-Tout, *British North America*, I, p. 51.

these elements. This is not more strange than the fact that the harem and the Christian household exist side by side at the present day.

Elements of marital unions.

This being so, we shall not attempt to trace one line of normal and continuous evolution of marriage. We must begin by ascertaining whether certain fundamental ideas recurring in various combinations may be traced as the elements of the institution. If such elements exist, the working of each one ought to be analysed as far as possible by itself before the ways in which it combines with other elements can be properly studied. The materials for such an analysis may be drawn from a broad and comprehensive collection of ethnological data, because it is only in this manner that we can make sure that nothing essential has escaped our observation; the conclusions will have to be utilized for our special study of the Aryan tribal system.

It can hardly be doubted that there are certain fundamental ideas which assert themselves in all forms of human marriage. For our purpose we shall, I think, have to consider four such fundamental ideas or elements.

1. Marital unions are the outcome of sexual *selection* and *restrictions*. Even casual intercourse is the result of some choice of mates, and involves at least temporary restrictions on other individuals of the same species. When more or less permanent unions arise, conditions of selection and restriction become very important, and form one of the chief elements of the institution.

2. The second elementary fact is *maternity:* although sexual intercourse may be transitory and irregular, its natural consequences are not casual, and it may be said that a mother is wedded by nature to her children even before she is wedded by law to her husband.

3. The third elementary fact is supplied by the *physical superiority of the male,* that enables him to obtain possession of females, to treat and keep them and their offspring as subjects to his rule.

4. Every marital union produces not only offspring but relationships, it provides points of contact between groups,

and the latter, in turn, react on the formation and regularization of marital unions.

Complexity of primitive culture.

One or two preliminary observations have to be made before we proceed to make use of the vast material provided by ethnographical research. Caution has to be exercised in our treatment of these data—especially in two directions. To begin with, it must be borne in mind that the expressions, primitive culture, primitive society, commonly used by anthropologists and ethnologists, are apt to be misleading: they are often taken to mean a state of things bordering on the condition of animals and almost undetermined by specific social habits or institutions. Yet such a state of things is not to be found anywhere on the surface of the earth, for the simple reason that the human race has been in existence for scores of thousands of years, so that even representatives of the rudest forms of civilization, say the natives of the Terra del Fuego, or the extinct aborigines of Tasmania, have had an exceedingly long series of generations and large stores of customs and inherited instincts, complicated by various influences from outside, behind their present moral and social order. They may be living in the conditions of the Palæolithic age as far as their arts and crafts are concerned, and their ideas and morals may be correspondingly distant from our own, but, in a sense, their "boomerang" culture is the product of the accumulated experience of generations, quite as much as our "steam engine" culture. Heredity and adaptation have stamped it with peculiar traits which may be as difficult to imitate or to modify as in the case of modern European culture. It is only by realizing this fundamental truth that one comes to understand certain striking facts of ethnology—for example, the rapid dying out of many aboriginal nations when they come into contact with European settlers or traders. Even apart from the ruthless methods of *conquistadores* and from the ravages of imported diseases, native tribes disappear because they are unable to accommodate their definitely stamped habits of life to new requirements and new conditions. Another result of the same process of specialization may be noticed in the exceedingly complicated institutions that may arise in the life of "savage" tribes by the side of the most rudimentary forms of husbandry and political arrangement: witness the confusing ramifications of sexual taboos and matrimonial classes in Australia and among the North American Indians. These remarks do not mean, of course, that there is no difference in quality and quantity between the social lore of the Hottentots and the arts of European nations, but rather that the lore of the Hottentots is the organic product of ages and therefore follows peculiar lines of evolution that cannot simply be wiped off the slate or treated as "passed viewpoints" that have to make room for something more advanced and perfect.

Migrations of customs.

Another qualifying proposition must be derived from observations of an exactly opposite kind. However much we may allow to the formation of distinctive psychological and social peculiarities of human races and tribes, this moulding of national types is counterbalanced in history by various processes of mixture and imitation. It would be unnecessary to dwell on the important results of conquest, of emigration, of intermarriage, of economic penetration; they are sufficiently illustrated by common experience. It is less realized, however, that the transmission and "reception" of devices and institutions of all kinds is constantly modifying the course of social evolution in all its stages. It is not only Roman law, the printing press, and firearms that have wandered through the world and been accepted by representatives of the most varied cultures: systems of script, funeral by cremation, the erection of megalithic monuments, may also be cited as cases in point. Archæologists and ethnologists have been very active lately in showing the remarkable currents of cultural influence running across the continents of the Old World or across the Pacific Ocean.[1]

Hence there arose a very important complication in tracing the ways and methods of evolutionist study. Instead of looking out chiefly for the natural correspondences between social results and environment, investigators have had to

[1] G. Elliot Smith, *The Migrations of Early Culture* (Manchester, *Memoirs*, vol. lix, no. 10, 1915); *Primitive Man*, in *Proceedings of British Academy*, VII (off-print), pp. 37 ff. Cf. Rivers, *Social History of Melanesia.*

take careful stock of the possible transmissions from abroad. All attempts at solving social problems either with the help of the one clue of *adaptation* or the one clue of *imitation* are sure to lead to one-sided systems: if one may be allowed a somewhat unusual comparison, the safe has to be unlocked with two keys. How and when each of these keys is to be used, is a delicate question that must be decided in accordance not with an abstract formula, but with the actual evidence in each concrete case. Such difficulties are indeed familiar to the unprejudiced social student, and there is nothing for it but to meet them with patience and attention to details. One guiding principle may, however, be pointed out even at this stage. It is clear that the more artificial and complicated the affinities between compared cases come to be, the more likelihood there is that the resemblance has been reached by influence or transmission. Migrations of words, of technical processes, of complicated institutions like representative government, are easily traceable in most cases. On the other hand, it seems against common sense to resort to the suggestion of imitation in order to explain the solution of simple and pressing problems of life; and the view that "inventions are made only once" may be grossly inappropriate in such cases. It is not necessary to look out for a foreign teacher in order to explain the building of shelters, or the construction of a boat, or the use of bows and arrows, or the discovery of the domestic properties of fire, or the rules of sexual avoidance, though in some instances each of these devices may disclose peculiarities suggestive of importation from abroad. These remarks may be sufficient as a preliminary warning against one-sided theories. It is now time to survey the actual field of the inquiry.

Unstable unions.

As it is of course impossible for us to obtain evidence as to the beginning of time, we cannot say with certainty whether there has ever been a definite period of sexual promiscuity. What we can say is that in no society that we know of at the present day or in well-recorded history, are the relations of the sexes marked by complete and unrestrained promiscuity. On the other hand, in a number of cases unions between the sexes are certainly unstable: sexual passion may assert itself occasionally without much restraint and lead to shifting unions between persons of the two sexes, while in other cases the instinct of jealous appropriation makes itself felt in attempts on the part of the strong partner to ensure the exclusive possession of wives. Which of the two tendencies obtains the upper hand for a time depends largely on material circumstances—the scattering of the tribe over a large tract of territory, or its concentration for a festival or a hunting expedition. "The life of the Australian societies passes alternately through two distinct phases. Sometimes the population is broken up into little groups who wander about independently of one another, in their various occupations; each family lives by itself, hunting and fishing, and in a word trying to procure its indispensable food by all the means in its power. Sometimes, on the contrary, the population concentrates and gathers at determined points for a length of time varying from several days to several months. This concentration takes place when a clan or a part of the tribe is summoned to the gathering, and on this occasion they celebrate a religious ceremony, or else hold what is called a corrobbori in the usual ethnological language.

"These two phases are contrasted with one another in the sharpest way. . . . The dispersed condition in which the society finds itself results in making its life uniform, languishing and dull. But when a corrobbori takes place everything changes. . . . The very fact of the concentration acts as an exceptionally powerful stimulant. . . . They are so far removed from their ordinary conditions of life . . . that they feel that they must set themselves outside of and above their ordinary morals. The sexes unite contrarily to the rules governing sexual relations. Men exchange wives with each other. Sometimes even incestuous unions which in normal times are thought abominable are now contracted openly and with impunity."[1]

[1] DURKHEIM, *The Elementary Forms of the Religious Life*, transl. by W. Swain, pp. 215 ff. Cf. Sir H. H. RISLEY, *Tribes and Castes*

It would be wrong to regard the erotic manifestations of tribe orgies as something exceptional and subordinate in the life of a primitive people: they give vent to one of the most powerful instincts of human nature and, as Durkheim rightly points out, they constitute a necessary element of the social and religious psychology of savage tribes. In a more specialized form the sexual passion appears in connection with phallic cults, which to millions of men represent the most striking manifestations of the life of Nature.[1]

The same root idea is apparent in the sexual licence of boys and girls at the age of puberty, which may lead to the concentration of these explosive persons in separate barracks.[2]

Such practices, in their universal spread, show conclusively how little our ideas of chastity, fidelity, and jealousy fit in with the indistinct notions of savages as to these matters. The elaborate arguments of Westermarck and Malinowski in favour of the patriarchal family and of individual unions supported by mutual affection seem at

of Bengal, II, p. 233: "The principal festival of the Santals is the sohrai or *harvest festival* celebrated in the month of Posh (November-December), after the chief rice crop of the year has been got in. Public sacrifices of fowls are offered by the priest in the sacred grove; pigs, goats and fowls are sacrificed by private families, and a general saturnalia of drunkenness and debauchery prevails. Chastity is in abeyance for the time, and all unmarried persons may indulge in promiscuous intercourse. This licence, however, does not extend to adultery, nor does it cover intercourse between persons of the same clan, though even that offence committed during the harvest festival is punished less severely than at other times."

Cf. Miss CZAPLICKA, *Aboriginal Siberia* (1914), p. 293, on the exchange of mates at the ceremonies dedicated to Keretkim the sea god.

[1] E.g., the Semitic cults of Moloch and Astaroth and the South Indian Dravidian cults.

[2] "A Naga village or town will sometimes contain as many as eight or ten communal houses or *pahs*, as they are called by some tribes, for the bachelors, and four or five such houses for the girls. Where the institution of these communal houses exists for the unmarried youth, the most complete licence is reported to prevail between the sexes up to the time of marriage, and this licence is not merely connived at, it is recognized by public opinion. No value is placed on youthful chastity; sexual morality in our sense of the word only begins with marriage, but after marriage infidelity is said to be very rare" (FRAZER, *Totemism*, IV, p. 300).

least one-sided[1] when applied to these relations, in which the most opposite feelings assert themselves side by side. On the other hand, if we renounce our accustomed standards in order to seek a right understanding of the origins of family life, we shall be less astonished to find whole peoples living in polyandry like the Todas or the Tibetans, or practising wife-lending as a form of hospitality.[2]

In these cases we reach another stage in the development of the subject. Instead of undifferentiated origins characterized by irregular manifestations of various tendencies of human nature, we have to deal with relations unfamiliar to us, but consolidated into regular custom. An even more striking case of customary development as the basis of shifting unions is presented by the subsidiary unions among the natives of Australia.[3] For instance, "Among the Dieri and kindred tribes there are two forms of marriage: there is the marriage of a man of one class to a woman of the other class, which may be spoken of as 'individual marriage,' or for convenience as 'Noa marriage,' using the Dieri term, which is equivalent to our word 'spouse.' There is also a marital relation existing between a man and a number of women, or between a woman and a number of men, the same rule as to the classes being observed. This latter connection may be spoken of as 'group marriage,' or for convenience the Dieri word for the practice may be used, speaking of it as 'Pirauru marriage.' . . . Neither

[1] It is impossible to present here a detailed criticism of their arguments, but I cannot help entering a protest against the singular method of *counting* extracts adopted by Dr. Malinowski.

[2] Cf. ROBERTSON SMITH, *Kinship and Marriage in Early Arabia* (1885), pp. 116-17: "In old Arabia the husband was so indifferent to his wife's fidelity, that he might send her to cohabit with another man to get himself a goodly seed; or might lend her to a guest, as the 'Asîr did up to the time of the Wahhabites (BURCKHARDT, *Travels in Arabia*, 8vo ed., II, p. 378), and as people of Dhahabân must once have done according to Ibn Al-Moghâwir's account (*circa* A. H. 630); or going on a journey might find a friend to supply his place, as the Yâm did in the time of Burckhardt (*op. cit.*, II, p. 386); or might enter into a partnership of conjugal rights with another man, in return for his service as a shepherd, as we read in the *Fotûh al-Shâm*, p. 238 sq."

Cf. CRAWLEY, *The Mystic Rose*, p. 478.

[3] N. W. THOMAS, *Kinship Organization and Group Marriage in Australia* (1906), pp. 130-3, 136; RIVERS in the *Encyclopædia of Religion and Ethics*, VIII, pp. 427-8.

of these two forms of marriage is permitted between persons of the same totem. . . . These also include the group relations. . . . A man or a woman becomes 'Noa' to each other by the woman being promised to him during her infancy by her father or by being allotted specially to him as Noa by the headman and the great council of the tribe. . . . Besides this Noa marriage there is also a form of group marriage which is called by the Dieri *Pirauru* . . . the heads of the totems and the elder men meet in council and after deliberation determine which of the people shall be allotted to each other as Pirauru. . . . This time is one of festivity, feasting and amusement. . . . Dancing is carried on, and besides this there is for about four hours a general licence in the camp as regards the Piraurus. Moreover the Piraurus are, when allotted to each other, always in that relation in the future, and as a new allotment takes place at each circumcision ceremony it follows that a man or a woman may after a time come to have a number of Piraurus. . . . A man may always exercise marital rights towards his Pirauru when they meet if her Noa be absent, but he cannot take her away from him unless by his consent, excepting at certain ceremonial times when general licence prevails between the intermarrying classes. . . . The consent of the Noa husband is seldom withheld from the male Pirauru."[1]

There is a similar practice among the Urabunna tribe, where "every man has one or more of these *nupa* women who are especially attached to him and live with him in his own camp, but there is no such thing as one man having the exclusive right to one woman; the elder brothers or *nuthi* of the woman, who decide the matter, will give one man a preferential right, but at the same time they will give other men of the same group to which he belongs—that is, men who stand in the same relationship to the woman as he does—*a secondary right,* and such *nupa* women to whom a man has the legal right of access are spoken of as his *piraungaru.* A woman may be *piraungaru*

[1] HOWITT, *The Dieri and Other Kindred Tribes of Central Australia,* in the *Journal of the Anthropological Institute,* XX, no. 1 (August, 1890), pp. 53-7.

to a number of men and, as a general rule, men and women who are *piraungaru* to one another are to be found living together in groups. As we have said before, 'individual marriage does not exist either in name or in practice amongst the Urabunna tribe.' In this tribe we have:

"(1) A group of men all of whom belong to one moiety of the tribe and are regarded as the *nupas*, or *possible* husbands, of a group of women, who belong to the other moiety of the tribe.

"(2) One or more women *especially allotted* to one particular man, each standing in the relationship of *nupa* to the other, but no man having exclusive right to any one woman—only a *preferential* right.

"(3) A group of men who stand in the relationship of *piraungaru* to a group of women, selected from amongst those to whom they are *nupa*. In other words, a group of women of one designation have, normally and actually, marital relations with a group of men of another designation."[1]

These cases are described with special details and by good witnesses, but there are many other cases in which similar features are recognizable in less precise notices.

If we renounce for a moment the conventional phraseology of our own time, we may discern in these primitive relations between the sexes, some fundamental facts which are not altogether unlike some of the conditions obtaining in our own society. These relations even now fall into two sharply contrasted classes: the regular marriage unions between older men capable of supporting a family and their somewhat younger wives, and the irregular unions between younger men and a certain number of women who have lost their standing in society. Ethnology shows us a similar dualism, with the difference that the regular, more or less monogynic, unions of the savages, the appropriation of young women by older men, is carried sometimes to the exaggerated form of acquisition of child wives,

[1] SPENCER and GILLEN, *The Northern Tribes of Central Australia*, pp. 72 sq Cf. *The Native Tribes of Central Australia*, p. 64: "A group of women of a certain designation are actually the wives of a group of men of another designation."

while the same importance is not attached to continence and chastity in the case of the girls, who are often allowed to indulge in the same licence as the boys without lapsing into the condition of habitual prostitutes.

However this may be, we may, I think, sum up the information on the subject of unstable unions in the view that there is plenty of evidence from all parts of the world as to states of society in which the operations of the sexual instinct are not firmly restricted by regular marriage arrangements, but find outlets in various forms of sexual licence and communalistic custom.

Restrictions on sexual intercourse.

In spite of the strength of the sexual instinct and of the disturbing influence it exerts in various forms in all stages of civilization, all human societies have striven and are striving to counteract these disturbing influences and to regularize the working of the sexual cravings. To a certain extent such restrictive rules may have been derived from another powerful and primordial instinct—that of *appropriation;* but this latter tendency, if taken by itself, gives rise to struggles, and thus it does not directly guarantee peace and order. In one way or another, however, either through deliberate guidance, or indirectly by way of compromise after struggle, human communities are bound to formulate and do actually formulate rules in respect of sexual unions intended to prevent offence and conflict.

The simplest device suggested by these rules is that of *avoidance*—the prohibition of ordinary intercourse between members of the different sexes [1] who stand in some recognized form of relationship to each other. Among the Veddas of Ceylon, this form of avoidance is strictly observed. "If a man met his mother-in-law in the jungle he would move aside off the track. He may, however, speak to her in the presence of others, though if he found her alone in the rock shelter he would not enter it till there were others present. Similarly, though a man may eat food

[1] There are exceptional cases of avoidance between persons of the same sex, but they seem results of the not unfrequent process of extension of taboo rules by analogy.

prepared by his mother-in-law, he would not take it directly from her, it would be passed to him by some one else, most probably by his wife."[1] "Among the Tetons, a Siouan or Dacotan tribe, a man may not look his mother-in-law in the face, nor may his brother do so, and she may not look at them. If a man sees his mother-in-law, he must put his robe over his head and shoulder and pass by on the other side of the road; also he must sit on the other side of the lodge. In like manner a woman dare not look at or address her husband's father."[2]

Customs of avoidance exemplified by the above-mentioned taboos do not admit of any other interpretation but that derived from a moral condemnation of sexual union between persons who ought to be bound by other ties. The feeling against incest, and the more or less strict prohibitions against it, spring from the same cause, and it is easy to conceive what a fertile source of strife and degradation the removal of such rules would be.

One or two cases of complicated restrictions on marriage between members of certain communities may be mentioned at once: they enable us to realize the social importance and wide diffusion of such prohibitions. Among the Omahas "a man must marry outside of his gens. . . . A man cannot marry any of the women of the gens of his father, as they are his grandmothers, aunts, sisters, nieces, daughters, or grandchildren. He cannot marry any woman of the subgens of his father's mother, for the same reason; but he can marry any woman belonging to the other subgentes of his paternal grandmother's gens, as they are not his kindred. The women of the subgens of his paternal grandmother's mother are also forbidden to him; but those of the remaining subgentes of that gens can become his wives, provided they are such as have not become his mothers-in-law, daughters, or grandchildren. . . . A man cannot marry any woman of his mother's gens, nor any of his maternal grandmother's subgens, nor any of the subgens of her mother, as all are his consanguinities.

[1] SELIGMAN, *The Veddas*, p. 68.
[2] FRAZER, *Totemism*, III, p. 112.

"A man cannot marry a woman of the subgens of the wife of his son, nephew, or grandson; nor can he marry a woman of the subgens of the husband of his daughter, niece or granddaughter. A man cannot marry any of his female affinities who are his ika^{n}, because they are the real or potential wives of his fathers-in-law, or of the fathers-in-law of his sons, nephews or grandchildren. A man cannot marry any woman whom he calls his sister's daughter. He cannot marry any woman whom he calls his grandchild. This includes his wife's sister's daughter's daughter.

"He cannot marry the daughter of any woman who is his ihañga, as such a daughter he calls his daughter. . . . He cannot marry his sister's husband's father's brother's daughter, as she is his itucpa; nor can he marry her daughter or her brother's daughter, for the same reason. He cannot marry his sister's husband's (brother's) daughter, as she is his sister's potential daughter, and he calls her his itija^{n}. . . .

"Were it not for the institution of subgentes a man would be compelled to marry outside of his tribe, as all the women would be his kindred, owing to previous intermarriages between the ten gentes. But in any gens those on the other side of the gentile 'unete,' or fire-place, are not reckoned as full kindred, though they cannot intermarry."[1]

In another case, "Each moiety is divided into two classes, one, which we will call moiety A, has the classes Panunga and Bulthara, the other, which we will call moiety B, has the classes Purula and Kumara. Every individual member of the tribe belongs to one or other of these classes—exactly which is determined by his father's class. . . . For example, a Panunga man marries a Purula woman and their children are Bulthara. A Kumara man marries a Bulthara woman and their children are Purula. Amongst Australian aborigines no man is free to marry just whom he

[1] J. O. Dorsey, *Omaha Sociology* (Third Annual Report of the Bureau of Ethnology to the Secretary of the Smithsonian Institution, 1881-1882), (1884), pp. 255-8.

likes. In the first place a man of moiety A can only marry a woman of moiety B and *vice versa,* and further still, a Panunga man can only marry a Purula woman and *vice versa,* a Bulthara man can only marry a Kumara woman and *vice versa.* . . . If we arrange them in a simple table the matter becomes clearer. Thus:

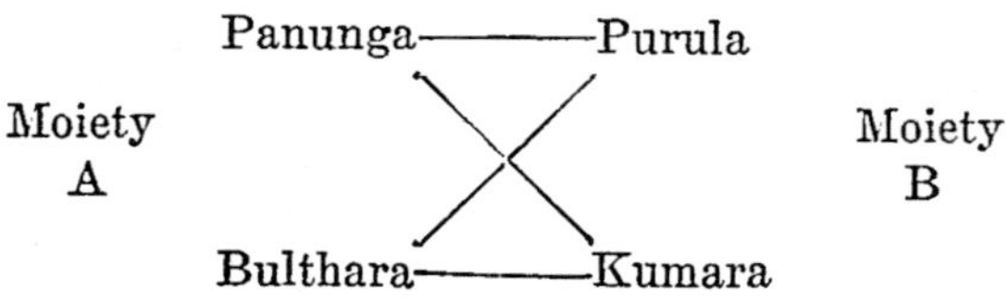

The horizontal lines indicate the marriages and the slanting lines, leading from the woman's class, the classes into which the children fall."[1]

Matrimonial classification.

These extensive prohibitions are connected with the arrangement of societies into matrimonial classes. Instead of proceeding by a gradual extension of the rule against incestual intercourse, they start from large tribal divisions and combine them for the purpose of restriction and selection in a way unfamiliar to us, accustomed as we are to tracing relations between single individuals and not between classes or groups. Once the principle of allowing unions between members of certain groups and forbidding them between other groups is grasped, the details become intelligible and need not trouble us by their many variations. It is more interesting to try to discover the motives which prompt all these primitive communities to frame their rules against incest by processes of classification and not by individualizing avoidance.

Exogamous practices.

The usual explanation is derived from the notion of *exogamy.* In so far as the designation is used to characterize the practice of seeking brides outside the social group of the bridegroom, there is nothing to say against the term, but the fact itself would still require an explanation. If,

[1] SPENCER and GILLEN, *Across Australia* (1912), p. 201. Cf. DURKHEIM, *Organisation matrimoniale australienne,* in *L'Année sociologique,* VIII (1905), p. 124, and RIVERS, *The History of Melanesian Society* (1914), II, p. 138, *Kinship and Social Organization,* pp. 61-2, 66.

on the other hand, exogamy is taken to mean that the youths have to look out for brides abroad, because their "sires" keep the women of their own group to themselves, such a construction cannot be supported by evidence. The Cyclopæan family can in no way be considered as the ordinary arrangement of primitive society, nor would the situation as conceived by Atkinson and Lang, lead to avoidance of women within the group, but rather to a contrast between endogamous seniors and exogamous juniors.

Epigamous practices. The facts, as we have them before us, are different. They point to general restrictions against marriage within the groups and might be ranged under the term of *epigamy*, as well as under that of exogamy. We are not yet in a position to speak definitely about the nature of the groups that are separated or combined by these prohibitions and directions. One thing we can perceive, however, even now, namely, that marital unions are allowed or forbidden in accordance with tribal organization. Three explanations may be suggested for such systems, and it is very likely that each of the three had something to do with its formation.

1. To begin with, there is an undoubted attraction in the foreign, the unfamiliar, an additional element of curiosity and desire, which may be illustrated from many incidents of our contemporary life and from numberless stories of the past. Finnish women (Kvens), for instance, had a special reputation as enchantresses of men among Norwegians and Swedes. Arabian tribesmen prized brides acquired by conquest,[1] and the world-wide diffusion of capture as a means of obtaining wives may be due in part to this taste.[2]

There are sometimes indications that the leading elders,

[1] Cf. Robertson Smith, *Kinship*, p. 73: "According to Ibn 'Abd Rabbih (*'Icd.* III, p. 296) the *hajîn*, that is the son of an *'ajamîya*, or non-Arab woman, did not inherit in the Times of Ignorance; but there was no such disability as regarded the son of a captive, nay, according to Arab tradition (*'Icd.* III, p. 290) the best and stoutest sons are born of reluctant wives."

[2] E.g., among the Wakelbura, Frazer, *Totemism*, I, p. 426; among the Araucanians, *ibid.*, III, p. 582; and among the Tasmanians, Ling Roth, *The Aborigines of Tasmania* (1890), p. 123.

medicine men, shamams or priests, perceive the bad effects of in-breeding which are recognized by our scientists and doctors. In Hadith it is said: "marry among strangers, thus you will not have feeble posterity." In Abd Rabtishi's Kitabal at Ikdalfarod (iii. 290), "he is a hero not born by the cousin (of his father); he is not weakly, for the seed of relations brings forth feeble fruit."[1]

We need not wonder at such "eugenic" considerations: the study of folk-lore discloses many cases in which traditional experience and close acquaintance with nature have suggested to ancient and primitive tribes views that have been confirmed by elaborate modern research. But quite apart from "eugenic" manifestations of folk-lore, the attraction of foreign women may be quite as powerful in social psychology as the fear of the "evil eye."

2. *A second root* of exogamic unions is to be sought in considerations bearing on internal order, which must have asserted themselves in every society when it attained continuous existence. If some form of political order is truly regarded as a necessary feature in the life of any human community, the prevention of conflicts arising from sexual competition must have formed the earliest and the principal object for the action of tribal authorities. We find this principle expressed in as many words by Arab commentators, and it is really not necessary to cite chapter and verse to prove its cogency and obviousness.[2] This point lies at the root of the Cyclopæan theory of A. Lang, but it has been developed by him and by his followers in too narrow a fashion. It was not only between fathers and sons that concord in this respect had to be established, but between brothers and other contemporaries as well, and stories of exceptional conflicts within families may serve to illustrate the cogency of the taboos. Cases of polyandry

[1] GOLDZIHER, in the *Academy*, XVIII (1880), p. 26.

[2] Amr. b. Kolthum's testament (*Kitâb-al-aghânî*, ed. Bûlâk, IX, 185): "Do not marry in your own family, for domestic enmity arises therefrom," quoted by GOLDZIHER, *loc. cit.*

are noted everywhere as astonishing products of local custom.[1]

As a rule, organized society guards against conflicts of jealousy within families by insisting on a clear separation between circles of near relationship and circles of possible sexual union; and one of the most important facts in this connection is that it is not only by alliances and compromises between various tribes that *epigamy* is arranged, but by artificial halving of complete units. The *veve* of the Australians, the matrimonial classes arranged in pairs, fours and eights, are the most remarkable expressions of this principle.[2] In regard to these matrimonial classes R. H. Matthews[3] writes: "In an article contributed to this society in 1905,[4] I illustrated the sociology of the Barkunjee tribe as comprising only two divisions, Mukunguna and Kilpunguna, the men of one division marrying the women of the opposite one. In studying the above table, we observe that there is a bisection of each of the two divisions of the Barkunjee so that in the Kurnu there are four divisions of the community instead of two.

"The Kurnu, like the Barkunjee, possess a further distinctive division into Muggulu and Ngipuru, with their feminine forms Mugguluga and Ngipuruga, meaning sluggish or heavy blood and swift or light blood respectively. Again, like the Barkunjee, the Kurnu are divided into Nhuné and Winggu, the Butt and the Branch shade. A man of the Muggulu blood and the Butt shade usually and normally marries a Ngipuruga woman of the Branch shade, subject to variations explained farther on. In regard to the offspring, a Mugguluga mother produces Muggulu children who take their mother's shade. A Ngipuruga mother produces Ngipuru children belonging to her own shade."

[1] Robertson Smith, *Kinship*, p. 133; Frazer, *Totemism*, II, p. 256 (among the Todas); Rivers, on Marriage, in the *Encyclopædia of Religion and Ethics*, VIII, p. 427 (among the Nayars).

[2] Frazer, *op. cit.*, II, p. 70; Thomas, *Kinship Organization and Group Marriage in Australia*, p. 128.

[3] In *Notes on Some Native Tribes of Australia*, in the *Journal and Proceedings of the Royal Society of New South Wales*, XL (1906), p. 96.

[4] *Ibid.*, XXXIX, pp. 118, 119.

Nor is this arranging into moieties and subdivisions of moieties restricted to Australian tribes. It is to be found in the Melanesian Archipelago and seems to underlie many of the constructions of matrimonial groups in America and South Eastern Asia.[1]

Uncertainty of fatherhood.

3. The third principle to be taken into account as explaining exogamic and epigamic practices is connected with the *uncertainty of fatherhood* characteristic of most primitive tribes. Whether we consider the effect of polyandric custom, of *pirauru* unions, of youthful licence and of other material expressions of social communism, or whether we merely take stock of the mystic views as to procreation current among the Aruntas[2] and in similar cases, it is obviously impossible in such cases to build up pedigrees and to formulate taboos on individualistic lines, while, on

[1] Frazer, *op. cit.*, II, p. 68; Rivers, *Kinship and Social Organization*, pp. 70, 72.

[2] Frazer, *op. cit.*, I, p. 188: "These semi-human ancestors, endowed with powers which are not possessed by their living descendants, roamed about the same country which is still inhabited by the tribe, and in their wanderings they gave rise to many of the most marked features of the landscape, such as the gaps and gorges which cleave the Macdonnell Ranges Each troop or band of these semi-mythical folk consisted of members of one particular totem clan, whether the totem was the wild cat, the witchetty grub, the kangaroo, the frog, the Hakea flower, or what not. And every man and woman of the band carried about with him or her one or more of the sacred stones which the Arunta call *churinga*, each of which is intimately associated with the spirit part of some individual man or woman. Either where they originated and stayed or else where, during their wanderings, they camped for a time, there were formed what the natives call *oknanikilla*, which we may describe as local totem centres. At each of these spots, which are all well known to the old men, who hand the knowledge down from generation to generation, a certain number of the *alcheringa* ancestors went into the ground, each of them carrying his sacred stone (*churinga*) with him. His body died, but some natural feature, such as a rock or tree, arose to mark the spot, while his spirit part remained in the *churinga*.

"Each local totem centre (*oknanikilla*) is tenanted by the spirits of one totem only. One spot, for example, is haunted by spirits of the wild cat totem; another by spirits of the emu totem; another by spirits of the frog totem; and so on through all the totems

"The natives believe that every living member of the tribe is the reincarnation of one of these spirits. Each of these disembodied spirits takes up its abode in some natural object, such as a tree or rock, at its own local totem centre: and this abode of the spirit is called its *nanja*. From time to time, when a woman approaches one of these haunted spots, a spirit passes from it into her body, and in due time is born as a child."

the contrary, the same results of guarding against incest and strife may be achieved without difficulty by drawing lines of demarcation between groups. This is what actually takes place among the "totemic" tribes of Australia, America, Asia and Africa. Although it is wrong to speak of *group marriage*[1] in the proper sense of the word, implying actual promiscuity as between the members of the corresponding groups, the notion is an appropriate one as indicating the correlation of possible unions and the manner in which the taboos of avoidance were drawn up. There is therefore reality in the notion; it is not a mere literary fiction devised by Morgan and popularized by his school: given the uncertainty of fatherhood, order as to sexual matters has to be either by arbitrary adoption, as in the case of the Todas, or by cleavage between groups, classes and sub-classes, as with the Australian, North Americans and other "totemic" tribes.

In the much discussed case of the Arunta I venture to suggest that the belief in reincarnation connected with certain local centres is not produced by ignorance as to physiological processes, but by the uncertainty of tracing descent from the father in a society where sexual unions are unstable. Even if savages were not sufficiently observant of the course of nature in the breeding of men, surely kangaroos and dogs must have supplied them with sufficient material for inferences as to the part played by both sexes in procreation. But it was not more unreasonable on their part to speculate on the spiritual transmission of personality than it was in the case of the Pythagoreans, the Brahmanists or any other believers in the transmigration of souls. A natural substratum for such views was provided for the Aruntas and other tribes with unstable unions in the uncertainty of descent from males, an uncertainty removed in the practice of the Todas by the ceremony of pointing the arrow, while with the Aruntas the magic rites of the *churinga* grew up on a similar background.

[1] RIVERS, *op. cit.*, p. 84, and in *The Encyclopædia of Religion and Ethics*, VIII, pp. 427-8.

In the examples of the Urabunna tribes referred to above [1] the marriageable (*nupa*) members of both sexes are clearly distinguished from the rest of humanity and supposed to belong to two classes strictly corresponding one to the other, so that the men of one moiety are destined to marry the women of the other moiety, and *vice versa*. In this way within each group the rule of *exogamy* obtains, but is matched by the rule of *epigamy* with the corresponding class. The basis for such rules of restriction and selection is to be found in the arrangement of these societies on the totemic principle, that is, conformity with religious belief in a mystic solidarity symbolized by the animal or other totem of the group. It is sufficient for our purpose to take note of the fundamental conception which lies at the root of such a grouping, without joining in the intricate controversies in regard to details of classification and ritual.

Unions between individuals of close kin.

One most important consequence of arrangement in classes is that it admits, within its broad distinctions, of *rapprochement* between individuals, who, according to our views, would be very closely akin to each other. Unions between persons closely related by consanguinity are possible and occur often under these regulations. It may be said that endogamy may be sometimes combined with exogamy. It is, for instance, a most common device among Australians, to obtain wives by exchange between offspring of brother and sister. Cross-cousin marriage is one of the most widely spread customs among primitive tribes of all the continents.[2]

[1] *Ante*, p. 174.

[2] RIVERS, *Kinship and Social Organization*, p. 20: "I propose to begin with a long familiar mode of terminology which accompanies that widely distributed custom known as the cross-cousin marriage. In the more frequent form of this marriage a man marries the daughter of either his mother's brother or his father's sister; more rarely his choice is limited to one of these relatives.

"Such a marriage will have certain definite consequences. Let us take a case in which a man marries the daughter of his mother's brother, as is represented in the following diagram:

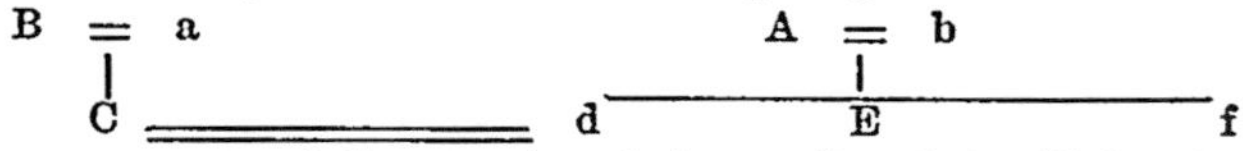

One consequence of the marriage between C and d will be that A, who before the marriage of C was only his mother's brother, now

In other cases the policy of preventing conflicts within the tribe prevails, while the eugenic consideration gives way before public convenience. Altogether economic tendencies and motives of self-preservation of the group are very noticeable in instances of so-called endogamy.[1] In these cases customs require, or at least allow, members of the same kindred or group to intermarry. This practice may be illustrated from the life of many tribes. It is very common among Semitic nations even in the form of marriage between half-brothers and half-sisters. In spite of the close degree of relationship in such cases, there is no obstacle to marriage, provided that the contracting parties are children of the same father, but they must be from different mothers. A conspicuous example of this principle is to be found in the Bible[2] : Abraham, it will be remembered, was married to his *half-sister* Sarah. While they were travelling together, she had passed as his sister, but when she is wooed by a stranger, Abraham has to explain that she is at the same time his wife. Although they are born of the same father, their marriage is regular and legitimate. Among the Egyptians even marriages between brothers and sisters of the same mother occur, at any rate in the reigning families of the Pharaohs.

The tendency towards marriages within a narrow circle of relations is clearly traceable to considerations of self-preservation, when there is a danger of being overwhelmed by outsiders, or when circumstances have brought about feelings of enhanced family pride and honour.[3]

becomes also his wife's father, while b, who before the marriage was the mother's brother's wife of C, now becomes his wife's mother. Reciprocally, C, who before his marriage had been the sister's son of A and the husband's sister's son of b, now becomes their son-in-law. Further, E and f, the other children of A and b, who before the marriage had been only the cousins of C, now become his wife's brother and sister. . . . Through the cross-cousin marriage the relationships of mother's brother, father's sister's husband and father-in-law will be combined in one and the same person, and the relationships of father's sister, mother's brother's wife and mother-in-law will be similarly combined."

[1] Cf. ROBERTSON SMITH, *Kinship*, p. 163.

[2] *Genesis*, chs xii and xx

[3] Cf. HILL-TOUT, *British North America*, I, pp. 162-3: "In one of the coastal tribes, the Bella Coola, the social organization was in some respects peculiar, particularly in the matter of marriage

In conclusion I should like to emphasize again the fact that *endogamous* customs do not stand in uncompromising opposition to exogamic ones. These practices shade off from one variety to the other without sudden break.

regulations. The tribe was divided into a number of local communes, each of which was very jealous of its own traditions and crests, and its rights to certain ceremonial dances, songs, etc. So highly valued and jealously guarded were these that it led apparently to the establishment of endogamous institutions among them. The members of each community were obliged by customary law to take mates only from among themselves, marriage outside the commune being forbidden. The custom would seem to have arisen from their desire to guard and retain within the limits of each group the legends, dances, etc. peculiar to that group.

"Under the common Salish rule of marriage this could not be done, a daughter not unfrequently, when she had no brothers, conferring upon her husband her father's rank and privileges, his crests and family legends; so to guard against the passage of these beyond the commune or body to which they belonged, they would seem to have deliberately established endogamous institutions, making it unlawful for a person to marry outside the limits of his or her own community."

CHAPTER II

THE MOTHER AND THE FATHER

The Mother.

The mother the centre of the household.

In modern systems of law it is admitted as a general rule that illegitimate children follow the mother's condition and belong to the mother's family. Children whose fathers are uncertain are illegitimate according to our view. Now in many primitive societies this is the normal state, on account of the fact that sexual unions are not entirely stable, and the question of uncertainty necessarily dominates the whole situation. This fact by itself is sufficient to explain the central position of the mother which we find expressed in many tribal organizations. Strangely enough, this fact was hardly realized by the learning of any centuries except the nineteenth and our own. It was only in the middle of the nineteenth century that the immense importance of motherhood as the centre of family organization was recognized. As often happens when a new idea comes to the fore, when recognized by Bachofen, Morgan, and McLennan, the importance of the principle was exaggerated in the sense that they spoke glibly of matriarchal institutions and pictured a society in which the family, centred round the mother, was ruled by women on the pattern of an Amazon commonwealth. It was soon perceived, however, that not only was it most unlikely that the rule of the weaker sex should prevail, but that as a matter of observation there was nothing to countenance the theory. The data show that though the institutions are not matriarchal as opposed to patriarchal, the women occupy a position of great importance not only in the household but in the tribe at large. The Seri of California are one instance to which such a characterization would to some extent apply. "The matrons participate with them in what we may call judicial and legislative functions. The executive power of the family seems to be exercised by the mother's brothers in order of seniority only through or in conjunction with her. And when she is a shaman of repute she is more reverenced than any man. To such an extent is this reverence carried that one of the most important considerations in the selection of the chief of a band is his consort's reputation for 'shamanistic potency.' The very name of the tribe expresses the predominance of woman. Seri is a foreign appellation—the native name is Kunkaak, which appears to mean womanhood, or rather motherhood.

"The tribe is made up of clans defined by consanguinity reckoned only in the female line. Each clan is headed by an elder woman, and comprises a hierarchy of daughters, granddaughters and (sometimes) great-granddaughters, collectively incarnating that purity of uncontaminated blood which is the pride of the tribe.

"The masculine element is merely supplementary to this. The huts are temporary shelters of the most modest kind. However rude it may be, both the hut and its contents belong exclusively to the matron. Her brothers, indeed, are entitled to places in it. A husband has in comparison with them no rights there. If there, his normal place is the outermost in the group, when he acts as a sort of outer guard or sentinel. Marriage, the permanent union of man and woman, is recognized. The candidate for a lady's hand, when provisionally accepted, after lengthy discussions, by the girl and her mother and matronly relations, is required to submit to a year's probation of the most arduous and exacting character. He must give proof of his ability and success in the chase. While himself continent, even when sharing his wife's tent and sleeping robe, he must recognize without a murmur her right to receive the most intimate attentions from his clanfellows. At the close of the year, if still approved, he provides a feast, and becomes a permanent guest in his bride's hut. As her husband, he is endowed with great personal privileges, the reward of his constancy and of his efficiency as provider and protector, but in regard to her family and domestic affairs he is wholly subordinate, without any authority even over his children. Such domestic authority as a man possesses relates not to his wife's household, but to that of his mother and sisters."[1]

Modified matrilineal arrangements.

This is a somewhat extreme instance, and we generally find modified forms in which, in contradistinction to patriarchal tribes dwelling side by side with matriarchal tribes, we notice the more important position of women. The tribal arrangements presented by the Iroquois, who are most reputed for prowess in war and hunting, are distinctly matrilineal not to say matriarchal. Women are admitted to the councils and consulted in all important matters. Here as with the Seri there is a disposition to regard women as more likely to practise magic arts, to prophesy and to give wise advice in the councils of the nations.[2] This extraordinary position of women is found not only among primitive people, but in a tribe which may have reached an advanced state of society and stood the test of centuries and of modern conditions of life. The Nayars of the Malabar coast, to the southwest of the Indian Peninsula, are tribes of mixed race, chiefly Dravidian, but with a possible admixture of Aryan elements. They form a prosperous and industrial community, with a highly developed

[1] E S. Hartland, *Matrilineal Kinship and the Question of its Priority* (*Memoirs of the American Anthropological Association*, IV, no. 1, January-March, 1917), p. 9; also *Primitive Paternity*, chs. iv and v.

[2] Cf. Frazer, *Totemism*, III, p. 15: "Marriages are contracted in such a way that husband and wife never quit their own family and their own house to make one family and one house by themselves. Each remains in his or her own home, and the children born of these marriages belong to the women who bore them; they are reckoned to the house and family of the wife and not to those of the husband. The husband's goods do not pass to his wife's house, to which he is himself a stranger; and in the wife's house the daughters are reckoned the heiresses in preference to the males, because the males have nothing there but their subsistence. Hence among the Iroquois a man's son was perpetually disinherited: he belonged to his mother's clan and tribe: he could never succeed to his father's property, titles, or office. If, for example, an Onondaga man of the Wolf clan married an Onondaga woman of the Deer clan, their children were all Deer, not Wolves. If a Seneca man of the Bear clan married a Cayuga woman of the Beaver clan, the children were all Cayugas and Beavers, not Senecas and Bears. The same rule regulated the hereditary transmission of the sachemship or office of high chief."

class of landowners and soldiers, in which the recognized centre of the family is the mother. Real property is held by her, and inheritance in regard to family (*tarwad*) property passes through her. The son belongs to the family of his mother. When his father dies, he does not wear mourning nor take part in the funeral, but if his mother or the brother of his mother dies, he is bound to wear the deepest mourning and to sit in ashes for weeks. Their pedigrees are like ours, and may be compared with the Roman agnatic family, except that succession is from female to female. Because the son marries into a family centring round another mother, property descends strictly through females. A *taivazhi* is formed by a married woman and her descendants either direct or, if indirect, descended from her through females. The mother, daughters and unmarried sons form an exact counterpart to the small patriarchal family, save that the daughters are more prominent than the sons. Eventually it is not even restricted to this small nucleus, but grows into a large joint family. This system is quite as prominent in Malabar as in the settlements of patriarchal India, only it is entirely conditioned by matrilineal descent.[1]

The mother's brother the standing protector.

Nevertheless a definite element of male influence, if not of rule, is represented by the brother of the mother. No family can do without the support of the man, for economic

[1] Cf. FRAZER, *Totemism*, IV, p. 243: "If a man die, the bulk of his property goes to his sister's son, not to his son; the reason being that of the blood-relationship of the nephew there can be no doubt, but the descent of the son may be questioned. The nephew is, therefore, looked on as a nearer relative than the son, and he is the heir, and should he die, more grief is felt than in the case of the son. A strange exception is made when a man marries a slave of his: the son then ranks first in this case, as the natives say that he is not only presumably the next-of-kin by birth, but also by purchase, as the mother belonged to the father." Similarly among the Kimbunda "sons begotten in marriage are regarded as the property, not of their father, but of their maternal uncle; and their own father, even so long as they are minors and under his protection, has no power over them. Also the sons are not the heirs of their father but of their uncle, and the latter can dispose of them with unlimited authority, even to the extent of selling them in case of necessity. Only the children born of slave women are regarded as really the property of their father and also his heirs"

Cf K KRISHNAN PANDALAI, *Succession and Partition in Marumakkatayam Law* (1914), pp. 3-5, 29 ff.

purposes and the performance of hard tasks, for defence and for protection before the tribunals, but the protector need not in all cases be the father. The standing protector is the brother; the mother remains in her own family and looks to him as her natural helper. This is recognized in law, and the brother is bound to help the mother in legal and economic matters beyond her capacity. When we renounce our set ideas about the relations between husband and wife, it is not difficult to realize, without any subversion of our ideas concerning the sexes, that the woman can lean on her brother as much as on her husband. This is the most prominent feature of the situation, and when the arrangement had already fallen to pieces and the transition to the patriarchal system was taking place, survivals of the matriarchal system might still be seen in the anomalous position of the brother in the tribe.

In Indian society the authority of the uncle over his nephews and nieces is in many respects greater than that of their own father. Thus, "The woman is the head of the Khasi family. So long as a man remains in his mother's house, whether he be married or unmarried, he is earning for his *kur* (i.e., his mother's family), and his property goes on his death to his mother, or, failing her, to his grandmother. Should the latter also be dead, his sisters inherit, and next to them his sister's children. In the absence of any of the above, the following relatives succeed in the order in which they are named, viz., his brothers, aunts, aunts' children, great-grandmother, great-grandmother's sister or children. The brother's children can never succeed, as they belong to a different clan. When a Khasi has left his mother's house, and gone to live with his wife, his property descends to her and her children, with the exception of his personal ornaments and clothing, which go to his own brothers and sisters. In the case of a female, the rules of inheritance are similar to those governing the descent of the property of a man living with his mother, except that in her case her children have a prior claim to succeed. All relationship is reckoned through the woman. The child takes the clan of the mother, and even the Seim (chieftain) is followed by his mother's or sister's child. His own offspring enter the clan of his wife, inherit her property and bear her family name. A man is thus in practice more nearly connected with his sister's children than with his own."[1]

The practice is the same among the North American Indians. For example, among the Choctaws, if a boy is to be placed at school, it is his uncle and not his father who takes him to the school and makes the arrangements. Among the Winnebagoes, a maternal uncle may require services of a nephew or administer correction which the boy's own father would neither ask nor attempt. Similarly with the Iowas and Ottoes an uncle may appropriate to his own use his nephew's horse or gun or other personal property without being questioned, which the sufferer's own father would have no recognized right to do.[2]

Thus the constitution of the family rests on the fact that family property and relationship are concentrated round the mother. At first sight it may seem odd that the mother's brother and not the mother's father is the male protector, but the brother is the contemporary and remains when the older generation, in the person of the father, has passed away.

In spite of the fact that this organization leads in most cases to the very independent position of the women,[3] there are tribes in which there does not seem to be any difference in the social status of women under a matrilineal and under a patrilineal system. For example, in Australia

[1] FRAZER, *op. cit.*, I, p. 259; GAIT, *Census of India*, 1891.

[2] FRAZER, *Totemism*, III, p. 25.

[3] The Nayar women show great independence of character and temper. As a consequence of the independent position of women in tribes practising mother-kin, we find cases in which a great latitude is allowed to women in regard to the dismissal of their husbands, e.g.: "In *Aghânî*, XVI, p. 106, in the story of Hâtim and Hâwîya, we read as follows. 'The women in the Jâhilîya, or some of them, had the right to dismiss their husbands, and the form of dismissal was this. If they lived in a tent they turned it round, so that if the door had faced east it now faced west, and when the man saw this he knew that he was dismissed and did not enter.' The tent therefore belonged to the woman, the husband was received in her tent and at her good pleasure."—ROBERTSON SMITH, *Kinship*, etc., p. 65.

Social status of women under matriarchal and patriarchal systems.

neighbouring tribes follow one or other of the rules of descent, and yet observers have found the women in the same condition of servants of all work and of beasts of burden under both systems.[1] This is due to the fact that the basis of society is the scattered household and the tribes congregate only for hunting and fishing. But the fundamental position is not to be shaken. In the reaction against the exaggerated views of earlier investigators, Westermarck and Malinowski have maintained that there is no matriarchal arrangement, only matrilineal descent, and that the family is always patriarchal. The question then is, how are we to harmonize this with the fact that the male sex is apt to exert its superior strength to obtain privileges and to push the weaker sex into the background? The development of the matriarchal system is not merely based on guesses, for we can see what makes the system so tenacious and why it can stand the test of thousands of years and of severe industrial competition. It is the effect of the division of labour that makes for the matriarchal arrangement of the household. Men are by nature destined for outside pursuits and women for housekeeping and inside pursuits. In primitive society also the woman not only cooks and carries, but manages the whole rudimentary culture of the soil, so that the characteristic implement of the Australian woman is the digging stick with which she digs round the house for roots, and that of the man is the boomerang. Even when the culture of the soil becomes less primitive, the sowing of the maize is regarded as women's work, and the women and children hunt small animals such as mice and opossums, while the man is the big hunter, of the kangaroo, buffalo and deer. The women rule the house, because the men do not care to meddle with small domestic matters. Thus the position of the mother as the economic centre is maintained in the

Influence of division of occupations.

[1] Cf. the situation in the Shortland Islands of the Solomon Group. "Although the system of mother-kin prevails in respect of the exogamous classes, Mr. Ribbe tells us that all the rights are on the side of the man. The woman is more the slave and beast of burden than the mate and companion of her husband."—FRAZER, *Totemism*, II, p. 117.

altered situation, and while progress strives to make more allowance for the predominance of the father, instinct and custom work the other way.

Transition between two systems.

Though the two systems seem opposed in principle, yet in a number of tribes we can see the transitional stages. As a rule the transition to the patriarchal system is an easy and gradual development. The main fact is *residence*. The Senegalese of Kandy follow two rules of marriage and inheritance. In a *Beena* marriage the descent is matrilineal, because it is constituted between a wealthy woman and a poor husband who lives with her kindred. But wealth is relative, and a brother of a poor husband may be rich compared with a poor wife whom he has married. In this case it is a *diga* marriage and the descent is patrilineal, as the residence is not in the house of the woman. Hebrew society was patriarchal, but the fact that Jacob lived with and served his father-in-law constituted a matriarchal arrangement. There is no inherent incompatibility in the two systems and it is possible to slide from one to the other.[1] The question is, what really decided the ultimate victory of the patriarchal or the matriarchal system? It is to be noticed that among all the more progressive nations the patriarchal system prevailed.

The Father.

The patriarchal system.

It is unnecessary to cite examples of the general aspect of patriarchal organization, because it is *the* organization familiar to us. It obtains among most nations even outside the circle of the civilized world. What is really important in an analytical survey is to ascertain the principal conditions leading to the formation of the patriarchal or-

[1] Cf. FRAZER, *Totemism*, I, p. 72: "Amongst the Banyai on the Zambesi, if the husband gives nothing, the children of the marriage belong to the wife's family; but if he gives so many cattle to his wife's parents the children are his. In the Watubela Islands between New Guinea and Celebes a man may either pay for his wife before marriage, or he may, without paying, live as her husband in her parents' house, working for her and her parents. In the former case the children belong to him; in the latter they belong to his wife's family, but he may acquire them subsequently by paying the price."

Cf on the Lalungs of Assam, *ibid.*, II, p 324.

ganization. From the outset one consideration is clear. It is evident that in all cases when violence and capture played a part, the result was bound to be coloured by the superiority of the husband, the captor. Among savage and primitive tribes and in the early ages of our own nations, capture led to the greatest number of marital unions. This is obvious, but another consideration deserves greater attention. In the case of capture, as the union is a one-sided assertion of force, there is no contract, though later, with the development of affection, a kind of contract may emerge. Women captured when their husbands or fathers have been slain become the unwilling wives of the conqueror. Suppose that no direct violence is employed, how are these marriages managed and what is the household arrangement? One particular circumstance may be decisive in shaping the case one way or the other. The important question is that of *residence* and whether the household is within the circle of influence of the wife's or husband's family. In this question, apart from the casual differences of wealth and power, the very fact of settlement is bound to play a great part. In a primitive society where the settlements are connected with scattered shelters, fatherhood is bound to assert itself with overwhelming force. There must be close proximity between husband and wife, and the wife is at a distance from her brother, who might otherwise become the male protector. Among the Veddas, who are called patriarchal and monogynous, the isolated household makes for fatherhood.

Influence of settlement.

Even among nomads there is a tendency to fatherhood. In hunting and fishing tribes the household has to follow the prey and wander about in pursuit of the means of existence, so that there can be no talk of isolated settlements; but when pasturage is the important point, the more settled existence produces clearer legal distinctions. In moderate and in northern climates the summer and winter appropriation of ground leads to a clearer mapping out of settlements and centres of residence. With an agricultural people the idea of the settlement growing into the soil is a basic factor, and the definite ground to till and to live on becomes the essence of the whole husbandry of the tribe. Isolation is the necessary consequence, and with the progress of the firm and isolated settlement fatherhood is sure to gain ground. A minority of cases, such as that of the Nayars, presents the curious feature of the survival of the ancient institutions of motherhood. As a rule, however, in the competition between mother-kin and father-kin, the latter eventually survives and predominates because of the influence of force, for the household organized round the father is a more strongly constituted centre of law and a more effective organization than is the more complicated arrangement which looks to the mother's brother for assistance. In the operation of the rule of the survival of the fittest, the more simple and solid patriarchal organization obtains the victory.

Marriage a form of property.

Since this is the general course of the development of the family, the next question is as to what shape the fatherhood principle takes in the hands of primitive tribes. It centres on *property,* for the law of marital union depends less on the law of relationship, not to speak of affection, than on the law of property and authority. The authoritative rule of the paterfamilias is self-evident, but it is less easy to grasp the importance of the fact that marriage is a form of the law of property. Inasmuch as marriage not only serves the purpose of sexual intercourse and the breeding of children, but is constituted on the lines of property, it may be compared with the soil, which is not only cultivated for the raising of crops, but is above all *property.* In all cases the principle obtains that the children belong to the male to whom the wife belongs. In the mother's case generation remains the dominant fact, but the relationship between father and child is ruled by the fact of property, and procreation is subsidiary in a way we have almost ceased to understand, save in the case of a stepchild who does not belong by procreation to the step-father. The working of the principle in primitive communities that it is immaterial by which man the woman taken as wife is pregnant, is illustrated by the frequent substitution for the licence of unmarried girls of the restrictions of married life. It is also admitted that if the father of the family (the owner of the wife) is sickly and unable to have children for himself, he may ask a stranger to procreate. There is also the curious custom of lending wives for the purposes of hospitality. According to the Arab proverb: "Children belong to the man to whom the bed belongs."[1]

Recognition of fatherhood.

One of the further results in law is the necessity of acknowledging the relationship between father and child when it is not regarded as natural. Primitive tribes demand a special acknowledgement, a "seisin," of the child. In the common form the taking up of the child by the father directly after birth, the performance of some ceremony connected with the ancestral hearth and the giving of a name, constitute the establishment of the legal relationship. More curious is the extraordinary custom of fictitious birth which prevailed in all parts of the world. The "couvade" has been found among the Basques of southwest France, in Guiana, in California, and among the Larkas of Bengal and many African tribes. This peculiar ceremony by which, when a child is to be born, the father goes into child-bed and undergoes a fictitious treatment, can have only one meaning, that of proving the right of the father in the child. There is no evidence that the prevalence of the custom is the result of migration from one continent to another, and it must be regarded as a remarkable instance of the similarity of the situation and thought in different tribes. As fatherhood was not a fact of nature, it must be established by an artificial ceremony, for property is the root of ancient fatherhood.

The Levirate.

The Levirate, the practice of marriage with a deceased brother's widow, is not the result of simple appropriation,

[1] ROBERTSON SMITH, *Kinship*, pp. 109-10: "A man is father of all the children of the woman by whom he has purchased the right to have offspring that shall be reckoned to his own kin. . . . The fundamental doctrine of Mohammedan law [is that] the son is reckoned to the bed on which he is born.

"Among the Arab customs of the time of heathenism we find a usage known as Nikâh al-istibadâ. When a man desired a goodly seed he might call upon his wife to cohabit with another man till she became pregnant by him. The child, as in the similar case in Hindu law, was the husband's son."

but is the outcome of the fact that the brother is under an obligation to take care of the widow and the property and movables connected with her and to prevent their dispersion. This is at the root of many customs of many tribes. To take one example from the Bible, Ruth, the Moabitess, widow of the Hebrew, Mahlon, came to the land of the Jews and approached Boaz, the cousin of her deceased husband, asking that he would marry her and take up the inheritance. Boaz acknowledged his duty as a kinsman:

"And now it is true that I am thy near kinsman: howbeit there is a kinsman nearer than I" (Ruth iii, 12). He then addressed the near kinsman and the elders:

"And the kinsman said, I cannot redeem it for myself, lest I mar mine own inheritance: redeem thou my right to thyself; for I cannot redeem it" (iv, 6). To this Boaz agreed:

"Moreover Ruth the Moabitess, the wife of Mahlon, have I purchased to be my wife, to raise up the name of the dead upon his inheritance, that the name of the dead be not cut off from among his brethren, and from the gate of his place: ye are witnesses this day" (iv, 10).[1]

Where polyandry, which is entirely contradictory to our own ideas, occurs not as an occasional practice but as the settled custom of regularly established and constituted Polyandry.

[1] On marriage with several sisters, see FRAZER, *Totemism*, IV, p. 141: "The general practice, as defined by L. H. Morgan, is that when a man marries the eldest daughter he becomes, by that act, entitled to each and all of her sisters as wives when they severally attain the marriageable age. The option rests with him, and he may enforce the claim, or yield it to another."

As to the Potawattamies, we are informed that "it was usual for them, when an Indian married one of several sisters, to consider him as wedded to all; and it became incumbent upon him to take them all as wives."

The customs of the Arapahoes in this respect are especially worthy of attention. Amongst them "a wife's next younger sister, if of marriageable age, is sometimes given to her husband if his brother-in-law likes him. Sometimes the husband asks and pays for his wife's younger sister. This may be done several times if she has several sisters. If his wife has no sister, a cousin (also called "sister") is sometimes given to him. When a woman dies, her husband marries her sister. When a man dies, his brother sometimes marries his wife. He is expected to do so."

tribes, it must not be treated as the expression of loose morality. It is necessitated by something in the life of the tribes, and the reason for it is clear. It is due to poverty, and in many cases brothers form a "joint-stock company" for the possession of a wife.

"The Bahima sometimes practise polyandry, several brothers marrying one wife and enjoying her in common. When a man is poor, when his herd does not yield milk enough to support a wife, or he cannot afford the number of cows required for a marriage dowry, he may ask one or more of his brothers to join him, and together they may raise the requisite tale of animals. A woman will readily agree to such an arrangement and become the wife of two or three brothers. The children born under such circumstances belong to the elder brother. The custom of polyandry seems to be rare among the Bantu peoples. The only other people known to Mr. Roscoe who practise it are the Baziba to the south of Uganda."[1]

"The Todas have a completely organized and definite system of polyandry, and in the vast majority of polyandrous marriages the husbands are own brothers. Indeed, when a woman marries, it is understood that she becomes the wife of his brothers at the same time. When the joint husbands are not own brothers, they may either live with the wife in one family, or they may dwell in different villages. In the latter case the usual custom is for the wife to reside with each husband in turn for a month. When a child is born in a family of this sort, all the brothers are equally regarded as its fathers; though if a man be asked the name of his father, he will generally mention one man of the group, probably the most prominent or important of them.

"When the joint husbands are not brothers, they arrange among themselves who is to be putative father of each child as it is born, and the chosen one accepts the responsibility by performing a certain ceremony called *pursütpimi*, 'bow (and arrow) we touch,' because it consists in the husband

[1] FRAZER, *Totemism*, II, p. 538.

formally presenting his wife with a little imitation bow and arrow."[1]

The holding of land as joint property by a joint family is an exceedingly common device among primitive peoples, and these polyandric unions stand on the same footing. McLennan has made a special study of them. In one particular aspect they are often found in conjunction with female infanticide. In difficult conditions of existence, when starvation is imminent, the sacrifice of daughters is not uncommon.[2] The *Aghânî*[3] has a description of a man who goes to the desert with his daughter and buries her alive. This practice of female infanticide results in the scarcity of women and the consequent necessity of joint marriages. They are not due to licence, but are as firmly established as monogamous marriages.

Influence of infanticide.

This is sufficient to illustrate the immense importance of property and economic considerations in the development of fatherhood. In the important question as to the elements with which we have to reckon in the formation of family life, we have discussed the selection of mates, mother-kin and the part played by generation, fatherhood and the facts of authority and property. The fourth question is, why has marriage in its historical development

[1] *Op. cit.*, II, p. 256.

Cf. ROBERTSON SMITH, *Kinship*, p. 133, on the practice among the Iberians: "All the kindred have their property in common, the eldest being lord; all have one wife and it is first come first served, the man who enters to her leaving at the door the stick which it is usual for every one to carry; but the night she spends with the eldest. Hence all are brothers of all [within the stock of συγγενεῖς]; they have also conjugal intercourse with mothers; and adultery is punished with death; an adulterer means a man of another stock."

[2] Cf. ROBERTSON SMITH, *op. cit.*, p. 279: "The practice of infanticide is spoken of and condemned by the prophet in several places. . . . The motive which he assigns is poverty; the parents were afraid that they could not find food for all their offspring" Cf. *The Koran*, transl. by Rodwell (Everyman's Library), *Sura* vi, 141; xvi, 60-6: "For when the birth of a daughter is announced to any one of them, dark shadows settle on his face, and he is sad.

"He hideth him from the people because of the ill-tidings; shall he keep it with disgrace, or bury it in the dust?"

Cf *Sura* lxxxi, 8: "And when the female child that has been buried alive. . . ." *Sura* xvii, 33: "Kill not your children for fear of want." vi, 152.

[3] xii, 150. The story is given in ROBERTSON SMITH, *loc. cit.*

reached, in all progressive communities, the stage beyond that of casual unions, and become a settled combination on the principle of agreement with actual or quasi-actual contract? We touch the line on which our description has to proceed from a different basis: we shall have to deal henceforth with marriage as an institution. The foundation of this development lies in the influence of the group.

CHAPTER III

RELATIONSHIP AND MARRIAGE

"Marital union" not the same as "marriage."

It is clear from our description of marital unions among primitive tribes that it would be wrong to describe them as marriages. It is a fundamental fact that there is inherent in our connotation of the term "marriage" an idea of reciprocal obligation which is not implied in "mating" or "marital union." For "marriage" something else is necessary, and even in savage society this additional element is sometimes present. The question to be answered is, how and in what surroundings is this contractual element developed? In the previous conditions with which we have dealt the unions were polygynic, that is to say, by legal custom—for it can hardly be termed law,—the husband attracts as many mates of the female sex as he can, and his right and desire to do so are limited only by the question of means. This is not even polygamy, for that involves an element of bilateral relationship. Among the Tasmanians of the first half of the nineteenth century, who have since disappeared, but who were then an exceedingly primitive people in the palæolithic period using only clipped stone implements, Lloyd "scarcely ever knew an instance of a native having but one *gin*. On the contrary, two or three were the usual allowance. I have known a grey-headed old savage to possess three wives of the respective ages of thirty, seventeen, and ten years, all betrothed to him from childhood, and from the time of their betrothal, become members of his family circle, entirely dependent on him for support."[1] But even when we start from the absolute conception of appropriation, the working of psychical and emotional intercourse on the higher plane of mutual regard may involve some sort of reciprocal arrangement even in

[1] Quoted by H. Ling Roth, *The Aborigines of Tasmania*, p. 124.

The contractual element in marriage due to the formation of relationships.

polygynous unions. The natural attachment of the man to his wife and children is in itself insufficient, and the decisive and most interesting fact from the jurist's point of view is that the obligation of marriage as a bilateral union is conditioned by the law of relationship. The germ of marriage lies in the fact that marital unions lead to the formation of circles of relationship reacting on the unions and tending to shape them in a less one-sided manner. Under the influence of groups of relationship, the wife becomes less a "thing."

Three systems.

It must not be assumed that the formation of the relationship is always on the same plan and as it now is. In a comparative survey of the collateral relationships developed from marriage, the whole immense material may be divided into three groups. In the first place there is the relationship of blood, consanguinity, in which the fact of procreation is translated into its social and legal consequences, and kinship is recognized by people born of the same mother, or, when the circle of observation is enlarged, of the same mother and father. This is the *cognatic* system.

The second important influence in the formation of relationship is the household, composed of one group dwelling together under one family name and tracing descent from the same original common household. This is the *agnatic* formation, the one-sided relationship which follows from union in a single household. Usually, as in our patriarchal system of descent, the relationship is through males, but logically it is equally right to build up the household system through females.

The divergence between the two types leads to important social results which may be expressed graphically thus. The cognatic relationship starts from a pair and is developed round this original pair in a kind of spider-web. The group is never quite compact, for at the beginning it starts from two, each of which is the offspring of two, so that there are four grandparents and eight great-grandparents. The apex of the scheme of an agnatic relationship, on the other hand, is normally the *paterfamilias*. The tree springs from one root and its branches extend in different directions. There is formed therefore a compact group of sons, grandsons and nephews, with the living grandfather at the top and all under his household *potestas* below.[1]

Thirdly, there is the *totemic* system which is neither entirely agnatic nor entirely cognatic, being based neither on procreation nor purely on the household, but on a religious system. It is found in all parts of the world and is an admission of kinship between locally neighbouring people, associated as a group and divided from other groups by the recognition of magic descent from a mythical ancestor, presented as an animal, a plant, or a meteorological phenomenon (e.g., cloud, rain). For instance, "Amongst the Black Shoulder (Buffalo) clan of the Omahas a dying clansman was wrapped in a buffalo robe with the hair out, his face was painted with the clan mark, and his friends addressed him thus: 'You are going to the animals (the buffaloes). You are going to rejoin your ancestors. You are going, or your four souls are going, to the four winds. Be strong.' Amongst the Hanga clan, another Buffalo clan of the Omahas, the ceremony was similar, and the dying man was thus addressed: 'You came hither from the animals, and you are going back thither. Do not face this way again. When you go, continue walking.' "[2]

We have seen how among the Aruntas the local association differed from the association in blood, and the whole system rests on the supposed connection between the locality and its inhabitants. Each man is the reincarnation of an ancestor whose identity is sought by local signs and magical rites. These are regarded as the regular and actual concrete facts of relationship. According to R. H. Matthews, "In the Chau-an as well as in all the other tribes reported by me, in the Northern Territory, succession of the totems does not depend upon either the father or the mother, but is regulated by locality, and I shall now en-

Reincarnation.

[1] Cf. RIVERS, *Kinship and Social Organization*, p. 79; and HILL-TOUT, *British North America*, I, pp. 158-9.

[2] FRAZER, *Totemism*, I, p. 35.

deavour to describe how this is carried out. The folk-lore of these people is full of fabulous tales respecting the progenitors of every totem. Some of them were like the men and women of our own time, whilst others were mythologic creatures of aboriginal fairyland. In these olden days, as at present, the totemic ancestors consisted of families or groups of families, who had their recognized hunting-grounds in some part of the tribal territory. They were born in the specific locality, and occupied it by virtue of their birth-right. Some of them would be, let us say, cockatoos, others dogs, others kangaroos, others snakes and so forth. The members of these family groups were subdivided into the same eight sections which we find among the people now. . . .

"In all aboriginal tribes there is a deeply seated belief in the reincarnation of their ancestors. The original stock of spirits, so to speak, perpetually undergo reincarnation from one human being to another. The natives are quite ignorant of the natural facts of procreation, and believe that conception is altogether independent of sexual intercourse. When a woman for the first time feels the movement of the child in the womb, commonly called quickening, she takes particular notice of the spot where it occurred and reports it to the people present.[1] It is believed that the spirit or soul of some deceased progenitor has just at that moment entered the woman's body. The entry may have been by way of some one of the natural openings, or through any part of the skin, the mode or place of ingress being immaterial to these ethereal beings. When the child is born it will have assigned to it the totemic name of the mythic ancestor belonging to the particular locality."[2]

Relationship on individual lines.

In the cognatic system it is possible to distinguish between two phases, the archaic and the modern. Ancient Roman Law was agnatic, but the cognatic system was admitted by the later Prætorian Law and is now practised by us. This is not, however, the ancient cognatic system, and there is a

[1] See *ante*, p. 183 n.

[2] *Notes on Some Native Tribes of Australia*, in the *Journal and Proceedings of the Royal Society of New South Wales*, XL (1906), pp. 107, 110.

fundamental difference between this system as the expression of matrilineal arrangements and as the expression of higher civilization. The cognatic system does not always point to ancient matrilineal arrangements, and it is a fallacy to argue that, because the Germanic system is cognatic, it must have been so from the beginning, and that it is impossible to suppose that it was at any time agnatic. Both the Greek and Roman systems were at one time agnatic, and the ancient Athenian matrilineal arrangements became patrilineal; and later, with increasing civilization, the γένος was broken up and a new form of cognatic system emerged. In both systems we can trace relationship on individual lines either from the definite and concrete fact of birth or from membership of the same household. In the totemic formation, however, the facts are different, for the essence of the reincarnation principle is a vague mythical idea. As we have here the notion of the group as the matrimonial class, it is impossible to construct relationship on definite individual lines. Relationship is formed not by actual marriage between single individuals, but by potential marriage between whole groups. A peculiar nomenclature, foreign to our ideas but evidenced all over the world, has arisen. In Australia, for instance:

"Like all other Australian tribes about whom we have exact information, the Dieri have the classificatory system of relationship. For example, in the generation above his own a man applies the same term *ngaperi* (*appiri*) to his father and to his father's brothers; and he applies the same term *ngandri* (*andri*) to his mother and to his mother's sisters. In his own generation he applies the same term *negi* (*niehi*, *neyi*) to his elder brothers, to the sons of his father's brothers, and to the sons of his mother's sisters; and he applies the same term *kaku* to his elder sisters, to the daughters of his father's brothers, and to the daughters of his mother's sisters. He applies the same term *noa* to his wife, to his wife's sisters, and to his brothers' wives; and on her side a woman applies the same term *noa* to her husband, to her husband's brothers, and to her sisters' husbands. In the generation below his own a man applies the

Classificatory system.

same term *ngata mura* (*athamoora*) to his own sons, to the sons of his brothers, and to the sons of his wife's sisters. Thus a Dieri man may have many 'fathers' who never begot him, many 'mothers' who never bore him, many 'brothers' and 'sisters' who are the children of neither of his parents, and many 'sons' whom he never begot. In the mouth of the Dieri these terms of relationship, while they include the relationships which we designate by them, also include many more: they mark the relationship of the individual not to individuals merely but to groups. It has already been pointed out that such classificatory terms, descriptive of group relationships, are only explicable on the hypothesis that they are directly derived from group-marriage. That inference has long been rightly drawn by Dr. A. W. Howitt, our principal authority on the Dieri and other tribes of south-eastern Australia."[1]

In the same way among the Urabunna: "Since in this tribe groups of women are thus common to groups of men, it naturally follows that the children born of such unions are also common to the groups. All the children born of women whom a man might marry, whether he has marital relations with them or not, call him 'father' (*nia*) and he calls them 'children' (*biaka*). Whilst naturally there is a closer tie between a man and the children of the women who habitually live in camp with him, still there is no name to distinguish between the children of his own wives and those of women whom he might marry but with whom he has no sexual relations. All children of the men who are at the same level in the generation and belong to the same class and totem are regarded as the common children of these men, and similarly the men are regarded collectively by the children as their fathers."[2]

The stages in the Malayan system of relationship are, according to Morgan: 1, The children of my brothers and of my sisters are my children. 2, All the children of several brothers and of several sisters are brothers and sisters as among themselves. 3, All the brothers of my father and of

[1] FRAZER, *Totemism*, I, p. 362.
[2] *Ibid.*, pp. 309-10.

my mother are my fathers, and all the sisters of my father and of my mother are my mothers. One general idea prevails throughout, namely, that relationship is traced not through individuals but through groups.

The system is based on potential, not actual relationship. The uncertainty of procreation is in the background and reincarnation takes its place. Morgan, who was the first to interpret this class relationship and its nomenclature, elaborated a theory of group marriage and consequent promiscuity between groups. This conclusion has been attacked, for no such promiscuity has been found, only occasional licence and subsidiary intercourse. The dividing lines are formed on class association, on religious lines.

The next question is, how does the fact that every marital union produces groups of relationship influence the institution of marriage? By-and-by marriage ceases to be only the relation between mates, and in all systems the relations are interested in the conclusion of right marriages and exert their influence to make marriage a legal institution instead of a casual sexual union. However, the forms which marriage does take in different tribes are not always conducive to contractual marriage.

Marriage by capture and *quasi* capture.

In archaic times the practice of marriage by *capture* was exceedingly prevalent. In all forms of marriage some traces of this may be found. There are, for instance, various ceremonies and customs, such as that of parting the bride's hair with a spear or of lifting her over the threshold. Capture shades off into elopement on one side, and on the other into an agreement accompanied by simulated capture, a compromise with real capture.[1] In Serbia at the beginning of the nineteenth century there were raids for wives at which real fights might take place, and the following account of a raid in the Caucasus is given by E. Rössler:[2]

[1] Cf. H. Ling Roth, *The Aborigines of Tasmania*, p. 123: "It was rarely the custom amongst them to select wives from their own tribes, but rather to take them furtively, or by open force, from neighbouring clans." (Quoting Milligan, *Beacon*, p. 29.) Cf. Frazer, *Totemism*, III, p. 582.

[2] *Zeitschrift für Ethnologie*, XXX (1898), p. 324.

"A raid had certainly taken place: but on this occasion it had been directed, not against the cattle of the villagers (as is generally the case), but merely against a girl! According to a common practice among the Tartars, the consent of the damsel is often obtained beforehand, and such was no doubt the case now. For if two lovers agree, the bridegroom waits for a favourable opportunity to abduct the lady of his heart. Having informed her secretly of his intention he appears during the night with his companions near the house of his beloved, who is waiting for him. He lifts her on to his horse and gallops away with her. Thereupon the parents and relatives of the damsel start in pursuit, and the whole village is roused. The chase which now begins is either feigned or genuine according as to whether the abductor is viewed with favour or disfavour by the pursuers. In the former case, the main object of the comedy is amusement, and much powder is expended in the firing of shots: in the latter, the bullets of course sometimes find their mark, and the wedding feast becomes a funeral banquet. If, however, the abduction is successfully carried out, the wedding takes place in a few days; there is a general reconciliation, and from that time onwards peaceful intercourse prevails between the newly married couple and their relations."

Marriage by elopement.

In other cases marriage by *elopement* is found. For instance among the Sikani, of the Déné tribe, "when a man has made up his mind to take a wife, he 'proposes' to the girl of his choice in the following words: 'Will you pack my beaver snares for me?' This is tantamount to asking her to be his wife, and is understood as such by the girl." [1]

Marriage by *purchase*, which takes the form of acquisition of a thing,[2] is really the beginning of marriage by

[1] HILL-TOUT, *British North America*, I, p. 182.

[2] Cf. ROBERTSON SMITH, *Kinship*, p. 77: "A woman of the Banū 'Amir ibn Sa'sa'a married among the Tayyi says:

"'Never let sister praise brothers of hers: never let daughter bewail a father's death:
For *they* have brought her where she is no longer a free woman, and *they* have banished her to the farthest ends of the earth.'"

In regard to women, the word "possession" is used in the same sense as of slaves.

Marriage by purchase the beginning of contractual marriage.

agreement. Presents are sometimes substituted for real purchase.[1] The contract of purchase opens a possibility of the introduction of certain conditions. The kin of the bride still keep a kind of authority and supervision over her life.[2] The obligation of revenge in regard to her remains with them. If the husband treats his wife unjustly, the father will probably wage war upon him. Possibly an agreement between the two kins may settle the extent of the responsibility on both sides. This double allegiance of the wife which leads to the maintenance of her relations with her father and brother, reacts on the children who are under the protection of the tribe of the mother also.

Summary.

It may be appropriate to sum up briefly the principal results of the analytical survey of primitive forms of marriage.

(1) It is not only impossible to trace one single course of development as regards family institutions, but it is most unlikely that such a single course could have been followed by the various tribes of mankind.

(2) There is no evidence as to general sexual promiscuity in any instance susceptible of exact observation, but there are numberless cases of occasional and seasonal licence.

(3) Exogamic restrictions in the selection of mates can be traced to one of three motives—the attraction of contrasting features of body and mind, the perception of eugenic laws as to cross-breeding, the policy of social order.

(4) Endogamy is to be accounted for by the wish of a group to keep together as against outsiders, and, more especially, by the tendency to prevent the dispersion of family property.

1 Hill-Tout, *op. cit.*, I, p. 188.

2 Robertson Smith, *op. cit.*, pp. 101-2: "The strength of the feelings of kinship bettered the wife's position, whether she were married in her own kin or to an alien, unless she were carried far out of the reach of her natural protectors: in *Agh.*, IX, 150, when the father comes to his daughter and says, 'This is Hârith ibn 'Auf a chieftain of the Arabs who has come to ask thy hand, and I am willing to give thee him to wife, what sayest thou?' the reply is, 'No! I am not fair of face and I have infirmities of temper, *and I am not his bint 'amm (tribeswoman) so that he should respect my consanguinity with him, nor does he dwell in thy country so that he should have regard for thee;* I fear then that he may not care for me and may divorce me, and so I shall be in an evil case.'"

(5) The position of the mother in the family is based on the patent fact of generation, and the elemental affection between mother and children.

(6) Matrilineal institutions develop under the influence of a sharply marked division of labour between males and females.

(7) In matrilineal arrangements the mother of the family leans on the support of her brother, instead of leaning on the support of her husband.

(8) The father's position in the family is primarily connected with appropriation and lordship.

(9) The transitions from matrilineal to patrilineal institutions are gradual and depend to a great extent on the condition of settlement.

(10) The patriarchal order has advantages in competition with the matriarchal, on account of its greater solidity and discipline.

(11) The institution of the family centre determines the formation of systems of relationship on the lines of affinity by blood (cognation), affinity through household ties (agnation) and affinity by consciousness of reincarnation (Totemism).

(12) The formation of groups of kinsmen reacts powerfully on the evolution of matrimonial unions by producing certain safeguards for contractual marriage.

PART II

ARYAN CULTURE

CHAPTER IV

ARYAN ORIGINS

Aryan linguistic affinities.

SINCE the days (1816) when Bopp traced the development of the *verb* among various nations of the Indo-European race, comparative philology, prehistoric archæology and ethnology have made great strides: it is possible to speak of Aryan or Indo-European origins with much more precision, and to place ascertained facts in better perspective, although most important problems still remain unsolved, and new problems arise in the course of investigation.

We know by this time that the chasm between the south-eastern group of Aryan nations and the north-western one is not so great as was supposed in the nineteenth century: ethnologists and linguists have to reckon seriously not only with Sanskrit and Avestic, but with Armenian, Tocharic, North Aryan, with Thracian and Illyrian, as intermediate links between the East and the West. What is even more important, the pedigree scheme of linguistic affinities sketched by Schleicher has given way before a view of intercourse extending in various directions,—a view that starts from the fact that certain terms of a particular language are common to it and to its eastern or northern neighbours, while other terms of the same language connect it with the speech of western or southern neighbours. For instance, Slavonic languages border on Iranian idioms on one side, on Lithuanian and German [1] on the other. This theory, again, has to be modified to some extent as against the absolute form in which it was propounded by Johannes Schmidt and popularized by O. Schrader, and recent philologists lay stress on the marked interruptions of continuity produced by consecutive migrations of sections of the Indo-European group. But, when allowance has been made for gaps and stages, the general view of the fluid relations between various gatherings of

[1] SCHRADER, *Sprachvergleichung und Urgeschichte*, pp. 92 ff. on Johannes Schmidt's theory.

the Indo-European ethnic mass still holds good and seems necessary in order to explain the curious cross-currents of linguistic affinity between the languages of the group.

Epochs of Aryan migrations. Some idea must be formed concerning the approximate epochs of Aryan migrations. Starting with the most recent historical movements of these peoples we have to notice that Pytheas (350 B.C.) testifies to the settlement of Teutonic tribes on the shores of the Baltic, and it is most probable that about the same time the Lithuanians and Slavs moved into north-western Russia to the east of the Teutons. The Celtic invasion of central and western Europe manifested itself about 600 B.C. The Italians cannot have reached the Apennine peninsula much later than 1000 B.C. As for the Greeks, their last Dorian migration, recorded as having taken place towards 1004 B.C. must have developed its initial stages somewhat earlier, while the Achæan occupation of the Balkan Peninsula and of the Ægean islands is synchronized by Mesopotamian inscriptions of 1275 B.C., mentioning the Danaiu, and inscriptions of Rameses III of 1234 B.C., mentioning the Achæans and the Æolians. These dates suggest that the union of the north-western group of the race can hardly be placed in an epoch more recent than 1500-1200 B.C. This would tally with the facts ascertained concerning the movements of the south-eastern group. While the Persians and Medes begin to exert a preponderating influence only late, towards the second quarter of the first millennium, there is already evidence in cuneiform inscriptions of Boghazkeui of the gods Mitra, Varuna and Indra as worshipped by tribes of invaders in Iran about 1500 B.C.; the Indian conquest of the Punjab reflected in the primitive Vedic language and lore probably took place about 2000 B.C.[1] And as we have to postulate an epoch of common existence preceding the disruption of the two great branches of the race, the south-eastern and the north-western, room has to be made for several centuries, perhaps some 500-700 years, of Indo-European union in the interval between 3000 and

[1] I follow Feist in this matter. Professor Macdonell places it not much earlier than 1200 B.C Macdonell and Keith, *Vedic Index*, VIII.

2000 B.C. Of course, the fixing of definite dates is merely guess-work, but the stages of development and expansion must have followed each other in accordance with some such sequence.

Geographical lines of the migration.

It is even more difficult to come to definite conclusions as to the geographical localization of these stages. The question as to the original home of the race cannot be considered as settled, and is answered in entirely different ways by leading antiquarians. In the main, opinions may be ranged in two rival groups: there are those who favour the view that the home of the race is to be sought in the vast plains of central Asia and south-eastern Russia, and there are those who contend that archæological and linguistic data point to northern Europe, and more particularly to the shores of the Baltic, as the place of concentration of the European branch of the race. I may say that the version of the steppes theory presented recently by S. Feist appears convincing to me. Apart from the discussion of details, it seems the only hypothesis that can account for the close relationship of the European nations with the Indians and Persians. A period of union in some central part of the old Continent has to be assumed, unless we are prepared to assign to the Asiatic branches an entirely subordinate place in the development of the race. It is in this connection that the existence of the intermediate groups—the N. Aryan, Tocharic, Sogdian and Armenian,—becomes very important. Is it conceivable that these various ethnic bodies should have been formed by pushes from a north European centre? On the other hand, the gradual deflection of late-comers from the central plains towards the north is easily accounted for, and, indeed, would have to be postulated *a priori*. A significant linguistic trait may be mentioned here at once. Expressions like *mare* (Latin), *meer* (German), *mere* (Old English), *morje* (Old Bulgarian),[1]

[1] The parallels are chiefly from S. Feist, *Kultur, Ausbreitung und Herkunft der Indo-Germanen* (Berlin, 1913). There are special references to H. Hirt, *Die Indogermanen* (Strassburg, 1905), O. Schrader, *Reallexikon der indogermanischen Altertumskunde* (Strassburg, 1901), and J. Hoops, *Waldbäume und Kulturpflanzen im germanischen Altertum* (Strassburg, 1905), as regards additions and variations.

point to expanses of water and may possibly have been meant for lakes and marsh-land; the specific terms for sea, navigation and fishing are specialized in various languages and stand quite by themselves in the Celto-Germanic group. Names of trees are generic, and their specific meanings are differentiated later on. Thus "beech" was originally any big tree, not necessarily a beech, and the parallel terms are as follows:

Latin	*Greek*	*Germanic*	*Russian*	*Kurdish*
fagus	φηγός	Buche	buk (buzina)	buz

For "pine" we have:

Sanskrit	*Greek*	*Latin*
pītu-dāru	πίτυς	pinus

for "oak":

Sanskrit	*Avestic*	*Greek*	*Gothic*	*Old Slavonic*	*Old Irish*
dāru	dauru	δρῦς (δόρυ)	triu	drevo	daur

for "birch":

Sanskrit	*Slavonic*	*Lithuanian*	*Old Icelandic*
bhūrjas	breza	beržas	björk

Linguistic and archæological evidence as to Aryan culture.

As regards the general standing reached by the Indo-European culture when the Aryan group was still united, there are curious indications in language and archæology. It is clear that the united race was at that time traversing the period of the stone age. Their implements were made of stone, but, chiefly through intercourse with neighbouring nations, they were acquainted with the use of metals, and certain objects manufactured from different metals were introduced among them. That the basis of their culture

[1] Cf. Hoops, *op. cit.*, pp. 117 sq.

was stone may be illustrated by the characteristic fact that the root word for "knife" or "axe" was "sax," the same word as the Latin "saxum," "rock."[1] These stone implements, especially sacrificial knives, have been found among burial remains.

Metals.

With the appearance of metals the culture of the outgoing stone and the beginning of the bronze period is reached. The linguistic parallels for "bronze" are:

Sanskrit	*Avestic*	*Latin*	*Gothic*	*Old English*
ayas	ayo	aes	aiz	ár

The immense importance of the intercourse with the nations of the East and South may be seen in the word "aes Cyprium," the bronze of Cyprus, i.e., copper. For "copper" the parallels are:

Latin	*Slavonic*	*Old Icelandic*	*Sumerian*	*Basque*
raudus	ruda	raudhe	urudu	urraida

The origin of these terms may be traced to the Phœnician trade, and the use of the metal was transferred from East to West, even when the West was in the hands of the Iberian predecessors of the Aryans. The eastern roots of the words are clearly marked and point to Sumerian—the primordial element of Babylonian culture. The teachers of metallurgy were Babylonian, Phœnician and possibly Egyptian. The parallels for "gold" are:

Sanskrit	*Avestic*	*Gothic*	*Old Slavonic*
hiranyam	zaranya-	gulth	zlato

[1]

Old Indian	*Greek*	*Latin*	*Lithuanian*	*Old Icelandic*	*O. H. German*	*Old English*
kšuras	ξυρός	saxum	skutu	sax	mezzi-sahs	mete-seax

for "silver":

Sanskrit	*Avestic*	*Tocharian*	*Greek*
rajatam	erezata	arkyant	ἄργυρος

Latin	*Gothic*	*Old English*	*Slavonic*
argentum	silubr	seolfor	serebro

for "iron":

Sumerian	*Assyrian*	*Hebrew*	*Old English* [1]
barzal	parzilla	barezel	bræs

Economic pursuits.

In the same way, with the help of linguistic parallels, something may be discovered of the general condition of their culture and economic state. When we ask what they were living on, we may conclude that they were a pastoral people with some beginnings of agriculture. The principal names of domestic animals are common to the whole group. Thus we have, "dog":

Sanskrit	*Avesta-Persian*	*Armenian*	*Greek*	*Latin*
śwā	spā	sun	κυων	canis

Old Irish	*Gothic*	*Lithuanian*	*Russian* and *Polish*
cú	hunds	szu	suka

"horse":

Sanskrit	*Avestic*	*Tocharian*	*Greek*	*Latin*
aśvas	aspa–	yakwe	ἵππος	equus

Old Irish	*Gothic*	*Old Icelandic*	*Old English*
ech	aihwa–	jór	eoh

"sheep":

Old Indian	*Greek*	*Latin*	*Old Irish*
avis	ὄϊς	ovis	ói

Old High German	*Lithuanian*	*Old Slavonic*	*English*
ouwi	avis	ovica	ewe

[1] Hirt, *op. cit.*, p. 686, and Schrader, *op. cit.*, p. 178, give:

Syrian	*Assyrian*	*Hebrew*
parzla	parzillu	barzel

"wool":

Sanskrit	*Greek*	*Latin*	*Old Irish*	*Gothic*
ūrnā	λῆνος	lana	olan	wulla
Old Slavonic	*Lithuanian*			
vulna	vilna			

"ox":

Sanskrit	*Avestic*	*Tocharian B.*	*Gothic*	*Cymric*
uksā	uxsam–	okso	auhsa	ych

Sometimes the same word is represented in nearly every case, but sometimes another root covers another whole set of terms. Thus we have for "ox" or "bull":

Greek	*Latin*	*Gothic*	*Old Icelandic*	*Old Slavonic*
ταῦρος	taurus	stiur	thjórr	tur
Lithuanian				
tauras				

and for "cow":

Sanskrit	*Avestic*	*Armenian*	*Lettish*	*O. H. German*	*Old Slavonic*
gāus	gav–	kov	guws	chuo	goved

while "g" is changed to "b" in:

Greek	*Latin*	*Old Irish*
βοῦς	bos	bo

These parallels indicate that the principal pursuits of the united Indo-Europeans were pastoral, but the curious analogy to be found among agricultural terms proves that they were not entirely nomadic, but were settled enough to carry on cultivation from season to season. Thus we have common expressions for implements of ploughing, as "yoke":

Sanskrit	*Greek*	*Latin*	*Cymric*	*Gothic*	*Lithuanian*	*Slavonic*
yugam	ζυγόν	iugum	iau	juk	jungas	igo

There are some indications as regards the ploughing already practised. The small original plough was suggested by a natural implement, the big branch with a small branch projecting like a horn. The original small, light plough was drawn by one horse or ox, later by two, the yoke. For this plough we have:

Sanskrit	*Old Irish*	*Gothic*	*O. H. German*	*Lithuanian*	*Russian* and *Polish*
sakha	cecht	hoha	huohili	szaka	socha

Then came the heavier plough, probably borrowed. Pliny refers to the big plough of the Rhætians, of east Switzerland and Illyria, with wheels, drawn by several heads of cattle "aratrum"; the parallels for the verb are:

Greek	*Latin*	*Irish*	*Gothic*	*Old Slavonic*	*Tocharian* [1]
ἀρόω	aro	airim	arja	oru	aren

For "sowing" we have:

Greek	*Latin*	*Gothic*	*Old Slavonic*	*Lithuanian*
ἵημι	sero	saia	seju	séju

The parallels for grains are:

"corn":

Sanskrit	*Latin*	*Old Irish*	*Old Slavonic*	*Old Prussian*
jirnas	granum	grán	zerno	syrna

"wheat":

Sanskrit	*Greek*	*Lithuanian*
pūras	πυρός	purai

and from a different root: [2]

Gothic	*Old Norse*	*Danish*	*O. H. German*	*Old English*
hwaiteis	hveite	hvede	weizzi	hwæte

"barley":

Latin	*Avestic*	*Armenian*	*Lettish*	*O. H. German*
hordeum	zars	gari	garsas	gerste

[1] Hoops, *op. cit.*, p. 506, gives:

O. H. German	*Old English*
pfluog	plog.

[2] *Ibid.*, p. 458.

The linguistic parallels are matched archæologically by the discovery of little stone hand-mills, especially in north Sweden and south Russia.

The Aryans before their dispersion therefore possessed a fairly high standard of economic culture based on pastoral pursuits and the beginnings of agriculture.

Relations with other races.

The fundamental point which must now be noticed is that nowhere, so far as our sources of information reach, does the Aryan race appear pure and isolated. It is never found by itself, but always on ground previously occupied by some other race. There is always therefore a mixture of races, and we have to take into account such elements as the Iberians, now represented by the Basques, the ancient Etruscans, the small, stout, stumpy, pre-Celtic race of Wales, and, in eastern and central Europe, the Finns. Often a population that from a political point of view seems to die, survives powerfully in language and the physical transmission of race. For example, the French do not possess the physical characteristics of the Gauls, the tall, fair-haired Aryans, but everywhere the small, dark, wiry type preponderates. The Welsh, the Irish, and the Highland Scots are thought to be typically Celtic, and yet among all these peoples we have to reckon with a strong infusion of pre-Aryan elements. Thus among the inhabitants of Britain, Cæsar noticed that it was a prevalent custom in the interior of the island for several brothers to have a common wife. Among the Picts [1] of Scotland and Ireland polyandry and descent through women were customary, and neither polyandry nor matrilineal institutions can be traced directly to Aryan usages. They are due, not to slow evolution from these, but to contamination arising from contact between an Aryan patriarchal people and primitive settlers whose construction of the family was different. The many stray evidences of matrilineal arrangements within the sphere of Aryan settlement do not necessarily imply that among the Aryans the matrilineal slowly developed into the patrilineal

Traces of matrilineal arrangements pre-Aryan.

[1] The name "Picts," "Picti," "the painted" is the Latin, not the vernacular name

system, but rather that there has been a collision of different tribes and that the influence of the vanquished has been asserted among the conquerors. The Aryans had certainly reached the patriarchal stage before their dispersion, and the few relics of ancient conditions, and of the influence assigned to the mother's brother, may be simply traces of matrilineal arrangements belonging to the older Iberian, Finnish or Dravidian settlers. The first discoverer of matrilineal institutions in Europe was Bachofen, and he lays special stress on a passage in Herodotus [1] referring to the Lycians of Asia Minor. The Lycians had a curious custom of taking their names from the mothers and not from the fathers.[2] They were a demonstrably mixed people, containing Aryan and non-Aryan elements. Matrilineal arrangements, due to contamination, not to slow development, were found also among the population in the neighbourhood of the Black Sea (cf. the legend of the Amazons), among the people of Locris, and at Athens under Kekrops.

Aryan organization patriarchal.

The central fact of Aryan culture is a patriarchal state of society. The nomenclature of parentage shows that all our principal expressions for members of the family were in existence five or six thousand years ago, with the interesting exception that there is no common name for "marriage." Each settlement seems to have adopted a different expression, that, for instance, in use among the Indians meaning "living together," and the Slavonic expression meaning "family." The absence of any common term is noted also by Aristotle. Otherwise all the principal "relationships" are represented in common in the Aryan languages. Thus the parallels for "father" are:

Family nomenclature.

Sanskrit	*Avestic*	*Tocharian*	*Armenian*
pita	pitar–	pacar	hair
Latin	*Greek*	*Old Irish*	*Gothic*
pater	πατήρ	athir	fadar

[1] Herodotus, I, ch. 78.
[2] Bachofen, *Das Mutterrecht* (1861), p. 1.

"mother":

Sanskrit	*Avestic*	*Tocharian*	*Armenian*	*Greek*
mātā	matar—	macar	mair	μήτηρ

Latin	*O. H. German.*	*Old Slavonic*	*Lettish*
mater	muotar	mati	mate

Similar words are found even outside the Aryan races, among Mongols and Turanians. There is another word also, for the wife, "the female head of the household," "she who has given birth to the child":

Sanskrit	*Tocharian*	*Greek*	
gnā	šen	(Bœotian)	βανα
		(Attic)	γυνή

Armenian	*Gothic*	*Old English*	*Old Irish*	*Old Slavonic*	*Old Prussian*
kin	qino	cwēn	ben	žena	genna

The parallels for "son" are:

Sanskrit	*Avestic*	*Tocharian*	*Gothic*	*Lithuanian*	*Old Slavonic*
sunus	hunus	še	sunus	sunus	syn

"daughter":

Sanskrit	*Avestic*	*Tocharian*	*Greek*
duhitā	dugedar	ckaćar	θυγάτηρ

Armenian	*Gothic*	*Old Slavonian*	*Lithuanian*
dustr	dauhtar	dshćer	dukté

"brother":

Sanskrit	*Avestic*	*Tocharian*	*Greek*[1]
bhrātā	brātā	pracar	φράτηρ

Latin	*Old Irish*	*Gothic*	*Old Slavonic*	*Lithuanian*
frater	bráthir	brothar	brat	broterélis

[1] ἀδελφός = Old Indian, *sagarbhyas.*

"sister":

Sanskrit	*Avestic*	*Armenian*	*Tocharian*
svasā	vahar	khoir	sar

Latin	*Gothic*	*Old Irish*	*Old Slavonic*	*Lithuanian*	*Old Prussian*
soror	swistar	siur	sestra	sesu	swestro

The hearth the centre and symbol of the united household.

As we get further from the fundamental notions the expressions are more varied. It is important to notice that, unlike the totemic system, there is no indication of a nomenclature based on class.[1]

The family is represented, not only in all its parts, but also as a whole whose centre is the hearth, the domestic fire. In the Vedic hymns there is mention of the fire on the heart—"*agni*" (Latin, *ignis,* Slavonic, *ogon*), and in Wales, "Whether the fire were of wood or turf, the hearth was swept out every night. The next thing was to single out one particular glowing ember, the 'seed of fire,' which was carefully restored to the hearth and covered up with the remaining ashes for the night. The morning process was to uncover the 'seed of fire,' to sweep out the ashes under which it was hid, and then deftly to place back the live ember on the hearth, piling over it the fuel for the new day's fire. This was the uncovering of the fire, which thus from year end to year end might never go out."[2] The hearth fire, therefore, symbolized the life of the generations, the worship of the ancestors of the household, and it was in conformity with this idea that the Greek colonists carried the fire from the mother-city to the new colony. The connection between the cult of the hearth and the cult of the ancestors lies in the fact that the ancestors, whose traditional cult forms the religious background of the family worship, are not taken indiscriminately; this place is reserved to those who have a definite connection with the

Ancestor worship limited to agnatic ancestors.

[1] Cf. DELBRÜCK, *Die indogermanischen Verwandtschaftsnamen.*

[2] SEEBOHM, *The Tribal System in Wales* (2nd ed., 1904), p. 92. Cf. *Hymne Orphique,* par. 84, quoted by FUSTEL DE COULANGES, *Cité Antique,* I, ch. iii.

household, that is, to agnates. The agnatic ancestors take the first place, and when the ancient Aryan—Indian, Greek or Roman,—made sacrifices and offered prayers to these ancestors, he had in view, let us say, his grandfather and great-grandfather on the father's side, who had lived and died by the house hearth, not those on his mother's side, though these were equally his ancestors. This is clear when we consider the ancient rules concerning tribal sacrifices. To begin with, Indian tribal sacrifices assume one of two shapes. Firstly the *pitaras*—the ancestors on the father's side—have to be propitiated by offerings of food designated *Pindapitriyajna, pinda,* meaning "bun," "cake" or "dough." Thus the *Sapindas* are the community of kinsmen bound to bring offerings of buns. In the second place there are the *samanodakas*—those who take part in common libations, or offerings of water (*udaka,* water), which are made to the ancestors by a secondary group.[1] In this second class may be seen the beginning of the recognition of the ancestors of the female side.

The essence of the ancestral cult is originally the propitiation of the ancestors of the household. Among the Greeks the *οἶκος* has to be kept up by the tradition of the ancestors, and thus organized on agnatic lines. The cognatic kin were to be found in other houses, for the house of the mother was not that into which she had married, but that into which she had been born.

In connection with this original ancestor worship of the household, there were some curious customs among the Romans, Lithuanians and Slavs. The Roman cult represented the household ancestry, *lares,* and though it is commonly pointed out that the *manes* also were worshipped, they were "good ghosts" in general, the more general protectors of the household, and the ancestors requiring the ancestral cult were the *lares familiares.* Among the Lithuanians this worship was visualized in the fact that in well-settled and ancestral households, a snake was kept in the

[1] SARVADHIKARI, *Principles of the Hindu Law of Inheritance* (1882), 31 ff.

corner and was deemed to represent the departed ancestors. The *paterfamilias,* the representative of the family tradition, brought food to this snake.[1] As regards the Germanic peoples, ancient examples are to be found on the linguistic side. For instance, in Scandinavian the same word, *erfa,* is used both for taking up an inheritance and for offering funeral prayers and rites, and *erf* means both "succession" and "funeral." Among the Slavs there were many quaint customs pointing to the fact that household ancestors were objects of veneration. Among the Russians *chur* distinctly indicated the household protector, the familiar god, the ghost of the ancestor. *Chur* as a popular exclamation is a kind of appeal for protection against evil spirits. *Chur mena* means " let *chur* protect me." Ancestor worship was connected with the boundaries of the household settlement; at the crossways, at Rome, urns containing the cinders of the corpse would be placed. Among the Russians it was customary to place wooden blocks, *churban,* as boundaries.[2] We ought not, therefore, to speak simply of "ancestor worship," but we must remember that Aryan customs point to the worship of the ancestors in the male line, the former rulers of the household.

Separate Aryan branches.

Now that the common traits of the united Aryan culture have been considered, their development in the separate races must be investigated. Our researches may have to be conducted on different lines. The whole history of the separate Aryan branches lies before us, in order that we should use it for comparative purposes. Certain precautions are necessary. When we begin to compare the situation between the various branches, the Indian, Greek, Roman, Teutonic and so on, we deal in turn with branches of the Aryan stock which have each taken up special positions, which have lived in particular conditions, unlike those of the other branches. Between the Indians, Teutons, Celts, etc., there are differences in climate, geography, mixture of races, conquests and other conditions, and, therefore, their develop-

1 SCHRADER, *Reallexikon,* s.v. Ahnenkult.
2 KLUCHEVSKY, *History of Russia,* I, 45 (Hogarth's transl.).

ment was bound to proceed on divergent lines. We cannot expect identical results, and we must always take into account the special conditions of economic, geographical and political development. The significant fact is that, in spite of profound differences in results, we do observe —especially in Family Law, and in that of Succession and Real Property—principles and rules that are varieties of the same leading ideas. There is a traditional and dialectic affinity, and, though we must make allowances for a variety of instances, we can yet treat the subject as one of connected development.

As regards the *Hindus*, three periods and three sources of information have to be considered. **Hindus.**

(1) In the *Vedic* period the Aryans had just occupied the basin of the Indus and the Punjab, and had not yet conquered the rest of the country. They were a pastoral people, constantly on the move, very primitive, very imaginative, expressing their religious and historical conceptions in the Vedic Hymns, which must be dated at about 2000 B.C.

(2) The *Dharmasutras* supply us with the juridical side of the picture and are commentaries on customary law. This period is the Middle Ages of the Hindus. They had moved to the Ganges and southwards and had conquered most of south India. The conquest of a population of different descent had resulted in a mixture of races, and in the beginning of *castes*. The differences between the *Arya-varna* and the *Dasya-varna* were developed in a rigid system of caste.

As for the *Avesta-Iranians*, the material is so scattered that it can be used only for occasional reference. **Avesta-Iranians.**

The principal fact about the *Greeks* and *Romans* is that their culture was a city culture, based on slavery. On this basis their upper class was established, thus forming a contrast to the caste system. There were profound differences in character and development between the Greeks and the Romans, the former being sensitive, imaginative and highly poetical, while the latter were logical and conservative by temperament. Roman Law is the best known **Greeks and Romans.**

part of Græco-Italian law, but it is, as a matter of fact, not really representative of the archaic form of tribal law. In early times it was apt to draw extreme and rigid consequences from principles, while later on it became the mould for the civil law of the world. Its origins have therefore to be studied in constant connection with Greek Law.

Celts. The *Celtic* group is less well represented in ancient tradition, but some information can be gathered from classical writers such as Cæsar and Strabo. A vast body of mediæval custom has been preserved by the Welsh Laws and the Brehon Tracts of Ireland. Besides, there are even now tribal survivals in certain Celtic districts. For instance, the clans of the Scottish Highlands still show vestiges of tribal organization, and the tribal system of the Welsh, which goes back to very early times, was fully described by the English conquerors in the fourteenth century.

Germanic races. Among the *Germanic* races, on the contrary, tribal arrangements were the rare exception, for when these tribes appear in history, they are constantly on the move and intermix with Romanized populations.

Slavs. The *Slavs* present excellent materials as regards the tribal system, but these are not evenly distributed in the different branches. The western Slavs, Poles, Czechs and Wends were drawn into the vortex of Teutonic migrations and much disturbed by conquests. They present, therefore, a mixed civilization strongly tinged by Roman and Germanic influences. The eastern and southern Slavs, on the contrary, present excellent examples of tribal arrangements. This is especially true of the southern Slavs: the Serbians especially continued to live under a tribal organization up to the nineteenth century. Their settlements of tribal clans may be compared with those of the Scottish Highlands. Settlements in a mountainous country naturally get fixed, and a small, secluded, easily defended valley may retain stiff tribal customs for thousands of years.

The Russians, though mixed with Finnish, Turkish and Tartar tribes, are predominantly Slavonic, and in the ancient traits of their land law show traces of tribal arrangements.

All these peculiarities will have to be taken into account in estimating the influence of tribal principles in the history of Aryan nations.

CHAPTER V

THE PATRIARCHAL HOUSEHOLD

The father the centre of the Aryan family.

OUR analytical survey of the elements of family life was necessary to prevent misconception and must be regarded as an introduction to the questions now before us. We shall have to deal now with a synthetic combination of these elements in the shape of the Aryan patriarchal system. The centre of this family is definitely the father, the "husband," in the ancient sense the "householder." In the Roman term, *paterfamilias,* the ancient genitive in *as* indicates that the word has been preserved in an archaic form, probably current about 1500 B.C. The power of the father (*patria potestas*) in the Roman family is well known: according to Gaius it was an unbending, absolute rule, so that the father could even put his son to death (*ius vitæ et necis*). His power over property was equally unlimited. As long as the father was alive, the grown-up son was not *sui iuris* and any property he was allowed by his father to manage was regarded as *peculium,* not different from the objects possessed on sufferance by a slave. These classical traits are familiar to every one, but as presented by Roman Law, they were exaggerated consequences of principles admitting of a more liberal application. It would be impossible to say that the statements of ancient writers on the subject are untrue, but they point to practices which were not in force among other branches of the race. The paternal authority was recognized among all the Aryans, but not to the same extent as among the Romans. As Gaius puts it, *fere enim nulli alii sunt homines qui talem in filios suos habent potestatem qualem nos habemus.*[1] With the Greeks the authority of the father is said to have been curtailed by Solon, Pittakos

Patria potestas.

[1] I, 55.

of Lesbos, and Charondas.[1] Indeed the whole conception of the relationship of the Greek father to his household differed from that of the Romans.[2] The father of the latter may be compared to an absolute king, while the former acknowledged the reciprocal rights and duties of a constitutional king. The Roman father had also to recognize moral and religious duties (*Fas*), but he was not answerable to any secular power for the exercise of his rule. Reciprocity was characteristic of the Greek system, and this has found emphatic expression in later law. The aged parent could claim support from the son, but his right of *γηροτροφία* could be established only if he had given the son a proper education.[3] If he had neglected his offspring or abused his rights, he could not claim support. From the Roman point of view such a reciprocity as regards rights and duties was unthinkable.

Again, as to *emancipation,* even in later Roman Law the son could be emancipated only by the death or by the volun-

[1] DIONYSIUS OF HALICARNASSUS, *Antiq. Romanarum* (Teubner), II, p. 26: "What therefore was to the advantage of women Romulus ordained by law . . . but as regards respect and uprightness on the part of children, with the intention that they should reverence their fathers and do and say everything which they should bid . . . there was a great divergence from our laws. For the founders of the Greek States gave instructions that for a certain short period children should be carefully ruled by their fathers, some until they were two years beyond the time of reaching manhood, while others remained youths till their names were inscribed in the registers of the public buildings, as I understand from the legislation of Solon, Pittakos and Charondas. . . . In regard to the punishment of the children, they ordered that, if they disobeyed their fathers, they were not to be driven from home . . . and not to be disinherited. . . . The Roman lawgiver, however, gave absolute power over the son to the father during his whole lifetime, even to the extent of shutting him up, flogging him, seizing the fruits of his labour, and deliberately choosing to put him to death, even if the son happened to be occupied in public business, subjected to examination in order to fill the highest public offices, and praised for his public distinction."

[2] Cf ARISTOTLE, *Politics,* I, p. 52 (p. 1259 b), Jowett's transl.: "A husband and father rules over his wife and children, both free, but the rule differs; the rule over his children being a royal, over his wife a constitutional rule. . . . The rule of a father over his children is royal, for he receives both love and respect due to age, exercising a kind of royal power. . . . A king is the natural superior of his subjects, but he should be of the same kin or kind with them, and such is the relation of elder and younger, of father and son." Cf. BEAUCHET, *Droit privé athénien,* II, pp. 76 ff.

[3] LIPSIUS, *Recht und Rechtsverfahren,* p. 343.

tary surrender of authority on the part of the father. In case of mental derangement, the insane or spendthrift could be put under a curatorship,[1] but otherwise the authority of the father normally ceased with his life. In Greek law the father's authority and economic sway came to an end when the son attained his civic majority—at eighteen years of age, on his enrolment in the armed force of the Commonwealth.[2] Tacitus mentions a similar view among the Germanic tribes, namely, that the sons became members of the republic when they took up arms, generally at about the age of twelve or fourteen. They were then no longer subject to the father's authority.[3]

The rule appears in a mitigated form in the history of other nations, but there is a characteristic reminder of the ancient full rule in the father's right to expose a child, which is found among all Aryans—Hindus, Greeks, Celts, Teutons, and Slavs. The right was used largely in the case of daughters, but also, though less frequently, in the case of sons. Thus in Sparta the Ephors had to decide whether a child was to be left alive or to be exposed. It is interesting to see that the decision had come to rest with a board and not with the particular parent. In the Greek system generally the child had to be definitely recognized by the father himself who performed the solemn act of taking it up (ἀναίρεσις), and carrying it round the hearth (αμφιδρόμια). After that ceremony the child became thereby a protected member of the household and could not be exposed.

Treatment of aged parents.

Another tendency, not derived from the state of filial dependence, but the outcome of the wish to organize the family as strongly as possible under the natural leadership of an efficient householder runs to some extent counter to the idea of *patria potestas.* What happened when the father was old, decrepit, incapable? Such old people either retired from active management and were left to vegetate until they died, or they were put to death. In the Vedic

1 M. VOIGT, *Die Zwölf Tafeln,* II, p. 729.
2 DARESTE. etc., *Inscriptions jurisdiques grecques,* I, p. 462.
3 *Germania,* XIII.

Hymns there is mention of a father exposed by his children.[1] Even in Rome, there are some reminiscences of the existence of a category of old men doomed to destruction. Festus the lexicographer, mentions that a man of sixty was incapable of any useful activity and should be thrown into the river.[2] The expression "de ponte," was understood in later times to mean "Voting Bridge," but the tradition as to the "removal" of aged parents by drowning is nevertheless a characteristic trace of ancient folklore. There is widespread evidence of a similar treatment among Celts, Teutons, Lithuanians and Slavs. The Baltic Slavs, or Wends, for example, got rid of their old men by placing them on a piece of bark, and thrusting them down into ravines in winter to die of cold and starvation. In a modified form the casting off of the authority of the aged parents has survived among the Norwegians, with whom a special house or room is constructed for the "pensioned" old people. Their allowance is called their *Fødéraad*. They renounce their authority, are given food, and live in retirement, while their sons take over the command and arrangement of the household. These customs indicate that the father's authority might be modified by considerations of household expediency by extraordinary measures. It

[1] *Rig Veda*, VIII, 51, 2.

[2] P. FESTI, *De verborum significatione* (Teubner), p. 66: "Depontani senes appellabantur, qui sexagenarii de ponte deiciebantur," and p. 450, Cf. LEWIS and SHORT'S Latin Dictionary, *Sexagenarius:* "Men sixty years of age were no longer admitted to vote in the saepta, and, if they attempted to enter, were thrust back from the bridge leading to them; whence arose the proverb, *Sexagenarios de ponte.* (Many Romans, at an early period, erroneously referred this expression to a religious usage, and even to original human sacrifices.)" *Varro ap. Non,* 523-21: "Quum in quintum gradum pervenerunt, atque habebant sexaginta annos, tum denique erant a publicis negotiis liberi atque otiosi. Ideo in proverbium quidam putant venisse ut diceretur, Sexagenarios de ponte deici oportere, id est, quod suffragium non ferant, quod per pontem ferebatur" But see also Ovid, *Fasti,* V, 621:

"Tum quoque priscorum virgo simulacra virorum
Mittere roboreo scirpea ponte solet.
Corpora post decies senos qui credidit annos
Missa neci, sceleris crimine damnat avos."

CICERO, *Pro Sex. Roscio,* 35: "Habeo etiam dicere quem contra morem maiorum minorem annis lx de ponte in Tiberim deiecerit."

was not an absolute right, but a means towards an end, namely, the maintenance of the family.

Manus mariti.

The power of the husband over the wife was not essentially different from that of the father over the children, and the *manus mariti* also expresses the fact that the lord of the household was considered as a proprietor as well as a ruler. This idea of appropriation is clearly manifested in three features.

Ownership shown in the *Suttee.*

The first of these is the *Suttee.* The burning of the widow with the deceased husband was practised in India till recent times, and it was suppressed only by the interference of the British Government. The notion at the root of it is that the wife so belongs to her husband that she cannot outlive him, but must follow him to the other world. It is sometimes said that the custom is the result of an exceedingly strong consciousness of the moral tie between husband and wife, but it may be noticed that the tie was not regarded as reciprocal, and the husband never died with the wife. The practice was by no means peculiar to Indians, but existed among other branches of the Aryan race. Herodotus [1] noted it among the Thracians of the Danube region, where wives were put to death on the decease of their husbands. It was prevalent also among Slavonic tribes: Bonifacius in the eighth century in a letter to one of his colleagues, insisted on what he thought a proof of the strong moral feeling of devotion and duty on the part of the Slavonic Wends who, though in other respects a cruel people, showed an amount of affection and devotion between husband and wife that might serve as an example to Christians.[2] Further evidence comes from the description of

[1] HERODOTUS, V, 5, Rawlinson's translation (1862), III, p. 178: "The Thracians observe the following customs. Each man among them has several wives; and no sooner does a man die than a sharp contest ensues among the wives upon the question, which of them all the husband loved most tenderly; the friends of each eagerly plead on her behalf, and she to whom the honour is adjudged, after receiving the praises of both men and women, is slain over the grave by the hand of her next of kin, and then burned with her husband."

[2] MIGNE, *Patrologia*, series II, lxxxix, 760: "Winedi, quod est foedissimum et deterrimum genus hominum . . . mulier, viro proprio mortuo, vivere recusat . . . ut in una strue pariter ardeat cum viro suo."

the funeral of a Russian chief which was attended by Ibn Fadhlan, an Arab traveller who visited south Russia about 900 A.D.[1] He tells us, among other things, that when the pyre was constructed and the dead chief laid on it, one of his wives was slain and placed beside him.

Ownership shown in partnership of wives.

The custom, however, was not the absolute consequence of the idea of *manus mariti,* and the fluidity of the institution must be noticed. Ancient rules and customs are often subject to oscillations of feeling. In the beginning they are more indistinct and neutral, but later they get settled in a stricter form. For instance, there is proof that the Suttee in India, where it was most prevalent, had not crystallized in Rig Veda times, about 2000 B.C., but was still only in formation. One of the Hymns [2] is composed of incantations and prayers connected with a funeral: the brother or son of the deceased takes the lead in the ceremony and addresses the gods and the community around him, and tells the widow to rise from the funeral pyre. Thus, although the widow has shown her grief by lying down by the side of her husband, she is not actually burned with him.

The second feature in which we find the ownership of the husband expressed, is the fact that curious habits of partnership as regards wives are recorded in Aryan lands. The explanation from sexual jealousy does not apply: that feeling is counterbalanced by other considerations. As regards the ancient Slavs, Christian missionaries and writers mention with horror that among the Baltic Slavs marriages between a woman and a father and his son were frequent; but this led mostly to cohabitation in succession, so that the wife was married to the father and inherited like property by the son.[3] Customs exactly analogous to this passage of the wife by inheritance are to be found among other primitive tribes.

Another consequence is the raising of progeny by substi-

[1] See *post*, p. 275.
[2] *Rig Veda*, X, 18, 8.
[3] *Codex Diplom.* (Stettin, 1748), pp. 286, 290: " . . . Cum enim pater aliquam uxorem de communi pecunia sibi et filio emerat, sibi pater hactenus servavit, ut mortuo patre uxor eius devolveretur ad filium, sicut alia hereditas de bonis communibus comparata."

tution, called in India, *Nyioga*. By this, when the wife is barren or the husband is unable to produce offspring, it is possible, and right, for him to employ a substitute. All the ancient Indian Law Books, the Dharmasutras,[1] admit this, and a protest against the practice is found only in Âpastamba.[2] Any opposition would be overborne by considerations of property and family power.

One more fact must be noticed. In the Aryan household there is emphatically no idea of strict monogamy. The Aryans were not polygamous as a rule, because the keeping of several wives is expensive, but they had no objection to the practice when economically possible. It is difficult to draw a definite line between the Mohammedan practice and the situation among the Aryans in the beginning of history: the development of monogamy was gradual, and it began at an early stage among those who had small means. The poor regarded a wife as a helper and beast of burden, and monogamy was imposed on them by economic considerations. However, the fact that the rich had full licence to take many wives shows that there was nothing in the juridical essence of the institution to prevent polygamy. Harald Harfagr, Vladimir of Russia, Samo of Bohemia, Meshko of Poland are all credited with many wives.[3] In the Indian codes it is expressly stated that any number up to ten may be kept, and four wives are attributed to a king, though the first is

[1] E.g., *Nârada*, XII, 55 ff.; *Manu*, IX, 31 ff., 167.

[2] *Âpastamba*, II, 10, 27, 2-5.

[3] For the custom among the Persians see HERODOTUS, I, 135 (Rawlinson's translation, I, p. 221): "Each of them has several wives and a still larger number of concubines."

The Wends renounced polygamy on their conversion to Christianity. Cf. HERBORD, *Dial.* II, p. 18: "Vos, qui usque ad haec tempora non Christiani sed pagani fuistis, sacramentum coniugii non habuistis, quia fidem uni thoro non servastis sed . . . plures habuistis uxores. Quod deinceps nobis non licebit. Si quis ergo in vobis est qui plures habuerat uxores ante baptismum, nunc unam de illis, quae sibi magis placet, eligat." Cf. *ibid.*, p. 22: *Cod. Diplom.*, 1249, p. 290; EBBO, *Vita Ottonis*, II, pp. 9, 12, 34. "Abdicta coniugum pluralitate." For the custom among the Thracians see STRABO, VII, 297.

the chief one and in the ritual of household prayer and sacrifice the *Patni* is mentioned, as a rule, in the singular. In the Germanic custom it seems to have been unusual to keep several wives, but, according to Tacitus, the nobles were proud to be able to afford two or three wives.[1] In the age of the Norse invasions it was the recognized thing for Icelanders to have two wives, one at home and one on their travels.

In the beginning, marriage was not considered a tie between one pair of conjoined mates only, to the exclusion of other relations, at any rate on the side of the husband. A consequence of this attitude is seen in the law of adultery, in which the whole stress is laid on the rights of the husband.[2] This conception, indeed, has had an influence which has continued till recent and even present times. Even now the husband and the wife do not stand on an equal footing in this respect.[3]

Evolution of *contract* in marriage.

We must now approach the interesting problem of the part played by the notion of contract in marriage: on this point there are still many misconceptions. Is marriage as constituted in Aryan legal custom to be described as essentially a *contract* between husband and wife, even though the preponderance is given to the husband? The answer seems to be that contract is not a necessary feature of Aryan marriage in general, but that it was gradually evolved from loose unions. Indeed, we have the curious spectacle of an institution which begins by being entirely fluid, but settles down more and more on a basis of contract with reciprocal rights and duties. The process is illustrated by sufficient evidence and the

[1] *Germania*, XVII: "Nam prope soli barbarorum singulis uxoribus contenti sunt, exceptis admodum paucis, qui non libidine sed ob nobilitatem plurimis nuptiis ambiuntur."

[2] CATO in AULUS GELLIUS, *Noctium Atticarum* X, 23 (Teubner): "Verba Marci Catonis . . . In adulterio uxorem tuam si prehendisses, sine iudicio impune necares; illa te, si adulterares sive tu adulterarere, digito non auderet contingere, neque ius est."

[3] Adultery on the part of the husband does not entitle the wife to claim divorce, although adultery on the part of the wife is sufficient ground for the husband to claim it.

causes producing the evolution may be discerned without difficulty.

The first point to notice is that in most cases we have to deal not with one kind of marriage, but with several kinds. Three groups of peoples may be especially considered: (1) the ancient Russians described in Nestor's Chronicle (twelfth century); (2) the Aryan Indians as described in the Dharmasutras and the Commentaries; (3) the ancient Romans.

(1) Among the ancient Russians.

(1) In such questions formal chronology is of no importance, and we may begin with the ancient Russians. Their chronicler, Nestor, describes a most archaic state of things. The different tribes which afterwards formed Russia possessed a variety of customs ranging from some which correspond to an exceedingly low standard of culture to others resembling Christian institutions. The Chronicler says that the Drevlians lived in forests like animals. They knew no marriage, but cohabited in the manner of beasts, making no distinction between near relations. This description may perhaps be superficial and exaggerated, but it is certainly not invented at random. Among the tribes of the Dnieper basin, the Viaticzi, the Radimiczi, the Kriviczi, and the Severians, marriage unions were somewhat more permanent, but still very informal. When the youths of the tribes congregated for games between the villages, they captured and carried off the girls. Such marriages by capture in connection with sports and festivities often develop from elopements, and may be prearranged by mutual understanding. The Polians followed a different practice: the bride was not fetched by the bridegroom, but was conducted at the close of the day to his home, and next morning presents were brought which were given *with* her, according to one reading, or, according to another, *for* her. They served therefore either as a purchase price or as a dowry, but the main point is that there was already an established understanding not only between the bride and bridegroom, but between the kinsmen of the parties.

(2) The forms of marriage among the Indians present a

(2) Among the Indians-

wide range of possibilities.[1] Eight forms are mentioned in the Sutras: [2]

(i) *Kshastria vi vaha* (*rakshasa* or devil's marriage) was specially attributed to the warriors and involved violence and capture.

(ii) *Paisaca vivaha* was not what we should call marriage at all, but rape leading to marital union. Seduction was employed, or the woman might be drugged. It was strongly deprecated by Brahmins, but took place sometimes among other castes.

(iii) *Svayamvara vivaha* was also chiefly practised among the warriors. It was a union arranged by agreement between the bride and bridegroom as a result of a competition of suitors. The epic songs give graphic descriptions of what happened in such a case. Sometimes the daughter of a king is proclaimed a bride, and the king invites her suitors to present themselves and to bid for her hand, in the manner of the suitors in "The Merchant of Venice." There might be competitions in solving riddles, or jousting. Personal consent was much to the fore and the choice of the girl was supported by her parents.

(iv) *Gandharva vivaha* is a love match, again a variety of personal union on wider grounds. It was practised not only by warriors and princes but by all classes and castes. The union sometimes took place in spite of obstacles, and commonly involved elopement.

All these four forms were most commonly used by the warriors, while the following two were devised to suit priests:

(v) the *Brahma vivaha* is a religious marriage in which the stress is laid on prayers and sacrifices.

(vi) *Daiva vivaha* is a particular development of the preceding form. In this case the priest who offers sacrifice is presented with a girl to be his wife.

[1] Jolly, *Recht und Sitte*, pp. 51 ff.

[2] Cf. the *Laws of Manu*, III, 20-35. *Sacred Books of the East*, XXV [1886], pp. 79-82): "The rite of Brahman (Brâhma), that of the gods (Daiva), that of the Rishis (Arsha), that of Pragâpati (Prâgâpatya), that of the Asuras (Asura), that of the Gandharvas (Gândharva), that of the Rakshasas (Râkshasa), and that of the Pisâkas (Paisâka)."

It may be added that the solemn ritual of this kind of marriage spread to other forms, so that now the Brahmin ceremonies are generally used in a ceremonial marriage, no matter what the caste of the bride and bridegroom may be.

The last two forms are evidently meant to suit less important people, the "plebs," as it were,—*vaisyas* and *sudras*—and this was evidently their most conspicuous feature:

(vii) *Asura vivaha* is emphatically marriage by purchase. The normal price of the bride is mentioned as a yoke of oxen, but among princes and nobles it might be increased, and a hundred cows are mentioned sometimes as presented to the parents.

(viii) *Pragapatya vivaha* closely resembles *asura vivaha*, but in this case it is the bridegroom himself who acts instead of the kinsmen.

The Brahmins were opposed to these last two forms, but they were so strongly rooted in popular custom that they could not be abolished.

It is evidently impossible to regard all these forms as varieties of one and the same contract. We have to recognize that marriage as a fluid institution shaped very differently according to circumstances. It may be due to violence or to a love match, or to a transaction on the part of the parents based on purchase.

(3) Among the Romans.

(3) The four forms practised among the Romans are described with some precision by Gaius:[1]

(i) the *confarreatio* marriage may be compared with the *Brahma vivaha* of India. It was the usual form among Patricians and involved ceremonies and sacrifice. Its essence was the transference of the bride from one household and cult to another with her personal consent.

(ii) *Coemptio* marriage was the most common form prevalent among the people and centred round purchase.

(iii) Marriage *usu* was a concubinate which by the prescription of a year and a day became recognized and established as a permanent union. There were two possibilities, however; the marriage might be accepted and confirmed on the same lines as the recognized *coemptio* form,

[1] I, 108-15.

or the wife might safeguard her personal independence by absenting herself from the house for three nights.

(iv) A fourth variety was constituted by marriage without *manus:* it seems that in this case there was from the first an agreement to renounce the *manus*, and marriage amounted to a personal arrangement for marital union.

Concubinate.

From the above enumeration, it is clear that it was difficult to draw a distinction between marriage without *manus* and concubinate. The legal distinctions between the concubine and the wife were chiefly the result of later development. There was indeed no reason for strict distinction. Certainly the Roman matron married by *confarreatio* or *coemptio* was not a concubine, but her marriage was the most advanced type of sacramental marriage recognized by Roman Law. On the other hand, the woman married *usu* before the year and a day was completed, and the woman married without *manus* were very similar to concubines. The cases in which concubinate shades off into marriage are important and interesting. Valuable evidence comes from the Greek Law, but it is supported by customary practices which may be observed even now among backward Aryans. For instance, the Ossetes, a Caucasian tribe descended from the Alani, who were driven into the mountains by the Huns in the fourth century A.D., even now have a curious practice of legal concubinate. The concubine (*Nomoulouss*) is only one degree lower than the legitimate wife. A definite price is set on her which, however, is less than that of the fully qualified wife.[1]

The Greek view can be illustrated in a fragment of an ancient law assigned to Dracon (lawgiver of Athens about 621 B.C.) which has been preserved to us in a speech of Demosthenes (*c. Aristostrat.* § 55).[2] This law enacts that a person who slays a man found in flagrant adultery with the wife of the accused, or with his concubine joined to him for the purpose of rearing free children ἢ ἐπὶ δάμαρτι . . . ἢ

[1] KOVALEVSKY, *Coutume contemporaine*, 166.

[2] Cf. Euktemon's threat, ISAEUS, on the estate of Philoktemon, §§ 21, 22 (W. WYSE, *The Speeches of Isaeus* (1904), Or. vi).

ἐπὶ παλλακῇ ἣν ἂν ἐπ' ἐλευθέροις παισὶν ἔχῃ), could not be punished, for though he had committed homicide, he had done so under the greatest provocation. Thus a concubine was placed next to a wife as regards fidelity to her mate.

There are also certain facts which show that from the position of a concubine a woman could be raised by economic ties and by usage to the actual standing of a wife. As we have already seen, the *matrimonium usu,* as described by Gaius,[1] is a case in point. It implies that two persons who have cohabited for a year and a day are deemed to be connected by marriage. Evidently the economic factor was most important. There was a corresponding Scandinavian practice, as is apparent from Valdemar's law of Jutland, according to which three winters sharing table and bed, lock and key, made a concubine a legitimate wife with claims to property; the children would be legitimate in this case.[2]

Handfast marriages.

From the north of England and Scotland come similar cases, which open up a most interesting prospect in comparative law. Here we find so-called *handfast* marriages in direct contradiction to marriage in Church. The cases recorded are late, but are not less interesting on that account, for they show how far the primitive customs of *matrimonium usu* had struck root in a fairly civilized community, and even led to legal decisions fully recorded in the fifteenth and sixteenth centuries. For instance, in 1471 there was a suit [3] between a person claiming the earldom of Murray, and the husband of a lady who also claimed the earldom in her own right. Her claim rested on the supposition that there were no legal male heirs. From the feudal and from the ecclesiastical point of view there was no doubt as to the absence of male offspring of a union recognized by the Church. The rival claim came from a man who claimed in right of a marriage celebrated not in Church but in the customary way of handfasting: he was the son of

[1] I, 111.
[2] *Jyske lov,* I, ch. 27.
[3] Robert Lindsay of Pitscottie, *The History and Chronicles of Scotland* (Scottish Text Society, 1899), I, p. 64.

one Isobel, who had married the former earl (the father of both claimants) by a handfast marriage. Troth had been pledged in the presence of witnesses, and the transaction was regarded as valid, so that regular cohabitation ensued. In the eyes of Church and Law the son was illegitimate and had no claim, but according to customary law he was the fully qualified heir by handfast marriage.

In 1509 the earldom of Sutherland was involved in a similar suit.[1] The offspring of a handfast marriage, Alexander of Sutherland, claimed the earldom "as one lawfully descended from his father Earl John the third; because, as he alleged, his mother was *handfasted* and fianced to his father." He was opposed by Adam of Gordon, the husband of his sister, who, on account of the handfast marriage, did not dare to press the matter, but made an agreement by which Alexander was bought off and renounced his claim.[2]

The marriage between the Earl of Angus and Margaret Tudor of England seems to have been dissolved on the ground that a previous union by handfasting had been formed between Earl Angus and the Lady of Trackquayre.[3]

In 1482 an indenture was made between "Lauchlane M'yntossich of Galeway and Donalde Angus M'yntossich. . . . And als sone as ye saide castell beys tane be ye saide Donalde, the saide Lauchlane sal gar incontinent, but ony langer delay, handfast Margret, his saide dochter, with the saide Donalde, and ly with him as scho war his lauchfull wiff; Ande als sone as the dispensacione cumys hame, the saide Donalde is oblist incontinent, but ony langer delay, to mary and spous the saide Margret, and to halde her in

1 Sir Robert Gordon, *The Genealogical History of the Earldom of Sutherland* (1813), p. 95.

2 "This renunciation was maid by Alexander, the bastard, judiciallie, in presence of the shirreff of Inverness, the 25th. day . . . of July, the forsaid yeir 1509." The deed of renunciation runs, ". . . quod ipse Alexander iure suo in et ad dictum comitatum in favorem Elizabeth Sutherland, heredumque suorum, pro certa compositione renunciaret, salvo tamen sibi Alexandro iure successionis, si contigerit de successione heredum Elizabeth penitus deficere." (Quoted by Sir W. Fraser, *The Sutherland Book* [1892], III, pp. 41-43.)

3 *Calendar of Scottish State Papers*, I, 1547-63, pp. 690, 694; E. W. Robertson, *Historical Essays*, p. 175, "Handfasting."

honour and worschip at all his power as his weddit wiff, for all the days of his lyff."[1]

We are told by Skene that among chieftains it was a very prevalent custom to give their daughters in handfast marriage, which "consisted in a species of contract between two chiefs, by which it was agreed that the heir of the one should live with the heir of the other as her husband for twelve months and a day. If in that time the lady became a mother, or proved to be with child, the marriage became good in law, even although no priest had performed the marriage ceremony in due form; but should there not have occurred any appearance of issue, the contract was considered at an end, and each party was at liberty to marry or handfast with any other."[2]

In a description of Scotch marriage rites given by Pennant, we notice the interesting variation that the contract confirmed by joining hands is made, not between the bride and the bridegroom, but between the bride's father and the bridegroom.[3]

Handfast marriage was not, however, peculiar to Scotland, and there are cases of it in the charters of Ripon and the records of the courts of York Cathedral. It was the secular preliminary to Church marriage, and definite formulæ were in use. In a Ripon case in 1471, witnesses told exactly what happened. A certain Margaret performed handfast marriage with two persons in one year, and a trial for the possession of the wife took place between the two. She confessed, and the one who had hand-

[1] *The Family of Rose of Kilravock* (Spalding Club, 1848), p. 147; cf. p. 36. I am indebted for this interesting notice to Professor J. A. Smith.

[2] W. F. Skene, *The Highlanders of Scotland*, ed. by A. MacBain (1902), p. 108. Cf. Sir Walter Scott's *Monastery*.

[3] Thomas Pennant, *Tour in Scotland*, 1769, II, pp. 205-06: "The courtship of the Highlander has these remarkable circumstances attending it: after privately obtaining the consent of the Fair, he formally demands her of her father. The Lover and his friends assemble on a hill allotted for that purpose in every parish, and one of them is despatched to obtain permission to wait on the daughter: if he is successful, he is again sent to invite the father and his friends to ascend the hill . . . the Lover advances, takes his future father-in-law by the hand and then plights his troth, and the Fair one is surrendered up to him."

fasted her first carried her off.[1] Again, at Easingwold in 1484 a man says, "Here I take the, Margaret, to my *handfast* wif, to hold and to have, at bed and at burd, for farer for lather, for better for wars, in sekenes and in heil, to dethe us depart, if holy kirk it will ordand, and thereto plight I the my trowth."[2]

Handfast marriage was based on consent, led to a kind of preliminary trial, and could be dissolved. At the same time, it was regarded as a *wedding,* and in the York Charters[3] the term "wedded wife" alternates with "handfast wife." "Wedded" means, of course, "bound" or "tied" by a contractual pledge, and so does "handfast."

The practice of "marriage on trial" may be further traced in Scandinavian, Germanic and Celtic customs. Thus in certain rural districts west of the Rhine, there was a practice of concluding a marriage which was on trial for a year. If there was offspring, the union became a regular marriage for life, but otherwise it was dissolved.[4] In Scandinavia, in the formula of Swedish marriage, the term was *at festa Konu* (i.e. to get a wife by contract). This marriage was not always necessarily for life, but might be only a temporary arrangement.[5] In ancient Ireland *coibchè* means the purchase of a wife by agreement. The arrangement usually lasted for a year, from May 1st or August 1st, and was set on foot especially at the Fairs of Lug in Ulster and Carman in Leinster.[6] For ancient Wales we have the testimony of Giraldus Cambrensis: "Matrimoniorum autem onera, nisi expertis antea cohabitatione, commixtione, morum qualitate, et praecipue fecunditate, subire non solent. Proinde et puellas, sub certo parentibus pecuniae pretio, et resipiscendi poena statuta,

1 *Acts of the Chapter of the Collegiate Church of SS. Peter and Wilfrid, Ripon, 1452-1506* (Surtees Society, LXIV, 1875), p. 159 ff.
2 *Ibid.*, p. 162, note i.
3 *Loc. cit.*
4 H. SCHURTZ, *Altersklassen und Männerbünde* (Berlin, 1902), p. 91.
5 AMIRA, *Nordgermanisches Obligationenrecht,* I, pp. 536 ff. The formula of Uplandslaga, p. 538.
6 H. D'ARBOIS DE JUBAINVILLE, *Cours de littérature celtique* (1895), VII, pp. 310 ff. Cf. O'DONOVAN, *Book of Rights* (1847), p. 243, note.

non ducere quidem in primis sed quasi conducere, antiquus in hac gente mos obtinuit."[1]

These cases are not curiosities of law, but are the outcome of the ancient conception that the relations between the two sexes need not be permanent, but can remain fluid. Sexual jealousy and chastity, as we know them, did not play a great part, and the background was entirely different from that of the modern Christian marriage leading to a permanent settlement.

Marriage by capture.

There are some generally known forms of marriage which have left more distinct traces in legal literature. The variety of forms in Hindu and Roman Law have already been noticed, and that of marriage by capture reappears, at least as a ceremony, in nearly all rites. One of the standing ceremonies in Irish custom was the meeting of the two parties of kinsmen as if in hostile conflict, and the throwing of bolts at each other before joining the wedding procession. These bolts were merely of light wood but they represented the spears of the original fight.

Marriage by purchase.

Marriage by purchase, the *coemptio* of Roman Law, is well established as the most common form. At first sight it seems exceedingly brutal, as if the woman were treated as a slave or an animal. Some notion of this kind underlies certain of the facts under discussion, but it is not the principal one. The object of the transaction was in reality not a person, but power, *manus* or *mund*. The most explicit commentary on this principle is supplied by Scandinavian law. The very name of a legitimately married wife in old Norse Law, *mundi kjöbt,* implies that the legal wife is one whose *mund* has been purchased. In Sweden, the passage of *mund* was effected by donation, "gift": hence the Scandinavian expression for marriage—*giftarmal.* The important point is that *mund* has to be transferred, and that this legal passage of power marks the line between concubinate and marriage. Where the formal transference of power had taken place, legitimate marriage was effected at once, while

[1] GIRALDUS CAMBRENSIS, *Descriptio Kambriae,* lib. II, cap. vi. (*Rolls Series, Giraldi Cambrensis Opera,* VI, p 213).

in the case of informal cohabitation it might be only brought about by a kind of customary prescription. Thus legal marriage is *prima facie* distinguished from concubinate by the element of the transference of power.

We have to ask next: who transfers power? The gist of the legal situation lies in the passage of power from one authoritative person to another. The view that the woman sells herself—*coemptionem fecit*—has been supported by reference to the forms of Roman marriage,[1] but the modernized use of the active form—*fecit*—is too slight a foundation for a theory according to which the bride would appear as both the subject and the object of the transaction. In normal cases the person to effect the transfer is the father, or, failing him, a brother or agnatic guardian. In Greece the subject of the transfer is κύριος. Thus marriage is originally not a transaction between husband and wife, but between the bride's guardian or father and the guardian or father of the bridegroom.

Distinction between *sponsalia* and *nuptiae*.

One fundamental consequence of the fact that the marriage was a contract between the guardians was the duplication of ceremonies and the distinction between betrothal and final marriage. This was fully expressed in the contrast between *sponsalia* and *nuptiae* of Roman Law. The *sponsalia* was the contract concluded between the guardians. The formulæ used on that occasion are frequently mentioned in ancient comedies of Plautus and Terence. Questions and answers were matched: *Spondesne*, "do you promise to give your daughter in marriage?"—*Spondeo*, "I promise,"[2] This was the betrothal of primitive law, traces of which survive even now in the modern ceremony of the "giving away" of the bride. The *nuptiae* consisted in conducting the bride to the house of the bridegroom; after the procession they join hands in front of the hearth. Here the personal element is very prominent. In the ancient Roman ceremony the bride, on the giving of hands, says *ubi tu Gaius, ibi ego Gaia*. This

1 KARLOWA, *Rechtsgeschichte*, 158 ff.

2 COSTA, in the *Bulletino dell' Instituto di Diritto Romano*, II, 28 ff.

formula expresses the fact that henceforth the two are joined as one person. It is sometimes said that this quaintly expresses the taking by the bride of the husband's name, by which she renounces her own name and kin. There is, however, one flaw in the reasoning: *Gaius* was never the name of a *gens,* it was always a personal name and at no time was there a *gens Gaia* in Rome. Besides, we know that Roman brides did not change their gentile name: the mother of the Gracchi, for instance, always remained a Cornelia. What was expressed by the formula was the joining, not of the *gentes,* but of the persons. It is an important point, which has not been noticed by commentators, that the significance of the *sponsalia* and *nuptiae* lies in the duplication of the bond of marriage: in the contract between the kindreds on the one hand, and in the sacramental agreement between two individuals on the other.

The Greek framework was similar: it started with the *ἐγγύησις,* the transaction between the guardians, after which the woman was *ἐγγυητὴ γυνή* (*δάμαρ*); [1] the second part of the ceremony, answering the *nuptiae,* was *γάμος* the process of taking the wife to the domicile of her husband and the beginning of their cohabitation and married life. This expressed the personal side which, from the legal point of view, was less important than *ἐγγυησις.* Thus in the trials reported in the speeches of Isaeus and Demosthenes, the answer to the question as to whether a woman was a legitimate wife or not, entirely depends on the evidence as to *ἐγγύησις* ; [2] *γάμος* is treated as a secondary feature. It is significant that the term *ἐγγυᾶν* is used for the action both of the *κύριος* who gives away the bride, and of the person who stands security for a debt and is expected to "hand over" the person of the debtor.[3]

The fact that the marriage that led to the production of legitimate offspring was a bond not only between persons, but between kindred, is expressed in the formulae used in

1 HRUZA, *Familienrecht,* I, pp. 40 ff.
2 E.g., ISAEUS. Or. III, 4, 70
3 PARTSCH, *Griechisches Bürgschaftsrecht,* p. 87 ff.

the marriage ceremonies in Greece, Rome and India. Thus when Kleisthenes, ruler of Sikyon, gave his daughter Agariste in marriage, he invited suitors to compete for her, and on giving her to the successful competitor, the Athenian Megakles of the Alkmaeonids, he pronounced the formula, "I give my daughter to thee, Megakles of the Alkmaeonids, for the breeding of legitimate children." [1]

Parallel features in Brahmanic and Roman marriage rites.

Curious features of the ancient ritual of the law of marriage are presented in the ancient Roman and in the Indian ceremonies. Brahmanic marriage, the most developed and sacred form, is fully before us, being practised even now, and as regards the ancient Roman marriage, the *confarreatio*, we have the notices of historians. If we compare the ritual of the two, we find that they are identical in all the chief particulars, which are so concrete and expressive that there can be no question of composing these rites at a later stage; it may be said, therefore, that we have here the old ritual of sacral marriage as practised five thousand years ago, before the division of the races. Three points must be noticed.

(1) The bride and bridegroom conclude the agreement as to common life and perpetual union by giving the hand (handfasting), described in Rome as *dextrarum prehensio*. In Indian ritual the corresponding rite is called *panigrahana* (handshaking).[2]

(2) In both rituals the bride and bridegroom sit down together on a seat covered with sheep-skin, thus establishing in a symbolical way the fact that both take part in the same act of housekeeping in a household in which pastoral pursuits are prominent.

(3) The bride and bridegroom partake of food in common. In the Brahmanical ritual the chief stress is laid on the sharing of "fire and water," but rice is also shared. The Roman ritual in this respect is more expressive and gives the name to the whole ceremony: *confarreatio* is the sharing of a cake made of *far* (spelt). The use of spelt is characteristic, and points to a period when wheat was

[1] HERODOTUS, vi, 130. The formula was: *ἐπὶ παίδων γησίων ἀρότῳ.*
[2] Cf. NÂRADA, XII, pars. 2 and 3.

probably unknown, while barley and spelt were the only sown grains. The cake shared in the Patrician ceremony was not an ordinary one: it is described as *mola salsa,* i.e., a baked cake of roughly ground corn,[1] and thus assigns the ritual to the later stone period.

There is another supplementary trait which is not mentioned explicitly in the Latin descriptions, but may be supposed to have been in use. The bride and bridegroom went round the hearth in symbol of the fact that the new hearth would be one and the same for both. In the Brahmanic ceremony this feature is very important and has developed on the line of making seven steps together (*hepta pada*); according to the judicial commentaries, when the seventh step is taken, the marriage is fully concluded. This does not appear in the narratives concerning *confarreatio,* but it is still recognizable in the ritual of the Eastern Church, as the newly married pair, led by the priest, walk three times round the little altar in the centre of the church, which corresponds to the altar of the domestic hearth of pagan custom.

The *confarreatio* ceremony became exclusive and purely Patrician. Other classes could not practise it at all, but members of the Patrician families, the old aristocrats, who wanted their sons to stand for ancient priesthoods, such as that of the *flamines,* had to prove that they were the issue of marriages by *confarreatio.* Let us notice also that in both rituals the greatest stress is laid on the personal factor. The sacramental marriage is between the bride and the bridegroom, and the part taken by the kinsmen is not apparent; it is really the last act of the *nuptiae, γάμος.* Thus it is in the betrothal, *sponsalia, ἐγγύησις* that the kinsfolk predominate, not in the religious acts which sanctify personal union.

A most curious description of a wedding according to Old English Law occurs in an Anglo-Saxon Formulary: it covers the whole ground of matrimonial relations. "If people want to wed a maid or a wife and this is agreeable

[1] Cf. *Germ. mahlen* and its linguistic parallels, and the evidence as to ancient stone hand-mills. SCHRADER, *Reallex.* 511.

Marriage by agreement between kindreds in Old English Law.

to her and to her kinsmen, then it is right that the bridegroom should first swear according to God's right and secular law and should wage (pledge himself) to those who are her forspeakers, that he wishes to have her in such a way as he should hold her by God's right as his wife—and his kinsmen will stand pledge for him.

Then it is to be settled to whom the price for upfostering her belongs, and for this the kinsmen should pledge themselves.

Then let the bridegroom declare what present he will make her for granting his desire, and what he will give if she lives longer than he does.

If it has been settled in this way, then it is right that she should enjoy half the property, and all if they have a child, unless she marries another man.

All this the bridegroom must corroborate by giving a gage, and his kinsmen stand to pledge for him.

If they are agreed in all this, then let the kinsmen of the bride accept and wed their kinswoman to wife and to right life to him who desires her, and let him take the pledge who rules over the wedding.

If she is taken out of the land into another lord's land, then it is advisable that her kinsmen get a promise that no violence will be done to her, and that if she has to pay a fine, they ought to be her next to help her to pay, if she has not enough to pay herself." [1]

The first paragraph states certain preliminary requirements. First the duties of the husband are defined—he must hold his wife according to God's law. Then the consent of the parties must be clear and definite: the marriage must be agreeable to the bride as well as to the bridegroom: thus the wife's personality is specifically recognized and respected. But the marriage must also be agreeable to the Kinsmen, and the parties who arrange the terms of the contract are not the pair to be wedded, but the bridegroom's kindred and the "forspeakers" of the bride.

The second paragraph relates to the price which is to be paid: note that this price is not for possession of the woman

[1] LIEBERMANN, *Gesetze der Angelsachsen*, I, p. 442.

herself as an object of property, nor even for *mund* over her, but it is for the expense of "upfostering" her. This is interesting as an evidence of transition, and clearly shows not only the roots of the transaction, but the process of transformation.

In the next paragraph another kind of price is referred to: it is money paid by the bridegroom to his wife for "granting his desire." This is a payment quite apart from the original sum agreed to be due from the husband to parents and kinsmen.

Next comes the third idea connected with the pecuniary obligations of the bridegroom, namely, that he must guarantee a certain maintenance to his wife if she survives him. Here we see the origin of *dower*, an institution familiar to Germanic law, and quite distinct from the Roman *dos*. If there is a child of the union, the wife is guaranteed a life-interest in the whole property of the husband; if there is no issue, she shall have an interest in half the property.

The next paragraph emphasizes the part which the kindred take in the transaction: while the individual contracts by *gage*, the kindred stand surety for him. Then we come to the actual ceremony of betrothal, which is effected by the giving of the *wed*, the gage or pledge, the symbol of obligations which are definitely undertaken by the parties to the union,—another reminder of the important fact that the history of marriage is intimately connected with the history of contract. He who rules the wedding—the umpire or middleman,—must also be taken into account in this connection.

Finally, after the actual wedding has taken place, we hear that the right of the kindred to protect the bride is not superseded when she passes into the household of her husband. There is a definite statement that the kindred retain a right to interfere for her protection and are under a duty to help her if she incurs a fine or a similar liability. This is very important, and it is one of the most firmly established principles of the *wergeld* fines that they are paid by both sides. This fact, not realized by former students,[1] that the wife did not belong entirely to the *gens* of her husband, and was not absolutely in their power, but that the protection of her rights rested on the lasting agreement made between the two kindreds by the transaction of the marriage, was the foundation of her position in right and in law.

Sources of women's rights as to property.

In regard to the position of women in ancient Aryan society a very important question concerns, of course, the exercise of rights of property. According to the ancient constitution of the family an unmarried woman was for ever dependent upon her curator, but the position of a married woman as to property rights was, as it were, double-edged. Although she was dominated by her husband, she was yet the *matrona, patni,* a personality under the protection of her former kin. In the higher forms of legitimate marriage as contrasted with concubinate and *matrimonium usu,* the wife's rights of property were recognized, even though she had to exercise them under the supervision and restrictions of her husband. There were two principal sources of these rights of property: (1) according to the Anglo-Saxon ritual, one item making for the recognition of the wife's proprietary rights is the present which the bridegroom gives the bride on the morning after the marriage "for granting his desire." In German law this is called the *morning gift,* and a similar custom is mentioned in Russian law. The agreement as to dower appears as a further development of the custom. (2) On the other hand, the bride is supposed to bring a certain number of things from her home. Thus in the Laws of Manu,[2] in all descriptions of the conclusion of a marriage the bride is said to proceed to the house of the bridegroom decked with jewels and well adorned. Besides an outfit of trinkets and festal clothes, she would be provided with articles of furniture, and, sometimes, with cattle. The married woman therefore draws her property from two sources—one being the dower assigned from the bridegroom's side, and the other the "*dos*" from father or guardian. In the Brehon Laws

[1] E g., FUSTEL DE COULANGES, in *La Cité Antique.*
[2] E.g., *Manu,* III, 27 and 28.

of Ancient Ireland, these two are contrasted under the names of *tinol* and *tinnskra, tinol* being goods brought by the bride from her old home, *dos,* her outfit, which is regarded as especially protected, and which never becomes the property of her husband. The wife's right is juridically recognized and protected, and her children have a special right of inheritance even against the father. *Tinnskra* is the bridegroom's allowance to the bride. Irish law demands that it should be equalized with the *tinol,* so that the bride receives as much as she brings with her.

These are the typical features of the ancient rights of the wife as regards property. When their full development is insisted on, there arises a conflict with the other rule—that the *paterfamilias* is the absolute ruler of the household—and compromises of various kinds between the two conflicting tendencies are devised among Indians, Romans, Greeks, Celts, Slavs and Teutons. We have thus in this case a curious example of the inconsistencies of ancient law: it does not generally follow up conclusions to absolutely consistent results. Even the most consistent system of all—Roman Law—recognizes customary rights in the shape of the *peculium:* the *paterfamilias* is absolute owner of property, yet his son and servant are protected by custom in the ownership of their stock of cattle and other goods. The wife is protected in the use of her *dos* not only by custom, but by the influence of her relations.

Celtic and Germanic law show that the different forms of family property were regarded from the point of view of daily use. Thus a strong distinction is made between the things that are in the ordinary use of the man—his military outfit and his team of oxen for ploughing [1]—and the things with which his wife is especially connected, such as the spindle, pillows, blankets, house furniture and jewels, her *Gerade.* The legal situation is adapted to simple economic considerations and to the natural division of labour.

[1] The Germanic designation of these things is *Gewaet* (plur. *Gewaete*), hence the *heriot* (Her-gewæt), the best horse or the best ox ceded to the chief.

An occasion when the separate rights of husband and wife assume a tangible form arises when, by the separation of the married pair, the rights of property have to be readjusted. How could it be admitted in the old Aryan society that marriage could be dissolved at all?—can one speak of divorce under a *régime* of appropriation by the husband? In a sacramental marriage it was impossible in principle, and *Suttee* is the consequence of the complete union. But this form is only one expression of marital union and is perhaps not the most common in ancient law. Contract or *quasi*-contract is more common, and just because the clauses of the marriage agreement are recognized to a great extent by the kindred concluding the agreement as subject to strict observation, the right to renounce it, if broken by the other party, is not entirely destroyed. Divorce or separation is produced not merely by the dismissal of the wife,[1] but also on her demand, or, rather, on the demand of her kin. How property is dealt with in the case of divorce may be seen from the Gortyn Code found in the ruins of a Doric city in Crete. It belongs to the sixth century B.C., that is, to a period soon after the time of the legislation of Solon in Athens. "If a husband and wife be divorced, she shall have her own property that she came with to her husband, and the half of the crop, if it be from her own property, and whatever she has woven within, the half, whatever it may be, and five staters, if her husband be the cause of her dismissal; but if her husband deny that he was the cause, the judge shall decide, confirming his decision on oath."[2] It is important to notice that the cause had to be established by a judge, who might decide that the husband was at fault. Thus the wife was not at the mercy of her lord, but had protected rights and a status before the Courts.

Divorce.

In the Brehon Laws we see a further development of the principle: the wife has certain rights as to things belonging to her husband. As regards succession there is an interesting distinction: if there is issue, the wife remains in

[1] Cf. the Roman practice.

[2] DARESTE, *Inscriptions juridiques grecques*, III, par. 14.

possession of what she had during the life of her husband; if there is no issue, she has an allowance. In ancient Greek law the rights of the wife to property were established by the State. In other cases, however, we must guard against exaggeration and must notice that in the Roman household we are dealing with an extreme manifestation of patriarchal absolutism.

The servants a part of the ancient Aryan family.

There is a third element in the Family besides the ruler and his wives and children: according to the general Aryan conception the servants are a part of the household. Even the slave is not regarded as an outside subject: he is a member, though an inferior member, of the family. Curious consequences from this principle arise in law. It is, however, necessary to make a clear distinction between periods: the slave of Cicero or Pericles, unlike that of the Iliad and of the Vedas, is a tool; but such a description would not be true of the ancient slave. In the archaic period he was an inferior member of the domestic cult of the hearth, not godless but sharing in the religion of the family to which he belonged. Though unable to perform the rites himself, he was present at them and might assist at subsidiary ministrations. In Greek law he is either *δμώς*, a captive, a prisoner of war who may have been a prince in his own land, or perhaps even a Greek and not a barbarian, so that there need not have been a fundamental distinction between him and his master: or else he was termed *οἰκέτης*, a *domestique*. Consequently we find in ancient times a milder expression of the relationship between master and slave than in later law.[1] Greek observers about the year 300 B.C., encountering the more archaic culture of India where the ancient views and customs were better preserved, were struck by this difference between slavery and the free condition of the *sudras*. Megasthenes, an envoy of one of Alexander's generals, Seleucus, gives a description of the India of the closing years of the fourth century B.C.[2] He comes to the conclusion that the Indians

[1] The human relationship between master and slave is illustrated, for example, in the *Odyssey* by the relations between Odysseus and his old nurse.

[2] Megasthenes in *Fragmenta Historicorum Graecorum*, II, 436.

did not know slavery. Indeed, the *pariahs*, the outcasts, in spite of their debased and miserable position, were not personal slaves, but subjects of the entire community somewhat similar to the helots of Sparta. The position of the *sudras* was better, as they were recognized as a lower caste of the people. In this matter the account of Megasthenes may be compared with Tacitus, who observed that subjection among the Germans did not amount to the abolition of personality, and was more in the nature of colonate than of slavery.[1] The subject *colonus* was a dependent rural farmer, paying tribute in kind or in money. The client had his own little household, of which he was master, but which was taxed for tribute, heavily or not as the case might be, in the shape of a certain number of measures of corn or part of the offspring of his cattle.

The typical Aryan slave a tributary client, *colonus*.

How then is ancient slavery to be characterized? It has been thought sometimes that complete exploitation on the lines of the slavery of Mohammedan countries or of the Southern States of America, where the negro was no better than an ox or a horse, has been the rule in primitive countries. But in reality, the primitive slave had a better standing, not on account of sentiment, but for practical reasons. The fundamental reason is economic. Ancient communities were based on natural husbandry, and so weak and insufficient was the concentration of society, that any complex organization of labour or exploitation of dependents could not be carried out. As every one was close to nature, the best way of using one's dependents was to fleece them, as it were, to take what they could provide in the easiest way. The master's demands as regards his servant were limited by considerations as to the latter's existence and health. There was not much choice in the matter, and the best thing to do was to settle serfs in their own homesteads and let them take part in cattle-breeding or the cultivation of the soil in much the same way as the master himself. The tributary

[1] *Germania* xxv: ". . . ceteris servis non in nostrum morem discriptis per familiam ministeriis utuntur. Suam quisque sedem suos penates regit. Frumenti modum dominus, aut pecoris, aut vestis, ut colono, iniungit; et servus hactenus paret."

form of slavery was therefore the natural one, especially among the Aryans who practised pastoral husbandry and primitive agriculture. It is hardly a paradox to say that slavery was intensified, up to a certain point, by the progress of civilization.[1]

Accordingly, in the Gortyn inscription, there is no distinction in quality between the superior and the subsidiary household. If the household is in danger of disappearing for want of heirs, succession goes over to the tributary clients (*Ϝοικεῖς*). There is no escheat, the community does not claim the property. In Sparta, for instance, the *περίοικοι*, the "dwellers round," may be compared with the *Ϝοικεῖς* of Gortyn. Thus primitive law is far from manifesting any sharp contrasts between the social orders and from degrading slaves to the position of cattle or tools. The lower classes were dependent, but they were not devoid of personal rights and juridical protection. The root of this lies in the necessities of the economic situation to which customs and morals had to adapt themselves.

[1] A remarkable exception occurs in the case of female slaves, whose value depended on sexual attraction, not on labour. The female slave—*cumhal*—was used by the Celts as a unit of currency. SEEBOHM, *Tribal Custom in Anglo-Saxon Law*, 97 ff.

CHAPTER VI

THE JOINT FAMILY

The persistence of family organization

We usually consider family ties and family property from the point of view of successive generations and of inheritance. This is, however, by no means a necessary or even a natural mode of approaching the subject. In ancient life the principal fact governing these relations was the continuity of a family organization, and there was no compelling reason for dissolving it in connection with the death of a particular member, even if the member in question happened to be the ruler or manager of the concern. We are quite familiar with the persistent maintenance of corporate units like the State, the Church, a town, a teaching institution, and there is no inherent reason for treating the combination of persons and things constituting a household unit in another way. As a matter of fact, every partition and dismemberment is bound to produce some loss and dislocation, and while such losses have to be incurred nowadays in order to satisfy the claims of individuals, the natural bent of ancient Aryan custom was in the direction of keeping up the unity of the household at the cost of curtailing individual tendencies. Strictly speaking, there should not have been any disruption of the family community by way of partition or inheritance, any more than there is a necessity for a party meeting for a meal to alter or abandon that common meal every time one of the members has to leave the table. In connection with this prevailing idea, we find among all the branches of the Aryan race manifestations of the so-called united family or *joint family* arrangement. The most extensive and best described practices of this kind are to be found in India and among the Southern Slavs, but there are many traces of similar institutions in the history of the Germans, of the Eastern Slavs and of Romance nations. To begin with, let us consider the Indian data.

The Joint Family in India.

In the Rig Veda we read in a Hymn (x. 85, 46) [1] of a bride who is invited to take charge of a household in which parents-in-law and other relations are mentioned as members. The Sutras often refer to the common management of families which have outgrown the stage of the primordial group of father, mother and children. The institution is considered in the Indian law books chiefly from the point of view of its possible dissolution by partition; [2] but this does not mean in any way that partition was the normal consequence of the decease of a householder. On the contrary, the sons of a householder generally continued to manage their affairs in common as before, but it was advisable from a juridical point of view to anticipate the possibility of partition, and to lay down rules as to the relative rights of interested persons. The supposition that, in the ordinary course of affairs, common management remained the usual expedient is supported by the fact that right through recent history, and up to our times, Indian families keep together as far as possible and submit to division only with great reluctance. It has been argued sometimes that the possibility of claiming a partition places these united families in the category of voluntary associations. Such a reading of the evidence, however, perverts the true state of things; it represents exceptions as the rule and the rule as an artificial contrivance built up by help of the exceptions. In these cases, as in many others, we have to take into account not so much extreme possibilities as the customary or usual development of affairs. From this point of view it is highly characteristic that brothers, cousins and nephews in India strive to keep up, as far as possible, the household

[1] H. H. Wilson's transl. (1888): "Be a queen to thy father-in-law . . . to thy mother-in-law . . . to thy husband's sister . . . to thy husband's brothers."

[2] E.g., *Manu*, IX, 104; *Gautama*, XXVIII, I; *Baudhâyana*, II, 38; *Yâjñavalkya*, II, 117. Cf. *The Law of Inheritance from the Mitâkshará*, transl. by H. T. Colebrooke in *Two Treatises on the Hindu Law of Inheritance* (1810), pp. 257, 259-61; J. D. Mayne, *A Treatise on Hindu Law and Usage* (4th ed., 1888), p. 256; West and Bühler, *A Digest of the Hindu Law of Inheritance, Partition, and Adoption* (3rd ed., 1884), I, pp. 59-60.

unit with which their claims are connected. During a recent visit to India I came across many significant facts of this kind: e.g., a large family of some seventy relatives was keeping up its connection with the central household of a judge of the High Court in Calcutta (Justice Chaudhuri). I was told that great gatherings of the members took place twice a year, that most distant relatives looked upon the household of the Judge as the principal stock on which they could rely in case of need, that considerable property was managed in common and that personal maintenance was provided for spinsters, widows, minors and other members who could not shift sufficiently for themselves. Similar arrangements could be witnessed in the daily life of some professors of the Sanskrit College, and of other Hindu householders with whom I came into contact.

The modern practice of the institution as reflected both in its customary peaceful development, and in occasional conflicts before the Courts, is marked by specific juridical traits which draw a definite line between this legal arrangement and forms of association known to the modern West. I have chiefly in view four consequences of the Joint Family system:

(1) The estimate of the shares held by the different members in the common concern.

(2) The method of managing property.

(3) Rights of maintenance.

(4) The relations between common and self-acquired property.

Shares: absence of privileges.

(1) The basis of the juridical conception in this case is the corporate existence of the family: there is originally no privileged right assigned to the father or to any senior member who acts as his substitute. Taking the case of the father as the most obvious, the fundamental fact is recognized that father and sons stand on an equal footing as members of the Joint Family. In this way the son cannot be said to be heir to his father, and does not take after the father's death property which did not belong to him before. The only change which occurs on the decease of the father

is the alteration which would follow from the fact that a family, say, of five members, would shrink to a family of four members and the surviving members would, therefore, each hold a fourth instead of a fifth. The same effect would be produced if one of the sons disappeared in his father's lifetime. This position is quite clear in the older system represented by the Yâjñavalkya and Mitákshará, and it holds good at the present time in the greater part of India.[1] In parts of the Bombay Province a more individualistic conception has taken root. According to the so-called *Dayabhaga* (partition) of this Western region, the father is recognized as the owner of the property during his lifetime. But even in this modernized arrangement the idea of the continuity of the family tradition is preserved, and there is no question of a purely individualistic treatment on the pattern of the Roman *dominium.*

Altogether the rights of members of a Joint Family appear as ideal shares: in order to understand the proportion in which these shares are allotted, we must keep clearly in view the fact that they follow the pedigree. Without going into the details of the question we have to notice that the right of representation holds good, so that the members of junior generations may have to wait for the realization of their individual claims till the decease of their parents, who, while alive, represent the whole branch. Such questions are, however, only particular applications of the general rule that shares are assigned to members in proportion to their relative seniority, and that the reckoning is carried out not *per capita,* but *per stirpes.*[2]

The policy of the manager supervised by the body of members

(2) As the father, or any substitute of his, acts as manager of the family and not as owner, his policy is subject to supervision and if necessary to correction by the body of members. There is a good deal of evidence in the Law Reports as to conflicts between managers and members. There are a good many disputed points as to the amount of

[1] Cf. COLEBROOKE, *Mitákshará,* pp. 254, 256, 257; WEST and BÜHLER, *op. cit.,* I, p. 69; II, p. 603.

[2] COLEBROOKE, *Mitákshará,* pp. 259, 264, 350-2; MAYNE, *op. cit.,* pp. 256, 259-60; WEST and BÜHLER, *op. cit.,* I, pp. 76, 339.

discretion to be left to the managers in dealing with current affairs and with emergency cases, but on the whole it is an established rule that alienations of valuable property, or mortgages which produce heavy encumbrances, should not be carried out without the consent of the whole body of members. At the same time, the conditions in which such consent has to be given or can be withheld are not set out very clearly. The customary tendency is towards unanimity; in practice such unanimity cannot always be attained and dissent is sometimes overruled, but there are no definite rules as to decision by the majority.[1]

The institution primarily a provision for existence

(3) The right of maintenance introduces a conception which is quite alien to modern European views as to property. The nearest analogy might be found in English Law in the position of beneficiaries under a general trust, such as the inmates of a charitable institution. In Continental law a similar situation is met by the rules as to foundations for definite aims (the German *Stiftungen*). The point in these cases is that a certain amount of property or its income is set apart for the maintenance of certain persons and cannot be diverted from that destination; nevertheless none of the beneficiaries can exchange his right for anything else or realize it as an object of property. In the same way, in the case of the Indian Joint Family, the stock of material goods belonging to it is regarded primarily as the basis for the economic position of the members, but not as a complex of things to be treated as materials *in abstracto,* from the point of view of ownership and possession. It would hardly do to conceive of the institution on the lines of the abstract notion of "corporation" as understood in the West: the aim and essence of the arrangement is to provide the means of subsistence for its members.

Turning back to Indian Law, we may say that this peculiar colouring of the institution, although present right through, is especially noticeable in the case of those members who stand in need of help and protection. If we take

[1] For the position of the manager see, COLEBROOKE, *Mitákshará*, p. 257; MAYNE, *op. cit.*, p. 288; WEST and BÜHLER, *op. cit.*, II, pp. 603, 618, 630, 634-5.

the fully-qualified householders or their grown-up sons, the usual correspondence between requirements and services, between meals and means, is expressed more or less on the same lines as in ordinary corporate property, but the fact that the Joint Family aims directly at establishing a material basis for the personal existence of its members, is strongly brought out in the case of the weaker members of the institution. A widow is entirely dependent on the assistance of the imperishable household to which her late husband belonged. In the case of a spinster, it is the duty not only of parents but of the Joint Family, to arrange a suitable marriage. Perhaps the most striking cases arise in connection with the requirements of education. In this respect there can be no definite limitation of individual claims: they depend entirely on capacity and opportunity.[1] A Joint Family would not think of refusing to spend money on an expensive course of education on the ground that the claimant was overdrawing his balance in the common fund. The other side of the matter appears when the community claims profits which are considered to be the result, not so much of individual exertions, but of the bringing-up by the help of the family.

Distinction between property acquired by personal labour and the communal stock.

(4) This leads to the difficult question of drawing proper distinctions between communal and self-acquired property within the sphere of action of a Joint Family. The development of modern economic ideas and relations is unquestionably breaking up the primitive conceptions of family solidarity, and it is unnecessary to consider in detail the various inroads which the interests of individuals make in the compact block of primitive conceptions as to property; but it ought to be noticed that the germ of the distinction is already definitely before us in the period of the Sutras. There is a famous saying in the Laws of Manu[2] that a ploughed strip of reclaimed land belongs as much to the tiller as a deer brought down by an arrow belongs to

[1] See *Nârada*, XIII, 5; COLEBROOKE, *Mitâksharâ*, p. 316; MAYNE, *op. cit.*, pp. 256-7; WEST and BÜHLER, *op. cit.*, I, pp. 255, 263; II, p. 65.

[2] IX, 43, 44.

the hunter. This saying has sometimes been cited in proof of the prevalence of private property in land in ancient India, but as a matter of fact it is nothing of the sort; it is neither land as such nor the animal as such that is claimed as property, but the result of the personal exertion of the tiller and of the hunter. We need not, I think, labour the point that a field which has not been appropriated by actual tillage would be out of the range of private ownership, in the same way as a deer which has succeeded in escaping from the arrow. As the stress is laid on concrete appropriation by some kind of exertion, the way is opened for a distinction between objects directly acquired by personal labour or prowess, and the store of goods which are potentially at the disposal of the family community.

Speaking in terms of modern economics, we may say that self-acquired property is directly derived from labour, while the capital from which labour starts remains in the hands of the community.[1] But, of course, all such translations from one set of terms into another and more modern set are only intended to call attention to characteristic distinctions and could not be followed with safety in working out details.

Similar features in matriarchal organizations.

A most interesting corroboration of the teaching as to the economic foundation and the natural history of the Indian Joint Family is provided by the fact that perfectly similar organizations arise on Indian soil in those cases where society is built up not on the patriarchal, but on the matriarchal principle. All the features which we have been examining in the life of the Mitákshará community recur in the practices of the Malabar *tarwads*.[2] The only difference is that we should have to substitute connection through the females for the agnatic skeleton of the Mitákshará Joint Family. The *taiwazhi* runs from the mother instead of from the father, and the management of pro-

[1] *Nârada*, XIII, 6; COLEBROOKE, *Mitákshará*, pp. 256, 278-9; MAYNE, *op. cit.*, pp 288-9.
[2] See KRISHNAN PANDALAI on *Marumakatayam Law*, 18 ff.

perty is complicated by the addition of a male protector, the *karnavan;* but in other respects we are met by the same problems as to unity and partition, as to ideal shares and representation, as to limits on alienation, as to maintenance and self-acquired property, which we have noticed within the domain of the patriarchal system. This shows convincingly that the necessity of holding together in large clusters of relations is the natural consequence of the social situation in India, and that systems of relationship built up on opposite lines have to take these necessities into account in the same way.

The *Zadruga* of the Southern Slavs.

No less instructive an instance is provided by the Southern Slavonic *Zadruga.* It has been proved, in spite of some captious criticisms, that this institution goes back to the tribal settlements of the Slavs, right from the earliest times, and that it is endemic among all the branches of this race.[1] But let us turn our attention first and chiefly to the development of the institution as presented by contemporary arrangements in Serbia, Montenegro, Bosnia, Herzegovina, Dalmatia and Croatia. Contemporary practices and absolutely trustworthy evidence as to the state of affairs in the earlier years of the nineteenth century make it possible to describe the working of the institution with great completeness and with clear indications as to the solution of problems which otherwise might have presented difficulties. In these regions, where the population had constantly to fight for existence against the Turks, the Albanians, sometimes the Hungarians, and where the economic struggle was also no easy matter in the absence of good roads, political security and commercial credit, the stress of social organization was laid emphatically on the communal principle as against individual action. According to a Croatian proverb, a single man does not get food nor work. Another saying likens a man devoid of communal support to a man without an arm.[2] As a result, all the provinces enumerated above were covered with Zadrugas, large families which had grown out of the narrow family, or

[1] A. Kadlec, *Encyklopedya Polska,* IV, 2, p. 67 ff.
[2] Krauss, *Sitte und Brauch der Süd-Slaven,* pp. 66 ff.

inokoshtina, composed of father, mother and children. The *inokoshtina* itself presents the features of a family corporation in its structure, and the father is anything but the absolute owner and ruler of Roman Law. He is in truth the manager and senior member who leads the family, but is included in its corporate existence. In this way there is no break of continuity when, after the decease of the father, the brothers and eventually the cousins of different degrees develop the *inokoshtina* into a *zadruga.* The feature of the family hearth is still preserved in the central *ognišće,* round which the members congregate in the common hall. It stands usually in the centre of a settlement shaped like a horseshoe and is surrounded either by *Kleti,* the bedrooms of the single families which constitute the joint household, or by separate cottages. In the latter case relations with the central hearth are nevertheless kept up. These communities are very different in size according to topographical conditions and customs, but they may be said on the average to include some thirty or forty persons of both sexes, not counting the children. Sometimes these clusters number even from fifty to seventy. At the head stands the elder or headman, *Glavar Domaćin.* His election is not regulated in a very formal way, and it may be said that seniority is taken into account as far as possible, unless there are definite reasons for passing over persons who are either senile or of weak character. Sometimes a dying *glavar* may point out his successor, and his recommendation in such a case would be treated with due respect. Sometimes, again, an especially capable or strong personality would win the seat of *domaćin,* even against senior competitors, as a result of an expression of public opinion. This is, however, not connected with any regular election or vote by majority. By the side of the *domaćin* leader stands the *domaćica,* the lady manageress in charge of the keys of the storehouses, the dairy and other household arrangements. In the settlement of all important affairs a council of the heads of the constituent family meets. Its decisions are reached by unanimity. It may appear strange to us that this seemingly vague idea of unanimity should

The position of the head-man, *domaćin.*

rule the proceedings, but what it really comes to is that votes are not counted but weighed, or rather that the moral influence of the elder and of the other leading family fathers is regarded with such respect that no action of the community is taken unless there is unanimity. The most prominent expression of this organic conception of management is to be found in the case of any alienation of property: it is impossible to imagine a *domaćin* acting in such cases by his single will without the assent of the other family fathers. On the basis of such an organization customary rules arise which are in principle identical with those obtaining in the Indian village communities. We might start from the position of the father in the narrow family (*inokoshtina*), as it contains the germs of further development. Professor Bogišić has summarized the customs in this respect in the following words: [1]

(1) The father, while living in the same household as his grown-up sons, has not the right to dispose of the family property.

(2) He has not the right to dispose of it *mortis causa* without the consent of his sons.

(3) The father is the head of the administration, but on important occasions he acts in concert with his sons. If, for any reason, he is not equal to the task of administering the affairs of the community, one of his sons may be put in his place.

(4) Sons who are of full age, especially if they are married, may demand partition during the life of their father.

The relations between members of large *zadrugas* were usually ruled by the sense of common interest and solidarity. In the exceedingly valuable collection of answers from various districts inhabited by the Serbian race, which have been published by Professor Bogišić, stress is often laid on the obligation of the elders to keep the fortunes of the community intact, so that the growing generations should in any case not receive less than their forefathers had left to their parents. Altogether the *zadruga* com-

[1] In an article in the (Russian) *Journal of the Ministry of Public Instruction.*

munities present a striking instance of the spirit of comradeship and union in the management of social affairs.

The possibility of partition is always open. For a general division, the consent of most members of the *zadruga* would be required, but single members and small families are constantly observed leaving the large unions on account of overcrowding or quarrels. Nevertheless the fact remains that this institution was up to quite recent times regarded as the customary form of peasant life in the country of the Serbians and Croatians. We have here, therefore, a case in which custom holds its own tenaciously in spite of the legal possibility of dismemberment.

Similar communities are reported to have existed among the Alpine Slovenes of Carinthia and Istria, although in these parts of the country they gave way to more individualistic management under the influence of German colonization.[1]

The Joint Family among the Russians.

Important facts of the same kind have to be noticed in the early development of the Russian race, both in the Northern forests and in the Southern steppes. The population of the Northern provinces, colonized from Novgorod, consisted of peasants who made clearings in the vast forests and moors of the provinces of Archangel, Vologda, Viatka, etc. The settlements were achieved by clusters of kinsmen, and the form of these settlements were repeated over and over again with the regularity of bee-hives. The unit was the so-called *derevnia,* comprising a Joint Family which usually extended to second cousins and sometimes to their children. Each *derevnia* consisted of six or seven *dvors* (crofts or courts) forming the dwelling-house and adjacent orchards of the smaller households. Several *derevnias,* again, formed a higher union called *selo,* and common husbandry did not reach any further than this. The *selo* and the villages composing it (*derevnias*) held wide tracts of moor and forest and fisheries in common, allowing each of the component householders certain gangs or entries, i.e., rights of exportation for the purpose of fetching wood, fuel,

[1] DOPSCH: *Die ältere Sozial- und Wirtschaftsverfassung der Alpen-Slaven,* 1909.

hunting, fishing, etc. Such tillage as there was had to be carried on in fields "snatched" (*terebit*) from the wilderness. Each of the householders took a certain number of strips in the different fields, so that each holding was originally equalized as between the brothers or companions (*siabri*, cf. *sobrini*). In the succession of generations some of the holdings were parcelled up into smaller parts in consequence of the allowance of claims by *stirpes*, but the idea of keeping up the communal union was strongly held, and occasional redivisions might take place under the pressure of insistent claims by members of the younger generations. Later on, with the growth of population and subjection to the land-tax, the *mir* system grew out of these tribal settlements. We shall have to return to that question later on. The South Russian arrangement is constructed on entirely similar lines, with the difference that the homestead is centred not in the *dvor* (court), but around the big oven (*pechische*). Again there recurs the fundamental feature of the enlarged household naturally growing out of the ordinary family on the death of the father.[1] Similar arrangements are recorded in the history of the Poles and Czechs. I may refer readers for information on this subject to the excellent monograph of Professor Balzer of the University of Lwów.[2] It is to be noticed, however, that with the Western Slavs *zadruga* arrangements gave way at an early period, and that from the fourteenth century the peasantry in those parts were organized on individualistic lines.

Communal tendencies among Germanic peoples.

The same observation may be made to an even greater extent in the case of the Germanic peoples. The geographical features of the land and the troubled history of migrations and conquests led to individualization in the earlier Middle Ages, but yet we find widespread vestiges of a tendency towards common management of family affairs on the lines of enlarged households. In all territories inhabited by Germanic tribes we find the practice of joint

[1] MRS. EFIMENKO, on *Peasant Land Tenure in the North* and on *Southern Russia* (Russian).

[2] *O Zadrudze Slowianskei.* Lwów, 1899.

management by co-heirs (*Ganerbschaft*) working in the same direction of solidarity in the difficult struggle for existence which is such a prominent feature in the life of *zadrugas*. The importance of voluntary co-operation and the more frequent partitions testify to a more mobile constitution of society than in the case of the Southern and Eastern Slavs. We read, for example, the following rule in the customary law of Skone: if a son is established with his wife in the household of his father, his property is added to that of his father. If he dies without having defined his property in severalty, his children share with grandfather and other co-heirs. It is clearly a case of a family which holds together under the authority of a grandfather after the marriage of some of its members.[1] A similar rule may be cited from the legislation of Liutprand of Lombardy,[2] and in the mediaeval Italian documents we often hear of *condomae* in the sense of joint households. Yet it is not always easy to say to what extent customary unions for the management of property, of which we get evidence in Romance countries, are to be traced to the gradual expansion of families, and in what measure they were the result of voluntary associations.[3] Altogether the Joint Family presents an interesting example of the value of co-operative action, and of customary restrictions on the free play of individual self-determination.

Traces of joint management in Romance countries.

[1] Brunner, *Rechtsgeschichte*, I², 105 ff. Seebohm, *Tribal Custom in Anglo-Saxon Law*, 276 ff. On this subject, see Sering, *Erbrecht und Agrarverfassung in Schleswig-Holstein*, Berlin, 1900.

[2] Viollet, *Histoire du droit civil français* (3rd ed. 1905), pp. 750 ff.

[3] Pertile, *Storia del diritto italiano*, Iv, 319 ff.

CHAPTER VII

SUCCESSION AND INHERITANCE

The natural law of succession refers to personal property

HOWEVER close the ties which bind the members of the association together, there is always a possibility of individuals going out; disruption of the group is a contingency to be faced, and therefore by the side of the joint household organization we find a system of laws which govern succession to property: it is clear that when a member of a group departs, his interests must be vested in somebody else. At the outset a fundamental distinction has to be made: the natural law of succession refers to *personal* property: it is, for example, in this basic principle that the English classification into real and personal property has its origin. There are many forms of property which are intimately connected with the person of the individual and the private uses which he finds for his possessions. A totally different set of interests is connected with *immovable* property: here the rights and interests involved are clearly of a more permanent character, and in many cases extend beyond the isolated individual. Succession to personal property arises very early in the history of societies: there are many things in which a man is conceived as having a distinctively individual interest—his shield, his sword, and so forth, are regarded almost as part of his personality. Hence among the most primitive peoples succession to personal property is governed by one set of rules, while totally different principles are recognized for real property. Very frequently the view was held that the dead man had the right to take with him into the next world a part of the possessions which had been his during life. He could not, as it were, claim all his property from the grave, for a compromise had to be made with the interests of the surviving members of his kin. But it was generally considered as a firmly estab-

"The dead man's portion."

lished principle that the deceased had the right to "a dead man's portion." The practice often took the form of putting in the grave those particular things which were considered *necessaries* for the life of the departed in the next world. This custom was very general in Egypt, and we find it in some form or other among most Aryan peoples. A familiar instance is the description of Scyld's funeral in Beowulf.[1] In the interesting and instructive description of the customs of the ancient Russians given by an Arabian writer, Ibn Fadhlan,[2] who lived in the tenth century, we are told that "the whole of the personal property was divided into three parts: one-third went to the family, the second third was used for making clothes and other ornaments for the dead, while the third was spent in carousing on the day when the corpse was cremated. The ceremony itself consisted in the following: the corpse was put into a boat, dressed in the most gorgeous attire. Intoxicating drinks, fruit, bread and meat were put by its side; a dog was cut into two parts, which were thrown into the boat. Then, all the weapons of the dead man were brought in, as well as the flesh of two horses, a cock and a chicken. The concubine of the deceased was also sacrificed, and ultimately all these objects were burned in a huge pile, and a mound thrown up over the ashes." This description is the more interesting because it starts from a division of the goods of the deceased, one part of them being appropriated, as it were, to his personal use. This rule continued to be observed in Germanic law in later times and became the starting-point of the doctrine of succession to personal property in English law. According to Glanville (vii. 5, 4) the chattels of the deceased have to be divided into three equal parts, of which one goes to the heir, one to his wife, and one is reserved to the deceased himself. "The same reservation of the third to the deceased himself is observed in Magna Carta (c. 26) and in Bracton's *De Legibus* (fol. 60), but in Christian surroundings the reservation of 'the dead man's part' was confined to the property which was

[1] I, 28-40.
[2] Harkavy, *Mohammedan Writers on Russia* (Russian).

to be spent for the good of his soul and of which, accordingly, the Church had to take care."[1]

Practical considerations prevented too much waste in the disposal of goods for the benefit of the deceased. A large part of them was, naturally, distributed among those who were nearest to him, and as regards cattle, money and other movable property, a division in equal shares between persons standing in the same degree of relationship to the deceased suggested itself as a matter of course. We find the same principle applied in cases where land was regarded as a marketable commodity and could be fairly easily sold. In the later law of Greece, Rome, and of Romance and Germanic nations, as far as they lived under economic systems based on cash nexus, equal partition of land among heirs is also recognized. This may be illustrated, for instance, from the customs of so-called *gavelkind* in mediaeval England.[2] It would be wrong, however, to suppose that the principle of equal sharing ever obtained unrestricted application in the customary law of Aryan peoples. It could not hold good in regard to commodities which formed organic units: it was out of the question to assign equal shares to three brothers in one bull or one horse. What is even more important, an estate, a farm, a holding, were also considered primarily from the point of view of the organic combination embodied in them, and this is where the idea of real property comes in to modify the abstract influence of personal claims of inheritance. On the one hand a farm is not regarded, and has never been regarded, as a mere complex of land and dwellings, but must have the necessary outfit of cattle, implements, seed, other stores necessary for production, and—labourers. In Roman terminology this stock annexed to the farm for the purpose of its working is characteristically called the "instrument" of the estate (*instrumentum fundi*). In the law of inheritance

Equal shares to nearest kin.

But personal sharing restricted as regards organic units.

[1] See my article on "Succession" in the *Encyclopædia Britannica*, 11th ed.

[2] *Gavelkind* is derived from *gafol*, rent, and the name therefore points to the prevalence of the custom among the rent-paying socmen of Kent, Sussex and other counties which had kept up a large population of small freeholders.

the same organic unity produces fundamental restrictions in the application of the principle of personal sharing. We need not go back to the question of joint management which has already been discussed. If such a joint management cannot be carried out for some reason or other—e.g., because the population of the estate would be too crowded, or because of dissensions between the members—if the land has to go by inheritance instead of continuing under joint tenure, the customary law of succession tends in one way or another to preserve the vitality of the farm or holding. This means that some of the claimants of equal degree have to waive their potential rights in favour of one among them. This may not happen by necessity if the estate in question can be easily subdivided, but in all cases of dismemberment difficulties arise, and at a certain stage actual partition may be quite impossible. Such situations are met in various ways. One of the best examples is to be found in Norse law—an example which provides an explanation for some of the more complicated institutions of Continental systems. The unity of the estate is recognized in the so-called *Odal* succession.[1] Not every estate is restricted by the land settlements of the Odal, but an estate which has been in the possession of a kindred for several (five) generations is reputed to be Odal.

Norwegian *Odal* succession.

There are all sorts of precautions against the Odal passing out of the kindred into the hands of strangers, but these precautions do not operate by way of an absolute prohibition. It is not said, for example "A stranger cannot buy the Odal"; the rule is that if the owner of an estate wants to sell it, he cannot simply go into the market and look for the highest bidder. He is first to offer it for sale to his own relatives and they can take it over even if there is some one else who will give more. They can have one-fifth of the price taken off in order to facilitate the sale to them. Even if they should not find it possible to avail themselves of this privilege, and consequently let the stranger purchase the estate, their rights do not disappear altogether,—they can come back and compel the stranger

[1] Cf. BRANDT, *Norsk Retshistorie*, I, p. 220 ff.

to sell the estate to them at a redemption price, should they have acquired the means and wish to resort to such redemption.

Odal right ought not to curtail the claims of the younger sons or of any heirs in a similar position. As a matter of fact, however, customary succession in Norwegian peasant-families sets great value on holding the property of the household well together. It is keenly felt that a *gaard* (farm) ought not to be parcelled into smaller holdings, and in the frequent case of several heirs succeeding to the farm, they generally agree among themselves who is to remain in charge of the ancestral household: the rest are compensated in money or helped to start on some other estate, perhaps in a cottage by the side of the principal house.

It is considered to be wrong for a son to insist on his right to get his share out of the actual estate; and in this way the organic unity of the estate is guaranteed in spite of the fact that it involves heavy charges on the land.

Ancient Welsh system.

The working of a similar competition between claims of relationship and requirements of *organic* husbandry is even more characteristically expressed in the Welsh system, where the original community of the *wele* or bed (*lectum*) becomes differentiated into *gavells* according to *stirpes*. Thus in the Introduction to the *Survey of the Honour of Denbigh, 1334*,[1] it is stated that, "In the surveys of the cantreds of Rewaynok and Roos, we find that the kindred appears as a rule to be differentiated into smaller units—the wele (*lecta*) and the gavells. There was no strict line of demarcation between these different terms. . . . In general the terms *wele* or *lectum*, meaning literally *bed*, might be rendered by the expression *stock*, and we can hardly go far wrong in assuming on the evidence of the Welsh laws that the term was usually applied in Welsh tribal custom to the descendants of a common father, grandfather or great-grandfather. Up to that point, a close community of interests was maintained not only as against

[1] Ed. by P. Vinogradoff and F. Morgan, *British Academy Records of the Social and Economic History of England and Wales* (1914), pp. xxii, ff.

strangers, but also as against more remote relations of the same kindred. A curious corroboration of this rule may be found in our Survey, where it is stated on two or three occasions that inheritance in land went on intestacy down to the third degree (*tertium gradum*); thus in the commote of Kaymergh it is stated that the son of a freeman on the death of his father must pay the lord ten shillings by way of relief, whereas a brother or nephew or more remote heir to the third degree shall pay twenty shillings for the same relief. Beyond the third degree, relations cannot claim the inheritance, and the land falls to the lord as an escheat; but if the lord wishes to let it, he has to offer it to the nearest in blood (*propinquiori de sanguine*) for its full price before he offers it to any stranger. The same principle of inheritance to the third degree is stated to exist in the commote of Yssalet. . . . Second cousins, as descendants of a common grandfather, would constitute this third degree, or, as we should put it, third generation. When that grade is passed, relationship still exerts a certain influence, but one which is limited at the time of the Survey to a preferential treatment by the lord in the letting of land. Reverting to the notion of common stock, we may assume that it was applied usually to the descendants of a person through males down to the line of great-grandchildren. One would have to go to the Laws to ascertain that such consequences were manifested both in regard to rights of property acquired by inheritance and to common defence. . . . As for the surveys, they inform us that the rights and functions of the lecta in regard to property were of the same kind as those of the kindreds (progenies), though more restricted in the sphere of their application. Still it must not be supposed that progenies and lectum are simply interchangeable terms. . . . On the whole, however, a general correspondence appears between the two units of organization in regard to rights of property. Thus we find that the co-parceners of a lectum appear as members of the same society of owners in various villages where the stock has rights of property . . . but by the side of such cases, we naturally find others in which the lecta broke up into differentiated settlements in the process of occupying and reclaiming land. . . . In such cases, the natural thing would be to speak of the lectum as broken up into gavells. . . . It may seem at first sight that the gavell was merely a subdivision of the wele, and it was in fact so treated by Seebohm. But it seems that the expression was really used on rather a different plane. If *lectum* roughly corresponds to the English stock, *gavell* might be appropriately rendered by the English *holding*. . . . What is evidently meant is the territorial basis of the kindred's rights, i.e., its holding or estate. . . . But the term is constantly employed, in the surveys of Yssalet and Ughalet, Ysdulas and Ughdulas, for the specific holdings among which the possessions of a kindred or wele are distributed. In this case, the gavell may be considered in two aspects—either as the closest and narrowest circle of blood-relations holding in common, or as the territorial basis of their holding. The first or personal aspect may be exemplified by almost any of the cases referred to in the Survey. The number of co-heirs and parceners . . . would sometimes be very considerable, and the tenement might be best described as a 'joint family holding.' . . . But the territorial aspect is also very prominent. From this point of view we get estimates of the number of acres which ought to have been apportioned to each gavell if the land were held not in ideal shares but in separate occupation. . . . It should be noted that the formation of communal unions and holdings on the basis of kinship is by no means restricted to the free population; the *nativi* (taeogs) are grouped in stocks and gavells in the same way as the free tribesmen. . . . But while we must recognize a general similarity in the economy of the free and unfree groups, it may not be purely accidental that in connection with *nativi* the term progenies, applied to an extensive kindred or class, is hardly ever used. We constantly hear of weles or gavells held by *nativi:* but the mention of a progenies of *nativi* is quite isolated and probably relates not to an organized kindred, but to a loose succession of generations."[1]

[1] Cf. VINOGRADOFF, *The Growth of the Manor* (2nd ed., 1911), pp. 13, 20-2.

The Indian *Pattidári* system.

In Indian custom we have indications of the treatment of the problem on lines determined by parentage. This is the so-called *Pattidári* system. Its main features are described in Baden-Powell's work as follows:[1]

"The principle of sharing is, or originally was, not one of 'democratic' equality of right in the area obtained, but one depending on the place in the table of descent from the founder or acquirer, the different heirs each taking the 'legal' share that belongs to him by the law or custom of inheritance. . . . Properly speaking, each takes his share in the land or in the proceeds, if the land is undivided, and pays the corresponding fraction of the revenue or other burdens. If the waste has remained undivided and is afterwards partitioned, the owners will share it in exactly the same fractions as have determined their holdings in the arable. This is the admitted theory; but naturally it often happens that in the course of years the strict shares have been forgotten or changed, and members not really of the founder's kin—perhaps members of the wives' families or other 'helpers in time of need'—may have been admitted to shares. Shares may also have been sold to outsiders under stress of necessity. Accordingly . . . where each now holds simply on the basis of his *de facto* possession . . . the village ceases to be *pattidári,* or 'ancestrally shared.' . . . This principle (*pattidári,* or ancestral-sharing according to the law of joint-inheritance) is simply the result of the joint-succession of all the heirs together. It is in villages of this class that it can truly be said that the village is the group which is held together by the land which it occupies 'in common'—i.e., as joint-heirs or co-sharers. . . . Inside the *patti* are the next grade of divisions called *thok,* and then the *tula* (or *tola*). Under one or other of such final or 'primary' divisions are grouped the many subordinate later families; but their divisions receive no new designation. So much may be ventured in this preliminary statement, as to say that in all probability the general prevalence of the three primary, or larger, divisions in descending grade is essentially connected with the

[1] *The Indian Village Community* (1896), pp. 29-31.

close-kindred of the first founders—representing the shares of the founder's son (*patti*), grandson (*thok*), great-grandson (*tula*)."

The sub-divisions in this case are the result of a competition between the principle of relationship as expressed in *stirpes* and the tendency to keep up organic estates. The inheritance is not cut up among co-heirs, but is made to serve as a basis for smaller estates estimated in accordance with the relative standing of the branches in the pedigree. In the Malabar arrangement which, as I have said before,[1] is exactly parallel to the patriarchal arrangement, the *taiwazhi* holdings are eventually made to grow into independent *tarwads*.

Unified tenure in Mediaeval Europe.

In mediaeval Europe we find yet another system of the economic organization of inheritance. It may be called the system of *unified tenure*, and we may watch its organization at work in Romance countries under the name of the *mansus*. The Polyptych of St. Germain-des-Prés[2] or the Cartulary of St. Bertin give excellent instances of that tenurial arrangement. We have before us peasant-farms evidently designed to serve the needs of small households consisting of perhaps half a dozen members of various ages. The peasant in question is a *colonus*, of free, half-free or servile origin, and the succession is regulated by the custom of the estate in such a way that casual disruption is impossible. The fact that the tenure is a tributary one does not change the economic condition of the farm, although, of course, it contributes to its fixity and continuity.

Among Germanic nations the same practice is expressed in the customs governing such units as the *hufe*, the *hide*, the *ból*. As we know in the case of the hide, which appears in Bede's *Ecclesiastical History* as a *terra familiae*, the

[1] *Ante*, p. 267.

[2] *Polyptyque de l'Abbaye de Saint-Germain-des-Prés*, ed. by LONGNON (1895), II, e.g., I, 14: "A. lidus et uxor eius colona . . . habent secum infantes iii. . . . H. lidus et uxor eius lida . . . habent secum infantes iii. . . . Isti duo tenent mansum servilem i, habentem de terra arabili bunuaria vi et dimidium, de vinea aripennum i, de prato aripennum i et dimidium. Facit in vinea aripennos iiii, manoperas, quantum ei iubetur; pullos iii, ova xv." Cf. I, 42; II, 2-5, etc.

estate was deemed to correspond to the work of one large plough-team of eight oxen and consisted generally of about 120-160 acres. The possibility of sub-division was not entirely excluded, and we find that these considerable estates were partitioned into yardlands (virgates) and oxgangs (bovates). There, however, the sub-division stopped, and smaller holdings, if they had to be built up, fell entirely outside the scheme provided by the plough team. In technical language, tenures in the fields (*in campis*) were contrasted with cottages or crofts. Here again the mode of tenure has been stabilized by feudal law, but in itself there is nothing inherently repugnant to free tenure in such arrangements. The contrast is not between free and servile tenure, but between farming under natural husbandry and farming under cash nexus. In the first case the organic unity prevails; in the second estates become broken up in consequence of various money arrangements. As a matter of fact, in Scandinavian countries and in northern Germany the unification of tenure has nothing to do with a servile status of the peasantry.[1] On the other hand, it must be noticed that the equalization of the units termed *mansi* or *hufen* or *hides* does not necessarily follow from their consolidation. Where these units arose from scattered farms like the Norwegian *gaards*, or the homesteads of *statesmen* in Northumberland, there was no reason why they should be equal: in fact their size depended on topographical features, on the quality of the soil, irrigation, etc. A certain tendency towards average sizes was produced by the usual constitution of the family, especially if this family happened to be a small one; but obviously there could be no standard measure in this respect. On the other hand, in "nucleated" villages, where the settlers lived in groups, there arose the requirement of apportioning rights and duties. As to rights, such apportionment was governed by various factors, such as the scarcity of meadows which led to their division into strips, to be occupied alternately by the various households.[2] Similar results followed in the common case of arable cultivation on the open field system.

[1] SERING, *Erbrecht und Agrarverfassung in Schleswig-Holstein.*
[2] Cf. *post*, ch. ix, p. 336.

Here again ploughlands and yardlands were formed by the apportionment of scattered strips in various fields according to certain common standards. In this way there was created a basis for a system in which both personal relations and agricultural needs entered as factors. The Welsh gavell is an especially striking example of this tribal combination. Some clauses of the Welsh Laws afford evidence of the view that a free member of a tribal community, a *boneddig,* was supposed to have a customary claim to a certain number of strips in co-aration.[1] Such a claim could not be an absolute one, but while there was a quantity of waste land, it was not uncommon nor impracticable. The actual units of tenure are, however, built up not from such individual *assignations,* but from the units of kinsmen called gavells. Their normal sizes, though varying from one locality to another, tended to become standardized within each local group.[2]

In correspondence with these assignments of claims and rights, we find assessment to various burdens imposed on the communities—the tunk-pound, the feasting of chiefs, the provision of victuals to the chieftains' halls, hospitality to officials and strangers, etc.

There is no necessary connection between servility and the unification of holdings. As I have already mentioned, the superimposition of a lord's power strengthened the unifying tendencies and contributed to give them definite shape, but their origin is to be sought in the requirements of the economic situation, which made for unity as against dispersion, and which was especially strong in primitive times when, as the Serbs have expressed it, "the single man is no person."

This digression into the question of the unification of holdings could not be avoided in a chapter on succession. All systems of unified holdings, except the Joint Family, start from the exclusion of some of the heirs in favour of others. This ruling consideration may develop in two dif-

1 SEEBOHM, *The Tribal System in Wales* (2nd ed., 1904), pp. 91-93; *Venedotian Code,* II, xvi; *Ancient Laws and Institutes of Wales* (1841), I, pp. 178-9.

2 *Survey of Denbigh,* pp. xix and xxv.

ferent ways. If *authority* is the most important element of the institution, then seniority and primogeniture are clearly indicated in the case of inheritance. This is the case in all *patriarchal* arrangements. We need not go back to the *paterfamilias* rule, except to say that the natural substitute for it is the rule of the eldest brother, and that for this reason the most common political institution of early ages is the rule of the eldest. Nor is it necessary to dwell at special length on primogeniture applied to military tenure. We might just point to a parallel to the Western knights' fees in the impartible succession to the Indian *raj.*[1]

Primogeniture.

The converse case of *ultimogeniture* seems more strange, and requires some explanation. The succession of the youngest son to the home of his deceased father is an exceedingly widespread custom.[2] The wealth of material in this case allows us to trace sufficiently clearly the principal idea which governs this institution: the youngest son succeeds his father because usually he is the last to remain at home when his elder brothers have already gone out and started their own households.[3] Our observation cannot, however, stop here. One is naturally led to ask in what states of society this separation of the elder brothers from their patriarchal home can have been so usual as to shape the normal course of succession. Sir James Frazer points to pastoral habits and to the rudimentary stages of agriculture when tribes cultivated their lands by destructive methods, such as burning down forests for the sake of fertilizing the soil with the cinders, and migrated to other fields when the fertility of the harvest began to fail.[4] In surroundings of this kind customs of ultimogeniture may easily arise, but we must not lose sight of the fact that in some of the most characteristic traces of pastoral and mi-

Ultimogeniture.

1 West and Bühler, *A Digest of the Hindu Law of Inheritance*, I, p. 157; II, pp. 735-41.

2 Sir J. G. Frazer, *Folk-lore in the Old Testament* (1918), I, pp. 433 ff

3 Frazer, *op. cit.*, I, p. 440. Bogišić, *Zbornik Pravnih Običaja* (1874), p. 1.

4 Frazer, *op. cit.*, I, pp. 442, 443, etc. Hanssen, *Agrarhistorische Abhandlungen.*

gratory life the patriarchal system arose and developed with great success. This was eminently the case in regard to the Hebrews, from whose condition Frazer's analysis starts. On the other hand, ultimogeniture in the shape of the *droit de maineté, Jüngstenrecht,* Borough English, etc., appears firmly established in the life of sedentary populations whose members were legally and economically *adscripti glebae.* The going out of the elder brothers in such cases cannot be regarded as a free movement in quest of waste land, and yet it is just among these half-servile peasants that ultimogeniture is especially common in Europe. A new link has therefore to be found in the chain of explanation.

Without denying in the least the possibility of ultimogeniture in fluid states of society, we have to notice that in the life of small peasants exploited by lords there were also elements making for ultimogeniture. One of these elements is the size of the holding: when holdings are parcelled out into very small units, their size puts a stop to any enlargement of the family on the lines of a *zadruga.* Whatever the relation of the holdings to one another, each single holding becomes emphatically a "one-man lot," and under these circumstances the struggle for existence suggested the keeping of the weakest at home and the attempt of the stronger to get out into his own independent walk of life, either as a settler under new conditions on reclaimed land, or as an occupier of a deserted holding, or as a sergeant or bailiff, later on as a labourer seeking wages.[1]

From the special point of view of succession, however, both primogeniture and ultimogeniture appear as effects of one and the same main cause—the necessity of keeping up organic units of an economic nature.

Let us now turn to the well-known disabilities of women

[1] For the revision of the population of manors by the bailiff see *Historia et Cartularium Monasterii Sancti Petri Gloucestriae* (Rolls Series, 1867), III, p. 213: "convocentur omnes nativi maneriorum . . . provideatur districte qui sunt apti retinendi in servitio domini, et in quo servitio, et ad quem locum . . . quandocumque placuerit loci ballivo, amoveantur ab uno loco usque ad alium ad commodum domini."

The exclusion of women from succession to land.

imposed by primitive law as regards succession to land. Norse law puts women and men on the same footing in regard to all forms of property equated to "movable money" (*Lösöre*), but as to land there is a prevalent idea that men should be privileged. Women are admitted to a certain extent, but always placed behind males of equal degree. According to the ancient provincial laws of Norway, estates are considered as belonging to the kindred with which they are connected historically. In order to keep these estates within the kindred they are to descend chiefly to males: women are admitted to them only in exceptional cases—when there is no male offspring of the same degree, e.g., if there is one daughter and no sons of the deceased, then the daughter will inherit; also the sister of one who has left no children and no brothers; nieces and first cousins may be admitted in the sense that they have to pass the property to their nearest male heir. The daughter's position will be altogether different from that of the daughter who has brothers. Instead of being provided with a dowry she is admitted to a man's share in the husbandry and the rights of revenge, and therefore is called in a characteristic manner *baugrygr*.[1] The notion is that through her the estate ought to pass by marriage to her son, and in this way to the male line again—a sort of engrafted male line, in the same manner as by engrafting a tree—the tree of kinship.

Frankish and Lombard law originally excluded women from inheritance in land, and this exclusion seems as ancient as the patriarchal system itself, whatever we may think about the position of affairs in pre-historic times when rules of matriarchy were prevalent. A common-sense explanation of one side of this doctrine is tendered by the law of the Thuringians (*Lex Angliorum et Werinorum*, c. 6).[2] It is stated there that inheritance in land goes with the duty of taking revenge for the slaying of relatives and with the power of bearing arms. The man who

[1] *Baug*, bracelet and *rygr*, woman. The *wergeld* was supposed to be paid in gold bracelets, and the heiress of a man who had no male descendants was entitled to receive such a *wergeld*.

[2] See *post*, p. 302.

takes land ought also to get the suit of armour and the sword. The land is practically reserved for the warrior.

Of course with progress on economic lines things change, and we actually notice in England, for example, that women do obtain parts of the inheritance in land at an early date. One of the most potent adversaries of the system of exclusion of women was the Church. It favoured, all through, the view that land should be transmitted in the same way as money and chattels. In Anglo-Saxon charters we consequently see that women hold and transfer land. The natural channel for their acquiring these rights consisted in the development of *bócland* property and of dower.

In the Norwegian system, the real proprietor is the person who gets a share in the *Baugs:* and if he dies leaving one daughter, she may succeed to the property; but she will transmit the right to her husband and eventually to her son. This view is even more fully expressed in Greek law, in the rights of the ἐπίκληρος, who is joined as a kind of complement to the κλῆρος: the fact that a man has not left sons who may succeed to his inheritance is remedied by the rule that his grandson may take the place of the natural heir. Again, a Frankish formula (*Marculf*) shows us a father who takes care to endow his daughter with a piece of land according to natural affection in spite of the strict law of his tribe.

It is hardly necessary to point out that the detailed Scandinavian and Germanic customs afford a good clue to the motives which underlie ancient Greek Law on the matter. The ἐπίκληρος of Athens and of Gortyn appears as a variety of the *baugrygr,* although it is the economic and not the military side of the institution which is prominent in the first case.

The Testament unknown to tribal custom.

One fundamental difference between the treatment of inheritance by tribal custom and by modern law consists in the fact that primitive organization leaves no room for the disposal of property by testament: volition is naturally supposed not to reach beyond the physical existence of the individual. A sentence in Tacitus, *Germania*,[1] serves admirably to summarize this view not only in the case of Teutons, but also in that of other Aryan nations: *heredes tamen successoresque sui cuique liberi, et nullum testamentum.* We find this principle at work even in comparatively late times. Indian law does not recognize testamentary power, in the proper sense of the word, apart from the law as to gifts.[2] Even now, although under the influence of English legal ideas the Indian law as to this subject has been to some extent developed, it is still limited and influenced by the rules as to gifts *inter vivos*.[3]

In ancient Greece the testament was the product of a comparatively late legislation. It does not appear at all in the inscriptions of Gortyn or of Naupaktos.[4] In Athens the power of disposing of property after death was introduced, according to tradition, by Solon. Originally the mode of procedure in the case of a disposal of family property after the death of the owner, was by adoption (ἐπίθεσις).[5]

The one marked and characteristic exception to this negative principle appears in the history of Roman Law. There can be no doubt that the Romans started from the same principle as the other branches of the Aryan family in regard to succession: *heredes successoresque sui cuique liberi, et nullum testamentum.* The conception of the unity of the household (*familia pecuniaque*) reflected by the cult of ancestors and supported by common property, is clearly expressed, among other things, in the standing of *sui heredes*, who are said in as many words to be masters of their property, successors in the administration of the household property as coming into their own.[6] The

The Roman Testament.

1 Ch. xx.

2 TUPPER, *Punjab Customary Law*, III, pp. 94 and 95; WEST and BÜHLER, *op. cit.*, I, p 182; II, p. 813.

3 *Tagore v. Tagore*, L. R. Sel. Ind App., p. 64, WEST and BÜHLER, I, p. 183.

4 DARESTE, HAUSSOULIER ET REINACH, *Recueil des inscriptions jurisdiques grecques*, I, pp. 180, 352.

5 SCHULIN, *Das griechische Testament.*

6 PAULUS, *Dig.* xxviii, 2, 11: "In suis heredibus evidentius apparet continuationem dominii eo rem perducere, ut nulla videatur hereditas fuisse: quasi olim hi domini essent, qui etiam vivo patre quodam-

heredium of two *jugera* assigned by Numa was regarded as a family share,[1] but the powerful development of the *patria protestas* opened the way for an early assertion of the personal will of the *paterfamilias,* the manager of the household. The XII Tables contain the definite rule: *si intestato moritur cui heres suus non escit, proximus adgnatus familiam habeto; si nec adgnatus escit, gentiles familiam habento.* These short sentences are well worthy of attention. To begin with, the case of a testamentary disposition is considered as a common one, and evidently confers the same right as the succession of the *suus* and of the *adgnatus,* the acquisition of the integral household (*familiam habento*). The direct aim of the rule was obviously to establish the sequence of claims to inheritance: as regards intestate succession the order proceeds from the *suus* to the *adgnatus* and then to the *gentiles.* It cannot be a mere accident that the *proximus adgnatus* is mentioned in the singular, while the *gentiles* appear in the plural: the law grants individual succession according to precedence of degree in one case, and provides for the return of goods to the *gentiles* as a body in the absence of agnates with a definite standing by pedigree. (Cf. Cicero, Top. VI, 29, on *gentiles.*) In view of such a careful distinction, it is hardly accidental that the *heres suus* also appears in the singular. It is known, of course, that Roman Law admitted heirs of equal degree to equal shares in the succession, but the phraseology of the XII Tables seems to suggest that it was customary in the older period to keep the "household" together as far as possible, and to provide in some other way for the satisfaction of current claims—possibly by arrangements like the unified succes-

modo domini existimantur. unde etiam filius familias appellatur sicut pater familias: sola nota hac adiecta, per quam distinguitur genitor ab eo qui genitus sit. itaque post mortem patris non hereditatem percipere videntur, sed magis liberam bonorum administrationem consequuntur; hac ex causa licet non sint heredes instituti, domini sunt: nec obstat, quod licet eos exheredare, quod et occidere licebat." GAIUS, II, 157: "Sed sui quidem heredes ideo appellantur, quia domestici heredes sunt et uiuo quoque parente quodammodo domini existimantur; unde etiam si quis intestatus mortuus sit, prima causa est in successione liberorum"

[1] CUQ, in the *Nouvelle revue historique de droit,* X, 537. *Manuel des institutions juridiques des Romains,* 683 ff

sion of the Norwegian *odal,* based on customary practice. It would be unsafe to rely too much on such indirect indications, but the hypothesis would tally with a well-established fact, namely, with the special position assigned to the *suus* in regard to a possible will. The *suus* mentioned in the rule of the XII Tables takes the property by a different title from the agnate, who claims only in the absence of *sui;* the former enters on the inheritance in his own right, while the latter has to establish his claim. The passage therefore implies that the right to make a will belonged only to such citizens as had no *heredes sui* (*cui heres suus non escit*). And indeed we know that in order to make a will against the interests of a *suus,* a son or grandson, a Roman citizen had to disinherit the latter in a formal manner (*exheredatio*). That such a procedure was not regarded as natural and easy is sufficiently indicated by the fact that Paulus compares it to the right of the *paterfamilias* to put his son to death (Dig. xxviii, 2, 11). In the light of this process one comes to understand the full meaning of the maxim—*nemo ex parte testatus, ex parte intestatus decedere potest.* It fits strictly the situation of *sui* in respect of a will. If a *suus* was disinherited, all his rights to the *familia* had to be disposed of: it was impossible to leave some of them to a disinherited person. What applied pre-eminently to direct descendants was naturally extended to other heirs *ab intestato.* One material difference there was between the exercise of the *ius necis* and the exercise of the power to disinherit by the *paterfamilias.* In the latter case, as the decision of the father had to take effect after his death and involved no alteration of the natural course of family relations, it depended for its validity on the consent of the assembly of clans presided over by the *pontifex maximus* (*comitia calata*).[1] It is not necessary to suppose that this oldest form of testament was derived from a practice of appointing a successor to the rule of a

Formal disinheritance of a *suus heres.*

[1] Gaius, II, 102: "Accessit deinde tertium genus testamenti quod per aes et libram agitur. Qui neque calatis comitiis neque in procinctu testamentum fecerat, is si subita morte urguebatur, amico familiam suam, id est patrimonium suum, mancipio dabat, eumque rogabat quid cuique post mortem suam dari uellet."

political association of the household.[1] There is no direct evidence of such a practice, and the analogy of the *interrex* and of the magistrate's designation may be explained on different grounds, though the view is not inherently impossible in theory. But the process as described by Gaius was clearly designed to meet exceptional cases, as it required the cumbersome interference of the *comitia calata* and could take place only on two days of the year.[2] It seems clear that it was originally reserved for cases of *exheredatio.* As in the kindred cases of *adrogatio* coupled with *detestatio sacrorum,* the federation of the clans had to pass a special decree in order to alter the usual course of family law.

This is the negative basis of the oldest Roman testament. Such a negative basis implies, however, a positive consequence. As one could not discard one's sacral obligations (*detestatio sacrorum*) without assuming obligations towards other *sacra,* even so one could not disinherit an heir without appointing another in his place. Hence the famous maxim, *heredis institutio est caput testamenti,* appears rooted in the oldest institution of the Roman will.[3]

Heredis institutio est caput testamenti.

The sacral and political side of the performance was, however, relegated to the background by considerations of a purely proprietary character. In the matter of intestate succession, the Romans, as well as other peoples, had to reckon with the plurality of heirs: their system did not favor either the growth of joint families or the formation of fixed holdings. The basis of their economic life was intensive agriculture,[4] and such husbandry leads to individual property in small farms. It would be needless to dwell on the part played by these small highly individualized plots in the social history of Rome.[5] Under these circumstances the fate of the *patrimonium* in all its aspects—as to land, stock, slaves, stores, pecuniary claims and debts,—became the chief object of succession, both intestate and by will.

[1] BONFANTE, *Bullettino,* IV, 97; VII, 157.
[2] MOMMSEN, *Staatsrecht,* II, 36; III, 318.
[3] Cf. MITTEIS, *Römisches Privatrecht,* I, 77
[4] Cato's directions to a husbandman were, *arare, arare, stercorare.*
[5] See e.g., WEBER, *Agrargeschichte Roms,* 81 ff; MOMMSEN, *Römische Geschichte,* I, 185, 441.

Bequests.

By the side of the institution of an heir or of several heirs by testament, there stood, as early as the forms of testament represented in the XII Tables, dispositions as to gifts after death, or bequests (*legata*). The famous passage as cited by Ulpian [1]—*Uti legassit super pecunia, tutelave suae rei, ita ius esto*—treats of bequests and wardships as of supplementary dispositions in the will, and for this reason restricts the source of such bequests to one part of the patrimony of the testator, namely, to his *pecunia*.[2]

The complete liberty to dispose of cattle and money and other movables was evidently in need of confirmation, and one can well suppose that many disputes between members of the family and strangers arose in connection with such gifts. Later on, legislation had to step in to protect heirs from the squandering of property by testators.[3] However, the power of bequest was admitted and expressed in the characteristic formula of the *legatum per vindicationem* preserved by Gaius. The expressions *mandatela* and *custodela* apply primarily to the trustee of an imaginary sale—the *familiae emptor*. They show not only that bequests were allowed within a wide range, but also that the function of the execution of the will was considered as a most important part of the performance. It fell naturally to the *heres* when the *familiae emptor* was degraded to a purely ceremonial participation in the proceedings.[5]

This is most evident in respect of the will *in procinctu*, which is represented by the sources as a substitute for the ceremony in the *comitia calata* conditioned by the exceptional circumstance of imminent battle.[6] In essence, it was not different from the full-dress performance before the

[1] GIRARD, *Textes de droit romain*, 3rd ed., p. 14, n. 3.

[2] MITTEIS, *Römisches Privatrecht*, I, 81 f.

[3] *Leges Furia, Voconia, Falcidia.*

[4] II, 193-200.

[5] I fail to see how the Roman system as regards testaments could have developed out of the *legata*, according to a theory first propounded by Cuq, supported by Ehrlich, and eventually worked out in a subtle manner by O. Lenel. It fails, as it seems to me, to account for the position of the *heres*. On the other hand, Bonfante seems to go much too far in assigning a purely political foundation to the *heredis institutio*. See LENEL, in *Essays in Legal History* (ed. by Vinogradoff), 120 ff.

[6] MOMMSEN—the will made in the interval between two military *auspicia* (*Staatsrecht*, III, 307).

curiae, though, as being made in haste, it was certainly emancipated from any strict forms and must have been confined in many cases to very elementary dispositions capable of being remembered and testified to by the comrades of the testator. This does not touch the essence of the transaction, however, which was meant to stand in lieu of the will made before the curial assembly.[1]

To meet the requirements of the new situation hingeing on the economic element of the *patrimonium*, a new device was brought in by practice, namely, the *familiae emptio*.[2] It consisted in the imaginary sale of the household to a third person who acted in the place of the heir (*loco heredis*). If we follow carefully Gaius' description, we can hardly escape the conclusion that the purchaser who was entrusted with the duty of carrying out the last will of the testator must have been originally exempted from the rule as to express disinheritance, as his function was derived from a simulated sale. As Gaius says, however, this was only a transitional stage which helped to vulgarize the process and to place it within reach of the plebeian community—a most important feature of this mode of proceeding. Once the practice struck root, it changed its character by absorbing some of the elements of the public testament. Safeguards were wanted against a possible misuse of his powers by the trustee, and as a result of such converging tendencies the "nuncupative" will *per aes et libram* arose and eventually became the typical civil law instrument of Roman jurisprudence in contrast to the still wider power conferred by the praetorian transmission of *bonorum possessio*. Here the *heredis institutio* and the freedom of making bequests are both represented, and in the formula addressed by the testator to the seven witnesses, who have taken the place of the *libripens* and his *classici testes*,[3] there is still a vestige of the ancient participation of the community.

1 ERDMANN, *Zeitschrift für vergleichende Rechtswissenschaft*, XXII, 14 ff.

2 GAIUS, II, 103.

3 GAIUS, II, 104. Ita do, ita lego, ita testor, itaque vos Quirites testimonium mihi perhibetote.

We need not follow further the intricate speculations of modern writers as to the time and conditions under which "universal succession," and especially the liability as to debts, were developed by Roman jurisprudence. This topic, though very important in itself, can hardly be reconstructed historically with sufficient precision. Nor does it belong properly to the domain of tribal law.

PART III

CLAN AND TRIBE

CHAPTER VIII

THE ORGANIZATION OF KINSHIP

The group in ancient society.

THE most profound difference between modern and ancient organization consists in the fact that modern society starts from individuals and adjusts itself primarily to the claims of the individual, whereas ancient society starts from groups and subordinates individual interests to the claims of these groups. There are two general reasons for this state of things. To begin with, there is the weakness and insecurity of the single man in barbaric surroundings, which drives him to seek companionship and to place himself under protection at any price. It is only by close union that tribesmen can survive in the difficult struggle for life against outsiders. A single man would be a lost man. In the words of Robertson Smith, "It is only by mutual help, by avoiding intestine quarrels and subordinating individual interests to those of the kin, that, in the hard conditions of desert life, and in a state of constant war with outsiders, a tribe can hope to hold its own (comp. *Agh.* ii. 170, 1). To get the full benefit of this mutual support, the group or *hayy* must not only fight together, but as far as possible move together."[1]

There is also a second reason which may not perhaps be so clearly perceived by those who deal with these matters. In modern society the State has assumed the monopoly of political co-ordination. It is the State which rules, makes laws, and eventually enforces them by coercion. Such a State, as a wide and more or less abstract union, did not exist in ancient times. The commonwealth was not centred in one sovereign body towering immeasurably above single individuals and meting out to every one his portion of right. Therefore the necessary political elements which are never absent from any human society, were distributed

[1] *Kinship and Marriage in Arabia*, p 37.

among formations which we regard now from the point of view of private law: churches, local bodies, kindreds.

Agnatic groups.

The organization of kinship for purposes of defence and mutual help is naturally dependent on the manner in which relationship is constituted in primitive societies. Of the three possible methods of treating relationship, the agnatic, the cognatic, and the totemic systems—we have to reckon in the case of the Aryan nations only with the first two. The totemic classification does not manifest itself, because the nations in question became known to us in the fairly advanced stage of development connected with separate households.

There is also a marked tendency towards agnatism which admits of a more compact and effective organization of the group under the household rule of a patriarch or of a substitute selected from his male relatives.

In order to see the process actually at work in historical circumstances, let us glance at the way in which this agnatic principle has been developed by some of the Aryan races.

Among the *Hindus,* agnatic relationship was certainly the prevailing one: and it should always be borne in mind in dealing with the Aryans in general that, as far back as we can look, we find the predominance of the patriarchal family. We need not necessarily conclude that the patriarchal family was a primordial institution. But apart from the question of absolutely primeval origins, it is incontestable that within that section of Aryan history which is known to us by actual evidence, agnatism arising out of the patriarchal family is certainly the social starting-point of kinship. Thus, according to Gautama,[1] "*Sapindas* (blood relations within six degrees), *Sagotras* (relations bearing a common family name), or those connected by descent from the same *Rishi* (*vaidika gotra*), and the wife shall share (the estate) of a person deceased with-

[1] XXVIII, § 21 (*Sacred Books of the East*—II, *The Sacred Laws of the Âryas* Pt. I, transl. by G. BÜHLER, 2nd ed., 1897). Cf. *Manu* IX, 187; *Âpastamba* II, 6, 14, 2; *Yâjñavalkya* II, 135-6; WEST and BÜHLER, *A Digest of the Hindu Law of Inheritance, Partition, and Adoption*, 3rd ed. (1884), I, p. 114.

out (male) issue (or an appointed daughter)." Cognates are indicated by the term *Bandhu*.[1]

Greek and Roman antiquities provide well known examples of the action of agnatism. The *γένος* (*πάτρα*) is as old as Greece itself: in these associations the patriarchal principle is clearly fundamental. Aristotle says: "The family is the association established by nature for the supply of man's everyday wants, and the members of it are called by Charondas 'companions of the cupboard' [*ὁμοσιπύους*], and by Epimenides the Cretan 'companions of the manger' [*ὁμοκάπους*]. But when several families are united and the association aims at something more than the supply of daily needs, then comes into existence the village. And the most natural form of the village appears to be that of a colony from the family composed of the children and the grandchildren who are said to be 'suckled with the same milk' [*ὁμογάλακτας*]."[2]

The period of the Eupatrids in Athens may serve as an example. The ancient constitution of that city before Cleisthenes was entirely based on a federation of phratries and *γένη*. All these alliances were essentially agnatic; they possessed the usual characteristic features—they started

[1] West and Bühler, I, pp. 486-8.

[2] *ἡ μὲν οὖν εἰς πᾶσαν ἡμέραν συνεστηκυῖα κοινωνία κατὰ φύσιν οἶκος ἐστιν, οὓς ὁ μὲν Χαρώνδας καλεῖ ὁμοσιπύους, Ἐπιμενίδης δὲ ὁ Κρὴς ὁμοκάπους. ἡ δ' ἐκ πλειόνων οἰκιῶν κοινωνία πρώτη χρήσεως ἕνεκεν μὴ ἐφημέρου κώμη. μάλιστα δὲ κατὰ φύσιν ἔοικεν ἡ κώμη ἀποικία οἰκίας εἶναι, οὓς καλοῦσί τινες ὁμογάλακτας* [*παῖδάς τε καὶ παίδων παῖδας*]. Pol. I, 2. 5-6 (p. 1252 b). According to Dikæarchos, as reported by Stephen of Byzantium, *πάτρα, ἓν τῶν τριῶν τῶν παρ' Ἕλλησι κοινωνίας εἰδῶν, ὡς Δικαίαρχος, ἃ δὴ καλοῦμεν πάτραν, φρατρίαν, φυλήν. ἐκλήθη δὲ πάτρα μὲν εἰς τὴν δευτέραν μετάβασιν ἐλθόντων ἡ κατὰ μόνας ἑκάστῳ πρότερον οὖσα συγγένεια, ἀπὸ τοῦ πρεσβυτάτου τε καὶ μάλιστα ἰσχύσαντος ἐν τῷ γένει τὴν ἐπωνυμίαν ἔχουσα ὃν ἂν τρόπον Αἰακίδας ἢ Πελοπίδας εἴποι τις ἄν. Φατρίαν δὲ συνέβη λέγεσθαι καὶ φρατρίαν, ἐπειδή τινες εἰς ἑτέραν πάτραν ἐδίδοσαν θυγατέρας ἑαυτῶν. οὐ γὰρ ἔτι τῶν πατριωτικῶν ἱερῶν εἶχε κοινωνίαν ἡ δοθεῖσα, ἀλλ' εἰς τὴν τοῦ λαβόντος αὐτὴν συνετέλει πάτραν. ὥστε πρότερον πόθῳ τῆς συνόδου γιγνομένης ἀδελφαῖς σὺν ἀδελφῷ, ἑτέρα τις ἱερῶν ἐτέθη κοινωνικὴ σύνοδος, ἣν δὴ φρατρίαν ὠνόμαζον. καὶ πάλιν ὥστε πάτρα μὲν ὅνπερ εἴπομεν ἐκ τῆς συγγενείας τρόπον ἐγένετο μάλιστα τῆς γονέων σὺν τέκνοις καὶ τέκνων σὺν γονεῦσι, φρατρία δὲ ἐκ τῆς τῶν ἀδελφῶν.*

from the household around a hearth fire, though the unit of association was frequently enlarged by adoption; but it was always thought that the adopted sons stepped entirely into the position of those naturally born. The marriage of the heiress (ἐπίκληρος) with the nearest agnate in Greece,[1] the succession and guardianship of agnates in Rome,[2] are striking expressions of the prevalence of relationship through males in the social organization of the classical world.

In the case of the Teutons the *sword side* has a natural and marked precedence over the *spindle side* in all matters concerning defence and ownership of land.[3] Among Scandinavian folk the Frostathing law may serve as an example. The customary law of tribes settled around Trondhjem in Norway treats wergeld from the agnatic point of view. All those who take the principal parts of the composition, the *baugar*, are agnates of various degrees; relationship through women is relegated to a subordinate position as the *nefgildi*. A woman takes a *baug* only exceptionally, when she is the only daughter and heiress of a slain man (*baugrygr*).[4]

Cognatism recognized as a subsidiary tie.

By the side of the principal ties of relationship which start from a patriarchal household and spread out in the ramifications of agnatism, the Aryan nations recognize in a lesser degree the value of relationship through women. There arises a dualism of relationship—on the side of the father (the *spear*) and on the side of the mother (the

[1] *Law of Gortyn*, X, § 45 (Dareste, *Rec. des inscrip. jur. grecques*, I, p. 375); Daremberg et Saglio, *Dictionnaire*, s. v. epikleros.

[2] Gaius, I, 155-6.

[3] *Lex Salica* (ed. Geffcken, 1898) LIX, p. 59: "De terra vero nulla in muliere hereditas non pertinebit, sed ad virilem sexum qui fratres fuerint tota terra pertineat." Cf. *Monumenta Germaniae*, LL. V, pp. 103 ff.: *Lex Angliorum et Werinorumn hoc est Thuringorum*, par. 26: "Hereditatem defuncti filius non filia suscipiat, si filium non habuit qui defunctus est, ad filiam pecunia et mancipia, terra vero ad proximum paternae generationis consanguineum pertineat" Par. 34: "Usque ad quintam generationem paterna generatio succedat. Post quintam autem filia ex toto, sive de patris sive matris parte, in hereditatem succedat, et tunc demum hereditas ad fusum a lancea transeat."

[4] Vinogradoff, *Geschlecht und Verwandtschaft im altnorwegischen Recht* (*Zeitschrift für Sozial- und Wirtschaftsgeschichte*, V).

spindle). If we proceed one generation higher, we have to reckon with an alliance of four families in the ascending line, because the descent from four grandparents converges in the case of every individual. If we go further back again to the great-grandfathers and great-grandmothers, we may get *eight lines* of converging descent, etc. The Frisians were actually organized on the basis of certain definite bodies of relationship called the *Klüfte* (corresponding to the four grandparents) and the *Fechten* (corresponding to the eight great-grandparents).[1]

The Germanic conception of the *Sippe* (*sibja*—Goth.) came to be applied to relationship on both sides—through males and through females, although there are clear traces of an earlier arrangement on strictly agnatic principles.[2]

The stream of feeling of union naturally diminishes with the remoteness of the degree of kinship. The further two persons are apart from each other in generation and household, the less powerful will be the bond of union between them: and we must therefore expect that in all systems of relationship it will be necessary to recognize certain concentric circles within which the rights and duties of the relations are more or less intense. On the evidence of actual facts, this is certainly true: we may observe everywhere this characteristic formation of circles.

The kindred in ancient Greek law.

A conspicuous example is to be found in Greek criminal procedure—the survival of the right of *accusation by the kindred*. Homicide was, in the view of ancient Greek law, chiefly a private wrong: or perhaps it would be more accurate to say that it was a public wrong which was inflicted not on the city, but on a clan. Hence came the rule of Greek criminal law that, when a man was slain, the accusation against the slayer should come from the relatives of the man killed. The principle is very definitely formulated in a law of Dracon of 621 B.C. The fragment was transcribed after the overthrow of the Four Hundred about 409 B.C.,

1 G-father = G-mother G-father = G-mother

Father ——————— = ——————— Mother

Ego

(See BRUNNER, *Deutsche Rechtsgeschichte*, II, pp. 114-6.)

2 AMIRA, *Grundriss des germanischen Rechts*, pp. 169 ff.

and thanks to this transcription we have an authentic record of the early law as to homicide: a law, it is to be remembered, which preceded the Solonian by one generation. The principal prosecutors are members of the ἀγχιστεία a circle of close relationship.[1]

"The lead in a prosecution of the slayer in the market-place shall be taken by all relations nearer than the degree of cousinship, and cousins and children of cousins, and sons-in-law and fathers-in-law and members of the phratry shall join in the prosecution. And if there be a question as to conciliation, then, if there be a father or brother or sons, they shall all join in allowing the conciliation, and if any one of them opposes it, he shall prevail."

Thus the initial accusation had to be made in the market by relations within the degree of first cousins once removed, and it is very important to note that in the next stage this wider kindred merges in the *phratry*, the extension of the γένος: so that ultimately these kindreds are conceived as big households federated in phratries. The next provision of the law is that, while the kindred can claim the execution of the offender, they are also empowered to enter into a compromise with him. But the decision as to conciliation must be unanimous on the part of the narrower family circle, and even one single dissentient voice is an effective bar to the whole proceeding. If there are no direct relatives, then the decision devolves solely on the phratry, ten members of which are empowered to declare for composition if they think proper.

[1] The ἀγχιστεία in the fifth and fourth centuries comprised the collaterals up to the degree of first cousins once removed or, possibly, of second cousins (corresponding to the Latin *sobrini*), both on the male and on the female side. In the case of succession we meet the same extension of the narrow household circle into the ἀγχιστεία comprising relations μέχρι ἀνεψιότητος that is, up to first cousins once removed, but in this case the claims of relations through females (sisters, aunts and cousins) are admitted, although the male side is preferred. In view of the constitution of the πάτρα or γένος it can hardly be doubted that the fourth century rule was an extension of an earlier agnatic arrangement.

See Caillemer, *Droit de Succession à Athènes*, pp. 7 ff.; Leist, *Graeco-italische Rechtsgeschichte*, p. 83; and in the opposite sense, Jevons, *Kin and Custom, Journal of Philology*, XVI (1888), pp. 95-8.

In this particular instance we are dealing with an advanced civilization: Athens about 621 B.C. had become not only very civilized, but to a great extent commercialized; the Greeks looked at relationship more or less from a point of view resembling our own; and yet the dependence of the individual on the kindred is strongly expressed. Among other races which developed much more slowly, we find the same idea of concentric circles of relationship more definitely connected with the growth of the households. A notable example appears among the Celts in the Irish *Fine.*[1] The principle of organization does not merely estimate the degree of proximity, but leads to a computation ascending to the heads of definite households.

The conclusion to be drawn from all these examples is

[1] *Gelfine*—own household descendants of the same father: brothers, nephews, sons, grandsons.

Derbfine—certain kin: descendants of the same grandfathers: uncles, first cousins, first cousins' sons.

Iarfine—further kin: descendants of great-grandfathers: great-uncles, second cousins and their sons.

Indfine—end of kin: fourth degree—third cousins.

					Derbfine Certain	*Iarfine* Subsequent	*Indfine* Final
						3rd degree	
					son of 1st cousin	son of 2nd cousin	son of 3rd cousin
						2nd degree	
					1st cousin Mac brāthar athar	2nd cousin	3rd cousin
						1st degree	
	Gelfine				paternal uncle Brāthir athar	grand-uncle	great-grand-uncle
4th degree,	3rd degree,	2nd degree,	1st degree,				
great-great-grand-son Indúa	great-grand-son Iarmúa	grand-son Úa	son Mac	father Athair	grand-father Sen-athair	great-grand-father Sen-sen-athair	gg-grand-father

Dóini, outsiders to the family, form a fifth class.

See Arbois de Jubainville, *La famille celtique*, p. 18.

that even in cases when the blood tie is recognized, relations are organized according to households, so that cognatism appears as the result of an alliance between patriarchally organized families. This is the essence of the *stirpes* or *parentelæ,* as they were called in mediæval times. The *stirps* consisted of descendants of one particular household: it could be the house of the father or mother,[1] but it could also be the house of an uncle, as the representative of a connection through the grandfather, or that of a great-uncle—the descendant of a great-grandfather.

Distinction between kindred and clan.

In its wider extension relationship becomes kinship. When organized into a group, it acts as a union for the purposes of self-defence and other vital social requirements. Let us notice the material distinction between a kindred and a clan. The latter embraces only agnatic relations: it is based on the idea of the ever-expanding household, and agnation is the fundamental principle which creates and maintains it.[2] In the kindred, on the other hand, cognation is admitted as a concurrent conception. But while it is both useful and necessary to observe these differences in terminology, which express very different notions and give rise to very different kinds of rights, it is not to be supposed that because clans come into existence, the kindred in the wider sense becomes impossible, or *vice versa.* It is necessary to emphasize this fact, because the contrast of the two principles has given rise to some misconceptions in the treatment of the subject. After studying social formations merely from the point of view of the clan, and realizing the fundamental difference between the principles of clan and kindred, many writers have supposed that the two things are to some extent mutually exclusive. Fustel de Coulanges, for instance, entirely disregards cognatic ties in the construction of the Roman and Greek family. On the other hand, even so authoritative a historian as

[1] The alliance between the household of the father and that of the mother is clearly expressed in Old Norwegian Law, as *fadherni* and *modherni.* See VINOGRADOFF, *Z. für Social- und Wirtschaftsgeschichte,* V.

[2] GAIUS, III, 17.

Maitland declared that as soon as men recognize the wide circle of cognatic relationship, we had better cease to speak of clans.[1] In reality it is erroneous to make the terms mutually exclusive in this rigid manner; for on examining the evidence we find that in innumerable cases the two formations overlap, as it were, and combine in all kinds of compromises suggested by utility. In many cases, though we find a very pronounced recognition of the clan principle, another powerful influence is also asserting itself: the necessity for alliances in self-defence makes it desirable to call in other clans or kindreds into association with the principal group.[2] In this way around a kernel of agnatic relationship supplementary cognatic alliances are formed. On the other hand, it is easy to realize that in course of time, as the individual becomes more and more emancipated and the State grows stronger, the strict principle of clan organization begins to fade. In proportion as it declines, individual relationship takes the place of the household bond. It is along such lines of transition that the history of social institutions is found to proceed.

The clan organization.

Let us look at the clan as the more consistent manifestation of agnatic kinship. All the members of the clan traced their pedigree from one original household and all regarded themselves as having a share by right in the territory held by the collective body of the clan. Thus there is a lively personal consciousness of the principle of combination between representatives of all kinds of social grades and occupations. The intensity of the feeling for the clan was best shown when attempts were made to disband this kind of organization. Scott provides us in *Rob Roy* with a vivid account of the circumstances under which the clan McGregor was outlawed and subjected to protracted persecution.

What were the leading features in the normal organization and management of a clan? They have been made familiar to us in literary form by Walter Scott. In some of his descriptions of Scotch life he has provided remark-

[1] *History of English Law*, II, p. 242 (2nd ed.); cf. Miss Phillpotts, *Kindred and Clan*.

[2] Vinogradoff, *Growth of the Manor*, p. 11. Cf. Arbois de Jubainville, *Revue Celtique*, 1902, pp. 358 ff.

able pictures of these arrangements, and his account is highly valuable not only for its intrinsic vigour and interest, but for the accuracy of the information it contains. In *Waverley,* for example, he gives us a picture of the clan of Fergus MacIvor, in 1745, and it should be remembered that this is not merely an imaginative description, but one which would have applied with perfect appropriateness to any of the great clans of Scottish history—the MacDonalds, Gordons, Mackintoshs, etc. In Chapter XX we are told that during the rising of 1745 a chieftain invited an English officer to a banquet. At the head of the table sat the chief and his visitor; then the elders of the chief's tribe, wadsetters and tacksmen, as they were called, who occupied portions of the estates as mortgagers or lessees, sat next in rank; lower down their sons and nephews and foster-brothers; then the officers of the chief's household, according to their order, and, lowest of all, the tenants who actually cultivated the land. Outside this group—on the green—was a multitude of Highlanders of a yet inferior description, who nevertheless were entitled to take part in the meal. "These stout idle kinsmen of mine," explained the chieftain, "account my estate as held in trust for their support, and I must find them beef and ale, while the rogues do nothing but practise the broad sword, or wander about the hills shooting, fishing, hunting, drinking and making love to the lasses of the strath."

The Welsh Clan.

We need not dwell further on these expressions of corporate life, for their meaning is fairly well realized in England. Let us consider in greater detail the internal organization of these social unions. No better evidence can be adduced for this purpose than that of Welsh documents. The strong ties of the *wyrion* or kindred are produced by the actual growth of households through many generations. In the Denbigh Extent, the Black Book of St. David's, the Record of Carnarvon, and similar documents, we can watch the progress of the clan organization from stage to stage. Let us take one simple and characteristic example of a Welsh clan-unit. It is the *lectum* or stock of a certain Rand

Vaghan ap Asser.[1] Its beginnings may be tabulated as follows:

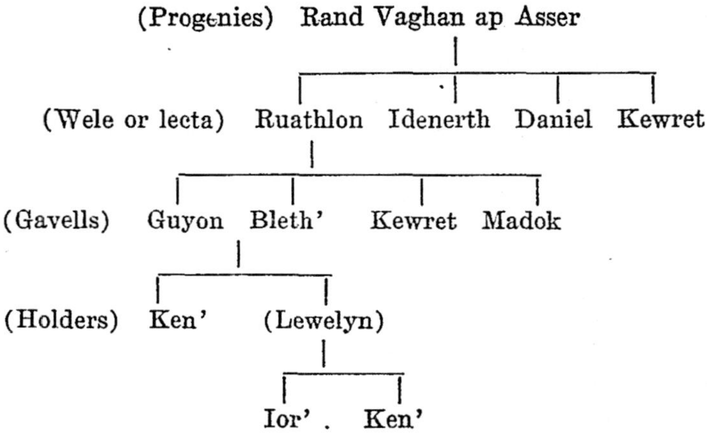

Such groups often represent something like sixty persons, counting only males. There is a definitely organized system of defence which includes the male members of the clan down to the seventh degree. The clan was by no means an amorphous and ill-organized mass. It is governed by certain strict rules of relationship, which form two inner circles: a narrower, limited to second cousins or to the fourth generation, and a wider which stretches to the seventh and to the ninth generation.[2]

The blood-feud.

The first and most obvious purpose of the clan organization is to provide an adequate defence for its members. This necessity expresses itself in the blood-feud, one of the most primordial institutions of society: it represents the vengeance taken by the body of kinsmen for a wrong inflicted on one of their number. Though its origin goes very far back in history, it is not confined merely to primitive communities: we can find notable examples of it in comparatively late society. For instance, this is how Domesday Book (I, 179) describes its occurrence in a Welsh district.

[1] *Survey of the Honour of Denbigh*, ed. by P. VINOGRADOFF and F. MORGAN, p. xxx.
[2] SEEBOHM, *The Tribal System in Wales*, 2nd ed., pp. 76 ff.

"If a Welshman slays another, the relations of the deceased assemble and harry the slayer and his relatives, and set their houses on fire until the corpse of the dead man is buried the next day about noon. Of the loot the king recovers one-third and they get the rest in peace." Certain police considerations are beginning to assert themselves as regards the exercise of natural right, but they culminate in a claim to a third of the booty and a limitation of the harrying in point of time.

Composition.

The blood-feud generally resolves into a system of *composition* or material compensation for the injury inflicted. It is easy to understand that in primitive societies, when a wrong done to a single individual might lead to retribution by a whole group of kindred, there was a constant danger of private war, which would be exceedingly injurious to society at large unless checked by *arbitration*. The incipient State did all it could to render conciliation acceptable to individual disputants, and it did not always have a very easy task. The desire for personal vengeance was very strong: and we must not suppose that because at a very early stage we find elaborate tariffs of payments for various wrongs, the principle of reconciliation was established beyond cavil.[1] The practice is described in a graphic manner by Miklosich as regards Southern Slavs:[2]

"The humiliating position which the guilty person assumes in the presence of the injured party, and which is indeed the main feature of the ceremony, is supposed to tame the savage mood of the avenger and to incline him to forgiveness. The same object is thought to be achieved by the bringing forward of innocent and helpless infants. The kerchiefs, mouchoirs, which Vialla describes as lying

[1] See Tacitus, *Germania*, xxi: "Suscipere tam inimicitias seu patris seu propinqui quam amicitias necesse est. Nec implacabiles durant, luitur enim etiam homicidium certo armentorum aut pecorum numero."—"It is as necessary to share the quarrels of a father or a relative as to share his friendships. Such quarrels admit, however, of reconciliation: even homicide is atoned for by a certain number of beasts of burden or heads of cattle." Cf. *Servius in Virg. Ecl.* IV, 43: "Si quis imprudens hominem occidisset pro capite occisi agnatis eius offert arietem."

[2] Miklosich, *Die Blutrache bei den Slaven*. Denkschriften der Kaiserlichen Akademie der Wissenschaften, Philosophisch-Historische Classe, Vienna (1888), XXXVI, p. 202.

in the cradles of these infants, are presents, the acceptance of which is the first indication that the injured party is willing to forgive. It is probable, however, that this interpretation rests on a misunderstanding, for according to J. G. Kohl, I, 432, each of the children is presented with a little cloth by the injured man as being his god-child. The murderous weapon hanging round the neck of the guilty person denotes that he is entirely in the power of the injured person. Vialla and Kohl, I, 434, state that the weapon is deliberately broken. The associations of god-parents and of chosen brothers are intended to confirm the friendship of the tribes. The presence of many members of both tribes gives the act of atonement the necessary publicity. The part played by the priest in the transaction in no way transforms it into a religious or ecclesiastical ceremony; his presence is to be explained sufficiently by the fact that the assembly needs the aid of some one able to write. So much for the rites of atonement in Montenegro and the neighbouring territories.

The corresponding ceremony among the Albanians so closely resembles that usual among the Montenegrins that an influence must undoubtedly have been exercised by one nation over the other. The fact that the Montenegrin ceremony differs in certain respects from that of other Slav nations, and that it is precisely in these respects that it coincides with the Albanian rites, would lead one to suppose that the influence came from the Albanians. Moreover, the Albanian act seems clearer. The priest adjures the injured person in the name of the Cross, the Book, and the innocent Blood. v. Hahn, on p. 206, calls attention in this connection to Justinus VII, 2: Illyrii infantiam regis pupilli contemnentes bello Macedonas aggrediuntur: qui proelio pulsi, rege suo in cunis prolato et pone aciem posito, acrius certamen repetivere, tamquam ideo victi fuissent antea, quod bellantibus sibi regis sui auspicia defuissent, futuri vel propterea victores, quod ex superstitione animum vicendi ceperant, simul et miseratio eos infantis tenebat."

In many cases there were among the people a strong feeling against "composition" and a marked reluctance to adopt it in practice. As an example of the disgust with which compensation was often regarded, we may take the famous story of the cursed treasure as told in the Edda and in Germanic Sagas.

Three gods, Odin, Hoenir and Loki, start on one of their usual wanderings round the world, and put up at the house of a certain Hreidmar. They sleep there, and in the morning go out to the stream which runs by the house and see an otter catching fish in the stream. They kill it, but it turns out to be the son of the owner of the house who had taken that shape for the purpose of fishing. The surviving kinsmen ought to take revenge, but prefer to accept gold as compensation. This gold is obtained from a dwarf, Andvari, who curses any one into whose possession his treasure, and especially a magic ring of his, may come.[1]

Evidently the practice of taking gold in compensation for blood was repulsive to the primitive mind. At the same time, there is the testimony of whole systems of law to show that the composition for injuries came to be treated in a perfectly business-like fashion and that individuals and wrongs to individuals were actually paid for in carefully estimated sums of cash. Let me quote an interesting fragment from the Anglo-Saxon laws.[2]

(1)	Twelfhyndes mannes wer is twelf hund scyllinga.	The wergeld of a 1200-man is twelve hundred shillings.
(1, 1)	Twyhyndes mannes wer is twa hund scill'.	The wergeld of a 200-man is two hundred shillings.
(2)	Gif man ofslægen weordhe, gylde hine man swa he geboren sy.	If a man is slain, let the measure of compensation be according to his birth.

[1] *Corpus Poeticum Boreale*, I, pp. 33, 156; MÜLLENHOF, *Deutsche Altertumskunde*, V, pp. 361 ff.

[2] *Die Gesetze der Angelsachsen*, ed. by LIEBERMANN, I, p. 392. The O.E þ has been rendered by th and ð by dh.

(3)	And riht is, dhæt se slaga, sidhdhan he weres beweddod hæbbe, finde dhærto wærborh, be tham dhe dhærto gebyrige: dhæt is æt twelfhyndum were gebyriadh twelf men to werborge, VIII fæderenmægdhe and IIII medrenmægdhe.	And it is right that the slayer, when he has given a gage as to the wergeld, should also find the pledges required by it: that is, for the wergeld of a 1200-man twelve men shall be pledges, eight from the father's line and four from the mother's line.
(4)	Dhonne thæt gedon sy, dhonne rære man cyninges munde, dhæt is dhæt hy ealle gemænum handum of ægdhere mægdhe on anum wæpne dham semende syllan, dhæt cyninges mund stande.	When that has been done, let the king's peace be established between them: that is, let them all of both lines of descent give sign by joining hands upon one weapon before an arbitrator that the king's peace is established.
(4, 1)	Of dham dæge on XXI nihtan gylde man CXX scill' to healsfange æt twelfhyndum were.	For twenty-one nights after that day let there be a payment of 120 shillings as a *Halsfang* from the wergeld of a 1200-man.
(5)	Healsfang gebyredh bearnum, brodhrum and fæderan; ne gebyredh nanum mæge dhæt feodh . . bute dham dhe sy binnan cneowe.	*Halsfang* falls to children, brothers and father's brothers: and that payment falls to no other kin save those who are "within the knee."
(6)	Of dham dæge, dhe dhæt healsfang agolden sy, on XXI nihtan gylde man	For 21 nights from the day when the *Halsfang* has been paid, let the

	dha manbote; dhæs on XXI nihtan dhæt fyhtewite; dhæs on XXI nihtan dhæs weres dhæt frumgyld; and swa fordh thæt fulgolden sy on dham fyrste, dhe witan gerǽden.	manbot be paid: then for 21 nights the *fyhtewite* (*id est forisfactura pugne*); then for 21 nights the frumgild (*id est prima redditio*) of the same wergeld; and so forth until full payment shall be made up to the time decreed by the *witan*.
(6, 1)	Sidhdhan man mot mid lufe ofgan, gif man hwile . . . fulle freondrædne habban.	Thereafter the slayer may abide in love, if he desire to have full fellowship with his friends.
(7)	Eal man sceal æt cyrliscum were be thære mædhe don, dhe him to gebyredh, swa we be twelfhyndum tealdan.	The same things shall be observed touching the wergeld of a ceorl, according to the sum that befits him, even as we have written concerning a 1200-man.

There are two points to be particularly noted: (i) the marked preponderance of the agnatic element, the influence of the male relations of the father. These kinsmen claimed two-thirds of the compensation of the *frumgild* portion of the *magbót,* and also stand security for the payment of two-thirds. They are therefore assumed to be interested in the affair twice as strongly as the kin on the mother's side. (ii) The nearest relatives of the deceased come in only for a share, and not a very large share, of the compensation: they take altogether one-tenth, the *Halsfang,* and possibly some portion of the *frumgild.* Two-tenths go to the lord and the king, while the kindred at large take no less than seven-tenths, although, probably, the closer circle of relations shared in this portion. If so, its members would take only as members of the general body of the kindred.

Icelandic law.

An interesting situation created by the conflict between traditions of kinship organization and settlement on individualistic lines is presented by Icelandic law. Their collection—the *Grágás* (I [a], pp. 193, ff.) makes a most elaborate statement as to the shares of wergeld (*nid-gjold*) to be received and paid by relatives of various degrees in case of manslaughter, when the slayer has been outlawed and has left the country. The payments are arranged in three sections, of which the first—to near relations—is particularly called *baugar*, in accordance with Norwegian terminology; but the general heading of the chapter treating of this subject, *baugatal*, and the mention of all the *baugar* in the sequel, indicates that all the fractións of the wergeld of 120 *öre* enumerated in it were *baugar* in a wider sense. The limit of kinship is drawn in this statement at the degree of fourth cousins (*thridhia brödhra ens vegna*).[1] This is not an isolated calculation of relationship. Icelandic "poor law" builds up its system of assistance to destitute people on a combination between income and relationship, and the latter is limited in the same way as in *baugatal*, namely, by the degree of fourth cousins (*Grágás*, I [b], pp. 3 and 26).[2] This establishes the fact that we have to deal with actual conditions, and not with mere reminiscences of Norwegian custom. In the twelfth century, at any rate, kindreds had grown into sufficiently extensive and ramified groups to admit of a reckoning of rights and duties stretching to the degree of fourth cousins, issued in the direct line from a common ancestor who may have lived some 150 years before. The tracing of descent from an *atavus* (great-great-great-grandfather) was a possible contingency, even if the original settlers of the *Landnama* are to be considered as single individuals: although in many cases brothers and cousins of various degrees had migrated together. However this may be, emigrants from a country where kinship was as strongly developed as it was in Norway, kept up the conception, and it naturally

[1] FINSEN: Mandlige slægtninge i femte led.

[2] See cap. 143, which treats of the obligations of fourth cousins, and is ascribed to Gudmund, *lögsögumadhr*, in the years 1123-24.

gave rise to a new crop of rules based on relationship in the new home.[1] I have to insist on these points of detail in order to guard against the extreme view that *baugatal* is unreal, and could not possibly be applied in practice in Iceland. It presents, of course, a kind of diagram or scheme, which covers all sorts of possible ramifications, and for this very reason must have been constantly modified in practice. But it would be rather reckless to reject such a deliberate statement of legal custom, which, besides, is entirely in agreement with similar rules in all varieties of barbaric law, and with statements in other parts of the Grágás. The fact that the Sagas do not allude in detail to the repartition of payment between the members of kindreds can certainly not invalidate the definite statement of the law-book: such minute questions did not interest the storytellers or their public, while the fact that those who helped in the feud were rewarded by shares in fines is not infrequently noticed in the Sagas.[2] As we know of many instances of increased payments (e.g. triple wergelds in Njála), we have to bear in mind that the official standards of payment and distribution were supplemented in many cases by voluntary agreements in which both the amount and the repartition must have greatly varied.

One problem remains, however: how is the statement of the *baugatal* to be reconciled or combined with the directions of the chapter immediately preceding it—the *vigslódi* (consequences of homicide) of the Grágás? The fine mentioned in the chapter is, however, specifically distinguished from the *baugar* and the supplementary payments of the *nidgjold.* It is a uniform fine of 48 *öre,* called *Rettr,* and is payable in cases of manslaughter, rape, wounding and assault.[3] For its application in cases of homicide we get a definite formula in the *Stadharhálsbók* version of the Law.[4] The accuser claims, besides, the

[1] Miss Phillpotts (*Kindred and Clan*) thinks that the insular situation of Iceland—and of England, too—prevented the development of relationship on agnatic lines; but what of the Scots, the Welsh and the Irish?

[2] For example, in Valaljotssaga and in the Njála.

[3] *Grágás,* I^a, p. 150.

[4] *Grágás,* II, p. 359.

property of the slayer. This procedure takes place only in cases of outlawry,[1] but outlawry is the starting-point for the application of all *vigslódi* rules. They are intended to regulate the claim of the nearest heir of the deceased, and are independent of the actual prosecution of the feud or suit,[2] as well as of the *nidgjold.* This fact in itself shows that we have to deal here with personal rights not covered by feud and composition. For this reason women take shares according to *vigslódi,* while they are excluded in *baugatal.*

On the whole, there can be no doubt that, although Icelandic conditions favoured scattered settlements and individualistic enterprise, the support of kinsmen was one of the most effective means of protection against aggression and violence. There are no traces of a clan system, but the Scandinavian kindred, the *aet,* is in full vigour, and its influence increases as generations follow one another in wider ramifications. The *thridhia brödhra* (fourth cousins) cannot be considered as a necessary element of every kindred, but their mention remains characteristic, even though it only marks a possible and occasional limit.

By a remarkable coincidence the same features are to be observed in the social organization of Celtic peoples. With the Celts of North Wales, the kin was organized much more stringently than among the Anglo-Saxons or Scandinavians. It was in fact a clan, but the fundamental provisions concerning the payment of composition are the same. The system observed among these Celtic tribes is recorded, for instance, in the version of the Venedotian Code; it estimates the shares of agnatic relations, or rather of the father's kindred, at twice as much as those of the mother's.

Welsh law.

The first third (of the *galanas*) falls on the murderer, and the mother and father and brothers and sisters with him, for those persons would receive with him a third of the

[1] Miss Phillpotts, *Kindred and Clan,* p. 41.

[2] Bötr allar om vigsaear ligo arftaco menn hvart sem theirero kazlar edha konor hvergi er söc söcir edha huergi adhile er. (Whosoever institutes the suit or is leader.) Gr. I^a, 171. It is improbable that this sentence should be referred exclusively to the time before the rule of 944 which forbade women to prosecute in slaying suits.

galanas if paid to them, therefore let them pay so with him . . . (one-third of it on the mother and father, one-third on brothers and sisters, and one-third on the murderer . . . males paying two parts and females one).

The remaining two-thirds fall on the kindred (two parts of it on the kindred of the father and one part on the kindred of the mother).[1]

The kindred for this purpose is confined within the seventh generation:

1. Brother =braut.
2. 1st cousin =keuenderu.
3. 2nd cousin =keuerderu.
4. 3rd cousin =keyuyn.
5. 4th cousin =gorcheyuen.
6. 5th cousin =gorchau.
7. Son of 5th cousin=mab gorchau.

Renunciation of kindred.

Feud and composition are by no means the only expression of kindred solidarity in ancient law. Some notion as to the extent of mutual support may be gathered for instance from a passage from the law of the Salian Franks (c. 60) which deals with the case of a man who has renounced his kindred—a case which may have occurred frequently, for it is easy to understand that, as individualistic conceptions began to assert themselves, a man might not wish to make himself responsible for the deeds of his kindred, and, *vice versa,* the kindred might not desire the presence among its members of particularly untrustworthy individuals. The ceremony of renunciation took the symbolic form of breaking sticks over the head of the man who quitted the kindred (*qui se de parentela tollere vult*).[2] He renounced his claims to inheritance and oath-help, and all other forms of solidarity with the kindred. After this renunciation by him, his former kinsmen could not claim either inheritance or composition in respect of this person.

Compurgation.

In this ceremony one of the most important features is the renunciation of oath-help. This was a most fundamental institution of tribal communities. We have seen

[1] SEEBOHM, *Tribal Systems in Wales*, 2nd ed., pp. 101 ff. Cf. 79 f.
[2] *Lex Salica,* LX.

that when disputes take the form of an actual feud, the kindred support the individual in the prosecution of his claim by force. In the same way, when the issue has to be decided not by violent means, but by the award of a regularly constituted court, a modified form of the struggle is usual: the claimant comes before the tribunal surrounded by his kindred, who take the responsibility of supporting him very much as in actual battle. They swear in support of his contention. This is the result of the view that collisions occur not between individuals, but between societies: and if one member of a kindred or clan has to come forth as accuser or accused, he appears in conjunction with his natural helpers, and the legal issue proceeds on the lines of assertion and compurgation in cases when there was a reasonable probability of the assertion being true. On the other hand, if appearances were strongly against a contention, the court usually awarded ordeal. Much depended, of course, on the manner in which the burden of proof was assigned by the tribunal.[1]

It is impossible here to consider the practice of compurgation in all its details: the important point for us to note is that here in court, as well as on the field of battle, kindreds were pitted against each other as unions.

Other duties of the kin.

There are a certain number of other functions and duties which arise as incidental to the main activities of the kindred organization. We find, for example, that the kin assume responsibility for the guardianship of minors. We are not told exactly who the guardians were, nor on what principle they were appointed to the office. It is a constant disadvantage of ancient evidence that it leaves us in the dark as to everyday occurrences, which are supposed to be known to everybody and therefore do not need to be recorded. It seems clear, however, that in early times the kin, besides providing individual guardians, exercised the same general functions of guardianship as are definitely assigned to the State by later law.

Again, as has already been mentioned, the kindred took and gave securities in connection with weddings, and it has

[1] *Die Gesetze der Angelsachsen*, ed. LIEBERMANN, II² 603.

been noted how provision is made that when a woman passes to the house of her husband, certain bonds are kept up which ensure her remaining in touch with her own kindred (see above, p. 211 f.).

In some instances the kin undertook the maintenance of destitute people. This appears, for example, in Iceland, where tribal arrangements were necessarily individualized, and the tribal principle resolved itself very largely into a succession of claims and duties.[1] In India, on the other hand, the weight of supporting needy members was thrown on the kindreds as groups, and on their natural subdivisons.

[1] *Grágás*, Ómaga bálkr, I^b, pp. 3 ff.

CHAPTER IX

LAND TENURE

SOLIDARITY between the members of a clan or of a kindred required in the beginning a close proximity in the occupation of the land and constant economic co-operation. The natural basis for social relations of the kind described above must necessarily be found in the soil. We cannot therefore avoid the discussion of the vexed question of the origin of landed property. It has sometimes been narrowed to sceptical remarks as to the lack of trustworthy evidence,[1] and to surmises as to the essentially selfish motives of savage tribesmen,[2] or the inherent instinct of individual appropriation.[3] It is evident, however, that the problem has to be approached in connection with a general view of social development in tribal societies. In this matter, as in the case of marriage or relationship, sundry variations depend on geographical and historical causes, but as the principle of kinship has exerted a powerful influence on all forms of tribal union, it is bound to manifest itself conspicuously in the history of land tenure.

We can safely start from the general proposition that in the earlier stages of development hunting, fishing and pastoral tribes do not know of any individual appropriation of the soil for permanent occupation and usage. There is no reason for carving out private plots when the whole system of husbandry is based on roaming about wide tracts of land.

Preponderance of Waste.

Even with the appearance of agriculture, territorial rights remain for some time in the communities of the

1 FUSTEL DE COULANGES, *Origin of Property in Land*, transl. by M. ASHLEY (1891).
2 K. HILDEBRAND, *Recht und Sitte auf den primitiveren wirtschaftlichen Kulturstufen* (1907).
3 POLLOCK and MAITLAND, *History of English Law*, II, p. 942, and VINOGRADOFF, *Growth of the Manor*, pp. 18 f.

households, kindreds or clans. An organization of this communal kind is to be observed in a number of hunting and pastoral tribes practising agriculture on freshly reclaimed land by the expedient of burning down trees or grass on certain plots, and cultivating them for a short time.[1]

On the borders of India, conquering tribes have been known to settle down on large tracts of land without allowing them to be converted into separate property even among clans or kindreds. Occasional or periodical redivisions testified to the effective overlordship of the tribe, and to the superficial character of agricultural husbandry.[2]

"Take the Tousoufzais, who are aboriginals of the country of Candahar; they did not arrive in the country of Svat until the end of the fifteenth century: they drove out, exterminated, or subjugated the inhabitants, Dilazaks or Svatis. Then their chief, the Sheikh Mali, counted the population of each tribe and divided the conquered territory proportionately in as many portions as were drawn by lot: and by the same method, the portion of each tribe was subdivided between the different clans which composed it.

"As it was impossible to parcel out sections of absolutely equal value, the apportionments were redistributed among the clans at certain fixed periods, so that the clans were constantly migrating from one district to another within the territory of the tribe. This custom, termed *vaich,* was still in use among certain tribes in the English territory at the beginning of the British occupation: it was in full force in Taghistan."

[1] Cf. FRAZER, *Folk-lore in the Old Testament*, I, p. 452: "Permanent occupation is essential to individual ownership, it is not essential to communal or tribal ownership. And as in human history the nomadic life of the hunter, the herdsman and the migratory husbandman precedes the settled life of the farmer under the more advanced systems of tillage, it seems to follow that individual ownership of land has been developed later than communal or tribal ownership, and that it cannot be recognized by law until the ground is under permanent cultivation. In short, common lands are older than private lands, and the transition from communal to private ownership of the soil is associated with a greatly improved mode of tillage, which in its turn, like all economic improvements, contributes powerfully to the general advance of society."

[2] DARMESTETER, *Lettres sur l'Inde: à la frontière afghane* (1888), p. 87.

Indian village communities

Let us now turn to the evidence of the influence of the arrangement by household, kin and clan on landed property in the case of the various Aryan nations. The ancient law and modern custom of the Aryan tribes in India provides evidence on this point.

"The great mass of the landed property in the Punjab is held by small proprietors, who cultivate their own land in whole or in part.

"The chief characteristic of the tenure generally is that these proprietors are associated together in village communities having to a greater or less extent joint interests, and under our system of cash payments limited so as to secure a certain profit to the proprietors, jointly responsible for the payment of the revenue assessed upon the village lands. It is an almost invariable incident of the tenure that if any of the proprietors wishes to sell his rights or is obliged to part with them in order to satisfy demands upon him, the other members of the same community have a preferential right to purchase them at the same price as could be obtained from outsiders.

"In some cases (technically known as *zamíndari* tenures) all the proprietors have an undivided interest in all the land belonging to the proprietary community. Their rights are regulated by their shares in the estate both as regards the extent of the holdings they are entitled to cultivate, and as regards the distribution of profits; and if the profits from land held by non-proprietary cultivators are not sufficient to pay the revenue and other charges, the balance would ordinarily be collected from the proprietors according to the same shares.

"It is, however, much more common for the proprietors to have their own separate holdings in the estate, and this separation may extend so far that there is no land susceptible of separate appropriation which is not the separate property of an individual or family." [1]

Of course, a great deal depends on the character of the settlement. When, as in the case of the Norwegians in

[1] TUPPER, *Punjab Customary Law*, III, p. 129, quoting *Punjab Administrative Report of 1872-3.*

Iceland, a few settlers occupy what is practically virgin soil, they scatter, and landed property assumes an individualistic character. However, the treatment of the waste and pasture remains the business of groups even in this case. But when, as is more usual, settlement takes place in connection with the movements of large tribes and centralized interests, then the settlers are inevitably driven to hold closely together for the control and maintenance of the landed property of the household. In point of settlement, the result of this kind of centralization is the *village* or *township* as opposed to the *farm* or *homestead.* In general, it may be said that wherever we are given the kindred as a unit of society, we find that one of its chief manifestations is *projection on the land.* Only on these principles can we understand more complex tribal organization. If we move from the North to the South of India, we get into a great mixture of elements. Everything is complicated by local castes: in a single place, there may be, say, twenty-five associations, each one of which is a very close and exclusive group, and the village community will not be identical with these groups.[1] These complications result from the fact that the Aryans became mixed with other races—in particular with peoples of Dravidian stock. But the general principle—the club life, as it were,—remains active throughout, and it is by the competition of component groups that unity is ultimately produced.

Viewed from the historical point of view, the clans begin by being combinations of kinsmen, and end by being territorial communities. It is on this basis only that neighbours can be considered as claiming a share in property or succession.

Tribal element in village life. The Hindu term for village, the *grama,* has also the connotation of a settlement of kinsmen.[2] It was primarily the seat of a joint family. While the population was in a fluctuating state, and agriculture was carried on as a more or less temporary pursuit, the appropriation of the soil was dependent on the application of labour, and a tilled field was as much an object of protected possession as

[1] Cf. Sénart, *Les castes dans L'Inde,* pp. 37 ff.
[2] Macdonell and Keith, *Vedic Index,* I, 245.

the product of the chase or of fishing. Such possession is fundamentally different from the notion of permanent *dominium:* it is as shifting as cultivation itself, and emphatically a subject of possession, and not of property.[1]

When the occupation of territory became settled in consequence of the increasing congestion of inhabitants, the appropriation of land assumed stricter forms, which were originally derived from the arrangement of kinship. Of the three kinds of village settlement known to modern India—the *raiatwarí* type, the *zamíndari* type and the *pattidári* type, it is the last that bears the stamp of greatest antiquity. The *raiatwarí* villages are nothing but casual concentrations of individuals: the population has been pulverized into a number of separate units by the grinding powers of the *rajas* and their tax-gatherers. It would be absurd to look to such human flocks as representing the original forms of village settlements. Some writers, for example Baden Powell,[2] lay special stress on the numerical preponderance of such local units in India in recent times. It is not from the status of the exploited subjects of the Moguls or of the Mahrattas that the student of social origins can derive information about the beginnings of land tenure.

The *zamíndari* type,[3] sometimes considered to be the most archaic, is also not likely to be the rudimentary form of village organization. It is closely connected with the principle of joint responsibility for taxes and services, and therefore presents a combination in which governmental influence is clearly traceable; although in this case it made not for the isolation of settlers, but for their joint responsibility. As in the later Russian *mir,* used by the central authority as a material basis for the burdens laid on the population, it is difficult to distinguish in the *zamíndari* arrangement what has to be ascribed to archaic communalism and what to the correspondence between rights

[1] *Manu,* IX, 43. Cf. the old Russian conception of the right to soil where the "axe and the plough have gone."

[2] *The Indian Village Community,* pp. 227, 241.

[3] MAINE, *Village Communities,* Lect. V, pp. 156 ff.

and duties produced by the pressure of State requirements. Many features in the *zamíndari* management probably go back to ancient origins, but it is impossible to ascertain what the exact share of such ancient elements may be.

The *pattidári* type, on the contrary, clearly presents the application of the same principles which we have found at work in the customs of the joint family. The group holds together as far as possible, and individualistic tendencies are counterbalanced by the overlordship of the whole and the claims of all members to a fair measure of maintenance. Very striking expressions of this solidarity are to be found in the tenacious survival of a common fund (*shamilatdeh*),[1] in spite of the tremendous congestion, and in the shaping of village custom and village husbandry by joint boards (*panchaiats*).

But the apportionment of claims proceeds mainly on the lines of estimates based on the reckoning by *stirpes* (*patti*). If indefinite subdivision of claims were admitted, the system would result eventually in complete individualization. But the most characteristic feature of the system consists in the resistance to such pulverizing subdivisions. The intense Indian feeling for group solidarity acts as a check on the process and produces *stirpes* (*patti*) which take care of maintenance and provide opportunities for all their members.

Vestiges of communal tenure within the tribe are scarce in the case of Greeks and Italians, because their culture developed at an early stage in connection with town centres surrounded by small plots of intensive cultivation.[2] Yet even in these cases some characteristic facts may be noticed. In Greece there was a widespread idea that land should be apportioned in equal κλῆροι, ancestral shares to be kept up as far as possible in accordance with an original division between households (οἶκοι). Even in Athens the first archon had to supervise such an arrangement, which may have been regulated by Solon. In other cities the main-

1 Douie, *Punjab Settlement Manual*, p. 70, cf. 62.
2 Aristotle, *Politics*, II c. 4. 1266b.

tenance of ancestral shares was carried to much greater lengths.

In Rome, a remarkable vestige of early communalism was preserved, however, in the ancient notion of a *heredium* of two *iugera* apportioned from the *ager publicus* by Numa.[1] Such a holding could only serve as a centre of grazing rights for a household chiefly dependent on pastoral pursuits.

Welsh tribal villages.

It is among the Celts that the tribal system of land tenure is most developed and best recorded. The detailed and accurate descriptions of tribal arrangements in the Welsh Surveys compiled for the use of English conquerors, give a complete insight into the principles governing a tribal community. I may be allowed to repeat some pages from the Introduction to the Register of the Honour of Denbigh.[2]

"Instead of the usual hierarchy of lords, freeholders, and villeins joined in a manorial system, we are met by tribal communities described in great detail. Their composition is dependent on the tie of blood, but they are essentially agnatic, comprising in their enumerations only males and noticing only relationships through males. Both the free and the unfree are grouped in kindreds. These kindreds hold land in communal ownership, and their possessions do not as a rule coincide with the landmarks of the villages (*trevs*), but spread spider-like through different settlements. For example, the progenies of Owen Gogh . . . is a very large aggregate of co-tenants (*coheredes et participes*) comprising as many as twenty-five male persons. It cannot be stated too emphatically that the tenure of the land is strictly communal; no particular individual is given a preponderant right, but they are all equally *priodarii*. Noteworthy consequences flow from this principle. To begin with, the members of the kindred of Owen Gogh, just mentioned, are not distributed in the five villages as holders of separate tenements, but appear together as lords of every single one of the five estates, which amount in all

[1] MOMMSEN, *Hist. of R.*, Bk. I. Ch. VI and XIII, pp 101 f. and 194 f.

[2] *Survey of the Honour of Denbigh* (1334), ed. by VINOGRADOFF and MORGAN, pp. xviii-xxxii.

to 733 acres. . . . These shares are ideal, and not actually marked off on the land: so that the compilers of the Survey, who were trying to turn the soil to account on the principles of English cultivation and delimitation, have constantly to make reckonings as to the exact number of acres which would be assigned to these various communities, if the land were actually meted out to them on equitable principles: for instance, in the case of Nanthyn Canon it is said that the portion of each gavell *secundum equam participacionem* should be 141 acres. . . .

"We hear of several cases in which either the English lords of the owners, or, in early times, the princes, have moved whole kindreds from one place to another. Thus in the villata of Skeybeon (Ysceibion), in the commote of Kaymergh, the lord holds the entire villata, one-half by way of escheat, and one-half by way of exchange with a certain David ap Griffith, whose progenies, the entry continues, has land allotted to it in the vills of Mathebrut and Trebothle in the commote of Ughdulas. Here the process takes the form of an exchange of land between the lord and the collective body of the kindred. In this instance we see again that the subjects of rights with whom the lord has to deal are not individuals but groups.

Welsh System Communal, not patriarchal.

"The system of communal estates which we have been considering was characterized by Seebohm as patriarchal. This description, however, is not borne out by the facts. The Denbigh Survey, like other Welsh surveys, always insists on the equal rights of the co-tenants, and on the uniformly communal nature of their holdings. Historically, of course, the different kindreds traced their descent from common ancestors; but these ancestors as a rule had long ceased to exist, and their exuberant progenies were held together by communal comradeship. The Welsh Laws tell us of chieftains of kindreds (pencenedl), but the authority of these chieftains did not supersede communal tenure of land. In the surveys, the chiefs of kindreds are not mentioned as such, and we catch a glimpse of their influence only in indirect ways. It sometimes happens that some particular person is mentioned as representing a kindred in specific transactions; e.g., in the exchange of territory in Skeybeon, mentioned above, David ap Griffith is referred to as if he were the only person who had to decide on behalf of the progenies. The explanation of this apparent inconsistency seems to lie in the fact that certain persons were considered as the leaders of the different kindred-groups. . . .

Subdivisions of kindred.

". . . In the surveys of the cantreds of Rewaynok and Roos, we find that the kindred appears as a rule to be differentiated into smaller units—the wele (*lecta*) and the gavells . . .

". . . In general the term *wele* or *lectum,* meaning literally *bed,* might be rendered by the expression *stock,* and we can hardly go far wrong in assuming on the evidence of the Welsh laws that the term was usually applied in Welsh tribal custom to the descendants of a common father, grandfather, or great-grandfather. Up to that point, a close community of interests was maintained not only as against strangers, but also as against more remote relations of the same kindred. A curious corroboration of this rule may be found in our Survey, where it is stated on two or three occasions that inheritance in land went on intestacy down to the third degree (*tertium gradum*) . . .

". . . The gavell may be considered in two aspects—either as the closest and narrowest circle of blood-relations holding in common, or as the territorial basis of their holding. The first or personal aspect may be exemplified by almost any of the cases referred to in the Survey. The number of co-heirs and parceners (*coheredes et participes*) would sometimes be very considerable, and the tenement might be best described as a "joint family holding," as in the case of Ithel Lloyd ap Cadugan and his *coheredes et participes* already mentioned. But the territorial aspect is also very prominent. From this point of view we get estimates of the number of acres which ought to have been apportioned to each gavell if the land were held not in ideal shares but in separate occupation; in the case of Pereyon (Prion), for instance, it is said that if the *nativi* held a share proportionate to their contribution to the tunk, each gavell would take a parcel of ninety-one acres in arable and wood, and fifty-three acres in waste; and in Postu (Postyn) the entry records that if all the gavells were equally divided among the three vills which make up the area of Postu, each gavell would have fifty-three acres. Then again, it is on this basis only that we can find an explanation for a description like that of Abergellue (Abergele), in which it is stated that the kindred of Edred ap Marghuyd was divided into four stocks (*lecta*), each of which consisted of one and one-half gavells. The expression would be meaningless if applied to personal and not to territorial divisions. It should be noted that the formation of communal unions and holdings on the basis of kinship is by no means restricted to the free population; the *nativi* (taeogs) are grouped in stocks and gavells in the same way as the free tribesmen, and we actually learn the technical Welsh denominations of these two classes of holding. They are described as "Rethe" and "Caythe" gavells. . . . The free gavells are in one case at least distinctly reckoned as twice the size of the unfree gavells. The villata of Beryn (Berain), says the Survey, consists of seven and one-half gavells; one-eighth of the area in question is in the tenure of the freemen *pro dimidia gavella,* and seven-eighths in the tenure of the *nativi* in seven gavells. In other respects, the working of these groups seems to have been essentially similar, and the distribution of the native holdings of Pereyon, for example, affords as good an instance of communal conceptions as any of the cases registered under the heading of free tenure; there we have seen that if the shares were equally divided according to the contribution to the tunk, each gavell of the *nativi* ought to have ninety-one acres of arable and wood and fifty-three acres of waste assigned to it. . . .

"When treating of communal organization, one is naturally led to ask in what ways the communal principle asserted itself in the actual occupation and cultivation of land.

". . . In the first place it is clear that the occupation

of the land in common was greatly facilitated by the fact that grazing of cattle and dairy farming were evidently the main pursuits of the Welsh peasantry. In some parts of Denbighshire, with which we are more immediately concerned, no other form of husbandry is possible; even at the present day, this kind of farming seems natural, on the precipitous slopes of the hills. . . . We read in the Survey of wide tracts held by stocks or kindreds, which might have been apportioned in acres, but were as a matter of fact claimed on the principle of equal rural opportunities for the gavells of these tribal groups. In these surroundings agriculture itself assumed a communal aspect. Seebohm[1] has rightly laid stress on the practices of co-aration so minutely described in the Welsh Laws. They fit in remarkably well with the joint family groups of the gavells." Thus (Venedotian Code, III, xxiv):[2]

Waste and co-aration.

"1. Whoever shall engage in co-tillage with another, it is right for them to give surety for performance, and mutually to join hands; and, after they have done that, to keep it until the tye be completed: the tye is twelve erws.

"2. The measure of the erw, has it not been before set forth?

"3. The first erw belongs to the ploughman; the second to the irons; the third to the exterior sod ox, the fourth to the exterior sward ox, lest the yoke should be broken; and the fifth to the driver; and so the erws are appropriated, from best to best, to the oxen, thence onward, unless the yoke be stopped between them, unto the last; and after that the plough erw, which is called the ploughbote cyvar; and that once in the year.

. . . .

". . . Our document shows us at the same time how tribal society is gradually modified by the introduction of new principles. It may be broken up by violent methods —a fact to which ample evidence is borne by the confiscations and escheats which followed on the conquest and on

Transition from tribal to village communalism.

[1] *The English Village Community* (2nd ed.), p. 120.

[2] *Ancient Laws of Wales*, I, p. 315. See also *Gwentian Code*, p. 354; and the *Leges Walliae*, p. 801.

the suppression of national risings. Castles and manors spring up before our eyes, and escheated tracts of land are let for rack-rents or farmed to villages by the new lords. But it is even more interesting to observe the gradual changes brought about by social growth and migration. These changes are effected by various processes. In the first place, let us notice the fact that tribal communalism is sometimes transformed into what may be called tenurial communalism. For instance, the use of waste land and waste pasture is as a rule vested not in particular kindreds or stocks but in the population of entire districts. Then again, it is quite the regular thing for the community of a trev to take over the occupation and management of the escheated portion of its territory. In the description of Prees, we hear of a tract of waste land no less than 8,878 acres in extent; it is treated as a common for all the tenants of the Honour of Denbigh in Roos, Rewaynok, and Kaymergh; the 'whole community of the villa,' we are told, may use the escheated portion of the waste (1,699 acres) for the grazing of their cattle, but nobody except the lord may depasture the beasts of *extranei*. In Pereyon, we read, 'of the part of the aforesaid gavell, which constitutes the escheat, there remains . . . an area of 111 acres . . . from which the lord takes no annual rent-profit; but the whole villata pays six shillings per annum for the pasturage.' Sometimes the *communitas villae* would farm not merely certain pastoral lands, but the whole estate of an extinct stock. In this way the *communitas villae* of Moghedreue (Mochdre) holds the Wele Guyon ap Madok and pays tenpence tunk for it; another wele which it holds, that of Bleth' ap Madok, was extirpated, so the entry informs us, in the days of the Earl of Lancaster. These manifestations of the 'village community' principle are the more remarkable because in the case of the Welsh trevs we have to deal not with 'nucleated' villages, or large settlements grouped along streets or round a green, but with scattered clusters of homesteads, which nevertheless display a considerable amount of economic solidarity.

"The next stage is marked by the rise of a village very similar to the English type, and yet connected historically with tribal antecedents. A case in point is the hamlet of Brenbagle (Brynbagl), which arises on soil laid out by the Earl of Lancaster for grazing purposes, but the occupiers made it into a complete rural settlement divided into eight shares resembling the ox-gangs of an English village, and the attungs of Swedish rural settlements. Thus we can see that the transition from the tribal to the rural community was a gradual and natural process. Another phase of it comes to our notice in the shape of the frequent substitution of outsiders in the place of the original members and stocks. In many of these cases the admission of outsiders was probably the result of marriages. The old laws refer expressly to inheritance by maternity, which arose either through the admission of husbands to the gavells of their fathers-in-law, or else in consequence of irregular and illicit unions. But in process of time, what may be called transfer of shares was evidently effected in the course of economic transactions—donations, sales, exchanges, etc. It will be sufficient to call attention to one or two characteristic instances. In two cases, the Master of a Hospital of St. John is mentioned among the members of regular gavells. As his place in tribal pedigrees is not traced in any way, he must have acquired his shares by donation or purchase.

"The history of the kindred of Rand Vaghan ap Asser presents several interesting features which illustrate our point. Of the four gavells which sprang from the first wele of this kindred, two have been concentrated in the hands of one group of kinsmen, descended from Bleth', the ancestor of the second gavell: so that the progeny of the first gavell, named after Guyon ap Ruathlon, has altogether disappeared. The third and fourth gavells of the same stock have also suffered great changes. The third, which ought to have contained descendants of Kewret ap Ruathlon, is as a matter of fact headed by a certain Bleth' ap Yeuan ap Madok, who may be connected with the eponymos of the fourth gavell (Madok ap Ruathlon). In this fourth gavell, again, there is only one man, namely, the leader (Iorweth ap David ap Madok), who can possibly be traced to the original occupier, while all the rest of the holders are outsiders—Ken' ap Bleth' ap Grono, Ken' ap Iorweth ap Tudor, Eden' ap Lauwargh ap Tuder, and Bleth' his brother (ff. 155-9). The description of Hendrenennyth gives rise to another curious observation. One of the six gavells of the Wele Goither ap Idenerth has entirely lapsed into the hands of the gavell, which is headed by Ken' ap Bleth' Vaghan, and consists beside himself of Iorweth ap Lewelyn ap Bleth', Ken' his brother, Ken' ap Bleth' Loyd, and Hoel his brother (f. 168).[1]

"To sum up, we may say that the Welsh surveys, of which our Denbigh record is the best existing example, present invaluable evidence as to the evolution of tenurial and individualistic groups out of tribal communities."

Slavs and Teutons.

In the case of the Slavs the passage from the tribal to the village community is most clearly expressed in the history of the Balkan peoples. It may be sufficient to quote the following description of customary arrangements. "In western Bulgaria some fifty or sixty years ago, each *zadruga* comprised scores of houses round one courtyard with from 30 to 80 working men (working spoons) and 50 to 25 inhabitants. Marinov quotes the reminiscences of an old man about the *zadruga* to which he belonged: for ploughing 10 to 15 ploughs were sent out; at the hay harvest 20 to 25 scythes went out; corn was cut with 40 sickles; the *zadruga* owned 100 head of cattle, 150 horses, 800 sheep. And all these persons were gathered round one hearth, sat down at one table."[2]

In the case of Germanic nations there is some distinct evidence of the communal practices as to land. Cæsar describes Teutonic nations on the move towards the West and the South, especially Suabians, and his description reads like some of the accounts of Afghan and Jat conquests

[1] Perhaps the most perfect example of the complicated ramifications of a progenies is that of Edred ap Marghuyd: see *Survey of Denbigh*, p. xxxii and Table II.

[2] SMIRNOFF, *Outlines of a Cultural History of the Southern Slavs*, II, p. 201 ff.

quoted above (on p. 322). The tribe acts in a state of war as a concentrated group, assigns land to its clans and kindreds for temporary occupation, and removes them to other places when convenient.[1] Tacitus' account presents a more settled state of society, but the distribution of land is still dependent on the action of the whole group (*universi*), and land is occupied for cultivation on a basis of temporary possession. Fields are ploughed up for some few years and left to lie fallow after some time. There is room for such shifting husbandry because there is plenty of land in proportion to the sparse population.[2] In Alamannic law we come across kindreds holding land and conducting contests in regard to it.[3] In Frankish law a curious manifestation of communal ownership by neighbours has been preserved by an Edict of King Chilperic (A.D. 571). The right of the neighbours, which is abrogated by the Merovingian king, as it is connected with succession, was obviously derived from the settlement of a kindred.[4]

Regulations as to shares

By way of exception, the tribal system developed in isolated districts into complete clans: the most notable instance of this is presented by the Ditmarschen.[5] But on the whole the constant migrations of the Teutonic tribes, the intermixture with Celtic, Slavonic and Finnish elements, and the influence of Roman culture, led to an early development of class distinctions and manorial lordships. As a result, in the regions of village settlements the tribal

[1] *De Bell Gall.* VI, 22: "Agriculturae non student . . . magistratus ac principes in annos singulos gentibus cognationibusque hominum quique una coierunt quantum et quo loco visum est agri attribuunt atque anno post alio transire cogunt."

[2] *Germania,* xxvi: "Agri pro numero cultorum ab universis in vices occupantur, quos mox inter se secundum dignitatem partiuntur . . . arva per annos mutant et superest ager." Cf. HANSSEN, *Agrarhistorische Abhandlungen* I, pp. 125 ff.

[3] *Lex Alamannorum,* c. 81.

[4] *Edict. Chilperici,* c. 3: "Placuit atque convenit ut quicumque vicinos habens et filios et filias post obitum suum superstitutus fuerit, quamdiu filii advixerint, terra habeant, sicut et lex Salica habet. Et si subito filii defuncti fuerint, filia simili modo accipiat terras ipsas sicut et filii si vivi fuissent habuissent. Et si moritur frater, alter superstitutus fuerit, frater terras accpiat, non vicini. Et subito frater moriens frater non direlinquerit superstitem, tunc soror ad terra ipsa accedat possidenda."

[5] AMIRA, *Grundriss des germanischen Rechts,* pp. 13 ff. BRUNNER, *Rechtsgeschichte,* I², 117 f.

communities are either dissolved, or transformed into communities of neighbours—village communities. Besides the substitution of strangers for kinsmen, so well illustrated in the case of Welsh *weles,* the process of transition involved a regularization of holdings, a change from apportionment of shares according to rules of descent to an apportionment according to economic standards. This side of the process is best exemplified by Scandinavian, more especially by Swedish and Danish, law. The original distribution of land for homesteads and cultivation was made by way of assigning irregular plots, *ut fons ut nemus placuit.* The old shifting (*forniskift*) was designated also as *hamarskift,* possibly from the act of throwing a stone hammer to mark the boundary. When population increased, it was found necessary to "stint" the holdings in proportion to requirements and means of cultivation. The result was a *sólskift* (distribution in order following the course of the sun). The rules adopted on these occasions are given in detail in some of the collections of provincial laws.

The distribution of plots in the villages regulated according to *sólskift* is carried out on a principle that corresponds to the subdivisions of the money unit—the mark. As the mark consists of eight *öre,* so the village ought normally to consist of eight *attungar.* The Westgötalag says expressly that a village shall be built in attungs (*Attungum skal by byggias*).[1] The *toft* or homestead which serves as a basis for the reckoning is described in the law as a plot occupying twenty ells along the street, with a corresponding extent of court and orchard adjoining it, and a certain number of equal strips (*tegtar*) in the fields. The *attung* is considered as the normal holding of a peasant, although allowances are made for certain variations by way of accumulation and diminution of the original shares. Yet the actual holdings do not become dispersed in irregular fractions, but are combined in more or less simplified proportions, all of them gravitating, as it were, towards

[1] Cf. Östgöta-Lagen, *Bygda B.,* XXVIII, § 3; Uplandslagen, *Witterbò Balk,* I (Schlyter, III, p. 215); Westgöta-lagen, *Jordair B.,* I, F, § 3, I, 4; Amira, *Nordgermanisches Obligationenrecht,* I, pp. 609 ff.

the normal *attung*. The same root idea of a normal holding (*ból*) "in scot and in lot" with a township which is expressed in the rules of Swedish provincial laws, is also clearly traceable on ancient maps. The Danish antiquarian, Lauridsen, has shown in a most interesting manner how the rectangular plans of Danish villages constructed according to *sólskift* are gradually transformed by accretions, intercalations and partitions to fit the requirements of a growing population. Yet the original plan is generally apparent in spite of gradual changes.

It is not to be supposed that these regulations were always followed, or could be kept up against the pressure of population and the diversities in the lie and the fertility of the soil. In fact, the above-mentioned studies as to village-planning in Denmark have shown conclusively in what manner the symmetric plans of regulated settlements became complicated and irregular.[1] But the attempts at systematizing the disposition of buildings and the distribution of shares in Scandinavian villages are characteristic of a state of customary law in which the tenure of land was considered primarily from the point of view of the group of settlers and not of individual owners. Whether colonization starts from regular allotments or is subjected to redivisions for the sake of regularity is a minor question. In both cases the superior right of the community asserts itself and produces material results.

The holding as a share in the village community.

Another symptom of the same principle of the overlordship of the village community is to be found in the widely recurring practice of estimating and assigning holdings as shares of a higher unit. The Scandinavian villages divide into eighths (*attungar*) for the apportionment of rights and duties. Now, the *attung* on one side corresponds to an *öre* assessment in money, i.e., to one-eighth of a mark, and to three *örtugar* as further subdivisions. As to seed, the mark is said to comprise 288 *skaeppar* (measures), at one penny each (24 to the *attung*-share). At the same time, as we have already noticed in the legal enactments as

[1] LAURIDSEN in *Aarböger for Nordisk Oldkyndighed*, 2nd Ser., XI, pp. 155 ff.

to settlement, the *attungar* were meant to represent actual holdings—the normal shares of householders in Swedish villages. In this way these arrangements, which seem artificial at first sight, express the views of the peasantry of Dalekarlia or Nörike as to the outfit and obligations of average householders.

It is curious to find a corresponding scheme in England, and to observe that in this case it is intimately connected with the composition of a large plough team or with the relation between large or smaller plough teams. I mean the well-known equations according to which a hide is supposed to fall into four yardlands and eight oxgangs. The Kentish *sulung*, though comprising a larger number of acres, is built up in a similar way as a complex of yokes. These fractions cannot have been uniform and measured to standard right through the country. As a matter of fact we hear of different standards in various localities; the poles, the ells, the perches, and roods are of varying size. Nevertheless in each locality economic and tenurial units are standardized on the basis of natural husbandry. It is in connection with commercial economics and cash nexus that individualistic tendencies prevail, and holdings are broken up or accumulated in arbitrary combinations.

The breaking up of holdings is represented in eleventh-century England by the social conditions of East Anglia and of the Dane-law, where the immense Danegeld payments and the loot collected by the Vikings had contributed to introduce cash payments and to mobilize landed property. In the greater part of England, as well as in Scandinavia, customary standards held their ground until the end of the Middle Ages.

The English evidence is especially worthy of attention as regards the correspondence of rights and duties in the formation of shares in the village community. The characteristic expression is—to be in *scot* and in *lot* with the village. The *scot* covers primarily payments, the *lot*—standardized claims to land and its appurtenances. The expression is quite usual, and may be illustrated in detail from innumerable documents.[1] It gives the clue to another set of typical terms of early England, such as *manlot, mantal, tenmanland,* etc.[2] Such a *manlot,* corresponding to the Latin *sors* and the Greek κλῆρος, was made up of *stikkas* and *gedals,* that is, of parts and strips.[3] While in the Welsh cases the connection with tribal arrangements is still very clear, in the English cases we have to deal with the purely territorial aspect of the process. It is not difficult to see, however, that there is an intimate connection between the two stages, and in the case of the *gavells* there is plenty of evidence to show that they gradually lost their tribal connotation and assumed the character of territorial associations.

Transition from tribal to village community.

The decisive point in the transition from the tribal to the village community is to be found in this way, not in the substitution of single outsiders for the kinsmen within the framework of gavells or hides, but in the reduction of holdings to standardized types independent of pedigree (*daddenhood*). This is effected partly by the crumbling of the larger units in accordance with the combined elements of the plough team, partly by the increasing pressure of duties which have to be made to correspond to outfit and available means. The pressure need not be a manorial one, in the sense of the subjugation of peasants by military lords, although such cases are very common. It arises also in the case of a heavy struggle with the sea, or with pirates or raiders, or by way of taxation. Frisian, Low German and English Fen practices may be taken to illustrate the first eventuality; border districts between England and Scotland—the second; the standardization of Swedish and Danish holdings—the third.

Very similar processes are apparent in the case of the Russian family communities. The term *siabr,* in the sense of a cousin or a relative, becomes an equivalent for the

[1] P. VINOGRADOFF, *The Growth of the Manor* (2nd ed., 1911), pp. 196 and 275.

[2] P. VINOGRADOFF, *English Society in the Eleventh Century* (1908), pp. 103, 281; *Villainage in England* (1892), p. 255.

[3] W. H. STEVENSON, *Yorkshire Surveys and Other XIth Century Documents in the York Gospels* (*English Historical Review,* January, 1912, pp. 19 ff.).

name for associate—*skladnik*. There is, for example, an act of division between six brothers from the north of Russia of the year 1640. They agree to divide bread and salt, house and liberties, money, cloth, and stores of all kinds, and to settle apart. As to arable, Shumilo is to take the upper strip in the fields by the settlement, and next to him Tretjak, then Maxim, then Zavial, then Shestoy, then Luke. In the big harvest furlong likewise, and in the small likewise, and by the meadow likewise, and so on through all the furlongs. Here is a clear illustration of the idea that everybody should have a share in the concerns of the community; and that an equitable division should be made among individual members; but it is clear that there is no exact estimate of mathematical principles on which the land should be split up. The basis of partition is simply a rough division into a number of furlongs, so that everybody may have the opportunity of enjoyment, in some part or other of the common property. But the system can only keep together so long as it remains *joint*. At a later stage shares are immobilized and redivided in accordance with the requirements of the State.

The open-field system.

At this stage of our inquiry the view may be expressed that it is to tribal custom that we must look for the principal explanation of the system of land-tenure which existed everywhere in Europe until the enclosures put an end to it —I refer to the open-field system. It was based on the distribution of the elements of an agricultural holding in such a way that every husbandman was, as it were, entangled in the economic arrangement of his neighbours; and the organization of village interests was not framed to meet the wishes of individual householders, but was concerned essentially with the regulation of conditions and interests in the open field. This degree of communalism may from our point of view seem almost absurd; for why, it may be asked, should people be expected to subject themselves to general rules which had nothing to do with their own private and individual affairs? But if this would seem to be a rational objection to the principle of the open field, on the other hand the system evidently arose out of some historic necessity, for it prevailed in practically all the principal countries of Europe, except the extreme South, and it continued in existence for thousands of years. If we look at an English village before the Enclosure Acts, we find an organization based substantially on the same principles as those which are to be found in Ine's Laws. It is in tribal custom as projected on the land that we observe the constitutive elements which explain the recognition and continuity of the arrangement. If we look, for example, at the Welsh communities in the ninth, tenth and eleventh centuries, we shall find one thing constantly recurring in different conditions: it is always insisted on that a householder, or free tribesman, who is starting in life, should get four *erws* (i.e., strips) for his use and enjoyment. Thus provision is made that the individual shall have the means and opportunity of profitable labour: but it is not the individual, nor yet the private household, which is regarded as *owning* the land; the ideal right of property is vested in the *whole clan,* and it is to that collective body that this direction is really addressed. The clan should see to it in its weles and gavells that every free tribesman gets four strips for cultivation. The provision has no practical meaning unless the land is virtually unlimited, and the individual allotments clearly cannot be parcelled out if the agricultural area is stinted—or even if it varies greatly in fertility, accessibility and similar qualities. That means that the abstract rule which regulates the enjoyment of individual portions must be adapted to the conditions of the land actually under cultivation. The result is a characteristic process of partition and distribution. Perhaps the most remarkable instance of this process is that of *meadows.* They are not allowed to follow the course of individual appropriation, but must be divided according to the number of households. The shares are taken sometimes by rotation and sometimes by lot. The practice may still be seen in full force in English villages, e.g., in Yarnton, near Oxford, where the distribution is made in each year in July, and the villagers take the meadow-land by lot. In the case of arable, a still more intimate connection is established between the land and the individual holder of it; the labour of sowing, fertilizing and reaping gives the husbandman a particular personal interest in the soil which is under his care; and it is natural that as the individual in this way is to a certain extent attached to the land, his holding tends to become hereditary. But it is not regarded as entirely separated from the communal groups: it is, for instance, considered as joint property when the crop has been taken from it. The whole system of division does not start from the convenience of the individual, but from that of the group, which takes care that an equitable division shall be made.

Continuity of Celtic and Saxon practices.

In conclusion, I should like to point out, on the strength of English evidence, one feature of rural life in which the continuity between the Celtic tribal system and the Anglo-Saxon township community arising from it is especially evident. This is the treatment of rents in kind, especially food rents. Every student of early English institutions is familiar with the "firms of one night" (*firma unius noctis*) imposed on ancient Royal estates and towns.[1] Corn produce was supplemented and even outweighed by dairy products, beer, honey, etc. The Laws of Ine supply the standard of these dues in the eighth century.[2] A consideration of the Welsh records makes it clear that such levies are simply a continuation of the arrangements by which Celtic chieftains maintained their household and retinue by levies from the free *priodarii,* and the more dependent *taeogs* of the country.[3] As we can trace the development of money rents and week work from these modest beginnings, even so the manorial system was slowly evolved from tribal customs.

Three main conclusions may be drawn from the survey of Aryan kinship organization:

(1) The kindred, as a variety of the clan system, was formed by the alliance between agnatic households for purposes of defence and mutual help. It involves a subsidiary recognition of relationship through women.

[1] *Domesday,* I, p. 75, etc. Cf. VINOGRADOFF, *Growth of the Manor,* p. 282.

[2] *Laws of Ine,* p. 70 (LIEBERMANN, *Die Gesetze der Angelsachsen,* I, p. 119).

[3] E.g. *Denbigh Survey,* pp. lxiv ff. Cf. SEEBOHM, *Tribal System in Wales,* p. 185.

(2) The arrangement of agriculture on the open-field system, based on the solidarity of the groups of neighbour cultivators, was originally conditioned by kinship.

(3) The transition from tribal to village communities was brought about by a standardization of holdings which aimed at establishing a fair proportion between the rights and the duties of the peasants.

CHAPTER X

THE LAW OF THE TRIBAL FEDERATION

Alliances between clans.

How was the clan or the kindred to maintain its existence as a unit of social organization? Although these unions comprised a greater number of members than the primary households, they cannot be conceived as entirely self-contained and self-supporting groups. In the process of evolution they had to combine with other clans or kindreds in tribal federations. This growth of larger groups can be clearly observed in many countries. In Albania, for example, the system of social organization is founded on the alliance of a number of clans in the larger body of the tribe. Among the southern Albanians, who conducted a determined struggle against the Turks, the clans which constitute the federations are so powerful that they may almost be considered as tribes in themselves. There is a recognized order of seniority, and the first among constituent groups —the *Hoti*—takes precedence at all general assemblies of the tribe. According to Gopčević, they number approximately 2,500 men, and have to provide 500 fighters in time of war.[1] Now as these family associations are so powerful and extensively organized, the question naturally arises how the government of the whole tribe is to be reconciled with the authority and compact organization of the clan? It looks at first sight as if the general association of the tribe may be described as a house divided against itself, for occasionally rivalry and strife arise among the influential members of the union. But usually some kind of reconciliation of the conflicting elements is effected for the sake of common defence: the lines upon which such

[1] The Clementi number 3,350 and send 500 warriors to the tribal host: the Gruda (2,200) send 200 warriors, and the Drekalovici (9,000) send 1,500 warriors: Gopčević, *Oberalbanien*, pp. 569 ff.

compromises are brought about are very similar in most cases.

Caesar on tribal authority.

In ancient history there are many instances of tribal federations and federal governments. Caesar, for example, gives us a remarkable description of the political state of German tribes—a description in which every word counts, as it was used by a man of action and is free from the influence of rhetoric or political prejudice: "Cum bellum civitas aut illatum defendit aut infert, magistratus, qui ei bello praesint, ut vitae necisque habeant potestatem, deliguntur. In pace nullus est communis magistratus, sed principes regionum atque pagorum inter suos ius dicunt controversiasque minuunt."[1]

The most striking feature in Caesar's account is that there is no common tribal authority in time of peace, though within the regional clans themselves, disputes are settled by the chieftains. As soon, however, as war breaks out, a common authority is elected for the whole tribe, and this representative (*magistratus*) of the union wields power over life and death.

A most important function of the tribal federation is the administration of law. Within the tribe, its constituent members, the clans, enjoy full autonomy, but in relation to outsiders—especially in the organization of defence—the tribe is a compact and undivided whole. In order to preserve this organic solidarity, careful provision must be made that the composite character of the aggregate does not lead to any irreconcilable conflicts. Thus the management of ordinary law in tribal society falls into two distinct departments. Within the clan, government is based on patriarchal authority, which in its turn recognizes the sway of religious and moral sanctions—those primary notions of right and justice which were termed by the Romans *fas* and *ius*. As between clans, the regulating forces are directed by principles which nowadays would be described as rules of positive international law. The adjustment of conflicts between members of the tribe belonging to different clans took primarily the form of *arbitration:* a judicial expedient

Arbitration.

[1] *De Bell. Gall.* VI, xxiii.

which is of enormous significance in all systems of ancient tribal law. The principal function of tribal authorities is to conciliate and to arbitrate between members of different clans. And this conception is not confined to very primitive states of society: even at a comparatively advanced stage of development, the judicial power of tribal leaders is plainly conceived and developed on these lines. Hesiod,[1] for instance, in the sixth century B.C. describes the function of kings sitting in judgment as the action of "middlemen" who conciliate contending parties by persuasive words, and induce them to make peace and not to resort to hostilities. Obvious considerations of utility dictate the policy of averting intestine conflicts if possible, and the duty of those in authority is to protect tribal solidarity against the disintegrating influences of dissension.

Compulsory arbitration.

But, of course, it is not always possible to achieve conciliation by persuasive words, and the rival parties may prove intractable to the suggestions of mediators. Then, if unity is to be preserved, the intervention of authority must take the form of *compulsory arbitration.* On the growth of this institution a great deal of early political development depends. The first step in this respect is to put an end to armed collisions between clans. The private feuds of individuals lead to hostilities between groups of clansmen, and the central authority must set itself resolutely against the action of these destructive forces. Ancient legal lore furnishes some interesting pieces of evidence which illustrate the connection between voluntary and compulsory arbitration, and the transition from one to the other. By chance a bronze tablet has been preserved which records a convention (*Fρατρα*) of the citizens of Elis: it concerns the case of one man accusing another of crime—probably homicide, though this cannot be definitely ascertained. It is quite plain from the first words, and the whole tenor of the enactment, that it is directed against a possible conflict between clans.

"Let the clan (πατριάν) and the kindred (γενεάν) of the accused and his property be secure (θαρρε̃ν) if any

[1] *Opera et dies,* 38, 202, etc.

one brings accusation against a man of Elis. If the chief magistrates and the kings do not provide legal remedies, each of those who have failed to do so shall pay ten minae to the sacred treasury of the Olympian Zeus. Let the Hellanodike pronounce judgment against them, and as to the rest (as to the subject of the claim), let the demiurgs deliver judgment according to law. If he (the Hellanodike) do not give judgment, he shall pay double at the rendering of accounts. If any one shall offer violence to the accused man, he shall be liable to a fine of ten minae, if he commit personal violence knowing that the issue is under judicial examination."[1]

A more familiar and no less striking instance of ancient arbitration is the procedure described in the famous account of the shield of Achilles in the *Iliad* (XVIII, 497). Two men are disputing about the blood price of a person slain. One asserts that he has paid the whole, the other denies having received anything. A witness is produced (ἐπὶ ἵστορι). The trial takes place before the people in the market-place. Some among the spectators side with one of the contending parties, others with his opponent. Ultimately the elders (γέροντες) rise in turn and each pronounces his verdict after taking up the sceptre symbolizing authority.

The case is one which turns on an agreement intended to take the place of an open struggle. The non-payment of the fine or blood price was in itself sufficient ground to take up arms and wage private war. Yet the decision is referred to a tribunal in which the popular element is not absent, and public opinion finds vent in the support given by outsiders to the parties. The question at issue is ultimately decided by the elders of the community, who deliver the verdict each one by himself. We are not told by what means the general result was consolidated and its execution was enforced.

A feature in the procedure which remains obscure consists in the fact that the elders who deliver the best judg-

1 SOLMSEN, *Inscriptiones dialecticae Graecae*, p. 84; GLOTZ, *La Solidarité de la Famille*, p. 248. Cf. ZIMMERN, *The Greek Commonwealth*, p. 10.

ment receive a prize in the form of money deposited as a wager. We do not know how and by whom the merits of the different judgments were estimated: possibly the standard was simply the number of votes cast in favour of each sentence; or the "persuasiveness" of the judicial dicta may have been measured by their effect on the popular audience. Although these problems remain unsolved, there are on the other hand many elements which are abundantly clear. The cardinal fact is that this is a suit which is brought before a public court on the principle of waging certain sums on the issue, and a final decision is delivered by tribal elders.

On the other hand, agreements might be arranged directly between the contending parties. An example of this is afforded by agreements in regard to *wergelds*. We see them reduced to regular tariffs in the laws of the barbarians, but originally they were the outcome of private and varying settlements. The public powers threw, of course, all the weight of their influence in the scale of such peaceful arrangements, and Charlemagne, for example, inveighed with severity against lawless people refusing to take the *wergeld* price and insisting on revenge in kind.

It is by no means only in cases of manslaughter and *wergeld* payments that people had to resort to agreements resembling international treaties. Every settlement of a dispute in tribal surroundings was in truth a treaty of peace. A treaty between parties was sometimes made the express condition for entering on a trial instead of fighting it out by force. This is the case with the Germanic *Gedinge,* a settlement to go to law binding on both parties and corroborated by the giving of gages. The gage is in this case usually the *festuca,* a staff as the symbol of the promise.[1]

The legal struggle.

This aspect of arbitration is also deeply ingrained in the constitution of ancient courts of law, and the forms of procedure. It may be said that an ancient trial was not much more than a formally regulated struggle between the parties in which the judges had to act more as umpires and

[1] GRIMM, *Deutsche Rechtsalterthümer*, II, 140 ff. Cf. KOVALEVSKY, *Coutume contemporaine*, 334. AMIRA, *Der Stab in der germanischen Rechtssymbolik.*

wardens of order and fair play than as investigators of the truth.

It is worth while to look somewhat more closely at the peculiarities of the different modes of legal proof, because they express the gradual substitution of judicial process for actual struggle. Of trial by combat we need not say much: the transformation of actual struggle into judicial litigation is so clear in this case that it is not necessary to labour the point.[1] It has been urged that single combat is to be considered as an appeal to God to manifest the right of one of the sides by giving it the victory.[2] This religious element is often strongly expressed: e.g., the Bavarian law expresses itself in the following manner:—"Let them accept the judgment of God, and the man to whom God gives victory, believe him." [3] But single combat was not only an appeal to God's authority; it was a substitute for private war and irregular self-redress. With the Norsemen it was regularly resorted to by agreement between the parties, and it might therefore take one of two different shapes: it was either a formless single combat, *einvigi,*—as it were an outlet for individual passion or resentment,—or else it took the form of an encounter according to fixed rules in carefully prepared surroundings (*holmgang*).

Another very characteristic and widespread mode of proof was the swearing of oaths. The swearer was to pronounce a formula which was supposed to call forth the action of divine Power, so that truth might be made known and untruth detected. These formulæ were occasionally very intricate, and a slip of the tongue was taken as a sign of divine interference to disclose the falsehood of an assertion.

The most striking trait of mediæval judicial oaths is certainly the fact that they were uttered not merely by the person making an assertion before the court, but also by a number of other persons acting as his companions—

1 G. NEILSON, *Trial by Combat* (1890).
2 LIEBERMANN, *Gesetze der Angelsachsen*, I, pp. 411, 517; *Iudicium Dei*, V and X.
3 BRUNNER, *Deutsche Rechtsgeschichte*, I², 262 ff.
4 Cf. STEMANN, *Dansk Retshistorie* (1871), p. 130.

compurgatores, consacramentales. The usual number was twelve, but it could be diminished or increased according to the importance of the suit and the social standing of the persons concerned in it. The oath-helpers had to be selected originally from among the kinsmen of the principal, or, in some cases, from his neighbours, but their statement was never brought forward as unbiassed testimony, but as an assertion of right, the strength of which depended mainly on the social standing of the body which made it. This assertion of the right on the part of a body of men is not a mere formality, because if the principal failed in his oath, his kinsmen had to suffer with him.[1] Eventually, in case of strong prejudice against a party, there remained the possibility of clearing oneself by an *ordeal*—a miraculous intervention of Providence out of the usual course of nature.[2]

The part played by the court is not without its importance on such occasions: it has to decide what mode of proof is to be used, and on whom the burden of proof shall fall; lastly, of course, there is judgment on the result of the proof attempted.[3]

Agreements as to fines.

If the parties have agreed to submit their dispute to the regularizing action of a court instead of prosecuting their interest by private means, and when they have given solemn promise to appear at the trial, the next step in Greek, Roman and Teutonic law was to provide for the amount of possible compensation and loss in the forthcoming struggle. It was not only a question of carrying through one's contention and retaining or acquiring the objects in dispute, or making good one's claim to the performance of an obligation, the conquering party meant to get compensation for the danger and risk of the enterprise, and for their efforts in carrying it out. The losing party had to incur a penalty for mischievous and useless resistance to the better right. Both parties usually made an agreement on entering on the trial to make a deposit with the court, in

[1] LIEBERMANN, *Gesetze der Angelsachsen*, II, p. 377 (*Eideshelfer*); BRUNNER, *Deutsche Rechtsgeschichte*, 2nd ed., I, pp. 123.

[2] HASTINGS' *Encyclopædia of Religion and Ethics*, s. v. *Ordeal*.

[3] An appropriate example may be taken from the *Russian Pravda*, Troitzky MS., § 17, p. 82.

order that the losing side should incur a fine at the end of the litigation. This pledge was symbolized in Greek law by πρυτανεῖα, in Roman law by *sacramentum* and in Teutonic law by *vadium* (*gage*). In all these cases we have the very elements which characterize international law at the present time: no direct compulsion, no necessity to bow to a superior or sovereign will, but a voluntary submission to rules established by consent of the parties and guaranteed by their good faith, and by a certain regard for public opinion as far as it represented the views of persons not directly affected in the struggle, and therefore better able to judge it with impartiality.

Tribal authority.

Looking back on ancient law, it may be said that criminal and civil procedure are still at a stage corresponding to a great extent to the modern state of international law and procedure. Procedure begins to develop at a time when the element of public compulsion is absent or insignificant. The transitions from one stage to the other—from a legalized struggle to arbitration and ultimately to full jurisdictional authority are very gradual. Two circumstances contributed powerfully to effect the transition from international law to a law regulated by the commonwealth: the growth of a mediating power to which parties were forced to submit, and the increasing strength of the view that even imperfect compromise is better than open struggle. The principle, then, of tribal federalism is sufficiently manifest: it remains to consider the actual political forms in which this principle is embodied. We might expect them to differ greatly according to nationalities, but in point of historical fact, they are remarkably alike. Throughout the tribal arrangements of different nationalities, we constantly find as rudimentary forms of political authority—*kingship, the council of the elders* and *the assembly of warriors*. It is difficult to establish a chronological order in the development of these institutions. In any case tribal kingship is not the most ancient. If it were necessary to establish an order of priority, I should be inclined to put the council of elders (γερουσία, senate) first, because it was originally a council of clan kings, and as clans were undoubtedly of more ancient origin than the federation of the tribe, this meeting in council is essentially antecedent to the institution of the tribal kingship. As in a modern state of the federal type, for example, in the United States of America, the Congress of the Union may be traced in its origin to meetings of plenipotentiaries, so in early society the clan kings made up the central body of federal representatives. It is important, however, to remember that in early societies a king did not represent merely political and judicial authority: his office was conceived as intimately connected with tribal religion, or rather, with magic, which was the characteristic form of religion in primitive society. The king was a kind of link or intermediary between the gods and the community, and his first duty was to secure by divine favour the welfare of the people under his care. His merit as a kingly ruler depended on the degree of his fortune in representing the people before the gods. One of the most fortunate kings of Norway was Halfdan, the Black. The importance which the people attached to his good fortune was shown by the fact that when he died, his body was actually cut up, and every district of his kingdom tried to obtain a portion of it.[1] The converse aspect is presented by the story of Olaf Trætelgya, a powerful ruler and a great colonizer, who at the end of his reign was pursued by ill luck: his sacrifices did not find favour with the gods. There was nothing for it, but to remove this source of offence, and to take some other ruler who was more pleasing in the sight of the gods. Olaf was therefore summarily dispatched, not on account of any wilful fault of his, but simply because he did not possess the necessary quality of kingly fortune.[2]

The assembly is no less vital to the organization of early society than the kings of the tribe and the elders or chieftains of the clans. We are not to suppose that there was anything approximating to a "democratic" feeling, in the modern sense, in the primitive community. The principle of the assembly is not that of political representation, but

[1] SNORRE STURLESON, *Heimskringla*, *Halfdans Svarta Saga*, K. 9.
[2] *Heimskringla*, *Ynglinga Saga*, K. 43.

of military organization. The general assembly of the people is identical with the army or host. Familiar examples in ancient history are the *comitia centuriata* of Rome and the armed assembly of the Teutons.[1] To what extent this collective assembly of the host was able to assert a superior power over the kings depended on the particular conditions of tribal life.

Self-help in the courts.

It is extremely difficult to enforce the rules of law and the decisions of courts of arbitration; this difficulty is felt even at the present time in international law, the rules of which are provided only with "incomplete" sanctions. All the acts of the parties and of the tribunals had to be formulated in an exceptionally strict and formal manner. The governing principle upon which the courts proceeded was not the investigation as to fundamental right, but the solution of conflicts between opposing parties. Its nature and methods are not directed towards an analysis of the complex contents of the cases. This latter form of judicial inquiry is difficult at all times, even when it is helped by the resources of an advanced civilization and of a scientific jurisprudence. For tribal societies it is impossible to tackle such problems, as the dominating influence of kin solidarity prevents the consideration of purely individual motives.

Hence most acts of a judicial character in early societies were directed towards settling the forms which were to govern legal contests. If, for example, a tribesman of the Salian Franks wished to prefer a claim against one of his neighbours, he was obliged to adopt a precise method in summoning his opponent.[2] He had to go to the house of his adversary, state his claim in the presence of witnesses and "set the sun," that is, name a day on which the party summoned was required to appear before the Mall, the judicial assembly. If the defendant did not appear, it was necessary to repeat the ceremony over and over again. Eventually, when he did appear, he could be called to account for his failure to answer the former summons, and

1 TACITUS, *Germania*, XI and XIII.

2 *Lex Salica*, ch. i, De mannire. Cf. the Roman *Condictio:* GAIUS, IV, § 18.

he might advance a number of pleas to excuse his default: for example, that he had been ill, or absent on a military expedition. Such a circumstantial procedure as regards summonses was rendered necessary by the weakness of tribal authority: it could not lay down and enforce stringent commands supported by the combined force of the whole social union.

So wide is the range of self-help in early society, that it may sometimes even go to the length of putting pressure on a tribunal, and, as it were, compelling it to give judgment. The litigant is bound to ask for the decision of a court to authorize his own action:—and this is evidence of the necessity of some control by constituted authority; but, on the other hand, the individual had to extract from the tribunal the judgment he desired;—and this is evidence of the power of personal self-help. In Frankish law, litigants frequently put pressure on the courts in order to obtain the required verdict. This seems a glaring anomaly to us at the present day, for we are accustomed to speak and think of the supremacy of the courts in litigation. The appeal to a tribunal had to be made by the particular means of a solemn formula, the "*tangano,*" and the arbitrators, or *Rachimburghs,* were required to deliver judgment in the manner specified by the claimant.[1] It would seem that in many cases they did so against their will: often the parties appearing before them were persons of great influence, and in primitive society it was no light matter for a judge to provoke powerful individuals by adverse decisions.

The actual settlement of a case depended on a treaty, each party giving pledges for the fulfilment of the judgment. But when this decision had been reached, there remained a further and no less important process: *execution* was still necessary to complete the course of law. It is here that we see most clearly the inherent weakness of tribal jurisdiction, for execution, the practical enforcement of legal decision, was not effected, as a rule, by sovereign authority, but left to a great extent in the hands of the

[1] *Lex Salica,* LVII.

individual litigant and his friends: it amounted to little more than self-help juridically sanctioned and approved by the tribe.

Self-help against wrong-doers.

Even now lynching is an outburst of outraged public feeling against some one who has grossly transgressed the rules of a community in regard to right and wrong: a negro guilty of an assault against a white woman is mercilessly lynched in America; a professional horse-thief is lynched by the peasants in Russia. One element of legal action remains intact and is strongly prominent in such cases; they proceed from the notion of a right emphatically recognized by the community.

An interesting expression of the view that an offended or persecuted person has to appeal to the community at large may be found in the history of Slavonic and Teutonic legal procedure. With the Czechs in Bohemia an accusation had to be instituted by a "complaint"—literally a plaint or wail before the people of the neighbourhood.[1] The Germanic *Klage*—plaint—which forms the first stage in proceedings against wrongdoers is of the same kind. The plaintiff adjures his neighbours and fellow-citizens to stand by him. I do not think that the famous practice of hue and cry in Normandy and England has any other origin. It was made use of by organized government to strengthen its police hold over the population, but it is undoubtedly connected with the natural cry for help of the victim of an assault. It appears in this special form in the *Sachsenspiegel* in cases of rape (II, 64, § 1). The shepherd is said to "shout" for help against wolves and against robbers (*Sachssp.*, II, 54, § 4). The menace of inundation is also announced by "Gerüchte."

Self-defence.

Another striking expression of this principle is afforded by the organization of self-defence in the matter of protection of life and limb. All the national branches of the Indo-European law recognized in one form or another the right of individuals to take the law in their own hands in certain cases. This is notably so in acts committed in a state of excitement, when it is recognized by the general

[1] BRUNNER, *Rechtsgeschichte*, I, 123. GRIMM, *Rechtsalterthümer*, II, 488 f.

sense of the community that provocation of a serious nature has been offered to the injured party. The most familiar instance is that of action against an adulterer. In regard to this even later Greek and Roman law allowed a summary slaying of the offender.[1] A noteworthy modification of this rule may be found in Greek law. For example, in the laws of Gortyn,[2] it is forbidden to kill the offender offhand, and the amount of fines to be paid in such cases is fixed by custom. If, however, the relatives of the culprit do not pay ransom for him, he remains in the hands of the offended kindred, who may do with him what they like.

The case of theft provides another striking illustration. If the thief is taken red-handed, he immediately falls into the power of his captor.[3] If he takes to flight and is tracked, the tribe exercises its influence on the procedure to be followed. The plaintiff has a right to demand a search in the house of the person suspected, and this search is carried out by the aggrieved individual, though he can only conduct it in certain forms which the law prescribes. Roman law recognized a similar form of execution. The pursuer was entitled to search in person, but again only if he observed certain precautions and ceremonies. He must wear the minimum of clothing, and carry a platter in his hands,[4]—this provision was perhaps intended to prevent the plaintiff from bringing some objects of his own into the house of an enemy, and then accusing the latter of having stolen it. The general tendency of these practices is obvious: theft was considered as a private rather than a public wrong, and it was the business of the party injured to secure redress for himself; but the commonwealth was anxious at the same time to prevent violent collisions and to ensure as much order as possible in the prosecution of the claims of aggrieved persons. It is significant that similar practices occur in widely different surroundings. A process resembling that which obtained in Greece and Rome was in operation in Scandinavian countries. The cere-

[1] LYSIAS, Speeches, XXX, On the slaying of Eratosthenes.
[2] §§ 8-13 (DARESTE, *Rec. des inscrip. jur. grecques*, ch. i, p 359).
[3] GAIUS, III, 189.
[4] GAIUS, III, 192-3.

monial is indicated by the word *ransack*, compounded of *ran*—loot, and *sökia*—to seek. Few people to-day realize that, when they ransack a cupboard for food, they perform an act which may be traced back to the ancient legal process of searching for stolen goods.

Distress.

Self-help is admitted by the ancient law of Indo-European nations in connection with civil as well as with criminal litigation. In fact it looks almost as if it were the orginal basis of possession itself. It is at least characteristic that some of the expressions referring to ownership in Indo-European language go back to the notion of conquest, the taking of booty. The Italian *roba,* meaning chattels, goods, is nothing but the Teutonic *Raub,* the produce of robbery, and the Latin *praedium,* estate, is related to *praeda,* booty. No wonder that the symbol of property in Rome came to be a spear, *hasta.*

One of the most common forms of self-help is *distress,* which, as is well known, is a recognized legal expedient even in such a highly developed legal system as the English. Here again the individual takes the law into his own hands, but he does not do so according to his own will and pleasure: if he is willing to conform to certain rules established by authority, his self-help will be sanctioned: if not, he will himself be guilty of a misdemeanour. Roman law provides many examples of legalized self-help of this kind. One of the most conspicuous is the process against an insolvent debtor. In the oldest Roman procedure for the exaction of debts, the debtor was bound to the creditor (*nexum*), and, if he failed to fulfil his obligation in regard to payment, he was liable to *manus iniectio,*—to be thrown into prison and chained. Gaius,[1] unfortunately, gives only a fragmentary account on this point, but the information given, though scanty, is plain enough if read in the light of comparative evidence. The procedure amounts to this: the creditor may lay hand on the debtor, with a solemn reference to the non-payment of the debt The presence of witnesses is necessary for the regularity of this ceremonial act. What guarantee was there that this power of self-help

[1] IV, 21 ff.

would not be abused? The only safeguard was that it might be met by self-help in the opposite direction. The creditor who takes his debtor in execution of a debt is liable to be stopped by a *vindex* acting on behalf of the debtor: and thus, ultimately, the procedure, instead of being a one-sided exercise of force on the part of the creditor, resolves itself into a judicial conflict between the claimant and the protector of the defendant.

Pignoris capio[1] was another familiar species of private execution in Roman law. It consisted in the taking of security, and could be employed even in the absence of the person who owned the chattel taken. Most commonly it took the form of impounding animals which were causing damage to the plaintiff's property. The analogous method in English law is to be found in the right of distress *damage feasant*. There is an obvious reason why in cases of this kind the injured party should have a summary remedy in his own hands. Strictly, it would be more in accord with modern juristic notions if he made a legal claim against the person responsible for the damage: but if injury is being inflicted by an animal, it would be absurd to expect the plaintiff to delay action until a trial could be arranged with the owner; it is only reasonable that he should be empowered to take immediate steps against the continuance of the damage. But here again he is bound to observe certain rules if he desires his remedy to be effectual and to receive the sanction of established law. The animal impounded must be placed in a particular enclosure: and various questions arise as to its maintenance, the possibility of its dying while in the charge of the plaintiff, etc.[2]

Public sanctions.

These examples immediately suggest an important problem to the modern observer. If so much depended upon private self-help, and if the intervention of the tribe or the city was so inadequate, how was the ultimate sanction of the community to be put into force? In the view of many modern writers on jurisprudence, the existence of a legal rule necessarily depends upon the sanction which can be

[1] Gaius, III, 77-81.
[2] St. German's *Doctor and Student*, c. vii, p. 19.

found to enforce it. But tribal systems present this vital element of law in a very remarkable light, and show in a striking manner that the enforcement of legal rules does not necessarily depend on the existence of indisputable sovereign authority. The sanction is desired and produced by public opinion, sometimes by indirect means, sometimes by private self-help, and sometimes by pressure from the tribe. But it is essential to understand that the origins of law in these communities depend on the *recognition of the community.* It is to this principle that we must look as the fundamental creative and regulative factor in early law. It is clear that in spite of all the commands of tribunals and all the ceremonies of execution, the enforcement of rights may remain difficult or impossible. If when all the stages of judicial process have been passed and all the formalities observed, the person against whom judgment is given remains obdurate, what is to happen? Will the State step in and use direct coercion against the recalcitrant individual? It will not do so in tribal society: It is at a much later stage that we meet this form of state power, and as soon as this period has been reached, we may recognize a great advance in social organization. In general, we may say that this is the case in Teutonic societies where *bann,* or public "*coercion,*" supersedes the *mannire* and private process. In the Roman system this notion of public coercion is rendered by the term *districtio.* The transition, naturally enough, only took place by very gradual steps. Even in the time of Charlemagne, public execution was only possible in specific cases.[1]

Outlawry.

Originally, when such execution takes place, it does not assume the shape of the direct enforcement of a certain course of conduct, nor of the direct exaction of a particular penalty, but is represented by the declaration of *outlawry.* If a man breaks his pledges and is not amenable to the force of private execution, the tribe declares that social intercourse is no longer possible with one who refuses to be bound by social rules, and that he is to be deemed equal to a wild beast, a wolf (*vargus, caput lupinum*). He must

[1] BRUNNER, *op cit.*, I^2, 200.

take to flight and dwell outside the protection of the law.[1] He has by his own rebellious conduct put himself beyond the pale of juridically organized society, and henceforth he can enjoy none of the rights which he had denied to others. The usual process, as we see it, for instance, among Scandinavian tribes, is that he betakes himself to the forest to live as best he can. The *skogar-men* are literally expelled from society: by means of solemn forms all ties which bind them to their fellow-tribesmen are severed. Not even their wives and families are allowed to help them in their helpless condition, and the communion of fire and water is forbidden to them.[2] Sometimes the disapprobation of society is evinced in even more drastic ways, and in ancient Russia, for example, it was customary not only to drive out the offending individual, but to destroy his house and loot his property.[3]

Outlawry, then, goes one step beyond private execution: it is a declaration by the commonwealth that a particular individual shall no longer enjoy the advantages of social intercourse. In the next stage, public authority proceeds to *direct* coercion, and the necessity for this form of execution is at least partially recognized even in rudimentary societies. There are certain offences which injure deeply the whole community as a collective body, and the tribe is bound to deal with them in its corporate capacity. Treason, for instance, is a menace to the whole system of social organization, and desertion from the army is an offence against the whole armed community, the military *host* in its broadest aspect. It is not surprising to find, therefore, that in nearly all tribal communities, both these offences have been considered as deserving direct punishment by society as a whole.[4]

Even apart from immediate retribution by superior force, there was another means of dealing with the more

[1] GRIMM, *Deutsche Rechtsalterthümer*, 4th ed. (1899), II, p. 335.
[2] Cf. HEUSLER, *Strafrecht der Isländer Sagas*, I, 24 f.
[3] Potok i razgrablenie, e.g. *Russian Pravda*, p. 30 (JIREČEK, *Svod Zakonov Slovanskyh*, 1880).
[4] TACITUS, *Germania*, xii. Cf. STRACHAN DAVIDSON, *Roman Criminal Law*, I, pp. 2 ff., 114.

serious forms of social delinquency—namely, by the force of *religion*. In one sense it may be said that a person who defies social morality outrages religion and offers a direct affront to the gods. But apart from this more idealistic conception, there are in tribal society certain elements of magic which exercised a powerful influence. One of the most deeply-rooted ideas of this kind was that the shedding of human blood is a *pollution* of the whole community. Public reaction against homicide asserts itself in the necessity for purifying the soil from that pollution. Primarily—in so far as the individual injury is concerned—homicide is a private wrong: but in the consequences which it entails, it affects the whole body of society.[1]

Formulation of tribal law.

In conclusion, it is interesting to inquire in what form the customs and principles of tribal law are embodied and enunciated. In spite of the fact that we are dealing with rudimentary conditions, these ancient formulations of legal principles are not without value to the modern student of general jurisprudence. The actual method of the declaration of the law was not so much the issue of a positive command as a process of ascertaining established views and customs. The ancient lawgiver never considers himself as issuing an order to particular persons or the community in general:[2] his primary function is to *find the law* and give expression to the sense of the community in regard to juridical acts. Among the Frisians, for example, who possessed little codified law, the task of formulating and declaring customary law was entrusted to a special functionary of high standing, the *asega*. He was not a judge, but a legal expert, a man versed in legal lore. Originally there were probably separate *asegas* for each of the three great divisions of Friesland, or even seven, one for each of the seven provinces. Later on, the office was concentrated in the hands of one man. The record of the oldest Frisian customs, the so-called Lex Frisionum, contains a number of

[1] See e.g., *Œdipus Rex*, 14 ff. Cf. ZIMMERN, *Greek Commonwealth*, pp. 98 ff.

[2] MAINE's criticism of the Austinian theory as to this point is hardly convincing.—*Ancient Law*, ch. i. Cf., however, *Early History of Institutions*, pp. 380 f.

paragraphs marked as additions made by the wise men, *additiones sapientum*,[1] and the names of two of these worthies, Wlemar and Saxmund, have been preserved for posterity.

Something similar occurred in Scandinavian countries. Both in Norway and in Sweden we find *laghmen*, legal experts elected from among the people, whose office was to lay down the law. The Swedish *laghman* was a professional, in the sense that he had to be versed in all the details and intricacies of the law, but he was chosen from among the ordinary laymen. He was not a clerk nor a student of foreign law, and he was even expected to represent more especially the interests of the peasant population in opposition to the court and royal officials.[2] A curious trait of his activity consists in the obligation to deliver not only consultations in cases arising by chance, but statements or lectures on legal custom in a more or less systematic form. This is termed the *lögsöga,* discourse on law, and it seems as if some of the provincial laws of Sweden owe their formulation to such discourses. At any rate one of them, the "Law of the *Östgöta,*" closes with the following words: "this is the end of the law discourse."[3] The institution of the "law discourse," which may be compared in some respects to the edict of the Roman praetor, was even more fully developed in Iceland, where the *lögsögu-madhr* was elected by the *Althing,* the assembly of chiefs, for three years and had to acquit himself of the task of proclaiming the law by lectures delivered in regular terms during these three years. It was expected that the entire domain of legal custom would have been treated by that time.[4]

The difference, however, from the edict of the Roman praetor is significant: the latter was, at least in theory, a

[1] LAMBERT, *Fonction du droit comparé*, 744 f.

[2] The *lagmen* of the Anglo-Danish borough, like Lincoln or Stamford, are representatives of the military class. Cf. VINOGRADOFF, *English Society in the XIth Century*, p 5.

[3] *Östgöta-Lagen*, Bygda B. LI; Nu er Laghsagha ithur lyktath og ut sagth.

[4] KONRAD MAURER, *Das Staatsrecht des isländischen Freistaates* (ed. by the Norwegian Academy, 1909), IV, pp. 263 ff.

prospective declaration, and was certainly not based on popular custom; the Icelandic edict, on the other hand, was a statement epitomizing and adopting customs, general views and opinions which had been formed in the past, and which were therefore accepted as principles applicable to the future. England has known a similar kind of judicial authority, for the *Witan* of Anglo-Saxon times presents many points of similarity to the *laghman* and the *lögsögu-madhr*. They met in the superior body of the *Witenagemot*, as well as in the *folkmóts* of the counties. It was not only their chief duty to decide particular cases, but they were also required to give verdicts in regard to general customs of the land.[1]

The "professional" function was to discover and declare the general opinion of society concerning certain fundamental institutions, such as succession. Social customs themselves obviously did not take their origin from an assembly or tribunal. They grew up by gradual process in the households and daily relations of the clans, and the magistrate only came in at a later stage, when the custom was already in operation, and added to the sanction of general recognition the express formulation of judicial and expert authority. In France and Germany, from the Carolingian age downwards, a special board of legal experts appears with certain characteristic duties. They are the *Scabini, Schöffen, échevins*, persons definitely elected for the purpose of máking out the law and holding office for life, or at least for several years. Such experts were, of course, of great help to the authorities in the settlement of all questions relating to local customs, but their standing is already so much a professional one that it would be difficult to treat their verdicts as pure statements of public opinion. Still they were supposed to declare customs of unknown origin assumed to have been created by popular tradition, and in this way they presented a marked contrast to the jurisprudence of royal courts and learned lawyers. The value assigned by public opinion to local customs in all Teutonic countries may be illustrated by a couple of lines

[1] VINOGRADOFF, *English Society in the XIth Century*, p. 8.

from the famous poem in glorification of Simon de Montfort: "*nec omnes provinciae sic sunt idiotae quibus leges propriae melius non sint notae*"—the people in the provinces, the local people, are not so peculiar as not to know better about their own laws.

Formalism of ancient law

When we turn from procedure and legislation to substantive rules, the feature which strikes the modern student most is the formalism of ancient law. The subjective psychological aspect of facts in law is ignored or relegated to the background—only results are considered, and results have to be presented in a definite and traditional form. The transfer of land in Norse law, for instance, had to be effected by throwing a symbolical object—a piece of turf or a stick—into the lap of the donee (*Sköjtning.*[1] Unless the ceremony was performed exactly according to custom and in the presence of witnesses, the donation or sale did not hold good. The spoken formulæ of different acts in law were strictly fixed, and a slip in their utterance would cause a breakdown in the act. For this reason the *Vorsprecher* (forspeca) was an important personage in ancient Germanic and Anglo-Saxon communities, as the instructed leader of the principal.[2] The practical importance of such solemn ceremonies may be illustrated by the custom prevailing in Bavaria and Alamannia, according to which transfers of land had to be performed in the presence of a certain number of small boys who, after attending the ceremony, were treated to boxes on the ear in order that they might keep a vivid remembrance of what had happened.

The decisive part played by form in legal acts made it necessary to provide in a specific manner for publicity and correctness in the performance of all customary requirements. A striking manifestation of this aspect of tribal custom is presented by the Scandinavian institution of the *fastar*. They are members of the folkmót or hundredmót

[1] See TARANGER, *Transfer of Land in Old Norwegian Law*, in *Essays in Legal History of the 1913 Historical Congress in London*, ed. by VINOGRADOFF. Cf. In laisum verpiri, *Lex Salica*, XLVI.

[2] BRUNNER, *op. cit.*, I, 126.

who must be present in case of any dealings with land, or of weddings, in order to testify to the performance of all rites, and to confirm the formal legality of the transaction. They are not witnesses (*vitni*) and are clearly distinguished from the latter. They act and make pronouncements in the course of the ceremony. The symbol of their activity is a spear or rod (*skapt*). In a charter of 1281 for instance, the principal *fastar madhr's* action is described in the following words: "*praedictam ordinationem esse legitime factam secundum leges terre et consuetudines approbatas.*"[1] The institution of the *fastar* was not restricted to the territory of Swedish provincial laws. There are traces of it in the Anglo-Danish region, especially in connection with the estates of the Abbey of Medhamsted (Peterborough).[2] It need hardly be said that this practice of solemn confirmation by the representatives of the community reminds us of the action of the *comitia curiata* in regard to arrogation and testaments in ancient Rome. It may be safely asserted that the formalism of tribal law had its roots not only in its intimate connection with religion and the reverence for traditional custom, but also in the federal organization of society. The latter laid stress on the interests and notions of groups, and for this very reason left the psychology of individuals in the shade. What is more, tribal law, as far as it was expressly formulated, was founded on treaties and conventions, and this origin made it necessary to keep strictly to details and formulæ.

Legal fictions.

The difficult problem for a law of this kind was the problem of development. How were necessary changes to be introduced? How were the traditional rules to be adapted to changing circumstances? The conservatism of ancient law was much greater than the conservatism of modern times, while legislative factors and methods were much less ready and effective. Hence the prominence of a peculiar method which has all but disappeared nowadays

[1] AMIRA, *Nordgermanisches Obligationenrecht*, I, pp. 273 ff.
[2] P. VINOGRADOFF, *Transfer of Land in Anglo-Saxon Law*, *Harvard Law Review*, 1909.

—the method of *legal fiction.*[1] The priests, or elders, or judges, who acted as guardians of legal lore, devised, or connived at, the substitution of altered contents within the forms hallowed by time and usage. The wisdom of the pontifical jurisconsults of Rome suggested and accepted legal reform under cover of an observance of old rites *dicis causa,* "for the sake of the term." Instead of requiring actual transfer of cash for the validity of an act of sale or emancipation, the jurisconsults admitted the confirmation of the transaction by the fictitious acceptance of a piece of metal in the presence of a *libripens* and five witnesses (*mancipatio per aes et libram*). Instead of insisting on the passing of an express law to allow a litigant to dispose at will of his inheritance, the jurisconsults introduced the fictitious sale of the household to a middleman (*familiae emptor*) who had to pass it on to the intended heir and to the legatees. Instead of liberating spinsters from the irksome *tutela* of agnatic relations, the jurisconsults advised them to get married to old men (*senex coemptionalis*), who would be declared their guardians for the sake of form, but who would be debarred from exercising any of the rights of actual husbands.[2] In Germanic law we find the same process in full vigour. In order to pass real property to some one out of the course of ordinary succession, the Salian Frank played a part in a little judicial drama—the *affatomia.*[3] He invited his neighbours to be witnesses to the fact that he left his house and court by jumping over the fence, in a bare shirt and with a staff in his hand, after having thrown some earth from the four corners of his homestead on a *salman* (middleman), and declaring that he had nothing left of his homestead either above the soil, or under the soil. Thereupon the *salman* remained in the house assigned to him for three nights, and treated his neighbours to a meal of porridge in manifestation of his

[1] Cf. MAINE, *Ancient Law,* ch. ii. I refrain from citing the well-known fictitious devices of English law, such as fine and recovery, the action of ejectment, the status of a king's debtor, the venue of Middlesex, etc. They are all products of judicial interference with obsolete law.

[2] CICERO, *pro Murena,* 122 f.

[3] *Lex Salica,* XLVI.

faculty as householder. The closing act was another transfer by the middleman to the intended donee. It is important to keep in mind that none of these acts or of similar fictions could have had any positive results, if the judges or magistrates did not make up their minds to connive at them, and to protect the beneficiaries from undesirable consequences of their formal acts. The Roman spinsters certainly wanted to be secure against possible enterprises of their pretended husbands, and they could obtain such security only through the protection of the tribunals which had allowed them to escape from agnatic *tutela*. Nor could a *salman* safely stop the dramatic performance of the *affatomia* at the second act and avoid the transfer to the donee in the third.

Legal fiction was undoubtedly not the only means of effecting changes in ancient law. Direct legislation and codification have left distinct traces in the history of Aryan nations from very early times. Even more potent was the exercise of the sense of justice and fairness by householders, elders and chieftains. The θέμιστες referred to in the Homeric poems [1] were decisions of this kind. The notion of θέμις cannot be rendered by our term "command": [2] it implies a pronouncement as to right, and a direction as to conduct [3]: it is the basis of Δίκη and is closely allied to religion. The *Dharma* of the Hindu Aryans is a collection and consolidation of such pronouncements. Later Brahmanic jurisprudence, as well as Roman and Celtic law, developed this notion in the shape of an extensive power of interpretation and formulation on the part of priests.[4] Some vestiges of a similar consolidation of sacred custom are apparent in Greek law. The ἐξηγηταί who had to preserve the traditions as to cases of homicide (δίκαι φονικαί) exercised similar functions in a restricted field.[5] But the rapid development of the City State in Greece arrested

Pronouncements as to right.

1 E.g. *Odyssey* IX, 112, 215; *Iliad* I, 238; IX, 99.
2 MAINE, *Ancient Law*, ch. 2.
3 HIRZEL, *Themis and Dike* (1907), p. 157.
4 JOLLY, *Recht und Sitte*, pp. 3 ff. The Brehons of Ireland were in this respect the successors of the Druids; ARBOIS DE JUBAINVILLE, *Cours de littérature celtique*.
5 DEMOSTHENES' speech against Euergos and Mnesibulos.

these beginnings, and as for the Teutons and Slavs, the introduction of Christianity acted as a bar to such developments.

Non-litigious custom.

There is yet another side of the formation of legal rules that has to be considered—a side which played a considerable part in ancient society. I mean the growth of *non-litigious* custom. If the most explicit expression of legal regulation is to be found in the treaties (ῥῆτραι) of federated clans, as distinct from the enactments and pronouncements of chieftains within their own kindreds, the latter again cannot be regarded as the simplest and original source of legal custom. It is not conflicts that initiate rules of legal observance, but the practices of every-day directed by the give and take considerations of reasonable intercourse and social co-operation. Neither succession,[1] nor property, nor possession, nor contract started from direct legislation or from direct conflict. Succession has its roots in the necessary arrangements of the household on the death of its manager, property began with occupation, possession is reducible to *de facto* detention, the origins of contract go back to the customs of barter. Disputes as to right in primitive society are pre-eminently disputes as to the application of non-litigious custom. The fundamental truth that a great deal of the law of Aryan nations goes back to the customs of non-litigious co-operation in the "Dark Ages," is a warning against the rationalism of narrow utilitarians, and an incentive to the historical study of law as a product of social conditions. The details of such a study must be left to legal historians, but it is of the province of Historical Jurisprudence to call attention to the consequences that result from the admission of one or the other principle as guidance for conduct. Jurisprudence even in its most modern phases, is bound to be historical in so far as it takes stock of the social conditions which call forth legal principles; it is also bound to be analytical in so far as it examines the logical consequences of these principles and their rational combinations. The results are

[1] See the chapter on *Ultimogeniture in* FRAZER'S *Folk-lore of the Old Testament.* On non-litigious practice, see EUGEN EHRLICH, *Grundlegung der Soziologie des Rechts*, passim.

never quite rational or simple: various side influences and cross-currents bring in unexpected turns and complicate actual developments. Opposition and compromises between conquerors and conquered, psychological peculiarities, industrial discoveries, the pressure of economic needs, produce all sorts of variations which it would be impossible to reduce by dialectic process to the evolution of one or the other principle. As a matter of fact the governing principles of jurisprudence, such as tribal solidarity, the City State, the Catholic Church, individualism, socialism, are synthetic in their nature and therefore subject to disruption and combination as well as to evolution. Yet in trying to understand the history of human society in its legal aspects we must begin by ascertaining the *leading themes* which recur in jurisprudential thought. As in music, they are not stereotyped in their manifestations, they vary in the course of conflicts and harmonizing attempts, but they are not numerous and are therefore amenable to definite observation and to reflective estimates.

ADDITIONAL NOTE

I HAVE not made any attempt to discuss in the text or in the notes the views of J. Ficker[1] on the family, marriage and succession among Germanic nations. His observations are sometimes interesting and generally startling; they have called attention to unexpected analogies between the legal customs of Scandinavian, Frisian, Burgundian and Lombard branches and the customary law of Spain, Portugal and France. But Ficker's method in stating his conclusions is so involved that it requires a great deal of patience to ascertain his definite meaning and, if one has apparently done so, it is usually found to rest on doubtful and even improbable surmises. It is quite impossible to consider any particular point of his theory without taking notice of innumerable threads connected with it and appealed to in support of the author's contentions. The only thing I can attempt here is to state some of the reasons why I cannot accept Ficker's general conclusions.

He deals with the subject on the basis of a comparison between legal customs formulated and practised in countries invaded by Germanic tribes during the Middle Ages. For the purpose of such comparison, he has selected, as the title of his work shows, the sequence and rights of heirs, but he treats, besides, of forms of marriage and property relations between husband, wife and children. In all these respects he discards the usual notions as to the prevalence of patriarchal arrangements and reconstructs on the strength of analogies between local customs certain leading principles derived from racial differences. Instead of the prevailing influences of Roman law and Salic law

[1] *Untersuchungen zur Erbenfolge der ostgermanischen Rechte*, I-V, VI (posthumous), Innsbruck 1891-1904. The clearest summary of the work in so far as it concerns mediaeval France has been made by R. Caillemer, *La formation du droit français médiéval dans les travaux de M. J. Ficker*, in the *Annales de la faculté de droit et des lettres d'Aix*, II, and *Annales de la faculté de droit d'Aix*, I.

he discovers right across Europe currents of Gothic custom, represented by Western Norwegian and Frisian laws to which, according to him, Danish law is allied. The most wonderful combinations arise from this reshuffling of ethnographic elements. Western France appears as the country of the Frisians in point of legal lore, while Britanny, Normandy and England are discovered to be under the prevailing influence of a current best represented in the customary law of Trondhjem (Frostathing lov).

This sounds adventurous enough, but the proofs adduced are quite as amazing. The derivation of the law of Britanny and Great Britain from Norway is chiefly based on the strongly agnatic character of the systems concerned,[1] as if patriarchal and agnatic tendencies could only be traced to these specific localities and had left no other vestiges in Europe. Again, the occurrence in Anglo-Norman and Saxon custom of a "Drittelrecht," of a habit of dividing property in three parts, of which two went to males or to the male line, while the third was reserved for females, is supposed to be specifically Danish and Norwegian.[2] A similar explanation is given to the rule of community in the administration of property between husband and wife after a year and a half has passed. It never occurs to Professor Ficker to look up the facts as to Celtic customs in these respects. If he had done so, he would have seen that the division among the male and female line in the ratio of two to one is equally prevalent in Anglo-Saxon and in Welsh law, and that it corresponds to the rights and obligations of the father's kin and mother's kin in regard to feud and *wergeld* (see above pp. 312 ff.). And as for the formation of community of possession by the year and the day it would have been worth while to notice that this custom looks like a natural outcome of the stabilization of marriage after the probationary year in the *coibchè* form of union (see above, p. 247). Altogether

[1] Vol. VI, p. 1 f

[2] FICKER, ss. 1176-1179; 1237, 1245.

[3] CAILLEMER, *Formation du droit français, Annales de la faculté de droit*, I, 208.

it seems rather odd that the legal lore of Britanny and Great Britain should be treated as a variation of Frisian or Scandinavian themes, as if a Celtic population had never existed there. Historians are too much in the habit of disregarding the Celtic and Iberian substratum for the sake of racial elements superimposed on it. We have seen lately several students of Roman Britain arguing in favour of complete Romanization. On the other hand Julius Ficker may certainly be cited as a conspicuous advocate of Germanization.

The source of all these fanciful combinations can be traced in the case of Ficker to one main fallacy, which has been rightly characterized by R. Caillemer: "Customary law in the south of France as well as in the north is a law of heterogeneous origin, the making of which depends on the fusion of Germanic elements with custom derived from vulgar[1] Roman law, but which contains chiefly elements of spontaneous growth, tending to satisfy new requirements—those of mediæval society, different both from the Roman and from the Germanic one which preceded the invasion."[2] Caillemer has illustrated in detail the truth of his remark by analysing the evolution of the very customs selected by Ficker in the south-east of France; and the materials cited by Ficker will have to undergo a similar process of critical sifting before they can be made to serve as basis for wide generalizations of Comparative Law.

[1] I should like to add: partly based on Celtic traditions.

[2] Les idées coutumières de la renaissance du droit romain dans le sud-est de la France, p. 175. (In *Essays in Legal History*, Proceedings of the section of Legal History of the London Congress of Historical Sciences of 1913. Ed. by P. VINOGRADOFF, Oxford, 1913.)

LIST OF BOOKS REFERRED TO IN THE VOLUME

I. INTRODUCTION

American Bar Association. Montreal Meeting, 1913. **Lord Haldane** on Higher Nationality.

Ames (J. B.). Law and Morals *in* Lectures on Legal History. Camb., Mass. 1913.

Anson (Sir W. R.). Principles of the English Law of Contract. 14th ed. Oxford. 1917.

Austin (J.). Lectures on Jurisprudence. 3rd ed. London. 1869.

Barbour (W. T.). The History of Contract in Early Equity. (Oxford Studies in Social and Legal History. Vol. 4.) Oxford. 1914.

Barth (P.). Die Philosophie der Geschichte als Sociologie. Leipzig. 1897.

Baudrillart (H. J. L.). J. Bodin et son temps. Paris. 1853.

Beccaria (C. Bonesana Marchese di). Dei Delitti e delle Pene. Monaco. 1764.

Bentham (J.). Works. ed. Bowring. 11 vols. Edinburgh. 1843.

Bergbohm (C.). Jurisprudenz und Rechtsphilosophie. Leipzig. 1892.

Bernatzik (E.). Polizei und Kulturpflege *in* Die Kultur der Gegenwart, II, 8. (Systematische Rechtswissenschaft.) Berlin and Leipzig. 1906.

Berolzheimer (F.). Strafrechts-Philosophie und Strafrechts-Reform. (Vol. V. of System der Rechts- und Wirtschaftsphilosophie, I-V.) München. 1907.

Beudant (R.). Cours de droit civil, I, II. Paris. 1896 ff.

——————— Le droit individual et l'État. Paris. 1891.

Boas (F.). The Mind of Primitive Man. Annual Report to Smithsonian Institution. Washington. 1901.

Binding (C.). Die Normen und ihre Übertretung. Leipzig. 1890.

Bodin (J.). See **Baudrillart (H. J. L.).**

Bosanquet (B.). Philosophical Theory of the State. 2nd ed. London. 1910.

Brandes (G.). Hovedströmninger i det XIX Aarhundredes Literatur. Köbenhavn. 1894.

Brentano (L.). Die klassische Nationalökonomie. Leipzig. 1888.

Brinz (A. von). Lehrbuch der Pandekten, II. Erlangen. 1860(71).

Buckle (H. T.). History of Civilization in England, I. (The World's Classics.) London. 1903.

Bücher (K.). Entwickelung der Volkswirtschaft. Tübingen. 1904.

Bufnoir (C.). Cours de droit civil, II. Paris. 1900.

Burke (E.). Reflections on the French Revolution. (Every Man's Library.) London. 1910.

Caird (E.). The Critical Philosophy of Imm. Kant. 2 vols. Glasgow. 1889.

Cannan (E.). History of the Theories of Production and Distribution. London. 1903.

Carlyle (T.). On Heroes and Hero Worship. (The People's Library.) London. 1909.

Carnevale (—). Critica Penale. Lipari. 1889.

Charmont (J.). Renaissance du droit naturel. Paris. 1910.

Coke (Sir E.). The Reports of, 117. London. 1777.

Colin (—) et Capitant (H.). Cours de droit civil. Paris. 1915.

Comte (A.). Cours de philosophie positive. Paris. 1830.

Croce (B.). The Philosophy of Vico. Translated by R. G. Collingwood. London. 1913.

Croce (G. C.). Filosofia della Pratica. Bari. 1909.

Dante Alighieri. De Monarchia. Oxford Text. ed. E. Moore. Oxford. 1916.

Dareste (R.). Études de l'histoire du droit. Paris. 1882.

———— Nouvelles études de l'histoire du droit. Paris. 1902, 1906.

De Greef (G.). Précis de Sociologie. Bruxelles. 1909.

Dernburg (H.). Pandekten, II. 7th ed. Berlin. 1884 ff.

Dicey (A. V.). Lectures on the Relation between Law and Public Opinion in England during the 19th Century. London. 1905.

——— Introduction to the Study of the Law of the Constitution. 6th ed. London. 1902.

——— Thoughts on the General Assembly of the Church of Scotland under the Constitution of 1690 (1690-1707), *in* The Scottish Historical Review, XIV, no. 55. Glasgow. 1917.

Duguit (L.). Études de droit public, I, II. Paris. 1901, 1903.

——— Manuel de droit constitutionnel. 3rd ed. Paris. 1918.

——— Le droit social, le droit individuel et la transformation de l'état. Paris. 1908.

——— Les transformations du droit public. Paris. 1913.

Durkheim (É.). De la division du travail social. Paris. 1893.

——— The Elementary Forms of the Religious Life. Trans. by J. W. Swain. London. 1915.

——— Les règles de la méthode sociologique. Paris. 1895.

——— Le suicide. Paris. 1897.

Ehrlich (E.). Grundlegung der Sociologie des Rechts. München und Leipzig. 1913.

Encyclopædia Britannica. 11th ed. Camb. 1910.

Encyclopædia of Religion and Ethics. Ed. by J. Hastings. Edinburgh and New York. 1914-18.

L'Encyclopédie, dictionnaire des sciences, des arts, et des métiers. Par MM. Diderot et D'Alembert. Vols. I-VII. Paris. 1751 ff.

Engels (F.). Socialism, Utopian and Scientific. Trans. by E. Aveling. (Social Science Series.) London. 1892.

Espinas (A.). Des sociétés animales. Paris. 1877.

Essays in Legal History read at the London Congress of

Historical Sciences, 1913, Legal History section. Ed. by Sir P. Vinogradoff. Oxford. 1913.

Ferri (E.). Criminal Sociology. Ed. by W. D. Morrison. London. 1895.

——— Sociologia Criminale. 3rd ed. Torino. 1892.

Fouillée (A.). L'Évolutionnisme des Idées-forces. Paris. 1890.

Fraunce (A.). The lawiers logike. London. 1588.

Garofalo (Baron R.). Criminology. Trans. by R. W. Millar. London. 1914.

Gény (F.). Méthode d'interpretation et sources en droit privé positif. Paris. 1899.

——— and others. See **Thaller.**

Gerber (C. F. von). See Jahrbücher für die Dogmatik des heutigen römischen und deutschen Privatrechts.

Giddings (F. H.). Principles of Sociology. New York and London. 1896.

——— Inductive Sociology. New York and London. 1901.

Gierke (O.). Johannes Althusius und die Entwickelung der naturrechtlichen Staatstheorien. Breslau. 1880.

——— Das Wesen der menschlichen Verbände. Berlin. 1902.

——— Genossenschaftsrecht. Berlin. 1868 ff.

——— Grundbegriffe des Staats *in* Zeitschrift für gesammte Staatswissenschaft. Tübingen. 1905.

Giffen (Sir R.). The Utility of Common Statistics. London. 1882.

Girard (P. F.). Manuel élémentaire de droit romain. 2nd ed. Paris. 1898.

Gray (J.). The Nature and Sources of the Law. New York. 1909.

Grundriss der Sozialökonomik, I. See **Schumpeter** and **Wieser.**

Gumplovicz (L.). Der Rassenkampf. Innsbruck, 1883.

Haldane (Lord). See **American Bar Association.**

Handwörterbuch der Staatswissenschaft. 3rd ed. VII. See **Löning.**

Harvard Law Review. Camb., Mass. 1887 ff.

Hastings (J.). Encyclopædia of Religion and Ethics. Edinb. and N. York. 1914-18.

Hatschek (J.). Englisches Staatsrecht. 2 vols. Tübingen. 1905.

Haym (R.). Die romantische Schule. Berlin. 1870.

——— Wilhelm von Humboldt. Berlin. 1856.

Hinneberg (P.). Die Kultur der Gegenwart, ihre Entwickelung und ihre Ziele. Berlin. 1906.

Hobbes (T.). Dialogue between a Philosopher and a Student of the Common Law of England. English Works ed. Molesworth. 11 vols. London. 1839-45.

——— Elementorum Philosophiæ. London. 1642-55.

Hobhouse (L. T.). Mind in Evolution. 2nd ed. London. 1915.

Holland (T. E.). The Elements of Jurisprudence. 12th ed. Oxford. 1916.

Hübner (R.). Grundzüge des deutschen Privatrechts. Leipzig. 2nd ed. 1913.

Humboldt (W.). Ideen zu einem Versuch die Grenzen der Wirksamkeit des Staates zu bestimmen. 1792.

Hume (B.). A Treatise on Human Nature. Part II. Ed. by T. H. Green and T. H. Grose. London. 1874.

Ihering (R. von). Geist des römischen Rechts auf den verschiedenen Stufen einer Entwickelung, I-III. Leipzig. 1852 ff.

——— Der Zweck im Recht, I, II. Leipzig. 1877 ff.

——— Scherz und Ernst in der Jurisprudenz. 8th ed. Leipzig. 1900.

——— Kampf ums Recht. 15th ed. Wien. 1903.

Jahrbücher für Nationalökonomie und Statistik, XVI. Jena. 1863. See **Knapp.**

Jahrbücher für die Dogmatik des heutigen römischen und deutschen Privatrechts. Ed. by C. F. von Gerber und R. Ihering. Jena. 1857.

Jellinek (G.). Allgemeine Staatslehre, I. Berlin. 1900.

Jellinek (G.). Die Erklärung der Menschen- und Bürgerrechte. Leipzig. 1895.

Jevons (W. S.). The Theory of Political Economy. 3rd ed. London. 1888.

Kenny (C. S.). Outlines of Criminal Law. 5th ed., revised. Camb. 1913.

——————— A Selection of Cases illustrative of English Criminal Law. Camb. 1901.

Kidd (B.). Social Evolution. London. 1894.

Knapp (G. F.). Die neuern Ansichten über Moralstatistik in Jahrbücher für Nationalökonomie und Statistik. Ed. by B. Hildebrand. Bd. XVI. Jena. 1871.

Korkunov (N. M.). General Theory of Law. Trans. by W. G. Hastings. Boston, Mass. 1909.

Kovalevsky (M.). Coutume contemporaine et loi ancienne. Paris. 1896.

Lambert (É.). Fonction du droit civil comparé. Paris. 1903.

Landsberg (C.) and **Stintzing (R.).** Geschichte der deutschen Rechtswissenschaft. München. 1898-1910.

Langdell (C. C.). Summary of Equity Pleading. Camb., Mass. 1877.

Lange (L.). Les émotions. Trad. par G. Dumas. Paris. 1902.

Lappo-Danilevsky (A. S.). L'idée de l'État *in* Essays in Legal History.

——————— On historical theories *in* the Bulletin of the Russian Academy of Sciences for 1917. Petrograd.

Law Reports:

(1907) A. C.	Law Reports, Appeal Cases, 1907.
4 Bing.	Bingham's Reports, Common Pleas, 1822-1834, Vol. 4.
36 Ch. D.	Law Reports, Chancery Division, Vol. 36.
10 Cl. & F.	Clark & Finnelly's Reports, House of Lords, 1831-1846, Vol. 10.
Co. Rep.	Coke's Reports, 1572-1616, Vols. 1 and 5.

24 Cox C. C. E. W. Cox's Criminal Law Cases, Vol. 24.

2 Den. Denison's Crown Cases Reserved, 1844-1852, Vol. 2.

2 Eden Eden's Reports, Chancery, 1757-1766. Vol. 2.

6 Eq. Law Reports, Equity Cases, Vol. 6.

10 Ex. Law Reports, Exchequer Cases, Vol. 10.

1 F. & F. Foster & Finlason's Reports, Nisi Prius, 1856-1867, Vol. 1.

(1917) 2 K. B. Law Reports, King's Bench Division, 1917, Vol. 2.

18 L. J. (Ex.). Law Journal Reports, Vol. 18 (Exchequer).

T. L. R. The Times Law Reports, Vols. 24 and 28.

Lieber (F.). Legal and Political Hermeneutics. Boston Mass. 1839.

Liszt (F. von). Strafrechtliche Aufsätze und Vorträge. 1905.

Löning (E.). Handwörterbuch der Staatswissenschaft, VII. 3rd ed. Jena. 1909.

Loria (A.). The Economic Foundations of Society. Trans. by L. M. Keasbey. (Social Science Series.) London. 1917.

MacDougall (W.). An Introduction to Social Psychology. 8th ed. London. 1914.

Maine (Sir H.). Ancient Law. London. 1860.

———————— Lectures on the Early History of Institutions. London. 1875.

Maitland (F. W.). Collected Papers. Ed. by H. A. L. Fisher. I-III. Camb. 1911.

———————— Domesday Book and Beyond. Camb. 1897.

———————— History of English Law. See **Pollock.**

Makarewicz (J.). Einführung in die Philosophie des Strafrechts. Stuttgart. 1906.

Marshall (A.). Principles of Economics. 6th ed. London. 1910.

Menger (A.). Neue Staatslehre. Jena. 1904.

Merkel (A.). Juristische Encyclopädie. Leipzig. 1885.

Merz (J. T.). A History of European Thought in the Nineteenth Century. Vols. 1-4. Edinburgh. 1896-1914.

Meyer (E.). Kleine Schriften zur Geschichtstheorie und zur wirthschaftlichen und politischen Geschichte des Altertums. Halle-a-S. 1910.

Michel (H.). L'Idée de l'État. Paris. 1896.

Mill (J.). Analysis of the Phenomena of the Human Mind. London. 1869.

Mill (J. S.). A System of Logic. 9th ed. 2 vols. London. 1875.

Mommsen (Th.). Römisches Staatsrecht, I-III (in five parts). Leipzig. 1887.

Morley (J.). Edmund Burke. London. 1867.

——— Rousseau, I, II. New ed. London. 1886.

Natorp (P.). Die Sozialpädagogik. M. Gladbach. 1912.

Nietzsche (F.). Werke. Leipzig. 1907.

Odgers (W. Blake). The Principles of Procedure, Pleading, and Practice in Civil Actions in the High Court of Justice. 8th ed. London. 1918.

Paley (W.). Moral Philosophy. London. 1838.

Paul (H.). Prinzipien der Sprachgeschichte. IIIe Aufl. Halle. 1898.

Petrazicki (L.). Lectures on the Theory of Law and Morality.

Phillpotts (Miss B. S.). Kindred and Clan in the Middle Ages and after. Camb. 1913.

Planiol (—). Cours de droit civil, II. Paris.

Plowden (E.). The Commentaries of. London. 1761.

Pollock (Sir F.). Principles of Contract. 8th ed. London. 1911.

——— and Maitland (F. W.). History of English Law, I, II. 2nd ed. Camb. 1898.

Post (A. H.). Afrikanische Jurisprudenz. 2 bde. Oldenburg. 1887.

Post (A. H.). Grundriss der Ethnologischen Jurisprudenz. Oldenburg and Leipzig. 1895.

Quételet (L. A. J.). Physique sociale. Bruxelles. 1869.

Ribot (T. A.). German Psychology of To-day. Trans. by J. M. Baldwin. New York. 1886.

Rickert (H.). Die Grenzen der naturwissenschaftlichen Begriffsbildung. Freiburg i. B. 1896-1902.

——— Naturwissenschaft und Kulturwissenschaft. Tübingen. 1912.

Roberty (E. de). La Sociologie. Paris. 1881.

Russian Academy of Sciences Bulletin for 1918. See **Lappo-Danilevski.**

St. Simon (duc de). Oeuvres choisis, I. Bruxelles. 1859.

Saleilles (R. de). Essai d'une théorie générale de l'obligation d'après le projet du code civil allemand. Paris. 1890.

——— L'Individualisation de la peine. 2nd ed. Paris. 1909.

——— Introduction à l'étude du droit civil allemand. Paris. 1904.

——— La personalité juridique. Paris. 1910.

——— L'œuvre juridique de. See **Thaller, Gény** and others. Paris. 1914.

Salmond (J. W.). Jurisprudence; or the theory of the law. London. 1907.

Schäffle (A. E. E.). Bau und Leben des sozialen Körpers. Tübingen. 1875.

Schulze-Gaevernitz (G. von). Zum sozialen Frieden. Leipzig. 1890.

Schumpeter (J.). Literary Survey *in* Grundriss der Sozialökonomik, I. Tübingen. 1914 ff.

Scottish Historical Review, XIV, no. 55. See **Dicey.**

Schmoller (G.). Jahrbücher für Gesetzgebung, Verwaltung und Volkswirtschaft im deutschen Reich. Leipzig. 1871.

Sigwart (C.). Logic. Trans. by H. Dendy. London. 1895.

Simmel (G.). Kant. Leipzig. 1904.

——— Soziologie. Leipzig. 1908.

Smithsonian Institution. See **Boas.**

Spencer (H.). The Man versus the State. London. (1884) 1886.

———— Social Statics. London. 1851.

———— Principles of Sociology. London. 1876.

Spinoza (B.). Tractatus Theologico-politicus. Hamburg. 1670.

Stammler (R.). Die Lehre vom richtigen Rechte. Berlin. 1902.

Stammler (R.). Theorie der Rechtswissenschaft. Halle. 1911.

———— Wirtschaft und Recht nach der materialistischen Geschichtsauffassung. Leipzig. 1896.

Steinmetz (S. R.). Ethnologische Studien zur ersten Entwickelung der Strafe. Leipzig. 1894.

Stephen (H. J.). A Treatise on the Principles of Pleading in Civil Actions, with preface by S. B. Williston. Camb., Mass.

Stephen (Sir J. F.). History of Criminal Law. London. 1833.

Stephen (L.). The English Utilitarians, I. London. 1900.

———— The Science of Ethics. London. 1882.

Stintzing (R.). See **Landsberg.**

Tarde (J. G.). Les lois de l'imitation. 2nd ed. Paris. 1895.

———— Penal Philosophy. Trans. by R. Howell. London. 1912.

———— Psychologie économique. Paris. 1902.

Thaller (E.), Gény (F.) and others. L'œuvre juridique de R. Saleilles. Paris. 1914.

Thayer (J. B.). Cases on Evidence. 2nd ed. Camb., Mass. 1900.

———— A Preliminary Treatise on Evidence at the Common Law. (Printed U. S. A.) London. 1898.

Thibaut (A. F. J.). Theorie der logischen Auslegung des römischen Rechts. Altona. 1799.

Times Law Reports, XXIII ff.

Trevelyan (G. M.). Clio, a Muse, and other essays. London. 1913.

Vinogradoff (Sir P.). Common Sense in Law. (Home University Library.) London. (1914.)

——————— Roman Law in Mediæval Europe. London. 1909.

——————— The Teaching of Sir Henry Maine. London. 1904.

——————— on Comparative Jurisprudence in Enc. Brit. 11th ed.

——————— Ed. of Essays in Legal History, q.v.

Vinogradoff (Sir P.). Ed. of Oxford Studies in Social and Legal History. Vols. I-V. Oxford. 1909-16.

Ward (Lester F.). Outlines of Sociology. New York and London. 1898.

Webb (S.). Socialism in England. London. 1890.

Webb (S. and B.). Industrial Democracy. New ed. London. 1902.

Weber (M.). Roscher und Knies *in* Schmoller's Jahrbücher für Gesetzgebung, Verwaltung und Volkswirtschaft. Leipzig. 1871.

Whetham (W. C. D.). The Recent Development of Mechanical Science. 4th ed. London. 1909.

Wieser (F. von). Theorie der gesellschaftlichen Wirtschaft *in* Grundriss der Sozialökonomik. Tübingen. 1914.

Windelband (W.). Naturwissenschaft und Geisterwissenschaft Begriffsbildung. Strassburg. 1904.

——————— Die Philosophie im Beginn des zwanzigsten Jahrhundert. Heidelberg. 1907.

Windscheid (B.). Lehrbuch des Pandektenrechts. 9th ed. Frankfurt. 1906.

Wordsworth (W.). Prelude. Boston, Mass. 1888.

Worms (R.). La Sociologie et la morale. (Annales de l'institut international de sociologie.) Paris. 1897.

Wundt (W.). Ethik. Stuttgart. 1886.

——————— Lectures on Human and Animal Psychology. Trans. by J. E. Creighton and E. B. Titchener. London. 1894.

——————— Logik. Stuttgart. 1880.

Wundt (W.). Völkerpsychologie. 2e Aufl. Leipzig. 1904.
Zeitschrift für gesammte Staatswissenschaft, XXX. See Gierke (O.).
——— für Rechtsgeschichte. Ed. by F. v. Savigny and Eichhorn. Weimer. 1861-78.
——— für vergleichende Rechtswissenschaft. Stuttgart. 1878 ff.

LIST OF BOOKS REFERRED TO IN THE VOLUME

II. TRIBAL LAW

Aarboger for Nordisk Oldkyndighed. See **Lauridsen.**

Academy, XVIII. See **Goldziher.**

Acts of the Chapter of the Collegiate Church of S.S. Peter and Wilfrid, Ripon. 1452-1506. Surtees Society, LXIV. 1875. London (1835-).

American Anthropological Association, Memoirs of the. See **Hartland.**

Amira (K. von). Grundriss des germanischen Rechts. 3rd. ed. Strassburg. 1913.

———— Nordgermanisches Obligationenrecht. Leipzig. 1882-95.

———— Der Stab in der germanischen Rechtssymbolik. Abhandl. der kais. bayer. Akad. des wissenschaften, philos., philolog. und histor. Klasse. München. 1909.

Ancient Laws and Institutes of Wales. Ed. by Aneurin Owen. London. 1841.

L'Année sociologique, VIII. 1905. See **Durkheim.**

Âpastamba. See **Sacred Books of the East, II.**

Arbois de Jubainville (M. H. de). Cours de littérature celtique, 1895. Paris. 1883- .

———— La famille celtique. Paris. 1904.

Archivio giuridico. See **Brugi.**

Aristotle. Politics. Trans. by B. Jowett. Oxford. 1885.

Atkinson (J. J.). Primal Law. *In* Social Origins. By A. Lang. London, New York and Bombay. 1903.

Aulus Gellius. Noctes Atticæ. 2 vols. Ed. by C. Hosius. Teubner Lips. 1903.

Bachofen (J. J.). Das Mutterrecht. Stuttgart. 1861.

Baden-Powell (B. H.). The Indian Village Community. London, New York and Bombay. 1896.

Balzer (O.). O Zadrudze Slowianskei. Lwów. 1899.

Beauchet (L.). Histoire du droit privé de la république athénienne. 4 vols. Paris. 1897.

Bogišić (V.). Zbornik Pravnih Obićaja. Zagreb. 1874. On the Inokoshtina. Offprint from the Journal of the Ministry of Public Instruction. (Russian.)

Bonfante (P.). *On* Hereditas *and* Legata *in* Bullettino dell' Istituto di Diritto Romano, IV, p. 97, and VII, p. 151. Roma. 1891 and 1894.

Book of Rights. Ed. with trans. and notes by J. O'Donovan. Celtic Society. Dublin. 1847.

Bracton (H. de). De legibus et consuetudinibus Angliæ. Ed. by G. E. Woodbine. Yale Historical Publications. New Haven, U. S. A. 1915.

Brandt (K. J.). Norsk Retshistorie. Kristiania. 1880.

Brugi *in* Archivio giuridico, Vol. 33, *on* Voigt, Die XII Tafeln.

Calendar of Scottish State Papers.

Brunner (H.). Deutsche Rechtsgeschichte. Leipzig. 1887.

Bühler (J. G.). See **West.**

Bullettino dell' Istituto di Diritto Romano. See **Bonfante** and **Costa.**

Burckhardt (J. L.). Travels in Arabia. London. 1829.

Caillemer (E.). Le droit de succession légitime à Athènes. Caen. 1879.

Caillemer (R.). La formation du droit français médiéval dans les travaux de M. J. Ficker *in* Annales de la faculté de droit et des lettres d'Aix, II, and Annales de la faculté de droit d'Aix, I. Paris. 1906 and 1907.

———— Les idées coutumières de la renaissance du droit romain dans le sud-est de la France, *in* Essays in Legal History. London. 1913.

Chilperici Edictum. See **Geffcken**, Lex Salica.

Cicero (M. Tullius). Pro Murena. Pro Sex. Roscio. Topica. Oxford Classical Texts.

Codex Diplomaticus. Stettin. 1748. See **Kotliarevsky** *on* Baltic Slavs.

Colebrooke (H. T.). Two Treatises on the Hindu Law of Inheritance. Calcutta. 1810.

——————— Mitákshará, a commentary on Yajña-valkya. Trans. by H. T. C. Calcutta. 1865.

Corpus Juris Civilis. See **Mommsen.**

Corpus juris Sueo-Gotorum antiqui. Ed. by H. S. Collin and C. J. Schlyter. Stockholm. 1827-

Corpus poeticum Boreale. Ed. and trans. by G. Vigfusson and F. Y. Powell. Oxford. 1883.

Costa (E.). I luoghi plautini riferentisi al matrimonio, in Bullettino dell' Istituto di Diritto Romano, II, 28 ff. Roma. 1889.

Crawley (E.). The Mystic Rose. London and N. York. 1902.

Cuq (E.). Manuel des institutions juridiques des Romains. Revised ed. Paris. 1917.

——— Sur le testament *per aes et libram in* Nouvelle revue historique de droit français et étranger, X, 537. Paris. 1886.

Czaplicka (Miss M. A.). Aboriginal Siberia. Oxford. 1914.

Daremberg (Ch.) et Saglio (E.). Dictionnaire des antiquités grecques et romaines. Paris. 1873-1917.

Dareste (R.), Haussoulier (B) and Reinach (T.). Recueil des inscriptions juridiques grecques. Paris. 1891.

Darmesteter (J.). Lettres sur l'Inde: à la frontière Afghane. Paris. 1888.

Delbrück (B.). Die Indogermanischen Verwandtschaftsnamen. (Abhandl. der philolog. histor. Classe der k. sächs. gesellsch. der Wissenschaften. Bd. XI, p. 379.) Leipzig. 1889.

Dharmasutras. See **Sacred Books of the East.**

Digesta. See **Mommsen.**

Dionysius (of Halicarnassus). Antiquitatum Romanarum quae supersunt. Ed. by C. Jacoby. Teubner. Lips. 1885.

Dopsch (A.). Die ältere Sozial- und Wirtschaftsverfassung der Alpen-Slaven. Weimar. 1909.

Dorsey (J. O.). Omaha Sociology. (Third Annual Report of the Bureau of Ethnology to the Secretary of the Smithsonian Institution.) Washington, U. S. A. 1885.

Douie (J. M.). Punjab Settlement Manual. Revised ed. Lahore. 1909.

Durkheim (É.). The Elementary Forms of the Religious Life. Trans. by J. W. Swain. (Social Science Series.) London. 1915.

———— Sur l'organization matrimoniale des sociétés australiennes. (In L'année sociologique, VIII.) Paris. 1905.

Ebbo. Vita Ottonis. See **Monumenta Germaniae Historica,** Scriptores, XII (Pertz).

Efimenko (Mrs.). *And* "Southern Russia." St. Petersburg, 1905 (Russ.).

Ehrlich (E.). Grundlegung der Sociologie des Rechts. München und Leipzig. 1913.

Encyclopædia Britannica. 11th ed. Camb. 1910.

Encyklopedya Polska. See **Kadlec.**

Encyclopædia of Religion and Ethics. Ed. by J. Hastings. Edinburgh and New York. 1914-18.

English Historical Review. See **Stevenson.**

Erdmann (W.). Die Entwicklung der Testierfreiheit im römischen Recht *in* Zeitschrift für vergleichende Rechtswissenschaft. herausg. F. Benhöft, G. Cohn und J. Kohler. Stuttgart. XXII. 1908.

Essays in Legal History read before the International Congress of Historical Studies in London, 1913. Ed. by P. Vinogradoff. London. 1913.

Fallaize (E. N. G.). On Family (Primitive) *in* Hastings' Encyclopædia of Religion and Ethics, V.

Feist (S.). Kultur, Ausbreitung und Herkunft der Indo-Germanen. Berlin. 1913.

Festi (Sex. Pompei). De verborum significatu quae supersunt cum Pauli epitome. (Ed. by W. M. Lindsay.) Teubner. Lips. 1913.

Ficker (J.). Untersuchungen zur Erbenfolge der ostgermanischen Rechte, Vols. I-V, VI (posthumous). Innsbruck. 1891-1904.

Finsen (V.). See **Grágás.**

Fragmenta Historicorum Graecorum. Ed. by V. Langlois. Paris 1870.

Fraser (Sir W.). The Sutherland Book. 3 vols. Edinburgh. 1892.

Frazer (Sir J. G.). Folklore in the Old Testament. London. 1918.

——————— Totemism and Exogamy. 4 vols. London. 1910.

Fustel de Coulanges (N.-D.). La Cité antique. Paris. 1864.

——————————— Origin of Property in Land. Trans. by M. Ashley. (Social Science Series.) London. 1891.

Gai. Institutiones Juris Civilis. Trans. by E. Poste. 4th ed. revised by E. A. Whittuck. Oxford. 1904.

Gait (E. A.). Census of India, 1891. Assam. Shillong. 1892.

Geffcken (H.). Lex Salica. Leipzig. 1898.

Gellius. See **Aulus Gellius.**

Gesetze der Angelsachsen. See **Liebermann.**

Gillen (F. J.). See **Spencer.**

Giraldus Cambrensis. Descriptio Kambriae. Opera. Ed. by J. S. Brewer. Rolls Series. 21[a-gh].

Giraud-Teulon (A.). Les Origines de la famille. Geneva. 1874.

Glanville (R. de). Tractatus de Legibus et Consuetudinibus regni Angliae. London. 1780.

Glotz (G.). La solidarité de la famille dans le droit criminel en Grèce. Paris. 1904.

Götz (L. K.). Das russische Recht, I, II. Stuttgart. 1910.

Goldziher (I.). *In* the Academy, XVIII, p. 26. London. 1880.

Gopčević (S.). Oberalbanien und seine higa. Leipzig. 1881.

Gordon (Sir R.). The Genealogical History of the Earldom of Sutherland. Edinburgh. 1813.

Grágás. Ed. by V. Finsen. (Nordiske Oldskrifter udgivne af det nordiske Literatur-Samfund.) **11, 17, 21, 22, 32.** Kjöbenhavn. 1850-70.

Grimm (J.). Deutsche Rechtsalterthümer. 4th ed. Leipzig. 1899.

Gwentian Code. See **Ancient Laws and Institutes of Wales.**

Hanssen (G.). Agrarhistorische Abhandlungen. Leipzig. 1884.

Harkavy (A. E.). Mohammedan Writers on Slavs and Russia. (Russian.) St. Petersburg. 1870.

Hartland (E. S.). Matrilineal Kinship and the Question of its Priority. (Memoirs of the American Anthropological Association, IV, no. 1. Jan.-Mar. 1917. Lancaster, Pa. 1917.)

——————— Primitive Paternity. 2 vols. London. 1909, 10.

Harvard Law Review. See **Vinogradoff.**

Hastings (J.). Encyclopædia of Religion and Ethics. Edinb. and N. York. 1914-18.

Herbordus. Dialogus. See **Monumenta Germaniae Historica.** Scriptores, XX. (Pertz.)

Herodotus. Histories. Trans. by G. Rawlinson. London. 1862.

Hesiod. Opera et Dies. 3rd ed. of Teubner. Leipzig. 1913.

Heusler (A.). Das Strafrecht der Isländer Sagas. Leipzig. 1911.

Hildebrand (R.). Recht und Sitte auf den primitiven wirtschaftlichen Kulturstufen. Jena. 1907.

Hill-Tout (C.). British North America. The native races of the British Empire. London. 1907.

Hirt (H. A.). Die Indogermanen, ihre Verbreitung ihre Urheimat und ihre Kultur. Strassburg. 1905.

Hirzel (R.). Themis, Dike und Verwandten. Leipzig. 1907.

Historia et Cartularium Monasterii S. Petri Gloucestriae. Rolls Series. 1867.

Hoops (J.). Waldbäume und Kulturpflanzen im germanischen Altertum. Strassburg. 1905.

Hose (C.) and McDougall (W.). The Pagan Tribes of Borneo. London. 1912.

Howitt (A. W.). The Dieri and other Kindred Tribes of Central Australia. (In the Journal of the Royal Anthropological Institute, XX, no. 1. Aug., 1890.)

Hruza (E.). Beiträge zur Geschichte des griechischen und römischen Familienrechts. Erlangen. 1894.

Ihering (R. von). Geist des römischen Rechts auf den verschiedenen Stufen seiner Entwickelung. Leipzig. 1852 ff.

Isaeus. Speeches. Ed. by W. Wyse. Camb. 1904.

Jevons (F. B.). Kin and Custom. *In* Journal of Philology, XVI, no. xxxi. Camb. 1888.

Jireček (C. J.). Svod Zakonov Slovanskyh. Prague. 1880.

Jolly (J.). Recht und Sitte. (Grundriss der indo-arischen Philologie.) Strassburg. 1896.

Journal of Philology. See **Jevons.**

Journal of the Royal Anthropological Institute. See **Howitt.**

Journal and Proceedings of the Royal Society of New South Wales. See **Matthews.**

Jyske Lov. Ed. by N. M. Petersen. Köbenhavn. 1850.

Kadlec (A.). *In* Encyklopedya Polska. Cracow. 1912-

Karlowa (O.). Römische Rechtsgeschichte. Leipzig. 1892.

Keith (A. B.). See **Macdonell.**

Kluchevsky (V. O.). History of Russia. Trans. by C. J. Hogarth. London and N. York. 1911.

Kohler (J.). Zur Urgeschichte der Ehe. Stuttgart. 1897.

Koran. Trans. by M. Rodwell. Everyman's Library.

Kotliarevsky (A. A.). On the Baltic Slavs. Works, in 4 vols. (Russian). Transactions of the Petrograd Academy. Section of Russian Language. Vols. 47-50. Petrograd. 1889-95.

Kovalevsky (M. M.). Coutume contemporaine et loi ancienne. Paris. 1893.

——————— Tableau des origines et de l'évolution de la famille et de la propriété. Stockholm. 1890.

Krauss (F. S.). Sitte und Brauch der Südslaven. Wien. 1885.

Krishnan Pandalai (K.). Succession and Partition in Marumakatayam Law. Trivandrum. 1914.

Lambert (É.). Fonction du droit civil comparé. Paris. 1903.

Lang (A.). Social Origins. Primal Law. By J. J. Atkinson. London, N. York and Bombay. 1903.

Lauridsen (P.). *In* Aarboger for Nordisk Oldkyndighed, II Ser., Vol. XI. Copenhagen. 1896.

Leist (B. W.). Graeco-italische Rechtsgeschichte. Jena. 1884.

Lenel (O.). Zur Geschichte der *Heredis Institutio, in* Essays in Legal History.

Lex Alamannorum. See **Monumenta Germaniae Historica.** Leges, V. Ed.

Lex Bajuwariorum. Ibid.

Lex Frisionum. Ibid.

Lex Thuringorum. Ibid. (Angliorum et Werinorum.)

Liebermann (F.). Die Gesetze der Angelsachsen, Herausg. im Auftrage der Savigny Stiftung. Halle. 1898-1912.

Lindsay (R., of Pitscottie). The Historie and Cronicles of Scotland from the slauchter of King James the First to the one thousande fyve hundreith thrie scoir fyfteen yeir. (Scottish Text Society.) 42, 43, 60 (1911). Edinburgh. 1899.

Lipsius (J. H.). Attisches Recht und Rechtsverfahren. Leipzig. 1915.

Longnon (A.). Polyptyque de L'Abbaye de Saint-Germain des Prés. Société de l'histoire de Paris. Paris. 1895.

Lysias. Speeches. Oxford Classical Texts.

Macdonnell (A. A.) and **Keith (A. B.).** Vedic Index of names and subjects. London. 1912.

McDougall (W.). See **Hose.**

McLennan (J. F.). Studies in ancient history. New ed. London. 1886. Second series. London and N. York. 1896.

Maine (H.). Lectures on the Early History of Institutions. London. 1875.

———— Village Communities in the East and West. London. 1871.

Maitland (F. W.). History of English Law. See **Pollock.**

Malinowski (B.). The family among the Australian aborigines. (Univ. of Lond. monographs on Sociology.) London. 1913.

Manu, Laws of. See **Sacred Books of the East.**

Matthews (R. H.). Notes on Some Native Tribes of Australia, *in* Journal and Proceedings of the Royal Society of New South Wales, XL. Sydney. 1906.

Maurer (K. v.). Das Staatsrecht des isländischen Freistaates. Publ. by the Norwegian Academy. Christiania. 1909.

Mayne (J. D.). A Treatise on Hindu Law and Usage. 4th ed. Madras. 1888.

Memoirs of the American Anthropological Association. See **Hartland.**

Migne (L'abbé J. P.) Patrologiae cursus completus, II, lxxxix., Ser. I-II. Paris. 1844-65.

Miklosich (F.). Die Blutrache bei den Slaven, *in* Denkschriften der kaiserl. Akad. der Wissenschaft. Philosophisch-historische classe. Bd. XXXVI. Vienna. 1888.

Mitteis (L.). Römisches Privatrecht. Leipzig. 1908.

Mommsen (Th.). Corpus Juris Civilis. Digesta. Berlin. 1872.

———— Römisches Staatsrecht *in* Handbuch der römischen Alterthümer. Ed. by J. Marquardt und Th. Mommsen. Leipzig. 1887.

———— Römische Geschichte. Berlin. 1868.

Monumenta Germaniae Historica. Leges. Scriptores. (Pertz.) Berlin and Hanover. 1877-

Morgan (F.). See **Vinogradoff.**

Morgan (L. H.). Ancient Society. London. 1877.

Müllenhoff (K. V.). Deutsche Altertumskunde. Berlin. 1870.

Narada. See **Sacred Books of the East,** XXXIII.

Native Races of the British Empire, The. British North America. C. Hill-Tout. London. 1907.

Neilson (G.). Trial by Combat. Glasgow. 1890.

New English Dictionary. Ed. by J. A. H. Murray. Oxford. 1884-

Nouvelle revue historique de droit français et étranger. See **Cuq.**

O'Donovan (J.). The Book of Rights. Celtic Society. Dublin. 1847.

Östgöta-Lagen. See **Corpus juris Sueo-Gotorum antiqui, II.**

Partsch (J.). Griechisches Bürgschaftsrecht. Leipzig. 1909.

Paul (H.). Grundriss der germanischen Philologie. Strassburg (Darmstadt). 1889-90.

Pennant (T.). Tour in Scotland, 1769, *in* Vol. I. of W. Mavor's British Tourist. London. 1809.

Pertile (A.). Storia del Diritto Italiano. Roma. 1894.

Phillpotts (Miss B. S.). Kindred and Clan in the Middle Ages and after. (Camb. Arch. and Ethn. Series.) Cambridge. 1913.

Pollock (Sir F.) and Maitland (F. W.). History of English Law before the time of Edw. I. 2nd ed. Camb. 1898.

Polyptyque de l'abbaye de S-Germain des Prés. See **Longnon.**

Punjab Customary Law. See **Tupper.**

Reallexicon der Indogermanischen Altertumskunder. See **Schrader.**

Rig-Veda-Samhitâ. Trans. by H. H. Wilson. 3 vols. London. 1888.

Risley (Sir H. H.). Tribes and Castes of Bengal. Calcutta. 1891.

Rivers (W. H. R.). History of Melanesian Society. Camb. 1914.

——————— Kinship and Social Organization. (Studies in econ. and polit. science.) London. 1914.

——————— On Marriage *in* Encyclopædia of Religion and Ethics, VIII.

Robertson (E. W.). Historical Essays in connexion with the land, the church, etc. Edinburgh. 1872.

Rössler (E.) *in* Zeitschrift für Ethnologie, XXX. 1898. (Verhandlungen der Berliner Gesellschaft für Anthropologie, 20. Bericht über seine für die kaiserl. russ. Archäologische Commission unternommenen Untersuchungen in Gouv. Elizabethpol.) Berlin. 1898.

Roth (H. Ling). The Aborigines of Tasmania. London. 1890.

Russian Pravda, Troitzky MS. See **Götz.**

Sacred Books of the East. Translated by various scholars and ed. by F. Max Müller. Oxford. 1879-

Sacred Laws of the Âryas. See **Sacred Books of the East, II.**

St. German (Chr.). Dialogue between a Doctor of Divinity and a Student in the Laws of England. London. 1532.

Sarvadhikari Rajkumar. Principles of the Hindu Law of Inheritance. (Tagore Lectures.) Calcutta. 1882.

Saxo Grammaticus. Vita et Passio S. Adalberti. See **Kotliarevsky** on the Baltic Slavs.

Schlyter (C. J.). See **Corpus juris Sueo-Gotorum antiqui.**

Schrader (O.). Reallexicon der Indogermanischen Altertumskunder. Strassburg. 1901.

——— Sprachvergleichung und Urgeschichte. 3rd ed. Jena. 1906.

Schulin (F.). Das griechische Testament verglichen mit dem römischen. Basel. 1882.

Schurtz (H.). Altersklassen und Männerbünde. Berlin. 1902.

Scott (Sir W.). The Monastery, Rob Roy, Waverley.

Scottish Text Society. See **Lindsay (R.).**

Seebohm (F.). The English Village Community. 2nd ed. London. 1883.

——— Tribal Custom in Anglo-Saxon Law. London (etc.). 1902.

——— The Tribal System in Wales. 2nd ed. London (etc.). 1904.

Seligmann (C. G. and B. Z.). The Veddas. (Camb. Arch. and Ethn. Series.) Camb. 1911.

Sénart (É.). Les castes dans l'Inde, les faits et le système. Paris. 1896.

Sering (M.). Erbrecht und Agrarverfassung in Schleswig-Holstein. Berlin. 1900.

Skene (W. F.). The Highlanders of Scotland. Ed. by A. MacBain. Stirling. 1902.

Smirnoff (J. N.). Outlines of a Cultural History of the Southern Slavs. 2 vols. (Russian.) Kazan. 1900.

Smith (G. Elliot). The Migrations of Early Culture. Manchester Memoirs, Vol. LIX, no. 10. 1915.

——————— Primitive Man. (Offprint from the proceedings of the British Academy, VII.)

Smith (W. Robertson). Kinship and Marriage in Early Arabia. New ed. London. 1903.

Smithsonian Institution, Report to Secretary of. See **Dorsey.**

Snorri Sturluson. See **Sturluson.**

Solmsen (F.). Inscriptiones Graecae ad inlustrandas dialectos selectae. 3rd ed. Teubner. Leipzig. 1910.

Spalding Club, miscellany of. See **Stuart.**

Spencer (W. B.) and Gillen (F. J.). Across Australia. London. 1912.

——————————— The Native Tribes of Central Australia. London and N. York. 1899.

——————————— The Northern Tribes of Central Australia. London and N. York. 1904.

Stemann (Chr. L. E.). Dansk Retshistorie. Kjöbenhavn. 1871.

Stevenson (W. H.). Yorkshire Surveys and other XIth century Documents in the York Gospels. (In the English Historical Review, Jan., 1912.) London.

Strabo. Ed. by A. Meineke. Teubner. Lips. 1895-98.

Strachan-Davidson (J. L.). Problems of the Roman Criminal Law. Oxford. 1912.

Stuart (J.). The Family of Rose of Kilravock, in the miscellany of the Spalding Club, 1848. Aberdeen (1841-52).

Sturluson (Snorri). Heimskringla udgivne for Samfund til udgivelse af gammel nordisk litteratur ved F. Jónsson. Köbenhavn. 1893-1901.

Surtees Society. See **Acts of the Chapter of the Church of S.S. Peter and Wilfrid.** Ripon.

Survey of the Honour of Denbigh. See **Vinogradoff.**

Tacitus (Cornelius). Germania. Oxford Classical Texts.

Taranger (A.). Transfer of Land in Old Norwegian Law *in* Essays in Legal History.

Thomas (N. W.). Kinship Organization and Group Marriage in Australia. (Camb. Arch. and Ethn. Series.) Camb. 1906.

Tupper (C. L.). Punjab Customary Law. Calcutta. 1881.

Uplands-Lagen. See **Corpus juris Sueo-Gotorum antiqui,** III.

Venedotian Code. See **Wade-Evans.**

Vinogradoff (Sir P.). English Society in the Eleventh Century. Oxford. 1908.

——————— Geschlecht und Verwandschaft im altnorwegischen Recht. *in* Zeitschrift für Sozial- und Wirtschaftsgeschichte, V. Freiburg i. B. 1896-99.

——————— The Growth of the Manor. 2nd ed. London. 1911.

——————— on Ordeal, Christian, Greek, *in* Encyclopædia of Religion and Ethics, IX.

——————— on Succession, *in* Encycl. Brit. 11th ed. Camb. 1910.

——————— Transfer of Land in Anglo-Saxon Law, *in* Harvard Law Review. Boston, Mass. 1909.

——————— Villainage in England. Oxford. 1892.

Vinogradoff (Sir P.) and **Morgan (F.).** Survey of the Honour of Denbigh, *in* British Academy Records of the Social and Economic History of England and Wales, Vol. I. London. 1914.

Viollet (P.). Histoire du droit civil français. 3rd ed. Paris. 1905.

Wade-Evans (A. W.). Welsh Mediæval Law. Oxford. 1909.

Waitz (G.). Deutsche Verfassungsgeschichte. Kiel. 1844-

Weber (M.). Die römische Agrargeschichte in ihrer Bedeutung für das Staats- und Privatrecht. Stuttgart. 1891.

West (R.) and **Bühler (J. G.).** A Digest of the Hindu Law of Inheritance, Partition, and Adoption. 3rd ed. 2 vols. Bombay. 1884.

Westermarck (E.). History of Human Marriage. 2nd ed. London. 1894.

Westgöta-Lagen. See **Corpus juris Sueo-Gotorum antiqi, I.**

Wissler (C.). Diffusion of Culture in the Plains of North America. (Congrès internat. des Américanistes, 15e session Tom. 2, p. 39. Quebec. 1907.

Yajñavalkya. See **Colebrooke.**

Zeitschrift für Ethnologie und ihre Hülfswissenschaften. See **Rössler.**

——— **für Sozial- und Wirtschaftsgeschichte.** See **Vinogradoff.**

——— **fur vergleichende Rechtswissenschaft.** See **Erdmann.**

Zimmern (A. E.). The Greek Commonwealth. Oxford. 1911.

INDEX TO VOLUME I